Staging Resistance

THEATER: Theory/Text/Performance

Enoch Brater, Series Editor

STAGING RESISTANCE
Essays on Political Theater

Jeanne Colleran and Jenny S. Spencer, Editors

Ann Arbor

THE UNIVERSITY OF MICHIGAN PRESS

To Those Born Later   —BERTOLT BRECHT

Megan Gentzler, James Weaver, Julia Weaver

A CIP catalog record for this book is available from the British Library.

Library of Congress Cataloging-in-Publication Data

Staging resistance : essays on political theater / Jeanne Colleran and
   Jenny S. Spencer, editors.
      p.   cm. — (Theater—theory/text/performance)
   Includes bibliographical references and index.
   ISBN 0-472-09671-0 (cloth : acid-free paper)
   ISBN 0-472-06671-4 (pbk. : acid-free paper)
1. Theater—Political aspects. I. Colleran, Jeanne M. (Jeanne
Marie), 1954–   . II. Spencer, Jenny S. III. Series.
PN2049 .S66   1998
792—ddc21   98-8958
                                                          CIP

Acknowledgments

As with most writing projects, more acknowledgments are due than can ever be given. The present collection had its beginnings in conversation between the editors during a 1991 National Endowment for the Humanities summer seminar on performance theory conducted by Herbert Blau at the University of Milwaukee, Wisconsin. We would like to recognize here the contribution such seminars make in bringing together scholars of similar interest and facilitating the kinds of collaborative research projects that keep our fields alive; we view the recent cuts in funding to the NEH and other government-funded arts agencies with grave concern. This project was also dependent on the lively and interested community of scholars who regularly attend the Women and Theatre preconference as well as the annual Association for Theatre in Higher Education conference. The initial call for papers distributed at these events was met with the kind of support and enthusiasm that made us believe the project worthwhile. The call also introduced us to important scholars on political theater—not all of whom could possibly have been published here. We found our own work enriched by contact with scholars who continue to do important work in the field of political theater: Robson Correa de Camargo, Claudia Orenstein, Ann E. Nymann, Angelika Czekay, Jan Cohen-Cruz, E. J. Westlake, Stacy Wolf, Jen Harvie, and Mary Karen Dahl among them. Others, such as Vicki Patraka, Susan Carlson, Katherine Burkman, Sheila Haney Drain, Brenda Wirkus, Maryclaire Moroney, and Krista Ratcliffe, have played a more long-standing, intellectually supportive role. We gratefully acknowledge the research support provided by John Carroll University, as well as the generosity of the photographers and theaters who provided the photos for this book without charge. Eve Merriam quotes and excerpts from *The Club* by Eve Merriam are copyright Eve Merriam and used by permission of Marian Reiner.

We are particularly thankful for the vision, support, and editorial expertise of LeAnn Fields at the University of Michigan Press, and for the assistance of Laurie Clark Klavins, Melissa Holcombe, and Mary Meade. David Dibble, John Panza, Melissa Zagata, Kate Fryer, and Karen Cardoza-Kane helped with research or editing at different stages of the process. Special thanks are due to Melissa Zagata and Katy Ryan, whose careful work during the book's final editing was invaluable. The contributors to the collection all deserve special tribute for their patience, friendship, and commitment to the project (for some of them, over several years). And finally, deepest thanks to Edwin Gentzler and Richard Weaver for their confidence that any and all resistances to the completion of this book could be overcome. Being so willfully optimistic about the future of political theater and the social transformations it can help to accomplish, this book is dedicated to our children.

Contents

Introduction

In 1929, Erwin Piscator declared that pure art was not possible in the reactionary context of his time.[1] Now, some seventy years later, Piscator might declare instead that *nonpolitical* art is impossible. To define political theater as a discrete category seems as difficult today as imagining what form a pure art might take, though we might agree that a reactionary context remains identifiable. The aesthetic-versus-political binary that underwrites such declarations is far easier to recognize than to escape. Theater performances, like other instances of cultural production, are decidedly "impure acts," simultaneously socially implicated and socially critical, an apparatus for the construction of meaning rather than an index to it. But what counts as political theater, how and if it can hold the line against political reaction, can remain an open question only if the category itself remains relevant.

The difference between Piscator's original utterance and our updated version is the difference between thinking of political theater as agitprop plays, of putting "politics on stage," and thinking of political theater as a cultural practice that self-consciously operates at the level of interrogation, critique, and intervention, unable to stand outside the very institutions and attitudes it seeks to change. Such a difference allows us to place under the rubric of political theater a range of theatrical activity, from theater as an act of political intervention taken on behalf of a designated population and having a specific political agenda; to theater that offers itself as a public forum through plays with overtly political content; to theater whose politics are covertly, or unwittingly, on display, inviting an actively critical stance from its audience. While hardly exhaustive, such definitions apply to each of the works discussed in this volume, although the essays themselves have stretched and challenged the conceptual frames with which the editors began.

If the category of political theater is for some commodious and for others uselessly ambiguous, so too are the terms of analysis we bring to its study. The title of this collection, *Staging Resistance: Essays on Political Theater* is meant, then, to indicate both the value and vulnerability of what political theater and criticism of it attempts. The editors share with the contributors a concern about the continuing usefulness of a cultural practice that, in so eluding definition, may have lost its ability to promote social change. But despite the impossibility of pinning down its perimeters, the writers in this volume believe in the capacity of theater to foment and assist in the broader processes of social transformation. The essays that follow offer numerous accounts of political theater that has successfully raised questions, prompted disruptions, and revised social agendas. Some, like Tom Burvill's description of two theatrical interventions that occurred during the Australian bicentennial, illustrate the power of theater to disturb particular moments of nationalist self-aggrandizement. Others, like Linda Kintz's examination of the abortion-rights drama *Keely and Du,* demonstrate that political theater as civic forum can at least provide what Herbert Blau has called an "estranged space in which we may realize . . . that what we think of as society or imagine as community is a more or less livable fiction that incorporates an *interrogation.*"[2] Emphasizing the continuing vitality of theater as a form of cultural intervention and political resistance, we draw here upon an international community of theater scholars working in various cultural contexts with differing critical tools and interests. Such a collaborative undertaking draws its strength from differences in material and methodology, as well as from its grounding in the careful observation of concrete, historically specific, culturally variable instances of political drama.

For the last three decades, both the discussion and the practice of political theater has been ghosted by Brecht's call for an epic theater of pleasure and instruction—for a theater that would activate its audiences, stage the movements of history as well as the agents who make it, and envision social justice as a necessary, not an impossible, task. While Brecht's legacy lives on, the conditions that gave rise to his specific forms of social critique have changed. Not only has the postmodern critique of the humanist subject undermined confidence in the very human agency on which social actions depend, but world political events in an age of "total television" coverage seem to outpace all adequate means of response. To speak now of cultural intervention through theater is also to speak of the resistance encountered by and within these very acts. Thus *Staging Resistance* also points to the limits of critique that arise when attention shifts from the micropolitical to the macropolitical, from the particular instance of local resistance to a broader awareness of global oppression. As Fredric Jameson has observed, we are facing a "new and historically original dilemma" for which adequate aesthetic or cognitive maps do not exist.[3]

Moreover, if the meaning and impact of theater are affected by everything from the conditions of production, to the geopolitical context of performance, to the sociological and psychic makeup of the audience, to the critical framing of the event, then the theater's effects will always be complex, historically variable, politically contested, undecidable. What is called for from the critic, and attempted by these writers, is something akin to the "complex seeing" that Brecht sought to produce for his audience. Appropriately self-conscious about the ideological positions that have informed their methods of critique, these writers are equally aware that their scholarship adds value to the material on which they work, that critical activity is itself a situated act of political investment. The result, we hope, is some useful, much-needed remapping of contemporary political theater.

Staging Resistance took shape from the initial concerns of its editors and a specific set of questions about the troublesome category that quite literally called forth the essays included here. In order to engage in discussions of "the political" that are pertinent to theater in an open-ended and thought-provoking way, we did not ask contributors to define the political, but rather to assume it in the subjects of their essays. Such a strategy implicitly recognizes just how much in this area has already been accomplished, as well as how much still needs to be done.[4] Our first set of inquiries invited speculation about how contemporary political theater builds upon or disregards its own history of radical theater practice, how specific political agendas might survive a theater group's institutionalization, and how the political efficacy of a dramatic work might be evaluated. We further pondered how best to address the social, geopolitical, and national contexts in which and against which particular performances situated themselves; and we asked contributors to think about how political theater implicitly requires that official versions of national history be reexamined. And finally, we wondered what happens when a political work is re-produced, evaluated, or read in geographically or historically different contexts. In various ways, all of these questions are deliberated in the essays that follow.

In retrospect, a number of interesting connections and related concerns have emerged—with a notion of place foremost among them. Whether conceived of in national, institutional, discursive, or intercultural terms, these essays inevitably return to an examination of place. Building upon particular and local examples, the collection itself aims, in a rather literal way, to clear some space for a renewed discussion of political theater. But with hindsight, it also seems apparent that the recurring emphasis on place has everything to do with the essential task of political theater—both to serve as an intervening space where revisionary projects can be undertaken and to reflect the historically shifting conditions under which they are made. The opening section, "Resituating Radical Theater," groups five essays, all concerned with gauging the effect of the particular theater events they revisit, and pays particular attention to the politics of location. Establishing concerns that will return throughout the volume, these essays remind us that "radical theater" is itself constituted as much from the institutional and geopolitical context of production as from specific intentions of individual theater practitioners.

In a revisionary project entitled "Irish Theater Historiography and Political Resistance," Lionel Pilkington opens this volume with an argument that traditional theater historiography is "fundamentally inadequate to the task of describing the existence and possibilities of a socially progressive theater in Ireland." Pilkington approaches the problem by examining the manner in which the Irish Literary Theatre—the "radical" act of cultural nationalism initiated by W. B. Yeats with the establishment of the Abbey Theatre—has been read as politically progressive despite the attempts by its founders to smooth over class conflicts and social differences. Pilkington's larger point is that adjudicating an institutional theater's political program is an impossible task when both the institutionalized theater and institutionalized criticism set standards of judgment in relation to national, culturally conservative agendas. A double failure ensues: alternative forms of theater that may challenge consensus-preserving ideas of nationhood become excluded from theater history, exclusions that in turn make it more difficult to see through the current critical paradigms and adequately account for contemporary instances of resistance theater.

Like Pilkington, both Lisa Jo Epstein and John Bell address immediate concerns about the fate and viability of long-established political theaters, the latter assessing the strategies through which "sixties" political theater has managed to survive into the 1990s. In "Beyond the Cold War: Bread and Puppet Theater and the New World Order," Bell suggests that the low-status tradition of puppetry itself, with its "exemption from seriousness" and particular use of imagery and spectacle, has allowed Bread and Puppet to accommodate itself as a postmodern theater practice that resists closure even as it enunciates a clear political position. The key to this seemingly contradictory state is Bread and Puppet's commitment to cheap theater, dependent on volunteer labor that often assembles itself literally hours before a production, endowing the theater work with a fragility that stands in opposition to any authoritarian tendency in its pronouncements on global economic concerns. While Bell discusses the resilience of one of the oldest leftist theater companies in the United States, Lisa Jo Epstein turns to the active, near legendary work of Augusto Boal's CTO (Parisian Center for the Theatre of the Oppressed) and Ariane Mnouchkine at Théâtre du Soleil, situating the two groups as highly diverging practices that nevertheless define the most influential political theater in France today. Keenly attuned to the importance of location, Epstein reflects upon the differing forms of politicized activity that have most recently occurred in their very different home spaces in order to illustrate "where, how, and *if* political theater resides in France today." Her firsthand account as an intern at both sites permits Epstein to see important connections between the work of these two groups, and her discussion of lost opportunities suggest just how much they could learn from one another.

The lessons of the two essays to follow are even more explicitly tied to the politics of place. Taking up the problem of cultural translation, both Una Chaudhuri and Eugene van Erven provide significant insights into the issues that arise for theater practitioners who seek, often with the best of intentions, to bridge national boundaries and break cultural barriers with dramatic work. Chaudhuri's essay, "Working out (of) Place: Brook's *Mahabharata* and the Problematics of Intercultural Performance," finds Peter Brook's project critically situated in the "discourse on interculturalism [at] a moment when one contextualizing ideology was giving way to another." In his attempt to honor an Indian epic largely unknown to Western audiences, Brook's adaptation linearized a complex hypertext into a universal narrative of "The Story of Mankind," offering up a liberal humanist "moral truth" against which the Indian terms were mere backdrop. In the uprooted version, however, Chaudhuri finds the experience of the performance itself salutary in ways Brook himself would not have predicted. If performative elements of the piece are disconsonant with Brook's vision of the text, the result is an unanticipated passage from a vaguely transcendent realm to a distinctly multicultural place in diasporic times. "Working Out of Place" could also have titled Eugene van Erven's essay, "Some Thoughts on Uprooting Asian Grassroots Theater." Reflecting on his 1988–89 experience organizing the "Cry of Asia!" tour, an Asia-Pacific grassroots cultural caravan that toured six European countries, van Erven's practical take on the event reminds readers of the importance of strong interpersonal communication, firm financial backing, equitable collaboration, and basic trust to any successful intercultural venture. The article also illustrates the particular problems faced by radical theater workers who attempt to use mainstream venues in order to reach audiences whose viewing habits and expectations have been influenced by entirely different kinds of theater. Finding even miscommunication instructive, both van Erven and Chaudhuri demonstrate how theater responds to the need, both within and between societies, to adjust to others' perspectives; and despite the inevitable, often overwhelming, difficulties involved in large-scale intercultural work, both find aspects of the experience rewarding.

If the broad category of *political theater* seems worth holding onto, it can no longer be one that neglects issues of gender, whether in relation to aesthetic practices or broader public policies. The writers grouped in part 2, "Gender and National Politics," all begin their analysis from a feminist perspective, one that affects both their method and choice of material. In "Re-Staging Resistance, Re-Viewing Women: 1990s Productions of Fugard's *Hello and Goodbye* and *Boesman and Lena,*" Marcia Blumberg revisits two of Athol Fugard's plays of stoic female heroism to raise questions about the appropriation of female voice, the dehistoricizing of the plays' incipient political moments, and the continued relevance of these works in the postapartheid dispensation. If the urgency of national liberation allowed Fugard's existential depictions of the suffering of the dispossessed to elude gender-based critique, the priorities of the African National Congress charter adopted by the Mandela government make such a critique imperative. Like others in this collection, Blumberg's essay insists on the connections between literary-intellectual behavior and the political-cultural sphere, and her analysis is consonant with the increasingly visible feminist movement within the South African academy. Tracy Davis's discussion of the first feminist drag play, Eve Merriam's *The Club,* both compliments and departs from the historicized reading Blumberg offers. The Fugard plays under consideration continue to appear on international stages, with Fugard himself an established model of a political dramatist, and the simmering volatility of reconciliation issues still thematically relevant to postapartheid South Africa. Eve Merriam's 1976 play has neither been revived nor much discussed, despite its anticipatory use of camp and cross-dressing to exact a gendered political critique during the height of the U.S. debate around the Equal Rights Amendment. With its compelling blend of theater history, social history, and feminist politics, "A Feminist Boomerang: Eve Merriam's *The Club* (1976)" models a reading of political performance that moves between current critical paradigms and those operative at the moment of the play's original performance date.

Just as Davis's writing, as well as her interest in Merriam's play, is necessarily informed by recent and widely disseminated scholarship on the socially constructed nature of gender, the essays by Josephine Lee and Linda Kintz place themselves within areas of debate in recent feminist scholarship. In "Pity and Terror as Public Acts: Reading Politics in the Plays of Maria

Irene Fornes," Lee explores the ways in which Maria Irene Fornes endows complex performative moments with immense political, specifically feminist, significance. Her close reading calls into question the most recent feminist appropriations of Fornes's work, dismantling the Brechtian-influenced distinctions between an empathic and distantiated theater. While Fornes's plays may be marked by a *failure* of agency or mastery within particular social situations, Lee finds her use of empathy a viable, partially redemptive social force that may help us revalue notions of empathy and emotional identification as a basis for politically effective theater. In "Chained to the Bed: Violence and Abortion in *Keely and Du*," Linda Kintz illustrates how this ostensibly realist drama reveals issues and impasses in current thinking and political organizing around the reproductive-rights debate in America. Like Fornes, the pseudonymous Jane Martin is interested in links between symbolic and actual violence; Kintz demonstrates how the "protection" of family values as argued by Phyllis Schlafly elides pro-life rhetoric with the language of national defense, a symbolic elision that has real-world effects. Kintz's powerful reading of the play makes it easier to see the relationship between the defining terms of the larger public debate and the actual violence perpetrated against women those terms make possible. *Keely and Du* is a politically significant play not simply because of its politically charged subject matter, but because of the way that subject is "impossibly" represented to both reveal and resist the logic of the radical right. Esther Beth Sullivan's essay "What Is 'Left to a Woman of the House' When the Irish Situation Is Staged?" returns to the issues of national identity raised in Marcia Blumberg's essay at the beginning of this section, as well as to Lionel Pilkington's essay on Irish theater. Looking at dramatic work by Irish women in relation to similar themes treated by British playwright Peter Shaffer, Sullivan explores the challenges peculiar to women writing in Ireland today, where feminist issues are routinely subordinated to nationalist causes that are themselves represented, in Ireland and elsewhere, in highly gendered rhetorical terms.

Paul Ricoeur claims that "a text is not without reference," and that it is "precisely the task of reading, as interpretation" to actualize the reference.[5] In some sense, the entire collection addresses the problems of stabilizing reference in acts of performance and reception, as well as the political consequences that follow from such stabilization. Not only is any given performance inflected by particular sociohistorical contexts and the general horizon of expectations audiences bring to the theater, but the semiotic system itself may differ in altered cultural spheres. As the essays so far have indicated, those differences may be traced along East-West or North-South lines, but just as likely, the process of cultural translation may be pursued *within* national boundaries where religious and ethnic differences, ferociously clung to in times of political assault, engender similar breaches of (mis)understanding. The essays grouped in the final section, "Toward a Civic Theater," both recapitulate these concerns and provide through their very different examples some models for a revitalized public drama. In "Playing the Faultlines: Two Political Theater Interventions in the Australian Bicentenary Year 1988," Tom Burvill explores two counterhegemonic theater interventions that occurred during the Australian Bicentenary, a year that highlighted the officially scripted nature of national identities. Both productions departed in differing ways from the respective groups' earlier community theater practices. In *Death at Balibo,* the Timorese Association used the entire border community to look at the undiscussed invasion of East Timor and the death of five Australian journalists, causing a real-life international incident in Australian-Indonesian relations. *Whispers in the Heart* by Sidetrack Theatre focused on the construction of Aboriginal identity in ways that exposed stereotypes and undermined the racist assumptions of much public discourse around Aboriginal issues in Australia. Like Epstein's essay, Burvill examines two very different theater practices that take their cue from the specific aesthetic needs of their particular audiences. Burvill's essay also points to the necessary conjunction of intercultural and postcolonial perspectives when examining theater works that take place in Commonwealth nations.

Given the severity of problems that confront audiences today, and the range of examples and cases over which we might linger, can we imagine a theater practice that is both engaged and engaging—with the kind of public power that makes investment in such cultural activity repay the effort? What might "successful" political theater look like, and how would we know? In "Personalizing the Political in *The Noam Chomsky Lectures,*" Elaine Brousseau considers the "instant success" of Canadian actors/playwrights Daniel Brooks's and Guillermo Verdecchia's first collaborative work. Described as a continual workshop piece, the play uses the icon of 1960s radicalism, Noam Chomsky, to address anew the coalition of government and media interests that Chomsky terms the "manufacturing of consent." Though the play initially appears as a dialogue along traditional lines of argument and debate, the performers undermine this model of political discussion as they mix in elements of stand-up comedy, theater of witness, and autobiography to urge the audience to a "continual battle with authority, beginning with the authority of the play itself." In addition to rethinking ways in which overtly political commentary can be incorporated into theatrical work, Brousseau's essay calls attention to the tenuous line between old political drama techniques and new, between high-profile success and politically provocative material, between ambitious theater artists and committed political activists. These lines are everywhere blurred in Harry Elam and Alice Rayner's cowritten essay "Body Parts: Between Story and Spectacle in *Venus* by Suzan-Lori Parks." Here attention to the crucial intersections between race and gender are played out against nationalist, and colonialist, discourses in a work that, as Elam and Rayner amply illustrate, necessarily implicates the viewing audience—an audience whose own histories are exhumed for display. In their provocative reading, Elam and Rayner suggest that Parks's project is not simply to reflect upon our historical past or pay tribute to lost victims of racial oppression—but rather to "reconstitute" that history in the performative present before an audience who cannot then so easily escape its consequences.

"Toward a Civic Theater" begins with three essays grounded in particularly productive examples of political theater from which very different kinds of historical lessons might be drawn. In contrast, Janelle Reinelt begins with a more theoretical look at the crises and opportunities the present historical moment may offer—if not for politically committed theater practitioners, then for their audiences. In "Notes for a Radical Democratic Theater," Reinelt claims that our current cultural crises, however disruptively experienced, may in fact be a time of "creative uncertainty" wherein a space of indeterminacy is opened up against formerly rigid categories of identification. Like many of the contributors to this collection, Reinelt believes theater may offer one of the last, live, civic spaces of dialogue in our "overscreened" societies, a space in which imaginative possibilities can be explored and enacted, a space where a consensual, if necessarily conflictual, democratic process can be affirmed.

Reinelt's closing thoughts return us to Jameson's observation that the possibility of actively contesting the status quo is sustained, in part, by both critics' and artists' willingness to provide "cognitive maps" to help spectators "grasp [their] positioning as individual and collective subjects and regain a capacity to act and struggle."[6] Those maps can never, of course, be "once and for all," for any audience at all times. A perfectly functioning political theater would signal the end of politics as we know it, perhaps of history itself. What the provisional mapping offered by the essays of *Staging Resistance* can do, however, is spark interest, action, and debate beyond the confines of a printed book. Read together, they weave a rather hopeful narrative about theater's relevance to the social sphere—as a forum for public debate, a gauge of national aspirations, an enactment of social critique, and a space for imagining alternatives.

NOTES

1. "It is scarcely possible to hold the line of pure art (the line of defense of political reactionaries) any longer." Erwin Piscator, *The Political Theater,* trans. Hugh Rorrison (Hamburg: Verlag Publishing, 1963), 323.

2. Herbert Blau, *The Audience* (Baltimore: Johns Hopkins University Press), 346.

3. Fredric Jameson, "Cognitive Mapping," in *Marxism and the Interpretation of Culture,* ed. Cary Nelson and Lawrence Grossbert (Urbana: University of Illinois Press, 1988), 351.

4. For example, see Graham Holderness, ed., *The Politics of Theatre and Drama* (New York: St. Martins, 1992); Philip Auslander, *Presence and Resistance: Postmodernism and Cultural Politics in Contemporary American Performance* (Ann Arbor: University of Michigan Press, 1992); Hal Foster, *Recodings: Art, Spectacle, and Cultural Politics* (Seattle: Bay Press, 1985); Liz Gunner, ed., *Politics and Performance: Theatre, Poetry, and Song in South Africa* (Wits: Witwatersrand University Press, 1994); J. Ellen Gainor, ed., *Imperialism and Theatre* (London: Routledge, 1995); Bonnie Maranca and Gautam Dasgupta, eds., *Interculturalism and Performance* (New York: PAJ, 1991); Baz Kershaw, *The Politics of Performance: Radical Theatre as Cultural Intervention* (London: Routledge, 1992); Johannes Birringer, *Theatre, Theory, Postmodernism* (Bloomington: Indiana University Press, 1993); Herbert Blau, *To All Appearances: Ideology and Performance* (London: Routledge, 1992); W. B. Worthen, *Modern Drama and the Rhetoric of Theatre* (Berkeley and Los Angeles: University of California Press, 1992); Sue-Ellen Case and Janelle Reinelt, *The Performance of Power* (Iowa City: University of Iowa Press, 1991). Though these works seem most germane to the issues that inform this collection, many others could be cited here.

5. Paul Ricoeur, qtd. in Edward Said, *The World, the Text, and the Critic* (Cambridge: Harvard University Press, 1983), 34.

6. Fredric Jameson, "Postmodernism, or the Cultural Logic of Late Capitalism," *New Left Review* 146 (1984): 91.

Resituating Radical Theater

Lionel Pilkington

Irish Theater Historiography and Political Resistance

It is not the play's effect on the audience but its effect on the theatre that is decisive at this moment.
—BERTOLT BRECHT

In "The Epic Theatre and Its Difficulties" (1927), Brecht argues that whereas traditional theater is marked by a "murderous clash" between theater and performance in which the theater "nearly always" emerges victorious, the aim of epic drama is to achieve the reverse: a political transformation through performance of the theater as a social and cultural institution. Brecht is emphatic that such a transformation cannot be solely a matter of aesthetics ("the result of some artistic whim") but must correspond instead to a revolutionary political project ("the whole radical transformation of the mentality of our time").[1] As well as underscoring the poverty of a theatrical analysis based exclusively on a reading of dramatic narratives, Brecht's remarks offer a useful reminder of the need for rethinking traditional theater historiography. Thus the recent groundbreaking scholarship of Marvin Carlson, Tracy C. Davis, Michael Hays, Loren Kruger, and Bruce McConachie suggests that the theater is not just a physical space for the performance of dramatic narratives, but an institution and social event in its own right: a cultural phenomenon to be analyzed politically for its playing out of dominant social, economic, and cultural conventions. Theater history, that is, must be considered in terms of a sociopolitical analysis and not merely as a "study of the production conditions of the already acknowledged major periods and accepted canon of the European literary drama."[2]

Despite what has been described as a Copernican revolution in theater historiography, the widespread application of a materialist and institutional analysis to individual national theater histories is still in its early stages. Ireland, in particular, is a case in point. With very few exceptions, narratives of Irish theater history and criticism relate a story of uncomplicated national development: from the anticolonial rejection of the "stage Irishman" proclaimed by the founders of the Irish Literary Theatre in the late nineteenth century to a modernist, "postcolonial" maturity following the establishment of the Irish Free State in 1922 and Ireland's departure from the British Commonwealth in 1948.[3] Moreover, as the first state-subsidized English-speaking national theater in the world, the Abbey Theatre dominates discussions of Irish theater to the extent that it is sometimes regarded as a synonym for Irish drama *tout court*.[4] Widely regarded as a national *literary* institution, Irish theater is seen as engaged in a modernizing educative project. Unsurprisingly, then, a concomitant feature of this national theater narrative is the recurring conclusion that Irish drama is inherently conservative: hence Nicholas Grene observes that Irish theater is characterized by a consistent opposition to militant Irish nationalism and imputes this to the "inherent" modernizing force of Irish history, while Philomena Muinzer and Rob Ritchie lament the lack of progressive contemporary Irish plays dealing with the political conflict in Northern Ireland.[5] These conclusions are unsurprising because they follow logically from a historiography bound to a narrative of national development. Not only does such a narrative restrict what criticism is able to recognize as political theater, but it obscures crucial ideological alignments by making mainstream or institutional theater appear identical to theater as such.[6] As David Lloyd points out in his critique of the antinationalist prejudice in twentieth-century Western historiography, a superordination of the state form of nationalism eclipses the recognition of a range of other political formations and cultural practices.[7]

The following essay reflects on these issues in the light of two different historical phenomena: the cultural nationalism associated with the Irish Literary Theatre (1897–1901) and the more dissident politics associated with the nationalism of the minority population in Northern Ireland from the early 1970s. In particular, I will argue that the application of a traditional theater historiography—one concerned primarily with narrating the development of a national, state theater as related by its main advocates—is fundamentally inadequate to the task of describing the existence and possibilities of a socially progressive theater in Ireland. The essay concludes by considering some instances of a political theater of resistance in contemporary Northern Ireland.

The year 1897 in Ireland was witness to two important but seldom related cultural and political developments: the Local Government (Ireland) Bill and the setting up of the Irish Literary Theatre. In May, the British Conservative and Unionist government announced the introduction to parliament of the Local Government (Ireland) Bill. Advocated by the British chief sec-

retary in Ireland, Gerald Balfour, as the linchpin of his policy of "conciliation," this bill provided for radical changes to the system of local and
municipal politics in Ireland.[8] Its principal feature was the replacement of
the "grand jury" system, whereby the landlords in any given vicinity would
monopolize the administration of local affairs by nominating bodies of jury-
men, with a system of democratically elected local representatives. Despite
some crucial limitations, control of the police, for example, remained in the
hands of the central (British) government. John Redmond, the moderate
nationalist leader of the Irish Parliamentary Party, came to describe the bill
as a "social revolution" because it made the "mass of the Irish people master of all finance and of all the local affairs of Ireland."[9] Irish unionist MPs
like Horace Plunkett and W. E. H. Lecky also welcomed the legislation,
regarding it as offering a sea change of political opportunity. If British government in Ireland could be made more acceptable to the majority population through the establishment of indigenous institutions and instruments of
national expression, then, many unionists argued, the desire for home rule
would diminish accordingly. Nationalists, on the other hand, saw such initiatives as an opportunity for demonstrating Ireland's integrity as an emerging nation-state and, thereby, furthering the cause of national self-government or home rule.

The Irish Literary Theatre, also announced in 1897, seemed to indicate
one way in which this attempt at social consensus heralded by the Local
Government Bill might be achieved. As early as 1892, Yeats had planned a
traveling theater as part of his national library project: its aim was to prose-
lytize literary values as a way of counteracting what Yeats regarded as the
tendentious and adversarial culture of popular Irish nationalism. The project
failed because of lack of funds, but in 1895, Yeats found evidence of the
newly energized literary and cultural revival that was now about to take
place in "the expectation of Balfours [sic] threatened emmense [sic] local
Government scheme," which had "nationalized the more thoughtful
unionists."[10] Two years later, following meetings between Lady Gregory,
W. B. Yeats, Edward Martyn, and Standish O' Grady, the Irish Literary
Theatre circulated its objectives:

> We propose to have performed in Dublin, in the spring of every year
> certain Celtic and Irish plays, which whatever be their degree of excel-
> lence will be written with a high ambition, and so to build up a Celtic
> and Irish school of dramatic literature. We hope to find in Ireland an
> uncorrupted and imaginative audience trained to listen by its passion
> for oratory, and believe that our desire to bring upon the stage the

deeper thoughts and emotions of Ireland will ensure for us a tolerant welcome, and that freedom to experiment which is not found in theatres of England, and without which no new movement in art or literature can succeed. We will show that Ireland is not the home of buffoonery and easy sentiment as it has been represented, but the home of an ancient idealism. We are confident of the support of all Irish people, who are weary of misrepresentation, in carrying out a work that is outside all the political questions that divide us.[11]

In this well-known formulation, Irish cultural nationalism and the Irish unionist policy of conciliation appear to converge. Indeed, it was the Local Government (Ireland) Act (the bill became law on 18 August 1898) that provided the actual legal mechanism that allowed for the Irish Literary Theatre to operate under license in the first place. Under pressure from Lecky, the British government agreed to include a special clause in the bill allowing the setting up of the Irish Literary Theatre at the discretion of the British lord lieutenant. Ireland, with its majority Catholic and nationalist population on the eve of limited local self-government, was the Irish Literary Theatre's idealized target audience. Under the guise of an authentic Irish identity, this audience would unite, or so it was hoped, "above all the political questions that divide us."[12] That dangerous passion for oratory—used to such destabilizing effect by nationalist leaders during the Irish Land War (1887–91)—would now be transformed (or "trained") into the more decorous, and less threatening, condition of listening.

For the founders of the Irish Literary Theatre, then, the theater was regarded as having a benign social effect, smoothing over social conflict and class difference through its convincing portrayal of an agreed national identity. But these ideological hopes were by no means unique to Ireland or, indeed, to the many ascendancy and unionist supporters of the Irish Literary Theatre.[13] In Dublin, and in the towns and cities of rural Ireland, the growing popularity of nationalist drama functioned to recuperate local traditions and methods of political and social organization into the more transparent, metropolitan terms of bourgeois nationalism. Whether it was the literary drama of Yeats and Lady Gregory or the more populist nationalist melodramas of Hubert O' Grady and J. W. Whitbread, nationalist theater—performed at different venues in Ireland and among Irish emigrant populations abroad—worked to consolidate what Benedict Anderson describes as the "imagined political community" of the nation-state.[14] That the experience of a play's performance would remain essentially the same whether it was performed night after night in a fixed venue or whether it toured from one location to another was so taken for granted that it was regarded as rudimentary to its status as theater. Similar to the way that the charisma of the stage action attempted to transmute the desire for individual and national freedom into a matter of specular projection and transcendence, considerations relating to the local context and occasion of a performance were thought to be subsumed by the apparent universality of the aesthetic experience. Social divisions experienced in terms of class and gender inequality—in Yeats's *Cathleen ni Houlihan* (1902), the woman's body itself—seemed to disappear in a cloud of nationalist transcendence. In each performance the theater as an institution conveyed precisely that simultaneity of time and space that is essential to a nationalism predicated in terms of the state.[15] In short, the alignment of cultural nationalism with Irish unionist conciliation in this period was blurred by the attractive guise of an authentic Irish identity, by a widely held view that the cultural role of theater was one of class unification, and by the privileging of emergent modernist "apolitical" values such as universality and transcendence.

Even those who were opposed to a national literary theater in favor of what they regarded as a more authentically nationalist and Irish-speaking institution still regarded the theater as fulfilling the crucial task of national homogenization: in the words of the actor Frank Fay, "set[ing] a standard diction before its audiences."[16] Theatergoing in late-nineteenth century Ireland was valued just as much in terms of the cultural modernization with which it was identified as it was in terms of an appreciation of the particular dramatic narratives that happened to be performed. The Irish theater begins, in other words, as an important instrument of bourgeois nationalist ideology. National theater is seen both as a sign of Ireland's economic progress and cultural modernization (here, the theater proclaims, is no underdeveloped colony but an emerging, cosmopolitan nation-state) and as a prefiguration of the individual's ideal relation to that state. A broad range of nationalist opinion in Ireland shared Yeats's frequently stated view that the cultural activity of theater existed in stark contrast to direct (i.e., non-constitutional) political action. As one writer put it in 1895 while attempting to explain the contemporary dearth of Irish drama: "We have been living through real dramas, and have no time for dramas of the imagination."[17]

One exclusion from the accepted definition of theater in this period are peasant "pretheatrical" forms such as mumming, Christmas rhyming, and folk rituals. Anthropologists Henry Glassie, Alan Gailey, and Kevin Danaher point out that these practices were intrinsic to traditional peasant culture in Ireland and that, until the mid–twentieth century, they were organized in conjunction with seasonal festivals, wakes, and weddings.[18] In a book dealing with the Whiteboys (Irish rural insurgents of the eighteenth and nineteenth centuries), the historian Michael Beames observes that folk drama traditions of mumming were, in fact, closely imbricated with the operation of rural political insurgency.[19] Beames points out that Whiteboys and mummers shared similar costumes (usually women's clothing and white smocks), certain terminology (such as the term *captain* to refer to the Whiteboys' or the mummers' leader) and a roughly simultaneous occurrence during the year (May Eve, November Eve, New Year's Eve, St. Stephen's Day). In addition, both groups shared an important crossover concerning methods of performance and recruitment. The administration of Whiteboy oaths of allegiance across a community and performances by the mummers took place by means of surprise nocturnal visits, the power and effect of which was partly determined by the extent to which the mummers/insurgents functioned metonymically for the community as a whole. Since the masked insurgent/mummer requesting political allegiance/admittance for performance could represent *anyone* within the community, the person addressed by the mummers or Whiteboys was answerable to the community as a whole. As Luke Gibbons has argued, such connections between Irish peasant drama and Irish agrarian violence in the eighteenth and nineteenth centuries suggests that agrarian insurgency was concerned not simply with economic issues but with the preservation of political values and social codes.[20] That these values and codes were oppositional and alternative to those of a state-directed, constitutional nationalism helps to explain the complete effacement of mumming from Irish national theater history.

The extent to which this effacement was accepted by a wide spectrum of nationalists may be gauged by an article on Irish mumming that appeared in January 1903 in a popular weekly newspaper, *United Irishman*. The article was written by Arthur Griffiths, a trenchant critic of conciliatory unionism, of the Irish Parliamentary Party, and (from 1903) of the institutional successor of the Irish Literary Theatre, the Irish National Theatre Society. Exhibiting all the traits of Frantz Fanon's second-phase native intellectual,[21] Griffiths's article expresses admiration for the folk elements of mumming but decries its hybridized combination of English plantation culture and Gaelic tradition.

> If the men and boys who indulge in this innocent amusement were prevailed upon to dispense with the rhymes altogether and act the figures only, the thing would lose its foreign and quickly assume its natural, national aspect, and the "Mummers' Dance" would become

immensely popular with Irish Irelanders, and find a fitting place at concerts and musical assemblies. The airs, mentioned by their nicknames, would find their rightful ones, which would be something towards rescuing from oblivion an ancient custom.[22]

Griffiths's critique shows his dedication to a narrative of national development. Local peasant practices such as mumming are deemed "natural" once they are without words and thus marked as conspicuously preliterate, while the fitting place for mumming is imagined as the urban concert hall or musical assembly. In conclusion, the beginnings of an Irish theater institution as represented by the campaign for a national theater in the 1890s and the announcement of the Irish Literary Theatre in 1897 coincide with a considerable narrowing of the definition of theater as such. In common with the more exclusive experimental and literary theaters in London in this period, the Irish national theater movement excluded from consideration a variety of forms of theatrical as well as paratheatrical activity that were perceived to be associated with forms of political agency inconsistent with the nation-state. As well as its much vaunted denigration of popular forms of theater such as the music hall—regarded as morally degenerate because of the high level of social and erotic audience activity that it excited'[23]—the campaign of an Irish national theater entailed a much more extensive range of theatrical exclusions.

This is not to conclude that Irish folk drama or mumming necessarily offers a more efficacious model for a theater of political resistance in Ireland today. Nor is it to imply that the problematic history of institutional theater in Ireland means that the forms and practices of the institutional theater cannot be used for the purposes of political resistance. My purpose has been to indicate merely the extent to which certain kinds of theatrical practice have been effaced from Ireland's national theater history because of their imbrication with alternative methods of social and political organization. If this has a critical consequence in terms of recognizing a contemporary theater of resistance in Ireland, it is in the suggestion that such a theater is most likely to be accompanied by a keen awareness of the sociopolitical contingency of the institutional theater's forms, conventions, and practices.

The relationship between the institutional theater and the widespread resurgence of minority (nationalist) protest in Northern Ireland comes into crisis in the early 1970s. Those responsible for theater policy in Ireland and Northern Ireland were torn between a need to show that minority protest could be represented in the theater, and could therefore be assimilated symbolically to the political interests of the state, and an anxiety lest in the course of such representation, the theater itself might be used as a forum of protest. Thus, to take only the example of the national (Abbey) theater in Dublin,[24] the artistic director, Tomás MacAnna, announced that the 1970–71 season of plays would be centrally concerned with "the question of the artist's position and responsibilities in times of political strife" and that "political satire, historical comment and documentary experiment" would be the season's principal ingredients. But the opening night of the theater's first production indicates the extent to which such "involvement" was circumscribed by political anxiety. This production—*A State of Chassis* by Eugene Watters, John D. Stewart, and Tomás MacAnna—consisted of a series of sketches that gave an impression of the equal absurdity of civil rights protesters and of loyalist reaction. The play satirized in particular the civil rights leader and Westminster MP Bernadette Devlin, who had recently been arrested in the course of a forty-eight-hour police siege on the Bogside, a working-class and nationalist district in Derry. Shortly after the play's interval, the performance was interrupted by a protest by two civil rights activists. One of them, Eamonn McCann, climbed onto the stage and condemned the revue for its caricature of the politics of the nationalist minority in Northern Ireland.[25] As the actors attempted to ignore the interruption and carry on with the performance, the protesters handed them and their audience leaflets calling for the release of incarcerated civil rights activists. The incident ended quickly when the voices of the protesters were drowned out by a slow handclap from members of the audience, and the two protesters were then physically ejected by management and a group of spectators. But the most interesting feature of this protest as far as cultural analysis is concerned is the terms with which it was immediately condemned. Describing the protest as a "riot," the *Irish Times* and the *Belfast Telegraph* characterized McCann's intervention as "crude and graceless" and as an "ignorant, stupid, and bigoted" attempt "to upstage" a legitimate performance.[26] Objected to in particular was the taking control and redefinition of the theater as itself a space for public protest. McCann's comment during the protest, "Nobody can act here in that it does not mean anything,"[27] implied both a repudiation of the methods of traditional theater *and* an implicit valorization of the methods of his own staged protest. It was this challenge to representation that, at least for the bourgeois press and for the theater management, needed to be violently and unequivocally rejected. Many leading writers and intellectuals agreed with this assessment, regarding McCann's protest as a major transgression because of its use of the confrontational and disruptive tactics of political protest and a theatrical "happening" in order to challenge the consensual, distancing process established by the revue.[28] Needless to say, insofar as the *State of Chassis* protest is mentioned in Irish theater history at all, it is written about as a disruptive spectacle: a propagandistic antithesis to the theater as such. Precisely what was at stake in the opposition to McCann's protest was the question of the theater's legitimacy. It was this that had to be violently protected, just as minority nationalist resistance to the Northern Ireland state was, and still is, portrayed in the press as a form of violent anarchy requiring stronger and stronger security measures.

A correspondence between state repression and the policing of aesthetic representation (in this case, the theater) can be further demonstrated by a brief consideration of the responses of the state and of the institutional theater to the events that occurred in Derry on Bloody Sunday, 30 January 1972. Bloody Sunday took place when thirteen peaceful nationalist civil rights protesters were shot dead by units of the British Army. The incident marked a turning point in the history of the present conflict. Immediate popular reaction led to protest marches organized in most cities and towns across Ireland, the announcement of a general strike, and the burning down of the British Embassy in Dublin. But the political irony of Bloody Sunday is that as well as galvanizing widespread outrage concerning the conspicuous criminality of "law and order" in Northern Ireland, the shooting dead of the thirteen civilians inaugurated the first phase of a counterinsurgency project that had the imprimatur of the Irish government.[29] The key strategy of this policy—later to become the main issue of the republican blanket, nowash, and hunger strike protests—was to attempt to contain "the troubles" by criminalizing all forms of nonconstitutional nationalist protest.[30] Lineaments of this policy can be traced across a wide range of social practices from legislation, such as the establishment by the Dublin government in 1972 of the juryless Special Criminal Court and the Offenses against the State (Amendment) Act, to the establishment of an (ongoing) propaganda war designed to influence media representations of the conflict toward a discrediting of republican nationalist politics.[31]

Plays performed within the institutional theater contributed directly to this process of discrediting. Thus, for example, Brian Friel's *The Freedom of the City* (1973) responds to Bloody Sunday with a satire on the British Government inquiry conducted by Lord Widgery but concludes with the suggestion that *any* representation of the Northern Ireland conflict will amount, inevitably, to a deleterious distortion. Indeed, if the overwhelming response of Irish nationalists to the publication of Widgery's *Report of the Tribunal*[32] was that this document confirmed their view that British military involvement in Northern Ireland was the main reason for the conflict, this is by no means the view that predominates in Friel's play. The play's action suggests that responsibility for the shooting extends to the entire community. Distorting representations of the three innocent civilians in the play are shown as emanating not just from the British authorities, but from characters who are ostensibly sympathetic, such as the priest, the Irish television journalist, the nationalist balladeer, as well as fellow civilians on the street. It is the cumulative effect of these distortions, so the movement of the play suggests, that gives rise to the shooting that takes place at the end. Friel's next play to refer to the conflict, *Volunteers* (1975), follows a similar pattern: in this instance, the action implies that militant republican resistance to the British authorities expresses an atavistic clinging to nationalist myth. Hence the eponymous political volunteers are revealed as the victims of a calcified and unchanging nationalist history. And in *Translations* (1980), Friel's most successful and best-known work, the play moves to a rejection of republican political resistance (either in terms of the politics pursued by Sinn Fein or the paramilitary campaign of the IRA) in favor of a nationalist project of ontological retrieval. But what is relevant for the purposes of the argument in this essay is that in each instance Friel's antirepublican[33] tendencies are based, tautologically, on the institutional theater's basic assumption: the ultimate passivity of the spectator. As in the case of the final moments of *The Freedom of the City* and *Volunteers,* it is the spectator's inability to do anything except watch passively the action on stage that serves as the proof that nothing, in fact, can be done. In *Translations,* it is the audience's acceptance of English as a theatrical convention for Irish—and the recognition that this convention is itself a matter of theatrical expediency—that serves as the play's most convincing demonstration of the inevitability of the loss of Irish as a spoken vernacular.[34] How else, after all, might the play be performed and understood in metropolitan centers like London, New York, Toronto, or Sydney?

The cosmopolitan anonymity of the spectator—a basic assumption for the institutional theater in the West—becomes the Irish theater's recurrent metaphor for the impossibility of radical political change. All that the institutional theater can do in the face of political resistance is reconfirm an identity that is recognizable as "true." To adapt the definition of counterinsurgency that appears in a British Army manual of 1971, the institutional theater in Ireland can be said to function like censorship or the imposition of a military curfew: a means of isolating a resistance movement "physically and physiologically from [its] civilian support."[35]

This consensus-making effect of the institutional theater is something that working-class republican communities in Northern Ireland have been aware of for some time. Because of its ability to strengthen solidarity in the face of censorship and systematic misrepresentation, theater is seen as an attractive cultural instrument for these communities while also remaining a constant reminder of their exclusion from cultural hegemony. This helps to explain certain ostensibly anomalous features of the theater of nationalist resistance in Northern Ireland. The Belfast People's Theatre from Anderstown in Belfast, for example, was established as a means of affirming the dignity of a nationalist community widely regarded as a ghetto, and yet is marked by early productions that take place as readings rather than theatrical performances. In the same way, many later (post-1984) productions for Belfast Community Theatre/Amharclann Mhuintir Bhéal Féiriste tended to adopt a performance style that is flagrantly "amateur" and nonprofessional and that sets out to travesty mainstream theater conventions. In *You're Not Going to Like This (Part 2),* for example, there are several scenes that parody theatergoing as a display of middle-class respectability and that expose what is portrayed as the factitiously literary quality of plays performed at the predominantly middle-class Lyric Player's Theatre in Belfast. Fr. Des Wilson, a founding member of the Belfast People's Theatre and Belfast Community Theatre, argues that both these groups were well aware, in fact, of the role of institutional theater in consolidating a counterinsurgency view of republican culture, but that they still regarded the theater as an important cultural resource for strengthening and maintaining the community's opposition to the state.[36] A similar point is made by Dan Baron Cohen, a scriptwriter and coordinator for the Derry-based theater and education collective Derry Frontline, who, while acknowledging the traditional exclusion of working class communities from the institutional theater, argues that the value of theater for an oppressed community lies in the potential that it allows for that community to remain subject and producer of its own protest: "Theatre's essential independence of capital ensures its potential freedom from external censorship."[37]

The most sustained development of a contemporary theater of political resistance in Northern Ireland arises from attempts to elaborate this ambivalent potential of the theater within the context of the prisons where republican activists are incarcerated. "Writers and Writing Today," an essay written by Eoghan McCormaic while incarcerated as a republican prisoner in the H Blocks of Long Kesh, discusses the extent to which literary culture in Ireland appears to be the monopoly of a dominant class. McCormaic argues for the appropriation of literary culture as a means of resistance but then adds a crucial qualification that the forms of bourgeois culture should not simply be appropriated but "corrupted" as well:

> Isn't it about time that the private writers in prison and in our com-
> munities began adopting such a policy of corrupting the enemy's lan-
> guage, not just English but the terminology and the built-in assump-
> tions on racism, sexism or class superiority and turned it to use against
> the enemy?[38]

The primary way in which such corruption occurs in the prison drama produced in the H Blocks, I want to suggest, is through this drama's repudiation of some of the fundamental terms of the institutional theater and its
redefinition of theater production itself as a cultural practice designed to
provoke the active participation of the audience or community to whom it
is directed. This development, which took place in the early 1980s, arose
both as a theoretical imperative and as a matter of political expediency.

Drama begins to be performed in the H Blocks in 1983 as part of the
general development of republican politics that followed the ending of the
hunger strikes in October 1981.[39] The British government's refusal to concede to the ten republican hunger strikers who starved to death in their
campaign for political status meant that the ending of the strikes resulted in
republican prisoners being placed in undifferentiated "nonpolitical" wings.
In most cases this meant mixing with prisoners who also came from nationalist communities in Northern Ireland but who had themselves been incarcerated for offenses that were not politically motivated. Plays were performed in the prisons as a way of introducing and recruiting nonpolitical
prisoners into the issues of anticolonial struggle and of establishing and reinforcing a culture of solidarity. In 1984, for example, the prison authorities
placed a number of "high risk" republican prisoners on a "red book" rota-
tion system whereby individuals would be moved from one cell to another
every ten days to three weeks. Designed to prevent the most active republicans from establishing an IRA-type command structure within the prison,
the prisoners responded by using the "red book" system as a method of
developing an extensive educational program. "Red book adjutants," as
these prisoners were known, took responsibility for different areas of cultural activity such as publication, book circulation, and theater. Those in
charge of theater circulated scripts written either by themselves or by fellow
republicans in the wings in which they were incarcerated. These would
then be brought to whatever new wing that the "red book" prisoner had
been moved. Scripts that were circulated were designed to be acted out by
different actors in each performance, and it was expected that the actors
involved would introduce changes to a particular script. (These were usually minor changes incorporating topical or local references to the wing in

which the play was being performed). Following the performance, the "audience" to whom the play was directed would discuss the performance and would sometimes contribute suggestions as to how the script or performance might be further changed or adjusted.[40]

What I have been describing is a theatrical practice that was designed specifically to elicit participation and to be altered according to the different place and occasion in which the plays were performed. In a practice in which there was no such thing as a final or finished performance, the actors and script writers were regarded as jointly answerable for the political content of the play. As with the forum theater of Augusto Boal with which some of the prisoners in this period would have been familiar, such plays were scripted in order to be adjusted according to the suggestions of their "spect-actors"[41] and in order to stimulate political debate. Theater in this case made possible a kind of "loose talk" in which traditional republican beliefs could be challenged and debated without the suspicion that the person initiating that challenge was trying to undermine the movement.[42] In short, drama was used as a means of developing a critical space for questioning many of the central tenets of republican beliefs while simultaneously functioning as a method of political recruitment.

Prison theater in the H Blocks also became a way of introducing cultural activists outside the republican movement to some of the central issues of republican politics. The prisoners in the H Blocks became familiar with the work of Boal, for example, through visits to the prison by members of Derry Frontline in the late 1980s while Derry Frontline was itself instigated by, and partly composed of, community and cultural activists from a working-class district in Manchester, England. Theater in these instances facilitates not only a politicizing of culture but the establishment of a broadly based network of political solidarity.

While attempting to integrate its participants into a discourse of anticolonial resistance, then, the emphasis of H Block theater on local issues and on local participation—and on this changing from one production venue to another—places an obstacle in the way of the bland homogenization of local issues that the institutional theater in Ireland appears so inevitably to achieve. In this respect, H Block prison drama fulfills what Barbara Harlow describes as a key feature of the prison writing of political detainees in general: a critique not only of the ruling systems responsible for such detention, but of "the very institution of literature as an autonomous arena of activity."[43] It is this critical and theoretical work, Harlow observes, that sometimes results in the political prison functioning counterhegemonically, as a "university" for resistance.[44] Ironically, then, it was the British government's "success" in consolidating the criminalization of republican prisoners in the early 1980s that created the conditions for an increasing emphasis among the prisoners on politicization, just as it was Prime Minister Thatcher's resolute "defeat" of the hunger strikers that led to unprecedented electoral successes for Sinn Fein in the early 1980s.[45]

The philosophy of theater that developed in the H Blocks in the 1980s may be said to be one of the most important influences on political theater groups in nationalist communities in Northern Ireland. It also suggests an obvious contrast to the depictions of republican culture that are commonplace within the institutional theater in Ireland. Whereas plays performed at the Lyric Player's Theatre, Belfast, or the Abbey Theatre, Dublin, tend on the whole to portray the culture of republicanism as sentimental, sectarian, and crudely propagandistic, plays written for the Belfast People's and Community Theatre, drama produced by republican prisoners in the H Blocks of Long Kesh prison, as well as the recent theater work of Derry Frontline—*Inside Out* (1988), *Time Will Tell* (1989), and *Threshold* (1992)—are concerned with issues such as choice on abortion, homophobia, racism, and liberation theology. This preoccupation with exploring issues that might be deemed controversial or taboo within the nationalist communities in which the plays are developed and staged is not fortuitous, but central to their political function. It exists both as a reflection of the political contexts in which these plays are developed and as an elaboration of the specific ways in which such plays seek to engage the critical and political involvement of their audiences. Moreover, this emerging theater of resistance is particularly interesting because of its skepticism—and sometimes outright opposition—to the conventions and practices of the institutional theater.

One striking illustration of this opposition occurred in July 1993 in Derry when a group of local theater activists performed an additional scene or ad hoc epilogue at the conclusion of Vincent Woods's award-winning play *At the Black Pig's Dyke*. Performed by Druid Theatre Company from Galway, Woods's play deals with what it sees as the insidious interpenetration of sectarian murder and mumming festivity amongst a rural community on the border between Northern Ireland and the Republic. At the blackout at the conclusion of the performance, two protesters (Actor One and Actor Two)—accompanied by a volunteer "technician" with an improvised spotlight—entered the stage area dressed as mummers and performed a short scripted epilogue. Actor One (Captain [John] Major) entered after five knocks, removed his mummer mask to reveal a hood made from a Union Jack flag, and then assumed a similar stance to that of the murderer figure in Woods's play. Actor One then attempted to award the Druid actor who played the part of the murderer with an Oscar on behalf of Margaret Thatcher, John Major, and [Taoiseach] Albert Reynolds. At this point, a number of the Druid actors took fright, and the protest/intervention ended in some disarray. It had been intended that the one- to two-minute protest would end with Actor Two removing the mock butcher's cleaver from the costume of Actor One, and then addressing the audience with the following short statement: "Peace is not the absence of war, peace is the absence of the conditions that create war." Ironically, the protest itself was regarded as an act of violence by raising the possibility that a British-affiliated Loyalist assassination squad could launch an attack on a visiting theater company from the Republic. The protesters were met with widespread condemnation in the local and national press (the intervention was described as a "riot") and in a motion of censure passed by Derry City Council. The protest, or "theatrical intervention" (as it was described by the protesters themselves), was intended to expose what the protesters regarded as the play's antirepublican and one-sided bias toward political violence. But the incident was also an implicit rejection of the theatrical decorum of passive, nonparticipatory spectators, which Woods's play takes for granted.

Resistance theater in Northern Ireland cannot be described, therefore, in a purely formalist way—that is, as a particular set of dramaturgical or technical innovations—but needs to be seen as a range of heterogeneous appropriations, interventions, and sometimes deliberate misuses or "corruptions" of the institutional theater. As a theater that is constantly adjusted to the strategic needs of local situations, to different political contexts, and to different methods of political organization, it is likely to fit awkwardly—if at all—in theater histories that are concerned exclusively with the nation-state.

NOTES

This essay is drawn from and revises an earlier article, "Theatre and Insurgency in Ireland," published in *Essays in Theatre/Études Théâtrales* 12, no. 2 (May 1994). I am grateful to Harry Lane and Ann Wilson for their comments.

1. *Brecht on Theatre,* trans. John Willett (London: Methuen, 1964), 22–23.

2. Marvin Carlson, "The Theory of History," in *The Performance of Power: Theatrical Discourse and Politics,* ed. Sue-Ellen Case and Janelle Reinelt (Iowa City: University of Iowa Press, 1991), 276.

3. David Cairns and Shaun Richards, for example, argue that the Irish theater should be seen as a trajectory of development: from what they regard as the crude nationalist propaganda of plays like W. B. Yeats's *Cathleen ni Houlihan* (1902) and Maud Gonne McBride's *Dawn* (1904) to the later, more sophisticated, and mainly postinde-

pendence drama of J. M. Synge, Sean O' Casey, Stewart Parker, and Thomas Murphy. It is argued that whereas the earlier nationalist plays by Yeats and McBride are marked by the ideological trope of representing Ireland as a woman, later plays such as O' Casey's *The Plough and the Stars* (1926), Parker's *Lost Belongings* (1986), and Murphy's *Bailegangaire* (1985) offer relentless exposure (or "deconstruction") of the way in which that nationalist trope ignores the particular material interests of women. See David Cairns and Shaun Richards, "Tropes and Traps: Aspects of 'Woman' and Nationality in Twentieth-Century Irish Drama," in *Gender in Irish Writing,* ed. Toni O' Brien Johnson and David Cairns (Buckingham: Open University Press, 1991), 136–37. Anthony Roche's recent book, *Contemporary Irish Drama: From Beckett to McGuinness* (New York: St. Martin's Press, 1995) advances a similar claim. For Roche, the modernist dramaturgy of mainstream contemporary Irish theater constitutes one feature of Irish drama's "postcolonial" status. A noteworthy exception to this trend in Irish theater history is Adrian Frazier's outstanding study of the cultural politics of the first six years of the Abbey Theatre, *Behind the Scenes: Yeats, Horniman, and the Abbey Theatre* (Berkeley and Los Angeles: University of California Press, 1990).

4. D. E. S. Maxwell, *A Critical History of Modern Irish Drama: 1891–1980* (Cambridge: Cambridge University Press, 1984), 6.

5. See Nicholas Grene, "Distancing Drama: Sean O' Casey to Brian Friel," in *Irish Writers and the Theatre,* ed. Masuru Sekine (Gerrard's Cross, Bucks.: Colin Smythe, 1986), 47–70; Philomena Muinzer, "Evacuating the Museum: The Crisis in Playwriting in Ulster," *New Theatre Quarterly* 3, no. 9 (1987): 44–63; and Rob Ritchie, "Out of the North," in *Rat in the Skull,* ed. by Ron Hutchinson (London: Methuen, 1984), 3–5.

6. The term *institutional theater* is used here to refer to a theater controlled by dominant class interests and the process by which it establishes or "institutes" itself as the legitimate place and occasion for theatrical activity within a given society. See Loren Kruger, *The National Stage: Theatre and Cultural Legitimation in England, France, and America* (Chicago: University of Chicago Press, 1992), 11–12.

7. See David Lloyd, "Nationalisms against the State: Towards a Critique of the Anti-Nationalist Prejudice," in *Gender and Colonialism,* ed. Timothy P. Foley, Lionel Pilkington, Sean Ryder, and Elizabeth Tilley (Galway: Galway University Press, 1995), 272.

8. See Andrew Gailey, *Ireland and the Death of Kindness: The Experience of Constructive Unionism, 1890–1905* (Cork: Cork University Press, 1987), 40–50.

9. Redmond, qtd. in Paul Bew, *Conflict and Conciliation in Ireland, 1890–1910: Parnellites and Radical Agrarians* (Oxford: Clarendon Press, 1987), 32.

10. W. B. Yeats, *The Collected Letters of W. B. Yeats,* vol. 1: 1865–95, ed. John Kelly and Eric Domville (Oxford: Oxford University Press, 1986), 455.

11. Lady Augusta Gregory, *Our Irish Theatre: A Chapter of Autobiography* (New York: G. P. Putnam's Sons, 1913), 8–9.

12. Gregory, *Our Irish Theatre,* 9.

13. In *Acts of Supremacy: The British Empire and the Stage, 1790–1930* (Manchester: Manchester University Press, 1991), J. S. Bratton points out that the ideological work of class conciliation was a characteristic feature of late-nineteenth-century imperialism subtending most theatrical practice of the time: "Much nineteenth- and twentieth-century debate about imperialism has been concerned with its manifest power, by the 1890s, to

override and even to supersede class consciousness, creating a unity of feeling which has seemed wonderful and reprehensible, inspiring or horrifying, according to the position of the analyst. Theatrical and quasi-theatrical presentations, whether in music hall, club-room, Shakespeare Memorial Theatre or the streets and ceremonial spaces of the capital, made an obvious contribution to that much-discussed national mood. They played a large part in the creation and propagation of the 'traditions' of the nation, supplanting local, fragmented and potentially subversive 'histories'" (5).

14. See Benedict Anderson, *Imagined Communities: Reflections on the Origin and Spread of Nationalism* (London: Verso, 1983), 15.

15. Anderson, *Imagined Communities,* 30.

16. Frank J. Fay, *Towards a National Theatre: Dramatic Criticism,* ed. Robert Hogan (Dublin: Dolmen, 1970), 57.

17. William Barrett, "Irish Drama?" *New Ireland Review* 3 (Mar.–Aug. 1895): 40.

18. The most extensive introduction to "folk" drama in Ireland can be found in Alan Gailey, *Irish Folk Drama* (Cork: Mercier, 1969). Further details of mumming and related cultural practices can be found in Kevin Danaher, *The Year in Ireland* (Cork: Cork University Press, 1972), and Henry Glassie, *All Silver and No Brass: An Irish Christmas Mumming* (Dublin: Dolmen, 1975).

19. Michael Beames, *Peasants and Power: The Whiteboy Movements and Their Control in Pre-Famine Ireland* (Sussex: Harvester, 1983), 72–101.

20. Luke Gibbons, *Transformations in Irish Culture* (Cork: Cork University Press, 1996), 140–41.

21. Frantz Fanon, *The Wretched of the Earth,* trans. Constace Farrington (London: Penguin, 1967), 179.

22. Arthur Griffiths, "All Ireland," *United Ireland: A National Weekly Review,* 31 Jan. 1903, 1.

23. See Tracy C. Davis, "Indecency and Vigilance in the Music Halls," in *British Theatre in the 1890s: Essays on Drama and the Stage,* ed. Richard Foulkes (Cambridge: Cambridge University Press, 1992), 38–57.

24. For a discussion of theater and the state in Northern Ireland in this period, see my "Theatre and Cultural Politics in Northern Ireland: The *Over the Bridge* Controversy, 1959," *Éire-Ireland* 30, no. 4 (1996): 76–93.

25. See *Irish Times,* 17 Sept. 1970, 1.

26. See *Belfast Telegraph,* 19 Sept. 1970, and *Irish Times,* 17 Sept. 1970, 1.

27. *Irish Times,* 17 Sept. 1970, 1.

28. See Brian Friel, "Plays Peasant and Unpeasant," *Times Literary Supplement,* 17 Mar. 1972, 305, and D. E. S. Maxwell, "Imagining the North: Violence and the Writers," *Eire-Ireland* 8, no. 2 (1973): 91–92.

29. Seamus Deane, foreword to *Bloody Sunday: What Really Happened,* ed. Eamonn McCann with Maureen Shiels and Bridie Hannigan (Brandon, Ireland: Brandon, 1992), 12.

30. See Liam O' Dowd, Bill Rolston, and Mike Tomlinson, "From Labour to the Tories: The Ideology of Containment in Northern Ireland," *Capital and Class* 18 (1982): 72–90.

31. See Michael Farrell, *The Apparatus of Repression* (Derry: Field Day Theatre Company, 1986), and Liz Curtis, *Ireland: The Propaganda War* (London: Pluto, 1984). For

an outstanding recent analysis of the pervasive relationship between the British military policy of "containment" and the practices of Irish writing and criticism since 1969, see Joe Cleary, "'Fork-Tongued on the Border Bit': Partition and the Politics of Form in Contemporary Narratives of the Northern Irish Conflict," *South Atlantic Quarterly* 95, no. 1 (winter 1996): 227–76.

32. Lord Widgery, *Inquiry into the Events on 30 January Which Led to the Loss of Life in Connection with the Procession in Londonderry on That Day: Report of the Tribunal Appointed under the Tribunal of Inquiry (Evidence) Act 1921* (London: H.M.S.O., 1972).

33. Sociologist Bill Rolston offers a concise summary of Irish republicanism: "The republican movement has a long history, dating back to the United Irishmen, founded in 1795 on identical ideals to those which inspired contemporary French and American revolutionaries. Its central aim has been the removal of British control of Ireland. Republicans engaged in an uprising in 1916 and a consequent War of Independence in 1919 and 1920 which ended with the partition of Ireland. The republican movement in the newly created state of Northern Ireland continued its struggle for the successful completion of the national revolution. Currently it has a political maturity which has rarely been matched in its long history, and a military capacity which even British generals admit ensures that it cannot be beaten by military means alone." "'When You're Fighting a War, You've Gotta Take Setbacks': Murals and Propaganda in the North of Ireland," *Polygraph* 5 (1992): 113.

34. See my "Language and Politics in Brian Friel's *Translations*," *Irish University Review* 20, no. 2 (1990): 282–96.

35. Qtd. in Curtis, *Ireland,* 229.

36. Fr. Des Wilson, letter to the author, 8 Jan. 1992.

37. Dan Baron Cohen, "Dan Baron Cohen: Resistance to Liberation with Derry Frontline Culture and Education," interview by Lionel Pilkington, *The Drama Review* 38, no. 4 (1994): 20.

38. Eoghan McCormaic, "Writers and Writing Today," unpublished ms., 1984–85, 6.

39. Rolston discusses the extent to which political art in republican prisons can be traced to the collective self-education that took place following the introduction of internment in Northern Ireland in August 1971. See Bill Rolston, *Politics and Painting: Murals and Conflict in Northern Ireland* (London: Associated University Presses, 1991), 74. For an account of the hunger strikes, see Brian Campbell, Laurence McKeown, and Felim O' Hagan, eds., *Nor Meekly Serve My Time: The H Block Struggle, 1976–1981* (Belfast: Beyond the Pale, 1994).

40. Eoghan McCormaic, personal interview, 11 May 1993.

41. Augusto Boal, *Theatre of the Oppressed* (London: Pluto, 1974), 119–56.

42. McCormaic, interview.

43. Barbara Harlow, *Barred: Women, Writing, and Political Detention* (Hanover, NH: Wesleyan University Press, 1992), 4.

44. Harlow, *Barred,* 5.

45. See Brendan O' Leary and John McGarry, *The Politics of Antagonism: Understanding Northern Ireland* (London: Athlone, 1993), 212–13.

John Bell

Beyond the Cold War:
Bread and Puppet Theater
and the New World Order

This is about Bread and Puppet Theatre, about how and why it continues
to make political theater in the 1990s, over thirty years after Peter Schumann began its work on New York's Lower East Side in 1963. Bread and
Puppet's political theater is part of the lineage of twentieth-century political
performance that has developed into a modern tradition. Bread and Puppet's longevity speaks to the effectiveness of its theater work, work that can
offer models for political theater of the next century.

"Sixties Theater" in the 1990s

On a February afternoon in 1995, Bread and Puppet Theatre director Peter
Schumann sits in the studios of WNYC Radio in New York City, about to
be interviewed on *New York and Company,* Leonard Lopate's popular arts
and entertainment chat show:

> *Leonard Lopate.* Papier-mâché puppets of all sizes, shapes, and colors
> will be invading our frozen city again starting tomorrow when the
> Obie Award–winning Bread and Puppet Theatre will return for five
> performances at the Theatre for the New City. After a year of trav-
> eling to Taiwan, Brazil, and Sarajevo, the internationally acclaimed
> troupe is opening the year with a production called *Mr. Budhoo's
> Letter of Resignation from the IMF: Fifty Years Is Enough*—long title!
> And with me now to discuss the colorful mayhem that will ensue is
> Peter Schumann, director of the company. I'm very pleased to wel-
> come you to *New York and Company.* Actually, you introduce your-
> self as Mr. Bread and Puppet. Is that how you see yourself?
> *Schumann.* No, I'm the baker. Bread and Puppet implies baking, and
> that's my specialty; I bake a mean old sourdough rye.[1]

Schumann has been somewhat reluctant to do the interview; he is cautious with Lopate, a bit wary of fitting in too finely with the gears of the typical mechanisms of culture promotion. But, in the end, there is no one in the mostly young Bread and Puppet company better fitted to do the interview than Schumann, and, after all, this is important: Bread and Puppet is not only trying to get an audience for *Mr. Budhoo's Letter of Resignation from the IMF,* but is in fact trying to get *volunteers* to *perform* in the show, only one day before it opens at Theatre for the New City (TNC).[2]

The situation is emblematic, both of Bread and Puppet Theatre's role as one of the oldest avant-garde political theaters in the United States and of Peter Schumann's ambivalent identity as a politically engaged theater artist—opposed to, but inevitably part of, the American society that has nurtured his work since he emigrated to the United States in the early 1960s.

The New York performances of *Mr. Budhoo's Letter of Resignation from the IMF* at a low-budget venue like TNC show how Bread and Puppet has managed to avoid "success" in the American theater. Not at all material for the "cutting edge" productions of the Next Wave Festival at Brooklyn Academy of Music, and too grandiose and politically blunt for the subtle, interior ambiguities of performance art that unfold at P.S. 122 (just across First Avenue from TNC), Bread and Puppet comes to New York on a shoestring: doing its own publicity, depending on volunteers to augment its nine-person company, and hoping that an audience for image-based political spectacle will materialize in the entertainment- and media-saturated island of Manhattan for—as the theater's publicity says—"Five Performances Only!"

The radio interview is also emblematic of Peter Schumann's own situation. Thirty-two years after he created the first Bread and Puppet shows with Bruno Eckhardt (a German painter) and Bob Ernsthal (an enthused American) in a loft on the Lower East Side, Schumann is, at the age of sixty, once more on tour, his reluctance to "push product" the American way effectively outflanked by the real need to fill the house. The necessities of promoting *Mr. Budhoo's Letter of Resignation from the IMF* as a good night out at the theater go against the grain of Schumann's desire to have his art recognized (as it so often is in Europe) *as* art. Put off by the mechanics of selling, Schumann nonetheless needs to market his wares on the airwaves, and so he does. Reluctant to explain with mere words the ambiguous juxtapositions of image and sound that characterize Bread and Puppet shows like the *Budhoo* piece (and perhaps, with his accented and German-syntaxed English, uncomfortable bantering with the glib Lopate), Schumann engages in rhetorical diversions. At times he portrays his work in high moral and political tones redolent of Brecht or Piscator, but if the rhetoric heats up, Schumann is ready with a feint: it's only puppet theater; he is just a baker.

Schumann's feint underlines the ambiguous status of Bread and Puppet Theatre, still an icon of United States political theater while at the same time a low-budget, low-status theater company struggling to survive in the budget-cutting atmosphere of the 1990s. Schumann wants to find opportunity and advantage in low cultural rank and even in low budgets; this is related to what he calls "the puppeteers' traditional exemption from seriousness" and their "asocial status," which, Schumann avers, amounts "to their saving grace."[3]

In a way, Schumann's rhetorical strategies are necessary in the 1990s. The witty, erudite Lopate, who two decades earlier was broadcasting on New York's radical radio station WBAI, is now on WNYC, a well-mannered and responsibly liberal voice. To Schumann he addresses the salient questions Americans have always been encouraged to ask about political theater: Isn't explicitly political theater propaganda? Isn't propaganda the opposite of art? Doesn't political theater preach to the converted and bore everyone else?

> *Schumann.* Puppetry was always political, if you want. Even medieval puppetry, it's considered coming from being thrown out of the churches, being inside the church and then opening the carnivals outside the churches.
> *Lopate.* But in most of that you read between the lines. Bread and Puppet Theatre is a bit more explicit. You don't force people to look for nuance.
> *Schumann.* No, it's true, we do a lot of propaganda, if you wish.
> *Lopate.* You call it propaganda?
> *Schumann.* Well, I would call this a denunciation show. A denunciation of the World Bank and the IMF, showing what type of criminals they are.
> *Lopate.* And *propaganda,* of course, is a word that is anathema to anyone who talks about being an artist. So how do you balance the arts and propaganda?
> *Schumann.* I'm a baker. I don't care particularly for the fine arts. We call ours the rough arts or the sourdough arts, or the sour arts.
> *Lopate.* So, you have a certain contempt for people who say, "Listen, I'm very vocal about my politics, but when I make art, politics have nothing to do [with it]"?

Schumann. We call our art "cheap art." We are cheap artists.

Lopate. But do you think art should be political?

Schumann. Yes indeed.

Lopate. All art?

Schumann. I think all art is political because if you abstain from politics, you make a political statement right there. So whether you realize that you are in a social context and a political context, whether you are naive about it or conscious about it, it makes you political whether you like it or not.

Lopate. But you said "political theatre that tends to be slogan theatre bores the equally minded and offends precisely those customers whose hearts it wants to win."[4]

Schumann. That's a big problem.

Lopate. So you really have to be careful here. You have to be entertaining or—?

Schumann. It's not carefulness, it's social sensitivities that come into play, it's something in between. Naturally, if you just hit people with a hammer over the head, or if you preach to the converted, that's a boring business, and I hope we are not in that business. I don't feel we are. First of all, our business isn't much of a business, so we are out of it in that way.

Lopate. Monkey business, mostly! Or, you're in the bread business, as you pointed out a number of times.

It is a question of focus. Lopate, asserting the need for a critical "balance" between "the arts and propaganda," maintained by a distinct border between art and politics, is bemused by the colorful subject matter of Schumann's puppet theater ("Monkey business!"). Schumann, reconciled to the constant permeation of art into politics and vice versa, worries about "social sensitivities" in a "denunciation show" about the "criminals" of the International Monetary Fund. In 1995, Bread and Puppet Theatre's low cultural profile, its concern with international political issues, and its straightforward attempt to make political theater, are remarkably consistent with the focus it has sustained since the 1960s.

"Sixties Theater" into the 1970s and 1980s

The longevity of the Bread and Puppet Theatre, Living Theatre, and San Francisco Mime Troupe companies does not fit the neat periodicity that theater critics and historians like to impose on twentieth-century theater.

Despite the constant work of these companies over several decades, it makes for a much clearer evolutionary narrative to peg them to "the sixties." Criticism can then focus on the postmodernist theater and performance art that developed out of and (to a degree) in reaction to the expansive and often excessive performance of the 1960s and that have been much more successful integrating themselves (back) into mainstream culture, an integration the political theater groups from the 1960s have instinctively shied away from.

The longest-lived leftist political theater in the United States is the Living Theatre, which Judith Malina and Julian Beck started in 1947 in New York as a direct result of Malina's studies with Erwin Piscator at the New School for Social Research.[5] The San Francisco Mime Troupe began in 1959, the Bread and Puppet Theatre in 1963. A unifying sense of opposition to the Vietnam War and to the Cold War path of United States society inspired 1960s political theater. Schumann, as a well-educated young German artist, was in a particularly apt position to understand the effects of war (as a child he was a refugee in wartime Germany), as well as questions of complicity and guilt; at the same time he had (in a tradition going back to German classicism) both a high-minded idea of the moral role of theater and an adroit sense of the effectiveness of popular theater techniques. This, and the enthusiasm of a changing roster of artists, musicians, actors, writers, and political activists in New York, made Bread and Puppet street shows, indoor productions, and street processions the theatrical center of anti–Vietnam War activity in the 1960s.[6] The strength of Bread and Puppet's work was acknowledged at a 1968 Radical Theatre Festival at San Francisco State University, attended by Bread and Puppet, El Teatro Campesino, and the San Francisco Mime Troupe. All three groups expressed their solidarity by each performing their own version of Bread and Puppet's *A Man Says Goodbye to His Mother*.[7]

The example and participatory support of New York antiwar activists such as Karl Bissinger (of the War Resisters League) and writer Grace Paley inspired and fueled Bread and Puppet productions. In 1968 Bread and Puppet first toured in Europe, beginning a long stretch of European popularity and financial support backed by veterans of the Parisian student/worker uprisings of 1968 (like Jack Lang, then director of the Nancy theater festival, and later François Mitterand's minister of culture), who were gradually working their way into the French cultural apparatus. A period of countercultural acclaim followed; the European tours were augmented by a storefront theater on Coney Island's boardwalk, and then in 1970 Bread and Puppet received an invitation to become theater-in-residence at Goddard

College in Plainfield, Vermont. Bread and Puppet's move to Vermont
coincided with the 1970s "back to the land" movement; but Peter and his
wife and partner Elka Schumann's relationship to that movement was not
superficial: Elka Schumann's grandfather, the radical economist Scott Nearing, and his wife Helen Nearing, had in fact first popularized the idea of radical, modern agrarian subsistence in the 1930s, when they left the city for a
farm in southern Vermont.

In Vermont, Schumann's image-based theater productions began to
reflect the powerful visual impact of the rural environment. In its initial year
there, Bread and Puppet inaugurated *Our Domestic Resurrection Circus,* a day-
long outdoor festival of puppet shows, circus, and pageant combining political theater with a celebration of nature, an event that has developed into
the theater's major annual production. Throughout these decades, the puppeteers building, creating, and performing with Schumann came and went
in cycles: New York companies, Goddard College companies, and then
companies based in the theater's second (and present) Vermont home in
Glover. Many puppeteers, such as George Konnoff, a San Francisco Mime
Troupe veteran who began working with Schumann in New York and
who now creates puppet spectacles with the Puppeteers Cooperative of
Boston, still maintain connections to Bread and Puppet; others, especially
those who worked in particularly tempestuous periods of the theater's history, chose a short career and a clean break from Schumann's theater.

The image of 1960s and 1970s avant-garde and political theater was
often tied to the image of the "Genius Male Director." The stars of the 1968
Radical Theatre Conference in San Francisco were Schumann, Mime
Troupe director Ronnie Davis, and El Teatro Campesino director Luis
Valdez. Julian Beck was as much (or more of) a celebrity of the Living Theatre as Judith Malina, despite the fact that she actually directed the company's shows. Part of this attitude, as Sally Banes shows in *Greenwich Village
1963,* her study of the 1960s avant-garde, reflects the ideology of mainstream
culture, in which talented men are slotted to play the role of visionary
geniuses, while women are cast as helpers, midwives to the men's creations.[8]
The Mime Troupe had a number of company members (Sharon Lock-
wood, Denny Partridge, and Joan Holden) who emerged as directors after
Ronnie Davis left the company in 1970; likewise, when director Richard
Schechner left the Performance Group six years later, Elizabeth LeCompte
emerged as director of its successor entity, the Wooster Group. Yolanda
Broyles-Gonzalez's fascinating reevaluation of El Teatro Campesino
specifically counters its long virtual identification with director Luis Valdez
by pointing out the fundamental contributions of women to its work, and

its dependence on the strong traditions of the Mexican popular performance she terms the "Rasquachi aesthetic."[9] Similar reevaluations could (and ought to) be made of other theater companies born in the 1960s. Such an evaluation of Bread and Puppet Theatre could valorize the contributions of its members (women and men) as fundamental elements of a cultural mix that, together with Peter Schumann's European sense of moral theater and his Brechtian confidence in the techniques of popular theater, created a unique theatrical hybrid.

The end of the Vietnam War in 1975 (which was also the end of the antiwar movement) affected all of the theaters associated with the 1960s. In Bread and Puppet productions there was an uncertain lull in political content, but this was soon followed by an increased awareness of other U.S.-influenced international policies, especially in Latin America. Like much of the post-Vietnam Left in the United States, Bread and Puppet began to focus attention there.

Working with a stable core company for eight years (1976–84), Schumann developed indoor and outdoor spectacles, smaller proscenium-arch shows built for leg-and-drop stages, street shows, processions, and pageants, all fueled by the annual *Domestic Resurrection Circus*.[10] An especially practical invention of this period was the creation of giant spectacles (beginning with the 1980 *Washerwoman Nativity*) that depended upon scores of local volunteer performers to augment the Bread and Puppet company in the creation of large-scale indoor or outdoor pageants. This technique, especially developed by Bread and Puppet companies of the 1980s and 1990s, was an economical and practical way to create spectacle theater on the scale of, say, Robert Wilson's extravaganzas (but without Wilson's extensive budgets), and to make the theater's connection to communities essential through the integration of local community members into the performances. The volunteer spectacles, together with Bread and Puppet's devotion to "cheap" means of making theater, were especially practical techniques in Latin American and other Third World locales visited by Bread and Puppet, where a lack of theater technology and even such resources as electric power was offset by an abundance of spirited volunteer performers.

While these developments were ongoing in Bread and Puppet Theatre, feminist theater and queer theater of the 1970s and 1980s developed expanded notions of the liberatory thrust of 1960s theater, and performance art and postmodern formalism (particularly the work of Robert Wilson and the Wooster Group) developed theater techniques that turned away from the "poor theater" aesthetics and the community-based focus of much 1960s political theater. Bread and Puppet, like any theater company at the time, was certainly aware of these expansions, but persisted in its basic approach—*Schumann's* basic approach—which was (and is) not overly interested in the politics of gender or sexuality, but fascinated by the global politics of capitalism and the possibilities of community performance. At the heart of Schumann's focus is a general critique not only of capitalism but of modern civilization in general, whether seen in the relative abstractions of history and fiction as in *Joan of Arc* (1977), Büchner's *Woyzeck* (1981), and Kafka's *Josephine the Singer* (1984); or in the more specific contexts of contemporary events, in productions such as *Swords and Ploughshares* (1981) about the Ploughshares Eight antinuclear activists, or *The Nativity, Crucifixion, and Resurrection of Archbishop Oscar Romero of El Salvador* (1984).

Political Theater and the New World Order

The International Monetary Fund, together with the World Bank, are global institutions for capitalist development set up as a result of the 1944 Bretton Woods Conference. Convened by the Allied powers to plan the postwar reconstruction of Europe and the "development" of Third World countries, the IMF operates largely through a closely supervised system of loans. With Europe "reconstructed" relatively soon after the war, the IMF turned its focus to the Third World, but critics of the IMF charge that its policies have done little to remedy the poverty of Third World countries and much to force them into "an accelerated spiral of economic and social decline."[11] Davison Budhoo, an economist from Grenada, was an IMF staff member working on development projects in Trinidad and Tobago until 1988, when he resigned because of what he termed the fund's "increasingly genocidal policies."[12] Not content with a mere letter of resignation, Budhoo delivered a massive, impassioned denunciation of the IMF that he later turned into a book, *Enough Is Enough*.[13] In a manner typical for Bread and Puppet productions, Schumann made this "real" document a central element of his theater piece.

> *Schumann.* We got hold of an unbelievable document last summer, which some friends from Burlington, Vermont, somehow got to us, and that was this Mr. Budhoo's—who is a Paraguayan economist— letter of resignation: a 118-paged document about the whys and the insights that made him step down out of being a high officer in the IMF.
> *Lopate.* So, this is, in a way, also a matter of investigative reporting here. There's no fiction in any of this. This is the real document!

Schumann. No, we are truly using the letter itself. It's a passionately
  written letter that—
Lopate. I don't know whether to believe you, Peter.
Schumann. Well, it's true. The man was a statistician who specialized in
  statistical fraud; Trinidad and Tobago was his specialty.

The fact that Budhoo's letter is the "real document" at the center of *Mr.
Budhoo's Letter of Resignation from the IMF* can help us focus on a number of
Bread and Puppet techniques that have allowed the theater to maintain its
highly individual form of political theater over three decades. Unlike the
actor-based techniques that characterize many Western theaters, Bread and
Puppet's central focus is on puppets, masks, and other objects, and this technique is worth considering for its efficacy in dealing with the post–Cold
War international issues that most often form the center of Peter Schumann's recent thematic concerns.

Puppet, mask, and spectacle theater have characterized theater traditions all over the world (unlike realistic actor's theater, which is a western
European invention); but Bread and Puppet's use of them to create contemporary political theater is a fascinating development, providing one of
the most successful examples of what Erwin Piscator and Bertolt Brecht
defined as epic theater. The fact that puppet theater by definition involves
a constant sense of separation between performers and their work creates
a kind of automatic *Verfremdungseffekt,* allowing a perusal of content as
political issue. This form of puppet theater involves the constant juxtaposition of objects and other stage elements (music, spoken text, light) in a
multilayered theater spectacle both grounded in real political issues (the
artifact of Budhoo's letter) and yet capable of abstract, open-ended meanings. Sincere moral outrage, which Schumann allows himself to express
clearly when, as Narrator, he recites Budhoo's text, is in a constant, tricky
balance with the sensual satisfactions of theater, clearly apparent in Schumann's beautifully painted heads for a chorus of African Gods, but also in
any number of other spectacular moments in the show that, in a way similar to Robert Wilson's work, use scale and rhythm to jolt the eye and ear
with "pure" spectacle.

Mr. Budhoo's Letter of Resignation from the IMF consists of large-scale
scenes inside a proscenium stage (featuring chorus movement, dances, montage of stage elements, and stationary tableaux) juxtaposed with a solo Narrator's performance outside the proscenium frame. The Narrator doesn't
simply identify what has been seen but complicates the images' meaning by
adding excerpts of Budhoo's text into the mix. To give an idea of how this

works, I present below a scenario based on the TNC production, 11 and 12
February 1995.

Mr. Budhoo's Letter of Resignation from the IMF

The show is staged in a large, open, high-ceilinged performance space, bor-
dered upstage by a black curtain. The Narrator (Peter Schumann) is positioned downstage left with violin, music stand holding texts, light illuminating his setup, and table with bread for the end of the show.

The cast includes thirty performers dressed in business suit and tie, with
other costumes or masks added when necessary; either sex can play any role,
although the African Women who sing are played by women. The dramatis personae are roughly divided into two groups—the International Monetary Fund and the Village—using various masks, puppets, and objects.[14] In
addition, the Natural World (a third element) is represented by ten six-foot-
tall Grain Puppets—flat, cardboard cutout paintings of bending stalks of
grain—and an eight-by-twelve-foot painted cloth landscape whose pre-
dominant color is green.

The show begins with the company's entrance, led by puppeteer Emily
Anderson, to perform an eight-minute introductory piece, a Bread and
Puppet cantastoria (show with banners) entitled *The Foot*.[15] At its end the
Narrator announces the title of the main show.

Scene 1

A two-person puppet Lion enters upstage right, roaring, with Budhoo's
over-life-size cardboard letter in its mouth, and climbs a step ladder; the
performers retreat stage left to put on their Pink Masks. The Narrator
attaches one end of a clothesline to the lion, leaving the other end at the
Narrator's station. The letter slides down the rope to the chorus of pink
faces. Choreography: letter drops, masks drop. The Good Demon (Linda
Elbow) enters with a megaphone and bundle of clothes; she transforms the
Chorus Leader (Emily Anderson) into an African Woman holding a rattle;
the other Pink Masks put on dresses over their suits and trade Pink Masks
for Black Masks. The African Gods enter stage right; the African Women
enter stage left, some playing "rough music" with pots and pans and others
carrying tables and benches, which they set up center stage.

Tableau: the Women sit around the table before the Gods; as the
Gods sway stage left to stage right, Anderson leads the Women in a call-
and-response spiritual, "There Are Angels Hovering Round." At the end

FIG. 1. Bread and Puppet Theater's 1995 production of *Mr.
Budhoo's Letter of Resignation from the IMF,* scene 1: Pink Masks,
led by Emily Anderson, confront the Lion carrying the letter in
its mouth. *(Photo by Liz Obert.)*

of the song, the Gods lean toward the African Women, and the forty-
foot-wide front curtain falls, revealing a black-on-white painting dominated by a giant image of a man whose outspread arms divide the curtain
into four quadrants, each filled with smaller images of daily life: houses,
animals, buildings, cars.

Accompanying himself on the violin, Schumann recites the following
text, excerpted from Davison Budhoo's *Enough Is Enough:*

FIG. 2. *Mr. Budhoo's Letter of Resignation from the IMF*, scene 1: the African Woman (Emily Anderson) calls in the African Gods. *(Photo by Liz Obert.)*

Today I have resigned from the staff of the International Monetary Fund after twelve years, and after one thousand days of official fund work in the field, hawking your medicine and your bag of tricks to governments and to peoples in Latin America and the Caribbean and Africa. To me resignation is a priceless liberation, for with it I have taken the first big step to that place where I may hope to wash my hands of what in my mind's eye is the blood of millions of poor and starving peoples.

Schumann turns out his light, and the curtain goes up—as it will after each Budhoo reading in the scenes below.

Scene 2

Two large brown cardboard-cutout feet (about five feet long and four feet high) are paused facing left just downstage from a flat, white, cardboard building. Two Women in dresses at the stage-left wall beckon to the feet and sing wordless syllables in harmony.

The suited chorus, now wearing Teeth Masks, crawls on their hands and knees down an auditorium aisle to the downstage-left corner of the stage. They pause on arrival and then turn their heads to the audience, revealing their masks for the first time. An alternating jumping dance ensues between the building and the Teeth Masks, who eventually push the building offstage right.

The two Women stage left begin singing, calling in the Grain Puppets. The Teeth Masks sit against the stage-right wall, then kneel in front of the Grain Puppets and begin howling like wolves; the Grain Puppets move first left, then back to the right, to reveal a door, stage left center. The Teeth Masks exit through the door; the Grain Puppet operators create a low rumbling sound by tapping on the backs of the puppets. This is silenced by the sound of a tin-can drum, and a parade of Teeth Masks enters and marches downstage with the implementation machine. One Teeth Mask wheels the machine to the downstage-right corner, then turns its crank, which erects a sign reading IMPLEMENTATION. Four Teeth Masks go to a Grain Puppet center stage and attach a blank sheet of paper to it with a staple gun, then mark the paper with a large X. The Grain Puppet operators tap on their puppets. Tableau: Teeth Masks standing at attention, facing stage right, in front of the Grain Puppets; the Grain Puppets slowly lean back, away from the audience, until they are flat on the ground, their operators having disappeared. The Teeth Masks exit.

Anderson's African Woman enters; she shakes her rattle and the lights dim. The African Gods enter upstage right; the African Women enter upstage left and set their benches in an arc facing the downed Grain Puppets. Tableau: the African Gods and the African Women view the harvested field of grain; Anderson leads the Women in "There Are Angels Hovering Round" as the Gods rock side to side. Curtain.

Schumann plays the violin alone, adds a whistling accompaniment, then stops to recite Budhoo's text.

The charges that I make are not light charges. They are charges that touch at the very heart of society and Western morality and postwar intergovernmental institutionalism that have degenerated into a fake and a sham under the pretext of establishing and maintaining international economic order and global efficiency. The charges that I make strike at the very soul of man and at his conscience. When all the evidence is in, there are many questions that you and me and others like us will have to answer. The first is this: will the world be content merely to brand our institution as among the most insidious enemies of

FIG. 3. *Mr. Budhoo's Letter of Resignation from the IMF,* scene 2: Teeth Masks, armed with their implementation machine and other tools, control the Grain Puppets. *(Photo by Liz Obert.)*

humankind? Will our fellow man condemn us thus and let the matter rest, or will the heirs of those whom we have dismembered in our own peculiar Holocaust clamor for another Nuremberg?

Scene 3

The Pink Masks, with wings, and the IMF Angel (center, attached to two ropes from the ceiling) lie on their backs on the floor. Other Pink Masks stand or sit at the stage-right wall—a sound chorus. They begin with short whistles, like peeping frogs, then tap on pots and pans; the IMF Angel begins to rise from the floor as the sound crescendos. The Angel hops up and down, begins to fly, and eventually ascends to the ceiling. The tapping stops; the sound chorus moans.

The Pink Masks, still lying on the ground, begin to flap their wings like birds struggling to learn to fly; intermittently they rise: first sitting up, then on their knees, then hopping into the air. After a crescendo of movement and sound, there is a decrescendo, and the Pink Masks end up back on the floor. Tableau: Two Torso Puppets are then carried in and set up; four Pink

Masks gather around each Torso and tap on the Torsos with hangers in a crescendo as the lights fade. Curtain.

Schumann begins to play his violin in slow, soft drones, and then recites.

In guilt and self-realization of my own worthlessness as a human being, what I would like to do most of all is to propel myself so that I can get the man-in-the-street of North and South and East and West and First and Second and Third and Fourth and all other worlds to take an interest in what is happening to his single planet, his single habitat, because our institution was allowed to evolve in a particular way in late-twentieth-century international society, and allowed to become the supranational authority that controls the day-to-day lives of hundreds of millions of people everywhere. [Interlude: short melodic solo.] More specifically I would like to enlighten public opinion about our role and our operations in our member countries of the Third World.

Scene 4

The cardboard-cutout Houses dance across the stage, passing each other in a lateral back-and-forth movement. The Bad Demon enters with a pot and a stick, and with his banging forces the Houses stage right, where they mill about in a tight group; African Women are intermittently revealed between the Houses. The Bad Demon bangs once, cueing the IMF Angel down from the ceiling, to hang in midair. In a similar fashion, the Bad Demon cues the rest of the action: Houses run left and right, fill the stage, freeze. The Bad Demon and the IMF Angel dance as the Houses begin to move, and the African Women peek out from them; the Houses then slowly fall to the ground. The IMF Angel drops to the floor, the Bad Demon catching it so it stands upright.

The Good Demon enters with her rattle and megaphone, blows into the megaphone, and forces the Bad Demon off stage. The Good Demon shakes her rattle; the African Women rise from the floor with their Houses. Together, they blow toward the IMF Angel; with each breath the Angel rises toward the ceiling, but then suddenly falls on the Good Demon, knocking her down.

Stamping, the Houses gather around the Good Demon. The Women try to grab the Angel as he flies back and forth over the Houses, and finally succeed. Tableau: the African Women look at the IMF Angel on the floor. The Women begin birdlike whistling as they raise their Houses above and behind their shoulders. Dance: the Women stomp with the Houses on their shoulders, finally freezing as they shout "Ho!" Curtain.

Schumann turns on his light, then plays a duet with his violin and a piece of trumpetlike plastic tubing. He drops the tube and plays the violin with strident bowing.

How in fact did we get into the game of giving farcical advice to member countries? Is the fund staff running amok with the unexceptional authority that they wield? Are we churning out despair after despair, hunger after hunger, death after death, in the name of our epistemology? Merely to satisfy a lust for power, and punish those who run against the grain or, for our personal political ideology, by rewarding those who think as we do?

Scene 5

The Gods stand grouped stage right; the IMF Angel lies downstage left. The Gods lean stage left; an African Woman emerges from the Gods, shakes her rattle over the Angel and then upstage. A parade of African Women playing pots and pans set up the table and benches on top of the IMF Angel.

Tableau: the Gods sway from right to left; the Women sing "There Are Angels Hovering Round." At the end of the song, the table is knocked over, spilling utensils and pots to floor. A Woman with a shopping cart enters from the Gods; she and other Women put the utensils in the cart as two Women lay out the landscape on floor. Three Women kneel downstage, each underneath a bicycle suspended from the ceiling; a rope hangs from each pedal, which they grasp. A chorus of Pink Masks enters and kneels facing the Landscape.

Dance: to the sound of blowing and breathing, three African Women begin to raise the Landscape slowly, giving it a billowing, wavelike movement. As the Pink Masks stand up and walk to stage right, the Women's Landscape dance moves downstage to conceal the IMF Angel with the Landscape and retreat upstage, leaving nothing where the Angel had lain. The Pink Masks slowly kneel face down on the floor. Tableau: the bicycle Women pull their ropes to turn the bicycle pedals twenty feet above them; the wheels make a loud whirring sound, and the Landscape recedes upstage. As the bicycle wheel sound dies out, lights dim. Final curtain, after which the cast returns, bows, and then passes out Schumann's rye bread to the audience.

The Complexity of Simple Images

At first glance, *Mr. Budhoo's Letter of Recognition from the IMF* seems a very simple show. In terms of plot, the IMF, represented by the Pink Masks and Teeth Masks, takes over a building and then attempts to control a Third World village. At first they appear to succeed, but they overreach themselves, and the Village of African Women, supported by the powers of their Gods, defeats the IMF, which, at the end, assumes a deferential, rather than authoritarian, attitude to the world. Schumann works with a strong but limited palette of images, basically divided into "good" (Third World) and "bad" (IMF) forces. The stage movements and musical elements are rudimentary (easy for a cast assembled in a few days to master); Schumann depends on the minimalism of basic movements, especially vertical ones: all kinds of rising and falling dominate the production. But the show is hardly simple to fathom, basically because the meanings of the show are abstract, often ambiguous, told in the multivalenced language of images that allow for, and in fact depend upon, the individual interpretation of each audience member.

To some, image-based political theater appears to be very simple, or simplistic: what could be more blatant than the blunt directness of puppets, which, in comparison to the nuanced characterizations of actors' theater, lack all sense of subtlety? In some aspects of Bread and Puppet work, especially in short street shows or parades, there is an obvious symbolism at work. Uncle Fatso, a 1960s-era puppet representing power, repeats the imagery used in Soviet street spectacle of the 1920s: he is a corpulent, larger-than-life-size man in a suit, a cigar clenched in his right hand. Wearing a stars-and-stripes hat, he undoubtedly represents a belligerent, almost comical, U.S. government. But even here there is subtlety and ambiguity: when Fatso first appeared in street parades, some watchers were sure his face was Nixon's. But in later years, other audiences were equally sure it was Lyndon Johnson's, and then Ronald Reagan's. Before the fall of the Soviet Union, when Bread and Puppet played in socialist countries such as Poland, Eastern European audiences took Fatso (wearing a simple black hat) to represent Russian domination.

It is the frisson of ambiguity, the bit of unclarity about what exactly an object represents, that allows the political theater of Bread and Puppet its possibilities of subtlety, of inexactness, of open-ended interpretation—despite popular American beliefs about the brutish simplification in which propaganda *must* be engaged. The natural inclination of puppet theater to refuse to fix meaning is similar to Schumann's verbal feints on the radio with Lopate: it allows the presentation of strongly held convictions but does not insist on the audience taking them as their own. Instead, it encourages contemplation. In the *Budhoo* show, what does each image mean? What do the bicycles mean? What do the feet leaving the building mean? What do the wings mean? Is Budhoo represented in the show? Where and how? Who is the Lion and why does it climb a ladder?

When I first saw the show, I had, off and on, been thinking about Islam, its representation in Western theater, and the horrors then being visited on Islamic Bosnians because of their religion. When the Landscape began its breezy scene 5 dance to remove the IMF Angel, and the Pink Masks all knelt facing it, I had the immediate sense that the scene represented an Islamic prayer scene, a feeling I further justified to myself because the Landscape was mostly green, the color of Islam, and because the suffering of Bosnian Muslims was preeminent in the news. Talking later with some of the puppeteers, I realized that my interpretation of the scene was not at all something the show sought to express. But my reaction to the green Landscape, I realized, was entirely fitting, because the situation that had come to my mind was in harmony with the rest of the show, which had in fact triggered my thoughts. My vision of suffering relieved, in the context of Islam and Bosnia, was not, I realized, exactly the vision of suffering relieved in the context of the International Monetary Fund's implementation policies. But in my mind, each instance informed the other, and I understood the connections, the similarities, between the two situations. In a strict sense I "misunderstood" the *Budhoo* show, but in another way, I had very much understood the show, because it inspired a train of thought that ended up illuminating Schumann's intent as well as allowing me to connect my migrating thoughts to it. The show rewarded my contemplation.

In *Mr. Budhoo's Letter of Resignation from the IMF* the various aural and visual elements of the show are presented, as it were, for the audience's delectation. Here, look at these objects, these artifacts, the show seems to say: we have put them together in some order—Budhoo's words, a gospel tune, Pink Masks, cardboard feet, an Angel, a chorus of Gods—but you need to make sense of them yourself.

This openness is hardly an abdication (as some postmodernist image theater is) from the artistic responsibility of expressing an opinion, a point of view. Peter Schumann definitely has one about the International Monetary Fund. But Schumann's Bread and Puppet shows are built on an idea about the relationship of audience and performance as dialogue. Schumann's work is capable of conveying the outrage, horror, or inequity of a situation, but at the same time it admits its own limitations, it admits its subjectivity, in fact glorifies that subjectivity, something that places Bread and Puppet work much closer to the emotional politics of the German expressionist theater of Ernst Toller, or Hugo Ball, than to the scientific objectivity Bertolt Brecht pursued. There is a kind of contradiction here, which often frustrates goal-oriented political activists who, one might think, would be the best audience for political theater. Such activists can object to the fact that Bread and Puppet's political theater does not "preach" to its audience, but the fact that it doesn't saves its integrity as art. Beth Cleary writes that in a Bread and Puppet show like *Budhoo,* "meaning is defied and thereby re-opened," and it is this defiance of meaning that inspires continued thought rather than a fixed political opinion.[16]

Realism as Artifact

With Bread and Puppet shows, despite their reliance on the artifice of cardboard representations of faces, buildings, bodies, and feet, realism *can* exist but does so simply, as artifact. "There's no fiction in any of this," Leonard Lopate says about Budhoo's letter. "This is the real document!" Characteristic of Bread and Puppet technique, Budhoo's words and the lyrics of "There Are Angels Hovering Round"—both "found" texts—are essentially the only words in the show. Schumann's authorial "voice" resides in his performance (and editing) of Budhoo's words, and in their juxtaposition with the images Schumann has created or assembled in the show. This textual "realism," which elevates Budhoo's words to the level of object, also pertains to such elements as the violin and bow Schumann uses in the show.[17] Both were made from matchsticks by Dale Brown, a convicted murderer serving a three-hundred-year sentence in a Kentucky prison. The folk-art fetish value of such objects always opens up the kind of spiritual meaning in the material world that Western culture has (vainly) sought to regain since the advent of the machine age. In a similar way, Schumann's rye bread, passed out to the audience at the end of the show, is its own symbolic object, here making connections to the use of food in Christian ritual, and to the more general signifier of food eaten together.

Like many twentieth-century artists—from classic early-twentieth-century proponents of collage and montage (Gertrude Stein, Sergei Eisenstein, Hannah Höch, Joseph Cornell) to more recent artists such as Reza Abdoh, Elizabeth LeCompte, and David Wojnarowicz—Schumann assembles his shows from many elements. Above all, they begin with his masterful sculptures and paintings, but they also involve objects, dances, characters,

and texts contributed by others. A Vermont political activist first sent Budhoo's letter to Schumann; puppeteer Trudi Cohen found the "Angels Hovering Round" song; Dr. Bert Francke, a Vermont neighbor and participant
in the summer circuses, gave Schumann the matchstick violin; puppeteers
Linda Elbow and Emily Anderson invented their own stage characters.
Schumann's uncanny ability to draw out these contributions, to depend
upon them, makes Bread and Puppet productions appealing to those creating them. Schumann does not command performers to visualize already
established ideas, so much as seek their collaboration in inventing movements and choosing the elements of performance.

As a director, Schumann has a strong sense of how spectacle works, and
his use of spectacle follows quite classic European theater models. The *Budhoo* show, for example, uses the framed image space that a proscenium stage
offers, with its simple but functional scene curtain that can suddenly reveal
stage images. Schumann's use of tableaux is taken from European stage traditions, and his use of an offstage narrator is a traditional device of both puppet and European popular theater, the kind of "epic" element Brecht
sought to employ. Schumann's use of epic narrative echoes Brecht's sensibility, but the Bread and Puppet's use of it comes not from 1920s epic theory, but, again, from the traditions of puppet theater that helped guide
Brecht. Schumann's skilled use of scale has connections to Greek classic theater's juxtaposition of the chorus to the individual, as well as to traditional
puppet theater's juxtaposition of the gigantic to the mere life-size (for
example, in the giant carnival puppet traditions of northern France and
Spain). Another classic (and rarely used) theater technique regularly
employed in Bread and Puppet shows is the stage machine, which in *Mr.
Budhoo's Letter of Resignation* appears in the form of the IMF Angel, quite literally a deus ex machina.

In addition to this age-old *machina,* Schumann uses machines with a
sense of their modern meanings as well, their existence as representatives of
the mechanized world. In *Budhoo,* there is an obvious difference between
two machines. The IMF's implementation machine is an invention whose
cranks and gears appear to succeed only in raising its own signifier, the sign
IMPLEMENTATION. This would be laughable were it not for the fact that the
implementation machine also magically cuts down the African Villager's
field of grain. In contrast to the Teeth Masks' destructive machine, the bicycles operated by the African Women at the end of the show offer some sort
of solace, not only because the whirring of their wheels is the last, pleasant
sound the audience hears, but because the bicycles seem to offer a compro-

mise: they are machines, but machines whose readily apparent functions are clearly of use to Third World societies.

Transformation is another classic theatrical device (a staple of English pantomimes, for example) routinely employed in Bread and Puppet shows. In *Mr. Budhoo's Letter of Resignation from the IMF,* however, it also becomes a device for dealing with issues of gender and racial representation. In the *Budhoo* show an all-white cast attempts to represent a Third World village. But while *un*masked actors are limited to the use of makeup to represent a different race and then forced to deal with the complications of such charged traditions as blackface, mask and puppet theater allows more subtle and distanced transformations that avoid the actors' claim to bodily imitation. In terms of gender, masks and puppets have always allowed their performers freedom to represent either sex. A performer provides the voice for a puppet of the other sex, or wears the clothes and mask of an other-sex character, but without actually impersonating that character the way unmasked cross-dressers do. In the *Budhoo* show these transformations with objects help create a multileveled performance. At the beginning of the show, Emily Anderson narrates *The Foot* as herself: a female puppeteer in a man's suit. As the *Budhoo* show begins, Anderson uses a pink mask to become one of the IMF men, but is soon transformed into an African Woman when she puts a colorful costume over her suit and wears a dark-painted mask. Anderson, like any other puppeteer, can perform a succession of race- and gender-crossing identities in relatively quick succession. This doesn't make her respectful investment in the seriousness of the characters any less, but that seriousness is taken care of by the integrity of the objects Anderson animates (their sculptural and painterly virtues) and the uncommon skill with which she operates them.

A Political Theater for the Future

At the close of his interview with Lopate, Schumann is finally able to get to his most important message, the real reason he has agreed to do the radio program: the quite practical task of seeking out volunteers to perform in the *Budhoo* show. Having withstood Lopate's cliché-ridden happy chat about puppets and politics, Schumann takes advantage of the radio's public address system to recruit performers.

> *Schumann.* We are looking for ten more mask wearers, puppet operators, manipulators, and people who want to crawl on their knees,

and people who want to sing a marvelous song and all sorts of participatory activities.

Lopate. Well, since this thing starts tomorrow, you'd better get these people soon.

Schumann. Right, they've got to come tonight.

Lopate. So, where should they go if they're interested?

Schumann. Theater for the New City, First Avenue and Tenth Street. And the rehearsal time that we absolutely need people for is tonight at six o'clock and tomorrow at four o'clock, possibly at three o'clock for dress rehearsal.

Peter Schumann's project in the United States has been to invent a twentieth-century method of political theater using puppets and masks and the energies of hundreds of different participants. By definition, this effort has operated at the margins of American culture, thriving both in the United States and abroad at moments when Bread and Puppet's techniques seem to present apt solutions to the challenge of performing effective political theater outside the channels of mainstream, electronically mediated culture. The persistence with which Schumann has pursued this effort underscores the extent to which Bread and Puppet has, in its own mind, defined itself quite outside clichéd concepts of "sixties theater." With its practical concentration on cheap, readily available materials, its reliance on community participation, its wide-ranging local and international focus, and its commitment to the creation of theater that is both politically and artistically challenging, Bread and Puppet offers a viable model for political theater of the future.

NOTES

1. Leonard Lopate, interview with Peter Schumann, *New York and Company,* WNYC Radio, New York, 7 Feb. 1995. All subsequent interview quotes from Lopate.

2. The Bread and Puppet company for the *Budhoo* performances in New York included, in addition to Schumann, Emily Anderson, David Lamoureaux, Sam Osheroff, Betsy Brock, Beliza Torres, Joseph Gresser, and Linda Elbow.

3. See "The Radicality of the Puppet Theater," *The Drama Review* 35, no. 4 (winter 1991): 75–76.

4. See Peter Schumann, "Puppetry and Politics," in Susan Green, *Bread and Puppet: Stories of Struggle and Faith from Central America* (Burlington, VT: Green Valley Film and Art, 1985): "The truth is, we don't know what good [puppetry] does. Political theater tends to be slogan theater that bores the equally-minded and offends precisely those customers whose hearts it wants to win. Our Bread and Puppet shows are not above that;

we fall into the same trap. But we try to voice our concerns anyway, with or without success, simply because we have to" (12).

5. This connection is elaborated by Judith Malina in her unpublished manuscript, "The Piscator Notebook" (1945).

6. For a concise record of Bread and Puppet's work in these and other years, see Stefan Brecht, *Peter Schumann's Bread and Puppet Theatre,* 2 vols. (New York: Methuen, 1988).

7. See San Francisco Mime Troupe, *Radical Theatre Festival* (San Francisco: San Francisco Mime Troupe, 1969), 5.

8. See Sally Banes, *Greenwich Village, 1963* (Durham: Duke University Press, 1993).

9. See Yolanda Broyles-Gonzalez, *El Teatro Campesino* (Austin: University of Texas Press, 1994).

10. See John Bell, "The Nineteenth Annual Domestic Resurrection Circus," *Theatre* 18, no. 3 (1987): 35–42.

11. Davison Budhoo, "IMF/World Bank Wreak Havoc on Third World," in *Fifty Years Is Enough: The Case against the World Bank and the International Monetary Fund,* ed. Kevin Danaher (Boston: South End Press, 1994), 20.

12. Budhoo, "IMF/World Bank," 192.

13. Davison Budhoo, *Enough Is Enough* (New York: Apex Press, 1990).

14. The International Monetary Fund used the following: Pink Masks, Teeth Masks (white cardboard face masks with the word TEETH painted where a mouth would be), wings (mounted on performers' shoulders), an IMF Angel (life-size suited dummy with a pink mask), implementation machine (a wheeled contraption whose cranks and pulleys reveal a sign reading IMPLEMENTATION), a building (cardboard cutout six feet tall and three feet wide), and a door (cardboard cutout the size of a real door). The Village was represented by ten African Women with black masks, head scarves, and simple dresses; ten African Gods (flat, cardboard cutout faces four feet tall, mounted on ten- to fourteen-foot poles, with simple costumes pieced together from scraps of cloth); a Good Demon (a black puppet head mounted on a stick and operated from within as a limping, bent-over character); a Bad Demon (horned mask with rag costume); two Torsos (cardboard cutouts, five feet tall); a wooden table and four benches; pots, pans, and other handheld kitchen utensils; a village of ten cardboard cutout Houses; and three bicycles (hanging twenty feet above the downstage edge of the performing space with a rope reaching the floor attached to each pedal). Additional objects included two cardboard-cutout feet (each five feet long and four feet high), a two-person puppet Lion (yellow papier-mâché head and cloth body), and an Envelope (a two- by three-foot cardboard cutout representing Budhoo's letter).

15. For a description and the text of this show, see Peter Schumann, "The Foot," and John Bell, "Bread and Puppet's Street Theater Picture Stories," *Theatre* 22, no. 3 (1991): 4–8.

16. Beth Cleary, Macalester College, personal communication, 28 June 1995.

17. To "elevate to the level of object" is a phrase coined by Erik Satie. See Ornella Volta, "Satie: 'S'Elever au Rang d'une Chose," *Puck* 1 (1988): 28–29.

Lisa Jo Epstein

Flexing Images, Changing Visions: The Twin Poles of Contemporary French Political Theater

The appropriation and use of space are political acts.
—PRATIBHA PARMA

In November and December of 1980, the Centre d'Etude et de Diffusion des Techniques Actives d'Expression–Methode Boal (CEDITADE) was welcomed into the space of the Théâtre du Soleil at the Cartoucherie on the eastern outskirts of Paris for four weekend workshops, coupled with presentations of two forum theater pieces, *L'anniversaire de la mère* and *Comme d'habitude.*[1] The presence of the CEDITADE in the Théâtre du Soleil space marked an important stage of development for Boal and his then fledgling Parisian group, who initially began working together in September 1978 when the exiled Brazilian found political asylum in France and established residency in Paris.[2] Without a central location in which to work, the Theatre of the Oppressed (TO) workshops at the Cartoucherie gave Boal and his group an extended period of time in a fixed, ample-sized space to share and explore the techniques of TO within the French context. However, because the workshops were being housed by Ariane Mnouchkine and Théâtre du Soleil in their home location, the placement of the TO workshops in this culturally prestigious, leftist performance space can be seen as a strategy by the CEDITADE; they not only hoped to draw participants from the established Soleil audiences, who had proven through vast numbers their interest in politically engaged theater, but more importantly, wished to increase the visibility and credibility of the politically invested, theatrical work of TO. The latter sought visibility within the same ideological frame of political theater as their famed host. Conversely, by offering their space to the TO group in which to work, the Soleil company members had a moment of possibility to partake in a challenging new form of political theater.

I consecrate space at the beginning of this article to describe how Mnouchkine and the Théâtre du Soleil welcomed Boal's first Parisian group into the Cartoucherie because the brief intersection of the two theaters points to the overarching issues with which I am concerned here in regard to contemporary French theater: simply stated, different cultural forms of representation and their inherent theatrical strategies for resistance need to be cultivated to coexist; definitions of political theater need to be flexible in order to allow such diversity to exist; and the respective theaters that are currently working (and sometimes barely surviving) in France need not only to accept their strengths and weaknesses, but to recognize the power—or not—that their form of theater might wield over theater approaches differ- ent from their own. Interning at the Centre du Théâtre de l'Opprimé– Augusto Boal and Théâtre du Soleil for almost two years and experiencing the juxtaposition of the work discussed below made me particularly aware of (1) how the interplay of location and space can define or shape concepts of political theater; and (2) how these two theater organizations can be seen as twin poles of the political theater world in contemporary France.[3] They are *twins* because both share the belief that their form of theater engages both the personal as well as larger sociopolitical realities that surround them, forming part of a larger constituency of cultural artists in France who desire a less oppressive and more democratic French and European society. They represent *poles* of political theater because of their divergent strategies, but the ideological resonances of each that exist in the other return the discus- sion to the concept of twins. I will therefore discuss the locations of these two groups and the forms of politicized activation that occur in the spaces that have come to embody the identity of each theater so as to demonstrate where and how these twin poles exist, and—despite their different approaches to the making of theater that is political—how each could learn something about the examination of power from the other.

By the time of the 1980 CEDITADE workshops, the Cartoucherie space of the Théâtre du Soleil had been transformed from a decaying, aban- doned government armory in the woods of Vincennes that the company had acquired in 1970 into an identifiable cultural space of aesthetic innova- tion and political engagement. After sixteen years of theatrical exploration and a particularly fertile decade of 1970–80, the Soleil's work had become publicly acclaimed both for its commitment to aesthetic creation of the highest professional standards and for its successful application of rigorously developed theatrical forms, to reconsiderations of history and the role/par- ticipation of (French) citizenry in its construction. In an interview with London theater critic Irving Wardle over two decades earlier, Mnouchkine

FIG. 4. Participants in a 1995 Theatre of the Oppressed workshop held in the
new Paris location of the Centre du Théâtre de l'Opprimé—Augusto Boal.
(Photo by Lisa Jo Epstein.)

described the company's core commitment to aesthetic creation and its relationship to political theater.

> What we have been doing until now is forging our instrument. We
> wanted to treat a political theme, but you cannot do that without a
> good instrument. The failure of political theatre—if it exists—is that
> it's often so bad aesthetically, thus of no service to politics. So our
> development has been to search for an improved means of expression
> before trying to express anything important.[4]

At the heart of the Soleil's philosophy was—and still is—the belief that
political issues cannot be adequately addressed unless the theatrical form is
aesthetically compelling because the staged production must stimulate the
audience's visual *and* intellectual needs. For Mnouchkine, a play and the
resultant staged production *is* the Soleil's instrument for political struggle,
but the theater space is not the place to rehearse *how* one must fight nor to
offer practical solutions. In 1996, when questioned about the Soleil's identity as a political theater, Mnouchkine quickly pointed out that such termi-

nology was reductive, as *political* had long since been evacuated of any profound meaning, and while the terminology of popular theater concurred more with the Soleil's mission, she preferred to articulate the identity of the company in terms of its process and how their endless exploration of different theatrical forms is fueled by its mission: to create a theater that learns from and confronts the contemporary world, brings to light its contradictions and richness, and offers both creators and audiences alike a visual, "intellectual and emotional workout just like a good meal at home."[5] The result of the Soleil's tremendous national and international success due to the company's adherence to this approach and its prominent placement in the French (and international) cultural canon has been an inhibition of growth and/or recognition of other forms of political theater in France. Most frequently, when these forms exist in Paris, they are overshadowed by the Théâtre du Soleil's work and/or judged in relationship to it. In the 1996 interview cited above, Mnouchkine recounted Bernard Dort's long-ago assessment of the Soleil as an impossible model for theatrical creation to follow and affirmed her belief that the Théâtre du Soleil had opened a route for exploration that has surprisingly been rarely traveled; therein lies the need to recognize the institutionalized power wielded by the extremely high aesthetic standards of the Soleil, not just for politically engaged theater but for aesthetic representation itself. As she decried the lack of other theaters concerned with civic responsibility, as well as the desperate situation of cultural creators in late-twentieth-century France, she also spoke passionately of the need to draw alliances among theaters in order to resist the takeover of for-profit culture.

In 1980, the mission of the early work of CEDITADE was unclear to French theater critics, who questioned whether Theatre of the Oppressed was in fact a form of theater or even existed on the same creative continuum. This critique prompted a vehement response from the then-new TO practitioners, who felt that the distinction between what the French call *animation,* or cultural trainings, and art, or artistic creation, was an incorrect and misinformed categorization of TO.[6] Because of its emphasis on aesthetic creation, critics and scholars easily positioned the Soleil's identity on the side of art, even though its work sought to animate the consciousness of spectators to their sociopolitical conditions. Yet, TO remained ambiguous because of the CEDITADE's goals to lead workshops, entertain, and engage audiences through Forum Theater shows, and still contemplate more professional productions.

Prior to the 1980 winter workshops, Jean-Gabriel Carasso of the CEDITADE wrote a passionate defense of the theatrical nature of Theatre of the

Oppressed in the *Information Bulletin* of the center. Carasso pointed out that French theater in general was facing a crisis and undergoing an examination of the relationship between itself, its audiences, and the larger political realm, as were the techniques of TO. Furthermore, Carasso underlined that they (of the CEDITADE) had no intention of abandoning their proper working space, which he considered *the theater* in all senses of the term. Part of their mission to bring the techniques of the TO from "the street" into a structured theater space was to investigate and

> question the ritual of theater itself, the writing, the acting, the scenography, etc. in order to envision spectator intervention. . . . For are we not also in part oppressed by ritualized, repetitive forms of performance that have been practiced up until now? Isn't this "return" of the audience sometimes cruelly missing when "traditional" forms of theater are shown?[7]

Because the Théâtre du Soleil was founded on the desire not to replicate mainstream, mimetic forms of theater nor the actual work structures and methods for creating theater that are traditionally applied, the Cartoucherie location seemed an ideal space to welcome the TO workshops. Carasso concluded his editorial by stating that only through the reintroduction of the Theatre of the Oppressed into an actual theater could the above-listed issues be addressed.

Whether consciously or not, Carasso's rationale for holding TO workshops inside the Cartoucherie belied a desire to have the TO workshops legitimated as a valid form of theater simply by the act of placement inside the Théâtre du Soleil's own space. The reasoning for such an attitude seems sound: since the Théâtre du Soleil's work involved crafting and refining stage images in order to flex audience's intellects and activate the mental process of linking theatrical image to contemporary, living subjects and situations, the public terrain appeared ready for the interactive TO techniques. However, being in residency at one of the only places in France where politically engaged theater retains an immensely popular following did not guarantee Boal and the CEDITADE sold-out workshops; in fact, they were almost completely ignored by the theater world. In order to mark the value of the workshops to those few who had participated, the CEDITADE shyly categorized them a "clandestine public success." Even after the CEDITADE was reconfigured as the Centre du Théâtre de l'Opprimé (CTO) in 1986, the need to be officially recognized—to carve out a distinct, acceptable, intellectual critical space (as opposed to category) between education and politics within the French theater world by somehow linking its work to established conventions of staged drama—would remain a problematic undercurrent of the center in the 1990s.

That a consciously activist theater form such as Theatre of the Oppressed had, and still has, difficulty getting recognized as a worthwhile form of theater in France may be due, in part, to the processual nature of TO work and the lack of a final product per se; is this where its politics lie? Is recognition difficult today because, with few exceptions, the 1990s members of the CTO are not theater artists or craftspeople first but primarily teachers, educators, social workers, and counselors with Theatre of the Oppressed as their only "official" theater training? Does this difficulty therefore indicate the limited definitions in France for what is authorized as effective political theater? The majority of French facilitators who have trained at, or with, the Parisian CTO over the past fifteen years are neither theater professionals nor university academics attracted to the dialogic, open-ended, self-critical, and performative nature of the work, as they are in the United States. In France, TO-informed individuals are mostly people committed to, or already working in, social and political terrains—most often social workers, trainers/animators, therapists, or educators—who come to a TO workshop, usually via word of mouth, curious about techniques that might complement and enhance their respective fields of work. For example, participants in some of the 1995 workshops ranged from an unemployed street educator, to the director of a branch of Amnesty International, to the president of Association Solidarité Algérie and founder of FAUED (Femmes Algériennes Unies Pour L'Egalité des Droits), who hoped to return to Algeria with a Theater Forum show that addressed women's rights and the establishment of peace in Algeria. Participants do not envision themselves as direct representatives of Boal, who must exclusively channel his theater techniques into the French context, but rather as independent workers who can utilize and adapt them as they see fit.

While the CTO's work does qualify as educational and social interventionist outreach, their workshops do not extend from either a "producing" theater organization or from a center for social research whose findings could be channeled back into French society. Because the CTO straddles the borders of social and cultural categories, its identity continues to be difficult to define, especially for the purposes of government funding through the Ministry of Culture. The hesitancy of the French cultural world to embrace the CTO is also linked to the historical lack in France of a grassroots, community-generated, popular theater movement in which people take local issues into their own hands via performative means. This is not to say that the French were or are apolitical; to the contrary, they are highly aware and very critical of both their immediate sociopolitical context and the more complex global political arena in which they are located and by which they are constantly effected. A long history and fervent belief in democracy, of privileging the voice and needs of the people versus that of the government, theoretically and sometimes practically pervades French societal practices. In the winter of 1995, for example, educators, teachers, students, and workers across the country teemed into the streets in greater numbers than they had in 1968 to form one of the largest nationwide protests against the government that France has ever experienced. Nevertheless, France's twentieth-century concept of popular theater—in terms of "theater of the people"— stems largely from (1) the Théâtre National Populaire, which sought to address Jean Vilar's belief that theater is "a public service in exactly the same way as gas, water and electricity,"[8] (2) Vilar's founding of the Avignon Festival and the now standard practice of government subsidization and decentralization that began in the 1950s, and (3) a long line of directors, companies, and creators across half a century, each of whom had varied ideas as to how theater should address the needs of the communities in which it was located.[9]

To this day, the French are theoretically steadfast about their commitment to fostering and promoting cultural and educational channels for popular voices, even as financial and political backing wane. In an attempt to reiterate and remind the theatergoing public of France's fecund tradition of "citizen's theater," the 1995 Avignon Festival showcased an exhibit entitled "Théâtre Citoyen: Du Théâtre du Peuple au Théâtre du Soleil" that traced the major trends (and alluded to the surrounding myths) of French theater created "for and by the people" from the turn of the twentieth century up to the present. This exhibit culminated in an installation devoted to the Théâtre du Soleil and posited that this company exemplifies the ability to keep popular, civic-minded theater alive.

Today as the right-wing government takes hold with President Jacques Chirac at the helm, the life of theatrical production in France, let alone that which is invested in critical dialogue and engagement with audiences and society, is threatened. Spectacle-oriented productions that gloss over the problematics of individual and collective existence, or slightly graze on pertinent issues with an opportunistic, politically correct, yet safe "liberal" hand, take precedence—and with it, increasing amounts of government funding. Yan Ciret, director of the journal of the Théâtre de la Bastille, one of the few theater spaces in Paris committed to alternative performance,

captured what is rotting in the state of French theater in the end of the
1990s.

> One essential question involves, far beyond just theater, all of civiliza-
> tion: the theater, born with democracy, will it die with it? In the face
> of this emergency, we must respond to the political and critical
> innocuousness of present-day theater and its downhill drift, even in its
> most radical forms, toward what the Americans call *entertainment*.[10]

Problems abound: in a country where the growing presence of social, political, and economic exclusion of the working class, high percentages of
unemployed and lower-income people, immigrants, young adults, and
handicapped have bred the all too frequently used buzz word *insertion* as the
social remedy, the ancient utterances of liberty, equality, and fraternity as
the ideological base of the cultural and political system no longer ring true.[11]
Not surprisingly, in 1995 sociologist and historian Pierre Rosanvallon edi-
torialized,

> Since the 1980s, French politics, one might say, have desocialized
> themselves. . . . The political system has at the same time turned into
> its self, the parties more and more having a rhetorical relation to the
> social. . . . [P]erhaps the greatest fault today is the lack of channels of
> expression, of the communication of social problems. You might say in
> other terms that an intermediary body is cruelly lacking.[12]

It is unsettling to discover the extent to which French theater, often thought
to be such an "intermediary body," has been affected by the political desocialization and the severance between the playing of politics and the playing
out of France's social realities, as well as the growing intolerance of free
thought in a country long considered a bastion for politically revolutionary
thinking.

Nevertheless, despite recurring unemployment and insufficient funding (albeit at different scales), both the Théâtre du Soleil and the Parisian
CTO strive to sustain their activities in order to serve as such intermediary
bodies. But since the encounter in 1980, little dialogue exists between the
two. The latter constantly moves around to different public locations and
theatricalizes unlikely places with small numbers of people in order to let
participants examine the oppressive mechanisms of power on the microlevel
of society, at their personal level, while the former creates epic-scaled,

staged theater productions for very large numbers of people with the goal of laying bare the contradictions of French political systems, its destructive societal practices, and the effect on individuals. Théâtre du Soleil productions want to stimulate audiences to activate their sociopolitical consciousness, while the work of the CTO empowers participants to enact their consciousness, partake in the construction of meaning, and, in doing so, come to understand the larger political themes inscribed in their individual stories.

While the Ministry of Culture receives 91 percent of the state budget, of which 27 percent is devoted to theater and musical production, this cultural output rarely engages with the concrete political realities of France. Yet by its seemingly large presence (over 100 theaters—state funded or not—are listed in the weekly entertainment magazines), theater seems now to exist as an extension of the rhetorical stance wielded by French politicians.[13] In 1995, 680 million francs were cut from the cultural budget, and, as a result, longtime alternative theaters are dying. In addition to provocative stage productions, an important aspect of the work that occurs inside the space of the Théâtre du Soleil is the mobilization of the populace around political problems. Capitalizing on the cultural clout and political history of the Soleil space and Mnouchkine herself in France today, the director of the Théâtre du Soleil organized a late March 1996 meeting of creators, artists, and citizens across different disciplines and from diverse countries in order to mobilize against the new conservatism of Chirac's government. This coalition of 450 people was motivated by concerns about "the danger of degeneration or destruction/annihilation that threatens not just this or that organization, this type of research training, this space of creation but all of the living fabric of intellectual and cultural production."[14] The meeting led to an urgent and impassioned emergency call the following June to theater practitioners, artists, educators, and researchers to join together at Peter Brook's Bouffes du Nord—either physically present or via fax and email—to express fears, brainstorm, and discover alliances in order to prevent the right-wing scalpel from further mutilating France's cultural body.

AIDA (Association Internationale de Defense des Artistes, Victimes de la Repression dans le Monde) is another element that informs the public of the politicization of the Théâtre du Soleil space. Founded by Theatre du Soleil actors in 1979 (the same year CEDITADE was formed), but dormant for a number of years, AIDA resumed its activities primarily in response to (1) the persecution and murder of women, artists, journalists, and intellectuals in Algeria by the Islamic Salvation Front and the lack of response by the French government; and (2) harsh changes by the French government of its immigration laws, which made procuring visas by endangered Algerians practically impossible. Functioning out of the administrative office at the Soleil, the AIDA staff receives calls and letters from artists asking for help; in turn, AIDA actively searches for lodging, organizes paperwork for visas, and seeks invitations for both short- and longer-term contracts that could enable the persecuted Algerian artists to take refuge in France.

With the cry that "all victims of persecution in the world have the right to asylum," AIDA brought hundreds of artists and concerned civilians, including exiled Algerians as well as prominent French artists and intellectuals, to a 27 February 1995 meeting at the Théâtre du Soleil. The highly charged and emotional assembled body who filled the bleachers of the performance space to capacity discussed the political situation in France and Algeria as well as the wording of a "Manifesto for the Right to Asylum and Hospitality for Algerian Artists" drafted by Mnouchkine and the AIDA team. Its final version, which was published in the 26–27 March 1995 edition of Le Monde, declared its refusal to accept the French government's reconfigured immigration and refugee policies that shut the door on Algerians who tried to obtain visas and refugee status in France (barely 1.5 percent of Algerians successfully obtain visas). The policies, ostensibly created in the name of the French people, made the government and by extension the populace collaborators in the assassination of Algerian culture.

Meanwhile, the previously homeless Centre du Théâtre de l'Opprimé–Augusto Boal (as it has been called since 1994) obtained its own space in February 1994 and moved into a period of transition and diffused energy as it sought solutions for its immediate needs and lost sight of committed engagement with the political problems that were plaguing the French cultural community (among others). Ironically this new place shares the address 75012 Paris with the Théâtre du Soleil, even though the CTO is not located in Vincennes but inside the Paris periphery in the 12th arrondissement. With its whitewashed walls and maze of little rooms, located amid a series of rambling warehouses in various states of renovation or disrepair, the CTO's new location is quite off the beaten Parisian track— behind the bustle of the Gare de Lyon train station—and ripe for regeneration. Installation in a fixed locale may seem contradictory for a theater that takes place in the field where conflicts exist, for a theater that thrives on repowering subjects within the formal structures that oppress them. As a genre, however, TO work is open to myriad styles and is powerful precisely because it can take place in innumerable spaces. Ideally, this new flexibility of having both a home site and countless locations could engender what political theorist Chantal Mouffe calls "the project of radical democracy" whose outcome would be "the articulation of the greatest possible number of democratic struggles."[15] Appropriation of a building could therefore be seen as a strategy to create a physical place in Paris to present the array of theater work engendered by fieldwork in various communities.

The current CTO team—not unlike their earlier CEDITADE counterparts—optimistically hopes that establishment in an identifiable location will finally enable it to stake out a recognizable conceptual space in the French theater world, as well as to expand their much-needed visibility with sociopolitical associations that work with marginalized communities throughout France. Will acquiring a home create the bridge to both the established theater world and the underprivileged communities they continue to serve? The encounter at the Soleil in 1980 did not initiate a dialogue between the two theaters nor among its audiences; long overdue, the CTO's connection with the leftist French theater world has been a critically missing element in the establishment of Theatre of the Oppressed as a viable form of socially invested "theater" in France. Even in 1994, the CTO was surprisingly absent from—and only mentioned in passing by—the assembled presenters at a minicolloquium on theater and social intervention sponsored by the Department of Theater at the University of Paris. As cultural organizers, the CTO team needs to be reminded that they themselves—as an organizing "body"—are situated in the troubled, politically charged space of France and that their theater-based work with its mesh of activist and therapeutic elements can offer an important tool for brainstorming solutions, especially for members of the extended artistic communities whose fates lie dangerously close to the conservative chopping block. Furthermore, the effectiveness and realm of political possibilities engendered through workshops coupled with the creation of several forums a year can only be intensified if, as individuals and as a collective center, the CTO steps up and dynamizes its *own* personal involvement in the political realities and struggles of the communities that most affect them.

If the CTO wants to partake in the French theater world and share knowledge and skills with the artistic community, now is the time, since dialogues about encroachment on freedom of expression and government oppression are circulating through networks of leftist artists and educators at all levels of the cultural hierarchy. The CTO team has already clearly defined the vast terrain wherein Theatre of the Oppressed can and should take place. Instead of participating in the pressing turmoils of the cultural community and raising awareness about the liberation dynamics of TO to revitalize the roles of both facilitators and participants alike, the desire to be recognized as a real theater in a real space has led the powerful work of the company askew. In 1995–96, the CTO team with Boal decided to reconfigure their work into a more recognizable, accessible theater form by mounting a traditionally staged production of Boal's adaptation of *Iphigenia at Aulis*. In it, the public played the role of traditional spectator, but with a twist. With the *Iphigenia* project, the CTO team idealistically sought to present a staged production of the drama to be immediately followed by a series of forums that would enable the assembled public to examine the ideological narratives encoded in the play and link these issues to the sociopolitical currents in France. Instead of successfully animating the interplay of politics and theater, however, the production undercut the strength of Theatre of the Oppressed as practiced by the CTO and devoured the team's already-diffused energy. Endless hours of physical labor were required to transform the new warehouse into an acceptable performance space by the opening date, while other members still had to organize and conduct TO workshops in order to secure and sustain the financial blood of the members. Moreover, learning how to rehearse the play co-opted critical time from the development of the most vital aspect of the project, which was the forum portion of the program.

In contrast to the underdeveloped theater activism of the CTO, the Théâtre du Soleil, ardently spearheaded by Ariane Mnouchkine, has continually created staged productions that have been outspoken about the policies, activities, or inaction of the French government. Despite the fact that 40 percent of their budget comes from government support, the remaining 60 percent is generated from ticket sales; hence, the Soleil is dependent—not unlike the CTO—on an active and activated public for whom stage productions that critically delve into the historical and sociopolitical constructs of their communities are considered vital. While the CTO longs (perhaps wrongly) for public recognition and financial support as a "theater," the sheer numbers of people over the decades who have journeyed to the cavernous hangars of the Soleil space (or respective replacement spaces when on tour) have created for the company an immense and diverse international community of spectators for whom the act of going to the theater space has become part of the process toward social change. Yet not unlike Boal's motivational political theories that fuel the work of the CTO, the Soleil wants to awaken this ever-changing spectatorial body to historical and sociopolitical contradictions and, in the process, activate audience members to discuss issues rather than resort to hollow communal consensus. As Mnouchkine described in a recent interview on contemporary tragedy and the political space of theater, "I would say that theater brings together in order to better illuminate. But, by illuminating, theater divides. That is its democratic function."[16]

While the CTO primarily works with people on the margins—of the city and of traditional forms of theatrical expression—the Soleil is literally located along the margin of the city and utilizes the power of the space's placement *outside* the established perimeters in order to devote extensive rehearsal time to delving *inside* dramatic texts that reexamine the very social constructs against which the Cartoucherie is situated. However, Théâtre du Soleil's goal to create "a theater taken directly from social reality, one that is not a simple account, but an encouragement to change the conditions in which we live. We want to recount our History to move it forward,"[17] resonates with the CTO's more humble mission to have *spect-actors* replay moments of their history in order to move out and beyond the confines of the personal or political structures that oppress them.

The principal working terrains of the CTO include prisons, poor suburbs, government-subsidized housing projects, centers for chemical dependency, rehabilitation halfway houses, and detention centers (to name a few) where disenfranchised and depersonalized inhabitants form what sociologist Rosanvallon calls an excluded "nonclass," "a shadow cast by the dysfunctioning of society, the residue of its decomposition and desocialization . . . without representation."[18] Having adapted TO techniques from their Latin American roots to the French context, then, it is not surprising that much of the CTO's most interesting work revolves around "person-personality-character" and focuses on the shift that individuals make as they play roles in different situations. It would be impossible to cite the range of work accomplished by all of the CTO members; the examples detailed below spotlight some of the more challenging current activities of the center that stretch beyond the confines of the techniques themselves.

In the first chapter of his book, *Méthode Boal de théâtre et thérapie,* Boal explains how human beings create a certain kind of ever-present trio that more or less constructs the spaces in which one exists and functions; this three-dimensional dwelling is comprised of the self who observes, the self in a situation, and the not-self or Other.[19] Implicit in the repowering of the political body is the movement of participants through each of these positions. In the aesthetic space, *spect-actors* reenvision notions of identity and negotiate personal and situational boundaries through physically resculpting and redefining the habitual or societally imposed images (or body masks) through which internal states are portrayed. In a thirty-hour CTO 1995 workshop with a group including actors, dancers, cultural animators, an art therapist, youth and emergency shelter careworkers, and a chemical-dependency counselor, Nicole Charpail (an experienced French actor) and Rui Frati (an experienced Brazilian-Italian actor and family therapist) integrated Boalian and other theater techniques to delve into the complexities and isolate the shifts in self-consciousness that accompany the transformation of the learned rituals and social masks that construct one's identity. Through a blending of image theater and Brecht-like character creation, the workshop sought to explore the passages between the aesthetic, the political, and the therapeutic, between "expression that comforts and creation that transforms."[20] Charpail and Frati pulled from a wide range of experiences, including work in prisons and with prostitutes (Charpail) and with unemployed and welfare recipients (Frati), where reconstruction of the participants' identities was a stepping stone toward understanding their personal identities in a political society. Through the process of moving from accustomed rituals to new ones, by foregrounding the "person" position to that of "character," passing "personality" along the way, the participants opened up previously untapped aspects of their personalities and imaginations—discovering different characters and capabilities that resided within them—from which they could then choose new strategies to implement in their daily lives.

Charpail's work in a detention center for women, many of whom were drug addicts between the ages of twenty-five and thirty-five, is an example of TO work conducted in places not normally considered theatrical. Charpail always applies her formal theater training to her TO work with "excluded" populations and so demonstrates the power of handing the mode of theatrical production—the means of theatrical expression via image theater and forum techniques—to participants physically and mentally trapped and living in oppressive mental and physical places. Through the course of one workshop, the women learned to imagistically analyze their everyday rituals with new perspectives. However, when the women became fed up with talking about "their crappy lives" (their words), Charpail introduced exercises with a neutral mask and asked them to make an effort "*to be* beyond all personality, all stories, without moving forward, without retreating, without stopping, without a future, without memory, an effort *to be,* short of any form-ulation, *without a name.*"[21] In combination with the TO exercises, the women realized their capabilities to reconstruct identities without falling into their customary performances of "prisoner," to push at the margins of what it means to be in prison, and to mobilize aspects of themselves that had been forced to be dormant.

Starting from the opposite pole, the Théâtre du Soleil interweaves issues of the "excluded" into the dramatic texts that they mount at the Cartoucherie. Yet Mnouchkine, and by extension the company, do not consider these issues as anything but their own, as concerned citizens who contribute to the health of French society. On the heels of the highly successful *Les Atrides* (1990–92), Mnouchkine wanted to speak directly about the present situation in France, where the erosion of moral conscience, widespread corruption, and personal ambition above the public good were key issues. Hence, the blood scandal *(l'affaire du sang)* of 1984–85 imposed itself as "the metaphor of the crime of our era. It's a new form of genocide."[22] Briefly, the affair involved hundreds of hemophiliacs who were contaminated with the AIDS virus through transfusions of unheated, untested blood supplied by the Centre National de Transfusion Sanguine (CNTS) with the tacit accord of the Ministry of Health, while other hemophiliacs who were already HIV-positive were given blood from the same stock, with unaccountable repercussions. It later came to light that the blood-screening test developed by the American Abbott Laboratories to detect the presence of the AIDS virus in donated blood was not put into immediate circulation because the French equivalent had not yet been completed by the Pasteur Institute; various administrative authorities consciously staved off implementation of the American test for fear it would flood the medical markets, thereby ruining the commercial marketability of the French analogue. Once the "affair" was publicly exposed, court testimony revealed probable cover-ups by public officials as well as various conflicts of interest involved in the case; newspaper articles surrounding the scandal have continued into the late 1990s.[23]

The Soleil's reading of the blood scandal resulted in Hélène Cixous's *La ville parjure (ou le reveil des erinyes)* [The perjured city (or the awakening of the Furies)], which could be considered the fifth episode of *Les Atrides* in which the blood spilt by Clytemnestra to avenge her daughter's sacrifice and the repercussions of matricide committed by a vengeful Orestes continue to flow into the 1990s and infect individual conscience and the mechanisms of democratic procedures. According to the program for the production, *La ville parjure* was written between December 1992 and September 1993, yet it proffered a situation "that took place between 3500 B.C. and the year 1993." Unlike the mingling of factual, historical events with fiction that characterized *L'histoire terrible mais inachevée de Norodom Sihanouk, roi du Cambodge* [The terrible but unfinished story of Norodom Sihanouk, king of Cambodia] (1985) and *L'Indiade, ou l'Inde de leurs rêves* [The Indiade, or India of their dreams] (1987), and without the spectacular visual and aural theatrical languages of *Les Atrides*, *La ville parjure* is a much more formal, ominous, and dark production than what the Soleil has trained its audiences to expect. Yet it is clearly in keeping with the political alarm they are trying to sound.

Because the French public has been inundated with newspaper articles and broadcasts of the real sequence of blood scandal events, this 1994

Cixous-Soleil creation didn't reproduce the story but offered a reading of events as "signs in the flesh in a very mythological universe. It is in that that *La ville parjure* is also *Le reveil des erinyes,* it is that that places us in the terri-tory of theater."[24] The Brechtian fable of the play revolves around the plight of an emotionally, physically, and financially ruined mother whose two hemophiliac sons have been killed by contaminated blood and who has fled to their gravesites in a dilapidated cemetery on the outskirts of the city. The cemetery is inhabited by a chorus of the marginalized members of society, its "undesirable shadows"—bedraggled homeless, errant drunkards, wan-derers, poverty-stricken immigrants—and is overseen by a gentle and aged, yet ageless, caretaker named Eschyle (Aeschylus), who notes down all that transpires there. Granted temporary refuge by Eschyle from the doctors' lawyers, who come charging into the cemetery in order to blackmail the mother into accepting money for silence, she listens to the chorus weave lyrical tales of who they are, their dreams and nightmares, and most of all, their desire for justice. Over the whole scene majestically reigns an androg-ynous graceful "Night" mother with trembling black wings and a face with a thousand wrinkles. The Night will later be responsible for sending the mother pietà-tinged visions of her dead sons, who enter manipulating mar-ionettes and accompanied by floating guardian angels cloaked head to toe in black. The Night will also call forth the three Furies to propel the mother's silenced, distraught cry of vengeance into action.

Stirred from their underground hearths, the Eumenides push their Fury selves to the surface, where appearances might have changed but only the telephone is different, where the sociopolitical system constructed by Athena in an effort to reign in acts of bloody vengeance and establish pathways of justice has become an immoral tool for unscrupulous corporatism and self-promotion by elected officials who get away with murder. Guided by the ageless Night, the Furies rumble back to the present to once again take up a mother's cause and recreate the scene of a crime from which justice was barred, an act that unleashes the true threat to the city. They kidnap X_1 and X_2, the perjured, cynical doctors (who broke the Hippocratic oath and claimed it was the fault of the state that children's deaths occurred), and turn the cemetery into a court of justice with the Furies as chief prosecutors and the spectatorial chorus (and audience) as jury. Accompanied by an outraged retinue of lawyers and counselors, X_1 and X_2 are confronted with the intan-gible charges of crimes of conscience, shame, cynicism, contamination, irre-sponsibility, and perjuring. The mother literally sits on the ground and waits, not for blood as desired by the three hungry Furies, but for the impossible request that the doctors admit they are sorry. The sheer vocalization and mobilization of the marginalized voices of the mother, Furies, and chorus—

FIG. 5. Juliana Carneiro da Cunha as the homeless Immonde in 1995 rehearsals for Hélène Cixous's *La ville parjure (ou le réveil érinyes)*. *(Photo by Lisa Jo Epstein.)*

heightened by the kidnapping of the doctors—exerts enough pressure to cause concern among the ruling politicians of the city on the pivotal day before, and then evening of, the ruling presidential elections.[25]

The principal political bodies whose actions theatrically resonate with their real-life counterparts are represented in the play as the following: the queen, who unsuccessfully pleads with her husband to take a stand on behalf of the mother and the injustices wrought by his administration; the aged king (considered by the French press as Mitterand) no longer capable of emotion, who exists as a stiff ceremonial figurehead, unwilling to investigate his own cabinet for fear of the truths that may surface, nor willing to take action for fear of political repercussions; Forzza, the clever and demonically portrayed fascist rival, who uses the cemetery event to manipulate voters and defeat the incumbent king and who, once elected, orders the cemetery to be destroyed along with all who reside in it; and finally, members of the medical profession of varying age, gender, and prestige who assemble in the middle of the night at the cemetery to consolidate their support of each other. The exception to the latter is Dr. Lion, who steadfastly refuses to sign a letter on behalf of the perjured doctors and, in separating herself from her professional circle, signs the end of her medical career.

By constructing a story in which a wide array of allegorical characters

FIG. 6. Shahrokh Meshkin Ghalam as *le roi* in 1995 rehearsals of
Hélène Cixous's *La ville parjure (ou le réveil érinyes)*. (Photo by Lisa
Jo Epstein.)

exist, the Théâtre du Soleil didn't explore how social mechanisms corrupt
individuals and drain democracy of its humanity, but instead showed the
societal masks performed at different levels of society. The theatricalized
bodies came to signify the different social actors of the drama but were *not*
the drama. In other words, due to the highly theatrically refined presentation of the characters, they were foregrounded as constructed, performative
identities whose interrelationships often seem denaturalized, unrealistically
heightened, and historicized, but in doing so, the mise-en-scène illuminated
the socioeconomic paradigm in which these roles were inscribed.

La ville parjure was forced to close long before predicted because the production did not fill the Soleil house with six hundred spectators on a regular basis as needed. Mnouchkine rationalized the forced closure by noting that

> this production needed a trumpet call that it didn't have, even if the reviews were favorable. The subject of *La ville parjure* made people scared. Perhaps both the press and ourselves didn't know how to explain that this production wasn't a television-like documentary but a tragedy on the erosion of conscience and the responsibility of our time, but with real characters.[26]

A key problem for the Soleil was how to captivate audience interest in a piece not only about a huge political scandal that was still making headlines at the time of the production's 1994 opening, but also about "individual conscience"—both of the spectators and the larger French political body. For Mnouchkine, the issue of conscience lay at the heart of *La ville parjure* as well as "at the heart of the current moral crisis in Europe." She sees "the crime committed by these doctors as the metaphor for the absence of conscience in our society" and believes "that we are raising a people with no inner voice and that democracy is threatened unless we instill a sense of individual responsibility in the new generation of Europeans."[27] The press easily identified the political players in *La ville parjure* and generally agreed on both the importance of the subject matter and the spectacular power of the play's imagery. However, the combination of the show's length (the production consisted of two four-hour parts) and Cixous's poetically dense, highly allusive, and meandering text mitigated the direct impact of an otherwise fascinating mythic depiction of contemporary France's sociopolitical subterfuges and machinations.

La ville parjure grandly aspired to delve into the invisible realm of personal responsibility and its relation to one's surrounding political context—to wake audiences up to how one's moral complacency can exist at once as an oppressor of others and the self and to show the negative repercussions of such complacency on the functioning of society. Had the Théâtre du Soleil remained in active dialogue with CEDITADE since their meeting in 1980 instead of eclipsing possibilities for exchange and mutual nourishment, the twin poles as well as their audiences might have benefited from working together to more clearly understand and untangle the central issues of the Cixous play that were correlative to pressing contemporary issues. Inviting the 1990s CTO into the Cartoucherie space during the run of *La ville par-*

jure or simply initiating TO workshops in its own new location around the emotionally difficult and politically charged themes might have created an innovative alliance between these two leftist French theater groups. Not only would such a joining have strengthened the impact of the Soleil's production—diffused through an overly ambitious spectacle and highly complex language—and rendered the urgency of the issues more palpable and immediate through the direct flexing of images that occurs in TO work, but it might have enabled the struggling CTO to revitalize its strength by focusing on political problems deeply rooted in the French community.

Like Foucault, both theaters recognize—and want those who participate in their theater to recognize as well—that "as soon as there's a relation of power there's a possibility of resistance. We're never trapped by power: it's always possible to modify its hold, in determined conditions and following a precise strategy."[28] However, it is the open dialogue—rather than the hierarchization of theatricality or political effectiveness—between these differing strategies that must occur among practitioners, no matter where their location, if resistance and change is to occur. When I was in France in 1994–95, some members of the CTO denigrated the processes of the Soleil although they supported AIDA's actions, and I was informed by company members at the latter not to bring up Boal's theater around Mnouchkine. I was never able to uncover the deeper personal differences that seemed to lie inside these remarks. Yet both theaters continue to represent twin poles of French leftist political theater that optimistically seek, through their respective spaces, to engender dialogue and open up discussion between individuals about their society. Such refusal to discuss each other's theatrical form seems to perpetuate reductive, oppressive attitudes at a time when cross-fertilization and renewed concepts and images of political theater in a late 1990s French context are sorely needed.

Postscript

When the first draft of this article was written in 1995, I was deeply involved in rehearsals and workshops at both the Théâtre du Soleil and the Parisian CTO and could find little critical distance with which to assess either company. As I moved back and forth from one space of cultural production to the next, I was struck by similarities in how bodies and corporeal images were exchanged among actors and repeatedly flexed in order to reconceive representation of a character's identity on stage. I was interested in how, concomitant to critiquing sociopolitical power structures on personal and historically material levels, the process of producing bodily images in each space offered new ways to look at what was actually "political" about each theater's techniques. That is to say, with each reconfiguration of body image came insights into the capability and necessity of channeling consciousness into a corporeal form in order to effect change.

As I continued to ponder the rapport between the development of consciousness and bodies, I was led back to the reality that such relationships were unique to, and contingent upon being in, a specific place, within a particular playing space embedded with its own political and theatrical history. Hence, I couldn't begin to explore how bodies and images were flexed and changed without taking the physical context into account; I first needed to define the particular spaces in order to situate their respective strategies. In placing the work of the Centre du Théâtre de l'Opprimé–Augusto Boal and the Théâtre du Soleil alongside each other, I recognize that identifying a location for "political" theater is itself problematic, and not just because political activism is defined and played out quite differently in France than in the United States or Latin America, or because all of these countries play a role in the political theater that comprises international relations. That said, a discussion of the location and space of each theater reveals how the CTO is in many ways constructed against the Soleil, which was itself originally constructed in opposition to mainstream theater. This study clearly manifests how a moment of possibility of real cultural exchange between leftist, politically engaged theaters was overlooked in 1980 and points to ways in which the work of the Théâtre du Soleil and the Centre du Théâtre de l'Opprimé–Augusto Boal could benefit from reviewing and flexing their agendas in order to shift attitudes and visions as to what are, and can be, valid forms of cultural, political expression.

NOTES

1. Boal and his Paris-based group had created the two pieces for a tour of Brazil earlier in the year.

2. The CEDITADE was officially founded in February 1979. In 1986, the group was reconfigured as the Centre du Théâtre de l'Opprimé (CTO), which was later changed to the Centre du Théâtre de l'Opprimé–Augusto Boal. I will use *CTO* to indicate the center as it has existed since 1986.

3. During 1994 and 1995, I participated in most of the activities that occurred in these two spaces. I was an intern at the CTO, which meant I was a regular participant in most workshops and also had various technical and administrative duties. After an initial period conducting archival research at the Théâtre du Soleil in 1993–94, I began working in a technical capacity during the run of *La ville parjure (ou le reveil des erinyes)* and later became a rehearsal assistant for the Soleil's production of Molière's *Tartuffe* from the fall

of 1994 through the summer of 1995. I returned to Paris in late January–February 1996 for three weeks in order to note developments since my departure, during which time I observed rehearsals for the CTO's production of *Iphigenia* and saw a number of representations of *Tartuffe* at the Cartoucherie.

4. Ariane Mnouchkine, qtd. in Irving Wardle, "Le Théâtre du Soleil: *1789,* an Interview with Ariane Mnouchkine," *Performance* 1, no. 2 (1971): 133.

5. Personal interview, Feb. 1995. Unless otherwise noted, all translations from the French are mine.

6. The literal translation of *animation* does not capture the breadth of this French term, widely used to refer to a variety of training and group activities used by knowledgeable facilitators to animate, enliven, or ignite the session participants.

7. "Théâtre de l'opprimé . . . et théâtre: Vraies ou fausses contradictions?" in *Théâtre de l'opprimé, Bulletin d'information du Centre d'étude et de diffusion des techniques actives d'expression (Méthodes Boal). Special Théâtre-Forum* 4 (1980): 26.

8. Jean Vilar, *Le théâtre au service pubic* (Paris: Gallimard, 1975), 145.

9. In a nutshell, after World War II and beginning in the 1950s, subsidization moved theaters from being privately run to largely government funded, which in theory enabled companies to lower their ticket prices and open up their theaters to audiences who previously had little or no access to cultural production (although by 1968, many state-supported theaters would be targeted as elitist and completely disconnected from the people due to their imposition of bourgeois ideology). It was also in the 1950s that Jeanne Laurent, a minister of fine arts, sought to establish a circuit of *centres dramatiques nationaux* (national dramatic centers), each with a permanent company, whose funding would be provided both by the government and by community sources from the center's location. By the 1960s, André Malraux, at the head of the then new Ministry of Culture, initiated the construction of fully federal supported *maisons de la culture* (houses of culture), to be situated throughout France, and for which directors were appointed because of their proven record and/or work in that region.

10. Yan Ciret, "Le théâtre au risque du spectacle," *Libération,* 1–2 Oct. 1994, 8.

11. While the word *exclusion* in French is equivalent to "poverty," it also has become a metaphor to designate a way of life due to massive unemployment that sweeps into its definition cultural, familial, sociological, political, and ethnic relations resulting from French social and political systems. *Insertion* (translatable as "reinsertion," "integration," or even "rehabilitation") has also become a key word to indicate a politics of employment created to help young people and longtime unemployed workers back into the job force and to ameliorate the living conditions of the very poor. Part of this policy revolves around the creation of professional and/or vocational workshops or internships called *stages* that are meant to provide necessary training for unqualified and/or unemployed workers, or to serve as a stepping stone for anyone into job placement. For more information about the politics and convoluted conceptions of the merits of French policies for rehabilitation of socioeconomically deprived people, as well as insight into grassroots-like organizations called *associations* that offer an array of practical training for the wide majority of "excluded" members, see Daniel Lenoir, "Les politiques sociales au risque de l'exclusion," in *L'etat de France '95–'96* (Paris: La Decouverte, 1995), 34; and Sylvia Zapp, "Les associations intermediaires cherchent leur voie," *Le Monde,* 9 Dec. 1993, xi.

12. Pierre Rosanvallon, "La société oubliée," *Libération,* 18 May 1995, 8.

13. Percentages taken from Joël Roman, "Politique de la culture, l'exception française," in *L'etat de France '95–'96* (Paris: La Découverte), 579.

14. EPOPEA, *"Appel."* Correspondence received via the Théâtre du Soleil, May 1996.

15. Chantal Mouffe, "Radical Democracy: Modern or Postmodern?" trans. Paul Holdengräber, in *Universal Abandon? The Politics of Postmodernism,* ed. Andrew Ross (Minneapolis: University of Minnesota Press, 1988), 41.

16. Ariane Mnouchkine, "Le tragique contemporain," *Théâtre/Public* 123 (May–June 1995): 13.

17. Théâtre du Soleil, *L'age d'or, première ebauche* (Paris: Theatre Ouvert, Stock, 1975), 14.

18. Rosanvallon, "La société oubliée," 8.

19. Augusto Boal, *Méthode Boal de théâtre et thérapie, L'arc en ciel du desir* (Paris: Editions Ramsay, 1990), 21. Now available in English as *The Rainbow of Desire,* trans. Adrian Jackson (London: Routledge, 1995).

20. Nicole Charpail, "L'art des marginaux, exclusion/création," *Art et Thérapie* (Blois) 46–47 (June 1993): 24.

21. Charpail, "L'art des marginaux," 25.

22. Martine Leca, interview with Ariane Mnouchkine, "Le sang contaminé est le crime de notre epoque," *InfoMatin,* 30 May 1994.

23. It was subsequently discovered that the general director of the CNTS also had a hand in satellite blood businesses that paid him a private salary beyond the government funds received as the publicly prominent head of the National Blood Center. Complaints have been lodged by many of the hemophiliacs and transfusion recipients against an array of doctors and past ministers on the grounds of poisoning, involuntary homicide, and nonassistance to a person in danger. Some of the accused received short prison sentences and fines, others did not. In January 1994, over one hundred prominent doctors petitioned Mitterand to grant Michel Garretta and Jean Pierre Allain, the two doctors most deeply implicated in the scandal, a state of grace; thirty-three Nobel Prize winners also interceded on their behalf.

24. Armelle Heliot, "Ariane Mnouchkine: Le sang des innocents," *Le Quotidien* 27 May 1994, 12.

25. It was undoubtedly deliberate that Cixous wrote *La ville parjure* to occur on the eve of an election so that the Soleil's production would parallel events of France's own election year. That the right-wing conservative candidate Jacques Chirac would defeat the Socialist candidate, Lionel Jospin, could not have been specifically foretold; ironically, the fictional drama forecast the political reality that its creators would soon encounter. All of the play's issues are listed in a glossary that comprises most of the program.

26. Ariane Mnouchkine, qtd. in "Soleil Voilé pour Ariane Mnouchkine," *Le Monde,* 21 Oct. 1994, 15.

27. Ariane Mnouchkine, qtd. in Julie Street, "Queen Ariane Triumphs at Tragedy," *European,* 10 June 1994.

28. Michel Foucault, "The History of Sexuality: An Interview," trans. Geoff Bennington, *Oxford Literary Review* 4, no. 2 (1980): 13.

Una Chaudhuri

Working Out (of) Place: Peter Brook's *Mahabharata* and the Problematics of Intercultural Performance

If the parentheses in my title have the slightly stale whiff of deconstruction, this is because the deconstructive method, stale or not, allows one to do what Peter Brook's *The Mahabharata,* at this historical juncture, most crucially calls for: that is, to see and say two (at least two) different things at the same time. *The Mahabharata* requires this double response because it is situated at a critical turning point in the discourse of interculturalism, a moment when one contextualizing ideology was giving way to another. Looking both backward and forward, *The Mahabharata* embodies the change that occurred in the course of the last decade, when intercultural performance shifted its grounds in Western liberal humanism and began to be recontextualized within the burgeoning critical discourse—inaugurated in 1978 by Edward Said's book *Orientalism*[1]—of postcolonialism.

This shift was registered in responses to *The Mahabharata* as the initial outpouring of lavish praise was increasingly tempered by harsh criticism, especially from Indian critics. Brook's baffled response to this criticism is clear evidence of the critical paradigm shift I shall be arguing for: he was, quite simply, amazed that there could be any objection to what he regarded as a labor of love—a desire to honor the Indian tradition, not to plunder it. Nothing could have been further from Brook's intention than the characterization he received in some quarters as "a self-appointed representative of a 'universal culture' [who] had pillaged world culture in search of new territories, then planted his own imperialist flag in the flank of [this] quintessential Hindu work."[2]

To recognize the historicity of interculturalism is, I believe, the best way to do justice to Brook's monumental achievement. We need, at this point in time, not to attack or defend Brook but rather to see how his

experiment opened up certain possibilities that other artists are now following up. If we can manage both to critique Brook's *Mahabharata* and appreciate it—that is, if we can conduct a critique that is not at the same time a
personal denigration—we shall see that Brook's achievement goes well
beyond what he himself attempted. I want to argue, in fact, that the very
thing that made Brook's *Mahabharata* so offensive to postcolonial critics—
namely, its universalism—also, and unwittingly, brought into play certain
representational options that show a way out of the apparent impasse of the
original critical debate. I shall argue that Brook's *Mahabharata*—*The Mahabharata* as performed, not the text in either Jean-Claude Carrière's French
original or Brook's English translation—employed certain performance
strategies that, if properly recognized, might be of use in negotiating the
problems interculturalism faces today, especially the problem of how to
avoid the essentialist trap of identity politics. This way out leads in a very
different direction from Brook's own philosophy; it is in no way a return to
a universalist humanist ideology, to a vision of the brotherhood of man.
Indeed, what I believe to be *The Mahabharata*'s greatest success may be, from
Brook's intellectual perspective, a failure. To me the value of *The Mahabharata* lies not in what its creator says about it but in what he did in it—or
rather, what happened in it, which is a quite different matter.

The term *interculturalism* covers a whole spectrum of borrowings from
foreign cultures, ranging from subject matter to texts to dramatic technique
to theatrical style, even to performance venue. When David Henry Hwang
writes a play about the encounter between a French diplomat and a transvestite Chinese performer, interculturalism resides at the level of subject
matter (and is often called, at least in America, multiculturalism). When
Tadashi Suzuki stages Euripides' *The Bacchae* using Japanese language, costume, music, and acting style, or when the Ark Ensemble Company in New
York stages Girish Karnad's modern Indian play *Hayavadan* with an American cast and a new English title *(Divided Together),* interculturalism is
located at the level of the text. When Ariane Mnouchkine puts the chorus
of her Greek tetralogy *Les Atrides* in Kathakali masks and costumes, one has
interculturalism of theatrical style. When a Japanese Noh company or an
Indian Kathakali troupe visits New York, one has interculturalism of the last
kind—based solely on a shift in venue. Rarely, of course, is interculturalism
restricted to only one of these possibilities—most works that deserve the
designation do so on several counts; Hwang's play *M. Butterfly,* for example,
is not only a case of intercultural subject-matter but also, in parts, of intercultural theater style.

The conceptual and practical development of intercultural theater that we have witnessed in the last two decades both reflects and is part of the changes that have swept this century and includes unprecedented movements and interactions of populations. Such immense social transformations have left their mark on all cultural activity, so that today not only theater but social life itself is increasingly intercultural, transcultural, multicultural. Among the conceptual categories that these changes have affected, perhaps the one that has been revised most thoroughly is place. The increasing dominance of space-based studies in the social sciences, elaborated by theorists like Henri Lefebvre, Michel Foucault, Fredric Jameson, Edward Soja (to name a few) has produced a whole new discourse of which the key terms are borders, limits, travel, rootlessness, territoriality, nomadism, *habitus,* migration, home, homelessness, exile, diaspora, position, location, situation, mapping; center-margin, open-closed, inside-outside, global-local. The immense significance of this new discourse is summed up by Fredric Jameson in his remark that "it is at least empirically arguable that our daily life, our psychic experience, our cultural languages, are today dominated by categories of space rather than categories of time, as in the period of high modernism."[3]

That the theater should respond strongly to this development is predetermined by its inherently spatial and local nature, its unbreachable bondage to space, place, and places. And among theater practitioners, who could be more centrally involved in charting the consequences of this new paradigm than the author of that hugely popular tract *The Empty Space*? Peter Brook's career can be described at one level as a lifelong inquiry into the potentiality of that empty space where he locates the origins of theater. The opening line of his book—"I can take any space and call it a bare stage"[4]—is so famous partly because it is so unlikely. We are used to thinking of the theater as a very specific and highly differentiated space, complete with a stage, an auditorium, seats, curtain, lights, and so on. Peter Brook's work has been devoted to liberating theatrical experience from traditional architectural confines, and the accounts of cultural experience they encode, a process that took him first from his native England to a warehouse on the outskirts of Paris and thence to places as distant as Shiraz in Iran, Africa, and India.

Among the things Brook brought back from India was a play that encapsulated the impulse of displacement that had motivated Brook from the outset. The commitment to working out of place—that is, to working outside of the places traditionally set aside for theater work—marks *The Mahabharata* at a profound level. What we can call for short the "outsideness" of this work has been literalized in some of its presentations, but it is a key feature of the play even when it is presented indoors. Here is David Williams's perspicacious summary of the spaces of *The Mahabharata:*

> A series of quarries (in Avignon, Athens, Perth, Adelaide), a boathouse on the shores of a Swiss lake, a film studio sound stage in Los Angeles, a disused transport museum in Glasgow, the newly renovated Majestic Theatre in Brooklyn, the Bouffes du Nord—these . . . settings outside or on the fringes of the conventional cultural geography of a city, most requir[ed] a certain effort to be reached—the extra-ordinary journey as act of literal and metaphorical displacement becoming an event in itself.[5]

Brook's theater of displacement—his way of working out of place—is also a way of "working out" place—that is, of exploring the status and meaning of place in human experience. He embarks on this exploration with a great deal of philosophical baggage—one might even say that he has decided in advance where he is going and what that place will be like—but certain conditions of this enterprise provide their own results, leading to a very different place from the one Brook claims to have reached. The place he works out is not the utopia he is looking for, not the undifferentiated and archetypal "deep space" that he believes all cultures share; rather, in working out of his own place he uncovers—stumbles upon?—a place more like what Michel Foucault called a "heterotopia"[6]—in which many distinct and different places are layered and combined, one on top of another or beside each other. The source of this heterotopia is not Brook's philosophy, which is resolutely utopian—but his theatrology, especially his casting choices and the resulting acting style these choices produce. The performative elements of *The Mahabharata* contrast strongly with the dramatic structure encoded in its text. The latter is conventional, linear, unified, simple; the former are differential, deconstructive, disjunctive, difficult. The text bespeaks a commitment to clarity and profundity; the performance speaks out the complex and clamorous claims of intercultural representation. It is this discrepancy between text and performance that accounts for the widely differing responses *The Mahabharata* elicited; it is also the site of its unintended passage beyond the impasses of 1960s and 1970s interculturalism.[7]

The Mahabharata as Hypertext

What attracted Peter Brook to *The Mahabharata* is exactly what got him into trouble over it, and it has to do with place: *The Mahabharata* is the founding text of Hindu-Indian culture, as deeply interlaced with that culture as the geography of the subcontinent. Like that geography, *The Mahabharata* seems not only to signify India but also to contain it and to create it: as Vijay Mishra remarks, "The Puranas, dramatic texts (both classical and modern), medieval romance, the Indian bourgeois novel and finally the Indian film all retrieve the rules of their formation from *The Mahabharata*. There is something so dreadfully imperialistic about this text that in a moment of willful generalization and enthusiasm we may indeed claim that all Indian literary, filmic and theatrical texts endlessly rewrite *The Mahabharata*."[8]

This "imperialistic" quality of *The Mahabharata* was translated by Brook into a characteristically benign metaphor, encapsulating his humanist theory of mythology. *The Mahabharata,* Brook said, has "its roots in the soil of India," implying that its branches and blossoms are elsewhere, or rather, everywhere.[9] But the organic metaphor is misleading, implying as it does that the epic reflects a natural order of things, complete with an evolutionary process of change. A more apt metaphor, one that was not available to Brook in the way it is to us, comes not from the natural world but from the field of contemporary communication. *The Mahabharata* is a hypertext, a field of textuality comprised of many distinct but interlinked elements—stories, characters, relationships, events, ideas—capable of infinite combinations and recombinations, and connected to its changing contexts and its readers by means of a complex web of social, philosophical, religious, and ideological discourses. Brook's decision to turn this dynamic force-field into a deep-rooted, towering tree was an act of translation that could not help but betray its source.

Besides suffusing its home culture as no other text does, *The Mahabharata* is unusual qua text, a work of such monstrous extension and hybridity as to seem to defeat the very notions of unity and stability that define a text. *The Mahabharata* is the longest poem in the world. It contains over one hundred thousand stanzas and runs to eighteen volumes in the Sanskrit original. It is fifteen times the size of the Old and New Testaments combined, and eight times the length of *The Iliad* and *The Odyssey* put together. Although tradition attributes authorship of the epic to the sage Vyasa, as does Brook's version, the text is clearly multiauthored, reflecting generations of priestly and literary additions, in which the original story is embroidered with material from folklore and legend and frequently interrupted with long meditations on matters of morality, ethics, theology, and statecraft. Although it reached its final form around the second century A.D., its earliest versions are thought to have arisen in the sixth or seventh century B.C., roughly contemporary, that is, with Homer. Between that conjectured origin and its final form, the epic "absorbed a large number of divergent

narratives, anecdotal and fantastic, as well as religious and theological"
material.[10] The hypertext that emerged is partially captured in the magiste-
rial Poona Critical Edition of 1959, which includes all the variant readings
and collates all the known manuscript recensions.[11]

The *Mahabharata* is the product of centuries of agglomeration and elaboration, with a compositional history that has registered India's long and
complex social history. In its earliest forms, it was a poem of triumph, sung
by the servants of the princely caste of Kshatriyas, at festivals and sacrifices
honoring a ruler, frequently gaining embellishments appropriate to the
occasion. From this early version, in all probability, is dated its insistence on
being a history *[itihasa]*, and the central events it records no doubt have
some connection to actual historical events. It was gradually disseminated
beyond the high castes and all over the subcontinent by wandering bards
who added details and commentaries in response to the cultural expectations and limitations of their changing audiences, as well as material from
local legends, myths, fables, and folktales. At some point in its evolution the
Mahabharata sustained extensive religious and philosophical influence from
the priestly caste of Brahmins, who incorporated into it material from
ancient Vedic scriptures, religious, philosophical, and ethical digressions,
and elements of customary law.

The Hindu cultural context, in which the original text has no auratic
status, made of the *Mahabharata* a living, changing cultural document, to
which the popular imagination has been free to add according to its spiritual, political, and aesthetic needs. Most importantly, this open-ended quality of the *Mahabharata* has allowed it to remain closely connected to the cultural and spiritual life of every generation of Hindus. The profound
significance that the *Mahabharata* holds for Hindus in India is voiced by
Gautam Dasgupta, who writes, "The *Mahabharata* I grew up with in India is
a vital source of nourishment, a measure of one's thoughts and deeds. It is
no mere epic constrained by literary and narrative strategies, but a revolutionary injunction, ethical and theological in purpose, that determines and
defines the social and personal interactions of millions of Indians."[12] This
fact—the mutual permeation of the *Mahabharata* and Hindu-Indian life—
has been the basis of most critiques of Brook's play, not because of the massive displacement involved but because of Brook's failure to adequately
address the consequences of his displacement of this text from its very insistent context.

Paradoxically, what critics see as Brook's failure to do justice to the
Mahabharata's Indian contextuality arises out of Brook's desire to honor
India, to close what he regarded as a lamentable gap between the status of

the epic within India and its status in the West. That this immense poem
could so saturate Indian culture and yet be virtually unknown outside it
struck Brook as somehow wrong and in need of redress. But Brook's mission was inevitably framed by his own philosophical vision, which, for all its
intercultural investments, is a Western humanist one. At its heart lies the
belief that Truth is universal and singular, and that this Truth can be recov-
ered from certain stories of other cultures—no matter how strange and
unfamiliar their outer form. In the case of *The Mahabharata,* this conviction
led Brook on a quest for what he called the epic's "core," its essential story,
which, as he put it, "on the one hand is universal, but on the other, would
not have existed without India."[13]

For Brook and Carrière, this double quality of *The Mahabharata* (Indian
but universal) entailed a choice, articulated as a distinction by Carrière in his
introduction to the published text: "Any historical or theological truth—
controversial by its very nature, is closed to us—our aim is a certain dramatic truth."[14] Carrière seems to be saying that the very thing that makes
The Mahabharata deep and complex (in his word, controversial) is somehow
by definition beyond his—that is, beyond, a Western reader's—reach. But
is this not like saying that the complexity of *Hamlet* is too much for a non-
Western reader, with the consequent implication that such readers would
be well advised to attend to the exciting plot of the play and leave the philosophical issues—controversial by their very nature—to others? Brook, of
course, would never say this; indeed, one of his defenses to the charge of
orientalism is his claim to be redressing a balance, bringing an Indian mas-
terpiece to the West "after a hundred years in which every educated Indian
was forced to know the works of Shakespeare and Molière and Racine."[15]
But in urging this parallel, Brook forgets that the works of Shakespeare and
company were not reinterpreted for Indians by Indians, nor reframed in
Indian terms; rather, Indians were expected to bring to bear on them the
same extensive knowledge of these texts' cultural and philosophical context
as Western readers did. There was no question of leaving their "historical
and theological truths" closed and apprehending them only at the level of
"dramatic truth."

Is there such a thing as a purely dramatic truth without serious attention being paid to its Indian context? Brook believes there is, and it forces
him into an oppositional construction that Indian critics have bristled at:
"To tell this story," says Brook, "we had to avoid allowing the suggestion
of India to be so strong as to inhibit human identification to too great an
extent."[16] The alternative formulation is articulated by Bharucha, who says,
"One cannot agree with the premise that '*The Mahabharata* is Indian but it

is universal.' . . . *The Mahabharata,* I would counter, is universal *because* it is Indian. One cannot separate the culture from the text."[17]

Brook, however, does want to separate the culture from the text, because he believes that the most valuable thing the text encodes is a universal, freestanding, transcultural, and transhistorical moral truth, of which the Indian terms are mere draperies. But I think it is at least worth considering if these draperies are not, like Draupadi's endlessly unfurling robe, the very fabric of *The Mahabharata*'s meaning. Perhaps there is no naked truth beneath them, with any claim to have uncovered that nakedness only putting other draperies in place. In making such a claim, Brook reveals that he regards the specifics of cultural difference as so many charming and quaint trappings. In the case of *The Mahabharata,* he goes so far as to relegate all these cultural elements to the status of a "flavor"—something like the exotic spices that turn English meat and potatoes into an exotic curry: "We have tried to suggest the flavour of India," he says, "without pretending to be what we are not" (xvi). But the flavor of India is not, as Bharucha rightly argues, alluding to Indian aesthetic theories of *rasa* (flavor), "some mystical aura that emanates from a culture."[18] It is the whole cultural complex, registered not only as sights and sounds and smells but also as narrative strategies, dramaturgical protocols, and philosophical orientations. Without these crucial elements of Indian flavor, any *Mahabharata* is destined to slip its moorings in its context, the very context that nourishes its meaning. Even more serious is the possibility that in distilling the epic's Indianness into a "flavor," one is concocting a homogenized image of India, a fiction of Indian sameness of the sort retailed by the Indian Government's Ministry of Tourism and Air India (both of whom were sponsors for Brook's work in India).

To be fair, Brook's tendency to remove *The Mahabharata* from its Indian context (and to transform that context into superficial atmospherics) was not merely a matter of individual choice. As the reviews of the productions show, Brook's audiences were, by and large, not looking for an encounter with radical cultural difference; indeed, many registered complaints against even the small extent to which Brook's play required them to depart from their usual theatrical experience. For example, the rigors of the long production—nine hours of playing time, divided into three evenings or experienced all together as one long "marathon"—produced much whining (Michael Feingold advised his readers to bring cushions and food and if possible their own Port-O-San) and was read by at least two critics (John Simon and Robert Brustein) as indicative of Brook's epic ego.[19] Several others complained about the accents of the international cast, including

John Simon, who noted, "These actors are recruited from the first, second, and third worlds, and some of them from out of this world. . . . How they sound in French at their headquarters I don't know, but in English, they enrich Hindu mythology with the story of the Tower of Babel, what with accents ranging from the opaque to the inscrutable and, even when scrutable, often cacophonous."

Given these kinds of responses, one cannot fault Brook for attempting to condense the epic (although the further condensations for the TV and movie versions, down to six and three hours, respectively, are quite disastrous). But much more problematic than the downsizing of the epic is Brook's structuring of it. Brook's choices regarding the scope, selection, and sequencing of his version of the epic, it can be argued, betray what is most fundamental to the work, its deepest meanings. *The Mahabharata* is a vast compendium of tales and scenes and intellectual treatises from which Carrière and Brook have distilled material appropriate to the construction of a three-act play. The process lasted ten years, beginning in 1975 when both men listened to the epic as told by French Sanskrit scholar Phillippe Lavastine. As Brook tells it, this initial exposure was a wonderful approximation of how the epic is transmitted in India itself. Having long ago heard about the *Bhagavad Gita,* Brook began by asking Lavastine to tell him "more about the Indian work where a warrior says, 'I am not going to fight.' To tell us who that warrior was, who he was fighting, and why he couldn't fight took my scholar friend three months. And so we received *The Mahabharata* in the traditional way, orally."[20]

The first text—a two-hour play—emerged from this narrative, and work began. Fairly early on, Brooks and Carrière decided that the Pandava-Kaurava story would provide their basic through line. Their reason for this choice encapsulates the intercultural problematic they were about to engage: "our basic through line was to tell the Pandava-Kaurava story. In India they don't need this—everyone knows the basic story. They can perform variations and fragments."[21] In making their key objective the telling of the core story—and furthermore, in telling it clearly, addressing it to people who had no inkling of it at all—Brooks and Carrière had committed themselves willy-nilly to working out of place. No matter how often they returned to India and to Indian *Mahabharata* performance traditions (and they returned to both repeatedly in the following years, witnessing *The Mahabharata* stories in the performance styles of Theyyam, Mudiattu, Yakshagana, Chhau, Jatra, and Kathakali) their *Mahabharata* would keep the mark of its initial displacement.

What has been disappointing is Brook's failure—or refusal—to adequately address the consequences of this displacement. People have been dismayed not so much by what Brook did—no one denies his extraordinary achievement, and even the harshest critics insist that this is not an issue of cultural property, of saying that a foreigner should not dare to treat Indian material—but in how he seems to have thought of it. As David Williams notes,

> Sadly Brook seems unwilling to confront the dangers concomitant with applying a culturally non-specific, essentialist/humanist aesthetic to such material. He has done himself a great disservice by never satisfactorily accounting in public for his production's relationship to Hindu culture in India, or teasing out the ideological repercussions of that relationship.[22]

Bharucha indicates one important direction that such teasing out would need to take: "for Brook . . . [*The Mahabharata*] is nothing less that 'the poetical history of mankind.' Within such a grandiose span of time, where does the Raj fit?"[23] Far from engaging such questions, Brook characterized the entire critique as a non sequitur, insisting that it was ill-placed in relation to the purely narrative intention of the work: "We are telling a story . . . If one enters to hear a story, and not to analyze it, or bring to it the kind of comparative criticism that one uses when one goes to see *Hamlet,* it is one of the richest stories one can experience."[24] As Glen Loney points out, though Brook "did not cite the biblical text, . . his appeal for a direct, even childlike openness to his *The Mahabharata* echoed the venerable piece of advice about being as little children in order to enter the Kingdom of Heaven."[25] Loney has identified what I think is one of the most troubling effects of Brook's position, impacting profoundly on the text of his play and on its meaning, namely the infantilization of the Indian epic, the tendency to treat it as a primitive folktale or a child's fairy tale—along with the unpleasantly orientalist suggestion that this material—unlike *Hamlet*—is best suited to a childlike—that is, naive and uncritical—mode of consumption.

The structural choices Brook and Carrière made in their presentation of the vast source material are perhaps best exemplified in the way they handled the narrative frame. In Brook's play, the story of the fratricidal rivalry between the Pandavas and the Kauravas unfolds as a story, told by Vyasa himself, the author designated by tradition. His listener is a young boy, who interrupts him periodically for clarification. Vyasa is helped in his narration by Ganesha, the elephant-headed god, who at one point removes his mask to become Krishna (one of the production's most inspired uses of theatrical semiotics to conjure the theological complexity of the material).

The Sanskrit *Mahabharata* is also equipped with a narrative frame, but in it Vyasa's narrative is richly contextualized. His listeners are Parikshit and Janamejaya, grandson and great-grandson, respectively, of one of the heroes of *The Mahabharata,* Arjuna. The story is told to Janamejaya just as he is about to commit a devastating sacrifice, in which he proposes to destroy all the snakes in the world. This ritual context positions the stories of *The Mahabharata* within an internally coherent world, where all are bound together with bloodlines and all sustain the consequences of the major action. By contrast, Brook's child has only the most abstract relation to the events: he lives, we are told, "centuries and centuries" after them. Instead of inhabiting the same ritual world as his forebears, "performing a snake sacrifice that recalls their sacrifice of battle," this boy is Everyman, the bemused and essentially alienated descendant of the epic's heroes. As Brook himself puts it: "In *The Mahabharata* this young man is a prince learning to be a king. If one takes a simple metaphor, the young man is us and the story is told to give us the seeds for our own development."[26]

But the metaphorical transposition of ancient prince to "us" is not really simple; the presence of the boy definitively situates *The Mahabharata* in a transcultural space, where its relationship to India is rendered as merely contingent, not determining. While this choice serves Brook's overall humanist project admirably, it cannot be denied that it distorts the epic's meaning. The presence of the boy literalizes the idea, expressed frequently by Brook and underwritten by Carrière's translation of the work's title, that *The Mahabharata* is not only for all people but also *about* them:

> *Maha* in Sanskrit means "great" or "complete." A *maharaja* is a great king. *Bharata* is first of all the name of a legendary character, then that of a family or a clan. So the title can be understood as "The Great History of the Bharatas." But, in an extended meaning, *bharata* means Hindu, and, even more generally, man. So, it can also be interpreted as "The Great History of Mankind."[27]

In the play, the boy is told repeatedly that this is the story of his "race," a term that is utterly out of tune with the social geography of the Sanskrit *The Mahabharata*. As Hiltebeitel puts it, "In typical colonialist terms, race stands in for caste as a means of rendering Indian social and historical dynamics intelligible."[28]

Before returning to the important issue of caste, I want to make one final point about the narrative frame. Not only does the frame alter the context of the epic story, but it constructs it *as a story*—a single linear narrative being told by one consciousness to another. This construction contradicts the inherent hypertextuality of *The Mahabharata,* the fact that its complex form makes it available to many readings, not just one telling. By making Vyasa the narrator, Brook and Carrière reauthorize this fictional author and situate their spectators as passive witnesses, rather than active readers, of Vyasa's (that is, Carrière's) version of the epic.

The erasure of caste from Brook's play is one of the main sources of its intellectual incoherence. The effort to ignore caste—always an uncomfortable system to Western minds—affects the characterology of the play in a way that makes much of the action seem downright bizarre. As Rustom Bharucha notes, "Indian characters do not merely act according to their feelings (which is what Brook's characters appear to do), but in accordance to how they are expected to act by virtue of their dharma, which in turn is determined by caste."[29] Carrière notes that he has left certain Indian words untranslated, including the word *kshatriya,* the name of one of the castes. But the word is not accompanied by any sense of the social status and ethos of that caste. Brook's *kshatriyas* are *kshatriyas* because they fight, but the inner code of values, the whole complex of behavior, thought, and feeling that lies behind the action of fighting as a *kshatriya* is never brought out. The result is that certain characters and events are distorted to the point of unintelligibility. Bharucha discusses the case of Karna as one example:

> As a *suta,* the adopted son of a charioteer, Karna will always be dependent on Duryodhana's magnanimity. His friendship will always be conditioned by servility. I don't think that Brook's audience had a clue about the intensity of Karna's humiliation as a *suta,* because he was never differentiated from the Pandavas or the Kauravas on the level of caste. True, he does refer to himself as the "son of a driver," but the rupture in his ritual status, and his consequent rejection of this status, have no resonance beyond the obvious fact that he has been wronged. Karna's dilemma seems entirely personal; it is not situated within the social and ritual structure of Hindu society, with its accompanying tensions and constraints.[30]

That caste is not a secondary and dispensable attribute of the characters but a crucial context for the intelligibility of their actions can be seen in another of Bharucha's examples, the fact that the Western audience laughed when

Yudhisthira is prevented from entering Heaven because of his companion—a dog. These spectators had no way of knowing that in the Hindu ritual universe a dog is associated with pollution. That Yudhisthira insists on
keeping his dog is no mere whim—and his exclusion from Heaven no mere
eccentricity—it is a mark of his extraordinary humanity, his daring self-
determination.

Brook's insistence on hewing closely to "the story" makes of his play a
Shakespearean drama, neatly divided into three parts—an Aristotelian
beginning, middle, and end with a vengeance—and burdened with a heavy
teleology. Whereas the Sanskrit original is structured recursively and non-
linearly, stories frequently doubling back on themselves, stories getting
inside other stories, stories leading off into new stories or simply pausing—
often for hundreds of stanzas, for meditations of an ethical nature, such as
the *Bhagavad Gita*—here all events seem to line up and press purposefully in
one direction, the direction of the great war. Especially in the third part,
where deaths follow each other with the brisk dispatch of a Shakespearean
tragedy, *The Mahabharata* is reduced to the level of an action-adventure car-
toon, the only difference being that the good guys have as rough a time of
it as the bad guys. To get a sense of how Brook's orderly narrative contrasts
with the hypertextuality of the original, one has only to compare it to a
description like the following, by Indologist Herman Oldenburg:

> Besides the main story, there are veritable forests of small stories, and
> besides, numberless and endless instructions on theology, philosophy,
> natural science, law, politics, practical and theoretical knowledge of
> life. [It is] a poem full of deeply significant dreamings and surmisings,
> delicate poetry and schoolmasterly platitude, full of sparkling play of
> colour, of oppressive and mutually jostling masses of images, of show-
> ers of arrows, of endless battles, clash after clash of death-despising
> heroes, of over-virtuous ideal men, of ravishing beautiful women, of
> terrible tempered ascetics, adventurers and fabulous beings.[31]

Furthermore, Carrière's tidy narrative structure signifies a view of time
and cosmic history that is much closer to the Christian tradition than the
Indian, which treats time as cyclical and recurrent rather than linear and singular, indicating a dramaturgy of simultaneity and eternal return rather than
of a sequential series of actions. The one instance of such a dramaturgical
principle in Brook's play shows how effective it might have been as a general principle: it is Arjuna's encounter with Shiva, watched by and reacted
to by Duryodhana and his brothers from another time-space. The density of

experience figured in this scene, where theological premises permeate individual actions, is sadly missing from the rest of the play. As Bharucha puts it,
"What one misses, however, is a sense of time that transcends chronology,
time that stretches into infinity. . . . [Here t]ime is truncated into blocks of
action, acts and scenes that have definite beginnings and ends."[32]

Carrière's purposeful narrativity is utterly alien not only to *The Mahabharata* but also to Indian modes of communication. As anyone who has visited India can tell you, the pleasure of a story for Indians is not in getting or
conveying its point but in embroidering its form. Digressions and circum-
locutions—of the kind that Salman Rushdie used to structure his modern
Indian epic *Midnight's Children*—are the hallmark of Indian narrativity, and
its absence from Brook's *The Mahabharata* is a major source of the work's
displacement.

The absence of the sense of an interpenetration of past, present, and
future derives not only from the structure of the play but also from its great
confusion about the meaning of the action. While searching for narrative
clarity, Brook pays insufficient attention to other kinds of meaning—most
seriously, to the philosophical tensions within the epic itself. In a very fine
reading of Brook's play, Vijay Mishra recalls that the great Indologist
J. A. B. van Buitenen identified genealogy as a major preoccupation and a
fundamental organizing principle of *The Mahabharata,* part of a complex
exploration of ideas of order, power, ownership, identity, and destiny. The
long opening section of Brook's play is a dramatized genealogy. Yet few
spectators of Brook's version are encouraged to recognize that this dramatized genealogy is also an illusory one, a kind of monumental fraud, turning
on the politics of gender. The official line of descent of the male heroes is
utterly contradicted by their biological descent, a secret that is known only
to the women. The dynasty of Bharata is in fact a matrilineal dynasty. King
Santanu's line dies with his two sons—Vichitravirya, so sickly that his half
brother Bhishma has to win him his wives, and Bhishma himself, who
vowed to remain childless in order to gain Satyavati for his father. Santanu's
dynasty then moves through his wife's son from an earlier affair with the
hermit Parashara, himself only remotely connected with the dynasty. This
son, Vyasa himself, is called in to give children to the dead Vichitravirya's
two brides, and the children he fathers are Pandu and Dhritirastra. Nor does
the line of patrilineal descent flow smoothly from this pair of patriarchs:
Pandu is cursed by a gazelle whom he accidentally killed in the act of love.
The curse says that his own lovemaking with either of his wives, Kunti or
Madri, will result in his death. Faced with childlessness, Kunti resorts to
magic to remedy the situation: her three sons, Yudhisthira, Bhima, and

Arjuna, and Madri's twins Nakula and Sahadeva, are not Pandu's children but the children of five different gods—Dharma, Vayu, Indra, and the twin Ashwins, respectively.

So genealogy is disrupted in several generations—and the genealogical connection of the main characters to the line of King Santanu is "symbolic, not real."[33] Thus when, during the war, Krishna helps the Pandava win, he is not asserting the principle of genealogical purity, as the plot and dialogue seem to suggest, but rather the superiority of gods over men. Yet even this principle is disrupted by the presence of Karna, another god-fathered child of Kunti, who is on the opposite side from her other divine children, and hence on the other side also from Krishna. As Mishra summarizes the situation, "The Epic is ambiguous in its claims on this score [the triumph of genealogy], seeming to confirm, and yet subverting, age-old genealogical principles, patriarchy and purity of race. That these ambiguities have been reduced to a perceptible order and continuity is a consequence of an [later] Indian regime of reading not necessarily endorsed by the text," a reading resistant to the text's suggestion that the real source of power and identity is woman.[34]

According to Mishra, Krishna's participation in maintaining the genealogical illusion stems from the cyclical temporality within which the action occurs. Krishna is aware that the conflict between the two sets of cousins is merely a version of a conflict between gods and antigods that has already been played out many times before. For him the present version is important not in terms of its outcome but in terms of its ideological significance: the war is, from Krishna's perspective, a game whose real purpose is to teach the principle of order, a principle that must be reaffirmed in every age. To affirm order, "Krishna must take the side of the righteous or the seeming righteous, even when the 'truth' of genealogy itself is in considerable disarray."[35] Thus the core story of *The Mahabharata* is not the pure or clear narrative that Brook imagines; it is fraught with contradiction, problematic to the core.

The Place of *The Mahabharata*

I want to turn now to the place of contradiction in Peter Brook's production of *The Mahabharata* and to argue that it is out of a specifically theatrical engagement with contradiction that this production works out its problematic of place and makes its most valuable contribution. In an interview after the production, Brook was asked why he chose an international cast for his play. He answered, "To increase the sense of contradiction."[36] The sense of contradiction is not a principle that belongs in Brook's philosophy—at least not in a positive sense—but it is, as this remark makes plain, a crucial element of his theatrology. Contradiction—along with difference, multiplicity, and choice—is the guiding principle of Brook's stage practice. At the intellectual level, he always refers this practical principle to his universalism (for example, the remark quoted above is followed by the insistence that the international cast generates "a fundamental harmony" and "helps to give the impression of universality"), but this is not necessarily, I believe, its effect. Rather, the sense of contradiction produced by the many accents and acting styles of his actors, along with the many musical and costuming elements taken from other cultures, gives the spectator a vivid experience of cultural difference.

In other words, the production of *The Mahabharata* reproduces the very sense of hypertextuality that Carrière's text tries so hard to restrict. This hypertextuality begins with the choice given to the spectator of how to interact with the production: in three separate events spread over three nights or in one nine-hour marathon session. In the case of the first option, two further options were available (at least in New York and a few other venues): one could attend on three successive nights, all in one week, or on three successive weeks. Each of these options, as Kent Devereaux notes, made for a markedly different "performance Gestalt,"[37] the marathon option maximizing the sense of otherness. In addition, the different venues also made for different experiences (although this was not usually a matter of choice for spectators).

But the greatest effect of hypertextuality was created by the cast itself. Watching and listening to them, one experienced not so much a group of characters but a collection of voices, "each trying," as Vijay Mishra says, "to assert its own utterance as logos,"[38] and each bringing on stage and into the drama its own cultural world. The intended interculturalism of *The Mahabharata,* the effort to create a McLuhanesque "global village," produced instead that paradoxical and quintessential space of postmodern experience: an "inside" filled with many "outsides." Like a postmodern city—like the Los Angeles that Edward Soja describes in *Postmodern Geographies*—or like the New York City and Los Angeles that come to life in Anna Deavere Smith's plays—Brook's *The Mahabharata* was (again, as performed) a model of interculturalism as *multiculturalism.*

I realize how preposterous, on the face of it, an analogy between Brook's crowded stage and Anna Deavere Smith's one-person shows might seem. Not only are the two utterly different in scope, but their respective subject matters could hardly be more unlike: the one an ancient story from a distant land, the other last week's headlines in our own inner cities; the one giving voice to heroes and gods who never existed, the other presenting the actual words of people alive today. Nevertheless, I think the two have much in common, and that an analysis of this commonality will give *The Mahabharata* the historicity that is needed to appreciate it.

Both Brook's practice and Smith's are, it seems to me, a response to the urgent challenge of living with and within cultural difference. Both show a way out of the essentialist trap of identity politics, the tendency, so perilously close to a rhetoric of stereotypes, to police ethnic representations and keep them contained within the narrow confines of a prescriptive group identity. In Smith's pieces, the radical particularity of the individual voices—reproduced by her in all the details of their rhythms, accents, diction, and style—is preserved. Her people never become mere representatives of the groups to which they belong: they never become, in fact, "characters" in the traditional realist sense, because they never sacrifice their individual identities to realism's myth of the universal-particular. Rather, they retain the full measure of their individuality while at the same time participating in collective identities. The ideological commitments and meanings that make up the social signification of those groups do surface in the speeches and behavior of the individuals but in a fragmentary, discontinuous and sometimes contradictory way, never as a seamless ideological discourse capable of wholly submerging and subsuming their individualilties.

Brook's international cast achieves a similar effect, though by different means. Here particularity is marked not by using the actual words of actual people but by actors performing in a non-native language. Brook's actors came from England, France, Turkey, Japan, Iran, India, Indonesia, Poland, South Africa, and Senegal. This is impressive, and not only, as Bharucha sneeringly says, as a "United Nations of Theater."[39] It is theatrically impressive, making a performance never heard before in a theater. The sound is that of the modern city in this century of diaspora. As Maria Shevtsova astutely observes, it is strange indeed to hear New York critics complaining about the diversity of accents, living as they do in a place where this many accents, and more, can be heard on any street any day of the week. More serious is the criticism made by Bharucha, who says that all these vocal signifiers of difference—like the play's other "eclecticism"—are there only to be dominated and homogenized by Brook: "Once he places his marks on his materials, they no longer belong to their cultures. They become part of his world."[40] I disagree: Brook may have wanted to harmonize everything, but (thankfully) he does not succeed in doing so. As Vijay Mishra says, the "non-native speakers bring to English a multiplicity of other voices, traces that supplement and add a discordance to the presumed univocality of the theatrical language, English."[41]

What many critics dismissed as bad acting was in fact a rupture in the norms of naturalistic acting, caused by using an unfamiliar language. Shevtsova further remarks, "The gestures that usually accompany a prescribed language and physically extend or translate verbal meaning change according to linguistic change."[42] But the change is not smooth: switching to English does not in itself produce the gestures that normally accompany that language. Instead, what is revealed is the gap between voice and body, speech and self, producing a kind of Brechtian effect in a non-Brechtian context. By contrast, the few English actors, most of whom have roles in the narrative frame (that is, Vyasa, the Boy, Ganesh, and Krisha), exemplify another kind of speech, in which "voice and consciousness are one."[43] Closer to us in terms of the textual structure, they are also more conventional in Western theatrical terms, more "realistic." The effect of familiarity they convey serves not only to draw spectators into the story but also to distance them from it by heightening the foreignness of the other characters. Thus while the narrative frame suggests—as Brook intended—that this is a story in the process of being told, the characterology generated by the international cast suggests that this is a performance in the process of being constructed, a representational project deliberately undertaken and inevitably contextualized within the problematics of interculturalism.

I have singled out the actors, but other performance elements—costumes, music, movement, props—all contribute to this staging of cultural difference. However, while all these other sign-systems are more marked by Brook's syncretic ideal, which converts the signs of other cultures into a generalized atmosphere of exoticism, the actors are not "colonized" in this way. Precisely because the roles and actions are all Indian, simple (stereotypical) national identification is not forced upon the actors; not required to function as representations of various nations or ethnicities, they retain their individuality. At the same time, as Shevtsova notes,

> the individual qualities they bring to the performance are traced over with cultural markers. The colour of skin, physique, gait, mannerisms, accent, intonation and cadence of speech and, above all, a way of seeing and doing, which are also acts of interpretations and affect how a role is performed, are markers in their own right. They are distinctive enough in the production to give the impression that delineated cultures, and not solely a mixture of individual traits, converge to produce a pluricultural composition. At the same time, because they are sufficiently distinctive, the cultures they evoke do not blur into an

indiscriminate, amorphous mass. The upshot of this is that plurality does not destroy singularity, even though the universal rather than the particular is sought from their conjunction.[44]

In short, the goal of universality is confounded by the performance of difference. In working out of place, the cast works out a new place.

To characterize this new place, I wish to conclude with a well-known piece of *Mahabharata* lore—Brook's first encounter with the epic, which I call "The Story of Peter Brook and the Likeable Indian."

> The day I first saw a demonstration of Kathakali, I heard a word completely new to me—*The Mahabharata*. The dancer was presenting a scene from this work and his sudden first appearance from behind a curtain was an unforgettable shock. His costume was red and gold, his face was red and green, his nose was like a white billiard ball, his fingernails were like knives; in place of beard and mustache, two white crescent moons thrust forward from his lips, his eyebrows shot up and down like drumsticks and his fingers spelled out strange coded messages. Through the magnificent ferocity of the movements, I could see that a story was unfolding. But what story? I could guess at something mythical and remote, from another culture, nothing to do with my life.
>
> Gradually, sadly, I realized that my interest was wearing off. After the interval, the dancer returned without his make-up, no longer a demigod, just a likeable Indian in shirt and jeans. He described the scene he had been playing and repeated the dance. The hieratic gestures passed through the man of today. The superb, but impenetrable image had given way to an ordinary, more accessible one and I realized I preferred it this way.[45]

In the spirit of the kind of misreading that my whole argument here has been proposing, I want to claim this text of Brook's for my own use and paraphrase as follows: whatever the magnificent philosophical vision behind his play, for me its performance gave way to an altogether different vision, not universal and eternal but very much of our diasporic times and our multicultural places. For me, the place worked out by *The Mahabharata* points to the possibility of a place where no one is out of place, where interacting does not mean assimilating, where being "unlike" does not automatically imply being "unlikeable." And, to quote Peter Brook one last time, "I realized I preferred it this way."

NOTES

1. Edward Said, *Orientalism* (New York: Pantheon, 1978).
2. David Williams, ed., *Peter Brook and "The Mahabharata"* (London: Routledge, 1991), 24.
3. Fredric Jameson, *Postmodernism; or, The Cultural Logic of Late Capitalism* (Durham: Duke University Press, 1991), 16.
4. Peter Brook, *The Empty Space* (London: MacGibbon and Kee, 1968).
5. Williams, *Peter Brook*, 21–22.
6. Michel Foucault, "Of Other Spaces," trans. Jay Miskowiev, *Diacritics* 16 (1986): 24.
7. One topic I propose to leave aside altogether is the question of Brook's personal and professional conduct while in India, particularly his treatment of various people—informants, performers, scholars—who helped him in his research. While I completely agree with Phillip Zarrilli that what he calls "the socio-economic-political-cultural-personal residue left in India by Brook and his company" raises issues "of accountability, power and ethics" that are "of vital importance to intercultural exchange" ("The Aftermath: When Peter Brook Came to India," *The Drama Review* 30 [spring 1986]: 92), I feel that their complexity and the factual contestation involved in them puts them beyond the scope of this paper. See also Alf Hilterbeitel, "Transmitting *Mahabharatas:* Another Look at Peter Brook," *The Drama Review* 36 (fall 1992): 151.
8. Vijay Mishra, "The Great Indian Epic and Peter Brook," in Williams, *Peter Brook*, 195.
9. Qtd. in Georges Banu, "The Language of Stories," in Williams, *Peter Brook*, 46.
10. Mishra, "Great Indian Epic," 195.
11. *Mahabharata,* critical edition, ed. Vishnu S. Sukthankar (Poona: Bhandarkar Oriental Research Institute), 1959.
12. Gautam Dasgupta, "Rites and Wrongs," *Village Voice,* 27 Oct. 1987, 76.
13. Banu, "The Language of Stories," 46.
14. Jean-Claude Carrière, *The Mahabharata,* trans. Peter Brook (New York: Harper and Row, 1987), xi. Page numbers from this edition hereafter cited in the text.
15. David Britton, "Theatre, Popular and Special and the Perils of Cultural Piracy," in Williams, *Peter Brook*, 58.
16. Banu, "The Language of Stories," 46.
17. Rustom Bharucha, *Theatre and the World: Performance and the Politics of Culture* (London: Routledge, 1993), 70.
18. Bharucha, *Theatre and the World*, 71.
19. See John Simon, "A Jungle Grows in Brooklyn," *New York,* 2 Nov. 1987, 110; Robert Brustein, "The Longest Journey," *New Republic,* 30 Nov. 1987, 26; Michael Feingold, "Brook of Life," *Village Voice,* 27 Oct. 1987, 111. All subsequent textual references refer to the reviews cited here.
20. Richard Schechner et al., "Talking with Peter Brook," *The Drama Review* 30 (spring 1986): 58.
21. Schechner et al., "Talking with Peter Brook," 58–59.
22. Williams, *Peter Brook*, 24.
23. Bharucha, *Theatre and the World*, 68.
24. Brooks, "Entering the Unknown," *Village Voice,* 1 Dec. 1987, 130.

25. Glenn Loney, "Myth and Music across the Continents and the Centuries," *Theater* 19 (spring 1988): 24.

26. Schechner et al., "Talking with Peter Brook," 61.

27. Schechner et al., "Talking with Peter Brook," 59.

28. Hiltebeitel, "Transmitting *Mahabharatas,*" 151.

29. Bharucha, *Theatre and the World,* 72.

30. Bharucha, *Theatre and the World,* 73.

31. Herman Oldenburg, qtd. in C. R. Deshpande, *Transmission of the Mahabharata Tradition* (Simla: Indian Institute of Advanced Study, 1978), 6, in Williams, *Peter Brook,* 22.

32. Bharucha, *Theatre and the World,* 75.

33. Mishra, "Great Indian Epic," 197.

34. Mishra, "Great Indian Epic," 197.

35. Mishra, "Great Indian Epic," 198.

36. Qtd. in Britton, "Theatre, Popular and Special," 56.

37. Kent Devereux, "Peter Brook's Production of *The Mahabharata* at the Brooklyn Academy of Music," *Theater* 19 (spring 1988): 228.

38. Mishra, "Great Indian Epic," 203.

39. Bharucha, *Theatre and the World,* 80.

40. Bharucha, *Theatre and the World,* 81.

41. Mishra, "Great Indian Epic," 203.

42. Maria Shevtsova, "Interaction-Interpretation: *The Mahabharata* from a Socio-Cultural Perspective," in Williams, *Peter Brook,* 219.

43. Mishra, "Great Indian Epic," 203.

44. Shevtsova, "Interaction-Interpretation," 218.

45. Brook, "The Presence of India," in Williams, *Peter Brook,* 41.

Eugene van Erven

Some Thoughts on Uprooting
Asian Grassroots Theater

Current discussions of intercultural theater tend to be performance-oriented or to focus on cultural property and the ethics of aesthetic appropriation. Often limited in scope to avant-garde experiments and theoretically bound by the ideas of Edward Said, Michel Foucault, Fredric Jameson, and a handful of other theorists, the intercultural aspects of grassroots theater are seldom considered, nor, indeed, are the intricacies of intercultural theater production processes and the class politics of North-South cultural relations.[1] Intercultural theater as intellectual debate seems at times the exclusive domain of formalistically oriented and socially privileged artists and academics on both ends of the North-South cultural divide. For me, however, the complex production processes involved in bringing explicitly political theater from the South to the North is both more pertinent and more interesting than the abstract debates that so often accompany allegedly avant-garde work. My own experience suggests that given the current lack of mass-audience interest in explicitly political performances from the South in the North, projects involving extended creative interactions between theater artists from the South and small groups of spectators, workshop participants, or occasional interns from the North seem to yield the most durable impact.

Before elaborating upon these opening remarks, I want to dwell for a moment on Peter Weir's *The Year of Living Dangerously,* a feature film that enjoyed popular success in 1982. Its dramatic tension is generated by two extreme attitudes toward Asian grassroots activism. One is represented by a physically handicapped Chinese-Australian photojournalist whose Asian cultural roots facilitate his ability to fraternize with the locals. He adopts an Indonesian pauper family and, after a gradual process of political radicalization, eventually unfurls a pro-Communist banner from a Western-style hotel before being murdered by henchmen of the dictatorial military. He has gone radically "native," and his stance is contrasted to a handsome

Anglo-Australian radio reporter, who regards his assignment in Jakarta on the eve of the 1965 anti-Communist coup as the biggest break in his ten-year career. After a romantic first encounter with Indonesian culture from a safe, air-conditioned, expatriate vantage point, he uses confidential information (obtained through flirtation with a British diplomat) to broadcast spectacular (and no doubt career-boosting) reports back home to Australia. The ethics of Third World–to–First World intercultural theater glides between similar poles of emotional (some would say romantic) identification and rational (or opportunistic) objectivity. The Australian movie, filmed, ironically, on location in Manila with Filipino actors at the height of the Marcos dictatorship, largely ignores Asian perspectives, which may be said to move along a similar sliding ethical scale as far as relations with the West are concerned.

It is no secret that I firmly believe in the empowering potential of community arts and grassroots cultural action. After discovering the people's art movements in various Asian countries in 1986, I reported enthusiastically about their effectiveness in countering totalitarian structures.[2] It could not hurt, I thought, to introduce this phenomenon to the West, for anything should be tried to revive grassroots cultural practice in our own "television-ized" realms. In addition, I figured, direct human contact between outgoing, talented Asian artists and Westerners could contribute to dismantling the persistent cultural stereotypes that play such an underestimated role in widening the economic and social abyss between North and South.

When considering the dynamics of Third World–to–First World intercultural theater projects, a number of half-truths present themselves as deceptively self-evident. For example, (1) the greater the geographical, cultural, economic, and class differences between partners, the greater the likelihood of friction and miscommunications; or (2) the more heterogeneous the participants, the more difficult the intercultural creative process. However, such simplistic assumptions usually undermine the very objective of increasing cross-cultural understanding, which is to bridge difference through mutual, open-minded exploration. At the end of the twentieth century, when cultural essentialism, ethnic cleansings, and more regional military conflicts than ever before threaten both North and South, the challenges posed by intercultural theater must be faced in all their complexity. In the absence of foolproof manuals and magic formulas that work under all circumstances, honest analyses of past experiments are the only way to improve future ones. As long as the gap between the poorest of the rural poor in, say, Bihar (India), and the richest of the rich in, say, Saint Tropez, continues to widen, humanity can ill afford *not* to build cultural bridges. Small-scale intercultural theater projects of a different kind than the Peter Brook variety offer promising opportunities to establish such connections, but these all-too-rare experiments are seldom frankly assessed. More often than not, they are documented in self-congratulatory reports solely intended to satisfy Western financial backers, who subsequently file them into oblivion.

One of the primary aims of South-North intercultural grassroots theater should be to break down cultural stereotypes in the North regarding the alleged intellectual, cultural, moral, and economic inferiority of the South. It is rarely considered, however, that negative stereotypes about Westerners and seemingly less sophisticated lower-class rural compatriots can be equally tenacious among middle-class Third World intellectuals from capital cities, those most commonly involved in the kinds of political intercultural theater projects I wish to address.

A Filipino Community Theater Workshop in New Zealand

While documenting the activities of the people's theater movement of the Philippines in February and March of 1986, I had noticed the eagerness of many cultural workers to foster contacts with like-minded artists in other countries. I already knew of international workshops in which artists from India, Indonesia, Japan, and the Philippines had collaborated in the late 1970s and early 1980s. In May and June 1986, I reported on the Philippine theater movement to theater practitioners and university students in the New Zealand capital, Wellington, where I was employed at the time. These public presentations generated sufficient interest to launch the idea of a workshop tour by three Filipino cultural workers for urban and rural Maori communities. Maori actress Roma Potiki would organize the venues, and I would write up a project proposal, raise funds, and recruit the three Filipino artists, Dessa Quesada, Chris Millado, and Nestor Horfilla. Potiki remobilized an ad hoc network that had been created for a rather ill-fated performance tour by an Anglo-Caribbean theater company from London the previous year. Our budget was less than twenty-five thousand dollars, a sum we painlessly raised with the assistance of the Queen Elizabeth II Arts Council, the Ministry of Maori Affairs, and several smaller funding agencies. I had met Quesada and Millado in Manila and knew them to be gregarious, competent performers as well as excellent workshop facilitators. Horfilla was reported to be one of the most experienced theater organizers from the southern island of Mindanao and possessed in-depth knowledge of tribal culture, an important asset for the proposed interaction with traditional Maori communities.

The preparations took eight months. The operational phase of the project lasted from early June until late August 1987, during which the three Filipinos conducted four workshops in rural Maori communities, two with urban youths, one with a Maori contemporary dance collective, one in a women's prison, and one for a multicultural women's theater. They also gave three well-received public performances of two drama pieces about the effects of militarization on a tribal and on a peasant community.[3]

The always delicate transition from preparatory fund-raising and organizing to production and tour management in this case went relatively smoothly. In the Maori communities, Roma Potiki presented herself as the main organizer; I assumed the role of driver, cook, and general assistant. It further helped my credibility that Maori target communities perceived me as a trusted Nordic European friend of the Filipinos rather than as a *Pakeha*, a European New Zealander whose motives would have been immediately suspected for understandable colonial-historical reasons. As a net result of the tour, at least one theater collective is still active (in Paekakariki near Wellington), and another workshop site (in the northern Hokianga region) has become the coordinating center for a fifteen-station nationwide Maori FM community radio network. Part of the reason for this nominal success was the relatively unproblematic interpersonal dynamics between the three Filipino visitors, who had all worked with each other before and had been thoroughly briefed by Roma Potiki on the Maori context they would be working in. The organizers in the host country were sufficiently familiar with structures and codes of the target communities, which themselves were quite homogenous in social and cultural terms. The target groups responded well to both the Filipino theater pedagogy and culture, which were presented in an upbeat, self-confident manner. Last but not least, financial arrangements were secure before the operational phase of the project began.

After New Zealand, the Filipino tour continued from August until November in Australia with a similar combination of community theater workshops and occasional performances in the states of New South Wales, Victoria, and the Capital Territory. Target groups were more heterogeneous than in New Zealand, ranging from Filipino migrants, Third World solidarity workers, and Aboriginal urban youths, to theater students, union activists, and community arts workers, although individual workshops were kept as homogenous as possible. The enduring fruits of the Australian campaign include long-term cultural exchanges and collaborative projects between Filipino and Australian artists, university courses on contemporary Asian political theater, and the formation of the Philippine Australian Cultural Interaction Network (PACIN), which still has active branches in most major Australian cities.[4] Keys to the success of these New Zealand and Australian ventures were careful selection of Third World partners, thorough cultural and political briefings at both ends of the intercultural partnership, transparent financial structures, small-scale productions (not exceeding five overseas visitors) in combination with workshops and low-key performances to avoid budget pressure and unrealistic aesthetic expectations. As the following case illustrates, however, ambitious large-scale projects can be considerably more risky.

An Asian Cultural Caravan through Europe: A Case Study

From early June until the end of July 1989, a group of fifteen performers, most of whom were linked to politicized elements in working-class and peasant communities of ten Asia-Pacific countries, created seven different theater pieces in a large chalet in the sleepy French alpine community of Hauteluce. They subsequently toured these pieces as a mobile political theater festival through six European countries. This project, called "Cry of Asia!" was multicultural, intercultural, and interdisciplinary. It featured drama, music, and dance and also involved the exhibition of six- by six-foot canvas paintings by progressive visual artists from the participating countries, community theater workshops for European solidarity workers and theater academies, as well as panel discussions on human rights. The original concept had also contained a parallel festival of radical feature and documentary films, but, due to organizational difficulties that haunted the project from the start, this crucial contextualization device never materialized. The idea was to hit the European public not only with entertaining performances but also with a variety of supplementary pedagogical, cultural, and informative components that would have a more enduring impact.

"Cry of Asia!" was a significant attempt to bring grassroots Asia-Pacific people's culture to western Europe on a massive scale. Its laudable aim was to spread awareness not only of contemporary Asian human rights abuses, but also of cultural movements with a vision and practice highly different from the exoticized Asian culture familiar to mainstream European audiences either through tours by the Royal Thai Ballet, Indian and Pakistani classical singers, or through the abstract, aesthetically oriented, pseudo-Asian multicultural experiments à la Peter Brook, Eugenio Barba, or Ariane

Mnouchkine. But the challenges posed by first getting mainstream theater managers on board, subsequently setting up the logistical, technical, and financial structures for producing all the separate components of this complex enterprise, and, finally, developing a new, broad-based audience for this kind of straightforward, de-exoticized Asian political theater proved, in some ways, forbidding.

In the preparatory phase of the project (March 1988–May 1989), the mood at both the Asian and European end shifted from initial optimism to stressful irritability caused by a combination of financial difficulties, intercultural misunderstandings, and lack of experience with projects of this magnitude. Once the caravan started moving, irritations were smothered in performance adrenaline and informal interactions with surprisingly sizable and receptive crowds and media representatives. By the time the Asian artists departed from Europe in November 1989, mixed feelings of exhaustion, frustration, pride, and satisfaction prevailed at both ends of the partnership.

Conceptualization Phase: March–August 1988

For all practical purposes, the project began for me in March 1988 in the office of Al Santos, executive director of the Asian Council for People's Culture (ACPC) in metropolitan Manila. A few days before my departure, I had just completed the third leg of several months of field research around the people's theater network in the Philippines. I had first met Santos in February 1986, after seeing his (and composer Joey Ayala's) highly acclaimed anti-American rock musical *Nukleyar* in a packed Manila university gymnasium the day after dictator Ferdinand Marcos had fled to Guam. During subsequent trips through the Philippines, many cultural workers had identified Santos as a talented playwright and an effective grassroots community theater organizer who had made significant contributions to the spectacular expansion of the national people's theater network. He seemed well connected with European and Japanese development agencies, which had subsidized some of his previous activities. ACPC struck me at the time as a useful initiative to share Philippine theater pedagogy and networking skills with progressive artists in neighboring countries. The "Cry of Asia!" project sounded like an effective way to acquaint European mass audiences with the power of Asian people's theater. Only later, after visiting several ACPC partners in South Korea, Thailand, India, and Pakistan, did I discover that their contacts with Santos had been minimal.[5]

The "Cry of Asia!" idea was not new, although bringing it to Europe in this format was. Since its foundation in 1984, ACPC had organized several international workshops and coproductions. In May and June 1986, three months after the fall of the Marcos dictatorship, ACPC had organized an international cultural caravan involving progressive artists from the Philippines, Japan, and Thailand. Inspired by similar tours through southern India, this ad hoc troupe journeyed through the northernmost Philippine island of Luzon with a mobile festival of street theater performances, workshops, a visual-arts exhibit, and films. Based on the success of this caravan, and on the experiences of the Philippine Educational Theatre Association's 1986 and 1987 tours through North America and Europe with a theater performance celebrating the Cory Aquino uprising, ACPC conceived the idea to travel with an intercultural Asia-Pacific caravan through Europe.[6] Calling the project "Cry of Asia!" Santos asked me to help recruit artists from New Zealand and Australia as well as from Thailand, India, and Pakistan, where I was heading to continue my own book research. He himself would search for candidates in the Philippines, Sri Lanka, South Korea, Japan, Malaysia, and Singapore. Upon my request, Roma Potiki invited Hemi Rurawhe, a young Maori musician and actor, to participate in the project. Stage and screen actress Madeleine Blackwell, one of the co-organizers of the Australian leg of the 1987 Filipino workshop tour, also committed herself, as did Dinasti Theatre from Yogyakarta, Maya Puppet Theatre from Bangkok, Mesca from Bangalore, and Punjab Lok Rehas from Lahore. Santos's recruiting efforts in Japan, South Korea, and the Philippines proved equally fruitful. People's theater activists outside the Philippines were clearly interested in "Cry of Asia!" but I had no clue as to how (or when) the project should be taken further.

I returned home to the Netherlands in May 1988, having been away for twelve years. Frantically searching for bearings in my own culture and preparing to teach new university courses, I was admittedly ill prepared for full-time involvement in "Cry of Asia!" which unexpectedly gained momentum. In June 1988, after not hearing from Santos for months, I received a letter from him indicating that several European funding agents had agreed to sponsor the caravan. Given the ease with which he had managed to obtain funds in the past, I had no reason to doubt his optimism, which later turned out to be premature. I did warn, however, that a project of this size required more preparation time than the nine months he had allotted. In September, Santos visited the Netherlands and, arguing that I needed to express my solidarity not only in scholarly writings but in practical terms as well, convinced me to produce the Dutch and French legs of the projected tour, as well as to organize a rehearsal space on European soil where the Asian artists could devise their shows.

Preparatory Phase: October 1988–February 1989

In order to apply for subsidies, I first established an officially registered foundation and recruited seven volunteers to help with administration, publicity, logistics, and tour management. We soon discovered that funding agents were reluctant to support us unless we could prove widespread interest for the project from professional cultural institutions. Because mainstream theater managers refused to negotiate until we could provide them with concrete visual documentation, we sent someone to Manila to produce a short video on the first "Cry of Asia!" workshop that Santos had meanwhile convened. This material proved instrumental in convincing theater managers that the project was real and helped us obtain firm bookings from a number of prominent Dutch theaters in May 1989. Although this commitment from theater managers gave us some financial security, the actual revenues could not be transferred until the Dutch leg of the tour had been completed. In addition, we awaited final word on several substantial subsidies until well into the summer of 1989, and those we did get paid only half of the sum up front, with half coming after presenting final accounts and project evaluation. With only a small start-up subsidy in our account, we had no choice but to draw on personal savings to pay for initial expenses.

Troublesome Finances and Intercultural Conflict

By early 1989, relations with ACPC began to sour, for Santos had interpreted our inability to send the U.S. $14,000 contribution to Manila and our criticism regarding the lack of information on participants and caravan components as evidence of a neocolonial attitude. Looking back, unrealistic Asian notions about Western wealth and, conversely, the resentment of unemployed lower-middle-class and working-class European project volunteers vis-à-vis (upper-)middle-class Asian performing artists enhanced intercultural tensions in the months leading up to the Avignon premiere. A predeparture conflict with the person we had dispatched to Manila to shoot the video and Santos's own domestic problems with his Filipino project administrator further fed negative rumors that were beginning to spread among the participating artists about the Dutch "Cry of Asia!" partners. It would take us well into July to regain some of their trust.

Withdrawing from the project was not an option: too much was at stake in terms of theater contracts, private loans, and personal responsibility toward Dutch volunteers and Asian performers who, in turn, had invested a year of their lives and considerable portions of their own savings to pay for international airfare. As it turned out, several of them had borrowed money from relatives and had left their families behind under politically stressful and, in the case of the Tamil participant, downright life-threatening circumstances.

In hindsight, the main obstacles in "Cry of Asia!" were financial, intercultural, and organizational in nature, and all three factors were closely interconnected. Whether for the sake of efficiency or for understandable reasons of psychological support, Santos had opted to give disproportionate responsibility in the "Cry of Asia!" project to Filipino artists and support staff, a move that partly preempted genuinely collective creativity and responsibility across the group. ACPC's employees were exclusively Filipino, as well as the three most prominent "Cry of Asia!" artists (Al Santos as overall artistic director, lead actress Grace Amilbangsa, and Father Eduardo Solang, the one genuine tribal elder in the cast). Only one of the two South Korean artists (Kim Myung Gon), one of the two Thai representatives (Ornanong Vongasawathepchai),[7] and one of the three Japanese participants (Nakko Kiritani, who had worked with Santos many times before) were eventually also given significant artistic or administrative responsibilities. As a result of this imbalance, some of the artists (particularly the participants from India, Sri Lanka, and Pakistan) came to resent their exclusion and ended up feeling artistically underused. In hindsight, the lack of equitable administrative and artistic representation among project participants prevented a constructive dialogue unhampered by ideological and intercultural prejudice. If more importance had been attached from the beginning to exploring cultural and class sensibilities between the different Asian and European partners, the composition of the cast and organizers might have been more egalitarian, the creative process more fruitful, the tour more efficient and effective, and the expenses tens of thousands of dollars lower.

One example of the financial complications caused by misunderstanding occurred before the artists' arrival in Europe. The progressive French arts organization Etats Généraux de la Culture had helped us get a discount on a chalet in the Alps where the Asian artists could quietly rehearse their shows and acclimate culturally and physically to Europe. Unilaterally canceling a previous agreement, however, ACPC ignored our cost-saving suggestion to let the Asian artists fly straight from their respective homes to Geneva, deciding instead to hold another extensive workshop in Manila before traveling to Europe by the end of June, a full three weeks behind schedule. As a further consequence of this miscommunication, ACPC and our own organization double-booked transportation for the trip from the Geneva airport to the French chalet, so valuable chalet rent, international airfares, and domestic transportation expenses were wasted. Clearly, the kind of miscommunication that can beset any group effort was in this case exacerbated on both sides by the long geographical distances involved, the increasingly "high stakes" of the project, and the difficulty of establishing and maintaining trust among partners used to more intimate kinds of collaboration.

In addition to helping the Asian artists settle into the exclusively rural alpine community of Hauteluce for their pretour rehearsal period, our work in the Netherlands continued during that summer. We consolidated and expanded our theater and workshop contacts and planned our publicity campaign, which we considered the key to the project's success. Putting together a program booklet in Avignon, only a few days prior to the Dutch premiere, was not easy. The photographs ACPC had brought were inadequate for European publicity purposes, and we did not obtain definitive curriculum vitas of all participating artists until a mere five weeks before the Avignon premiere. Even after the rehearsals in July, we had only scant insight into the form and content of the different country acts, a fact that not only hampered publicity but also jeopardized production of the absolutely indispensable, multipurpose program booklet planned for the tour; at the very least, we needed to include detailed plot synopses to help European audiences across formidable language and culture barriers.

Most of the Asian participants would later agree that they had underestimated the cultural and linguistic differences between the various European countries on the tour. Sensitive issues like appreciating that a Francophone Genevan does not accept being addressed in German, or that Austrians do not want their country equated with Germany, or that few French speak English, not to mention more subtle regional and class variations, were initially dismissed by the Asian partners. The European organizers could ill afford such callousness. In their shows, all Asian performers would speak and sing in their own respective languages, and there was no budget for high-tech projection of subtitles or a Walkman with an audio soundtrack in the listener's language. Producing low-cost instruments for facilitating intercultural communication, then, were mistakenly given low priority, as were the previously promised contextualization devices in the form of feature and documentary films. At the time, the Asian partners no doubt felt more acutely pressured to find sufficient money for airline tickets and to get their shows ready on time. However, without the necessary consideration of different audience needs, the tour suffered a continual dilution of its original concept and an unfortunate undervaluation of certain crucial caravan components. Clearly, in such projects production schedules for all elements must be carefully planned and adhered to; delaying or omitting even one can reduce the total impact of the event.

In July, Australian actress Madeleine Blackwell withdrew from the project after an insurmountable conflict with Santos over personal and artistic matters. Her country act on Australian nuclear and Aboriginal issues (entitled "Maralinga . . . Terra Nullus") was replaced by an undefined contribution by Japanese actress Nakko Kiritani, who would join the caravan in September. The absence of a poster design forced us to improvise one for France, Germany, Austria, and the Netherlands in three different languages within less than three weeks. With the help of the Paris-based international graphic design collective Grapus and a sympathetic Dutch printer, we managed to produce a poster just in time for the Avignon Festival. We solved the lack of adequate photographs by sending a professional Dutch photographer to Avignon. Until mid-August we were also left in the dark about the availability of the films and murals for the Dutch leg of the tour. Due to lack of funds, the murals had been left behind at the Manila airport and did not arrive in Europe until mid-September. The films never came.

The Performances

After Avignon, the cultural caravan traveled on to London's Riverside Studios, Leicester's Phoenix Arts Center, Glasgow, Edinburgh, and tens of venues in Germany and Austria, before arriving in the Netherlands on 11 October 1989. The common cultural thread that connected all participating artists in the full-cast, main-stage show was the pan-Asia-Pacific myth of the solar eclipse told in terms of a battle between good and evil spirits. The main plotline and stage imagery had been conceived by Santos well before rehearsals had started, leaving space particularly for Korea's Kim Myung Gon and Japan's Masahiko Uchizawa to create their own characters during improvisation sessions in France. The resulting show fused traditional and contemporary Asian theater forms in an easily accessible ninety-minute event that did not require subtle knowledge of Asian politics and concepts of time, space, gesture, and nonlinear narratives to be appreciated. The plot involved the corrupt tribal priest Inao, who sells his soul to the diabolical bird Minokawa in order to obtain dictatorial power over his people. At first, Inao manages to win his people's trust with all kinds of magical events, including the spectacular solar eclipse. But eventually he and Minokawa are defeated by the rebellion of the united tribal people led by a courageous village woman named Suwana. At Avignon, this full-cast show was performed twice in the courtyard of the lycée Frédéric Mistral and three times in an Avignon chapel. The average attendance in France was fifty and postperformance discussions revealed that the spectators were largely enthusiastic. In the Netherlands, the show was performed once in the Amsterdam Municipal Theatre, once in the Royal Theatre of The Hague, and twice in the Utrecht Municipal Theatre for an average audience of five hundred per show.

On nights that the big show was not performed, the group split up to perform their so-called country acts in smaller theaters. Thus "Ahurangi" was basically a concert featuring Maori musician Hemi Rurawhe, Balinese dancer Gusti Putu Alit Aryani, and Pakistani singer Musadiq Sanwal, all of whom performed contemporary political and traditional songs from their respective cultures. The aim of the show was to explore differences and points of convergence between Balinese, Maori, and Punjabi cultures.[8]

"Bodong" was a dance drama on the theme of sovereignty for Filipino indigenous tribes. It featured Manila-based mainstream stage and screen actress Grace Amilbangsa and Father Eduardo Solang, an Episcopalian priest-activist, tribal elder, and amateur performer from the Cordillera mountain region in northern Luzon. In the first part of their show they performed traditional songs and dances from the Muslim South and from Solang's native area. In the second part they both acted in a dance drama, telling the story of a courageous tribal chief who is eventually killed by opportunistic foreigners intent on gaining access to lucrative mineral deposits in ancestral burial grounds. The performance was always musically supported by two or three additional "Cry of Asia!" artists.

"Arirang" was a theater production on the theme of the divided Korean nation. Participating artists were film star and Pansori singer Kim Myung Gon and student activist Seung Jin Jung, occasionally assisted by the Japanese artists, Grace Amilbangsa, or Koreans residing in Europe. The performers worked with traditional instruments, masks, and dance. The first part of their show, which thanks to Kim Myung Gon's extraordinary stage presence was by far the most impressive of all country acts, consisted of a fable performed by Kim in the Pansori folk opera style. After the intermission, the two Korean artists performed a *Madang* theater piece on the colonial and neocolonial history of Korea.[9] In a mixture of traditional Korean theater, shamanistic rites, and contemporary satirical scenes, Kim and Jung

FIG. 7. Touring with "Cry of Asia!" Kim Myung Gon performs in "Arirang," a theater piece on the theme of the divided Korean nation. *(Photo by Michael Kooren.)*

expressed their country's yearning for reunification. In France, "Arirang" was performed once at the Maison du Off in the context of the Avignon Fringe Festival (attendance: forty) and once in Paris for a capacity crowd of several hundred, which included many expatriate Koreans. In the Netherlands, "Arirang" was performed five times: three times in De Balie (Amsterdam), once in Theater Kikker (Utrecht), and once in Schouwburg Kunstmin in Dordrecht with an average of thirty in attendance.

FIG. 8. Thai puppeteer Ornanong Vongasawathepchai performs as one of the rebellious village women in the mainstage production of the 1989 "Cry of Asia!" tour. *(Photo by Michael Kooren.)*

"Dance on the Southeast Asian Border" explored stylistic similarities between Thai, Indonesian, and Philippine dance. Participating artists were Thai puppeteer and visual artist Ornanong Vongasawathepchai, Grace Amilbangsa, and Gusti Putu Alit Aryani. From dances portraying women as submissive, the performance gradually evolved to images of more combative women in a series of war dances. In the Netherlands, the dance show was performed five times at lunch time in Theatre Bellevue, once in Rasa (Utrecht), and once in the Muzisch Centrum (Emmeloord) to an average attendance of fifty.

"Proletaria Aishu Gekijo" consisted of two short drama pieces from the repertory of Tokyo's popular political theater collective Black Tent. The first piece featured Masahiko Uchizawa playing the part of a newspaper reporter who gets conned by a hustler in Tokyo's red-light district. In the second piece, Nakko Kiritani performed a parable about a white elephant who is exploited by a greedy landowner. "The Puppet Show" was an improvised puppetry production put together from existing Indian and Thai pieces. Participating artists were visual artist Shashidara Adapa from Bangalore (India), theater director Kandasamy Sithamparanathan from Jafna (Sri Lanka), Ornanong Vongasawathepchai, Thai actor Vitidnan Rojanapar-

nich, and London-based Malaysian actress Foo May Lyn. The performance
began with a traditional golden swan finger dance and was followed by a
brief fairy tale about nature involving plants, animals, and a young boy. Subsequently, the Malaysian and Thai puppeteers performed a shadow puppet
play about two old people who are chased from their village by bulldozers
intent on destroying the rain forest. The final part of the show was performed by the puppeteers from India and Sri Lanka, who told a story about
the broken dream of Ramu, a child laborer. In the Netherlands, the puppet
show clearly was the most popular of the separate country acts, attracting an
average of one hundred spectators per show.

By the time the "Cry of Asia!" caravan reached the Netherlands, the
artists had been performing or conducting workshops on the road for almost
three months. Though physically and emotionally drained, the strained
internal group dynamics and earlier tension with the European organizers
had mellowed. In the course of the Dutch leg, the atmosphere improved
considerably, culminating in an extraordinary intercultural fraternization
with old Friesian folk dancers after the final European performance in
Emmeloord and a warm farewell at Amsterdam airport.

Almost five thousand spectators attended the combined Dutch and
French theater performances of "Cry of Asia!" In addition, in the Netherlands, the artists offered workshops with the specific aim of expanding
Western knowledge about the social and cultural dimensions of the countries participating in "Cry of Asia!" and exploring possibilities of applying
Asian cultural action pedagogy there. Target groups for these workshops
were students of performing arts academies, members of solidarity groups,
ethnic minority artists, and Asian migrants. A total of 124 people participated in the nine Netherlands workshops. These workshops provided effective opportunities for in-depth dialogue between the Asian artists and the
Dutch public.

Several Dutch organizations and institutions took advantage of the
"Cry of Asia!" tour by organizing events to politically contextualize the cultural festival in their country. For example, Amnesty International–Holland
organized public forums in Amsterdam and Utrecht on the role of culture
in combating human rights abuses in Asia, which drew approximately seventy people. The Malaysia solidarity group organized a forum on the grassroots environmental protection movement in Malaysia, attracting fifty people. Utrecht University's bureau for public lectures organized a symposium
on the theme of "Theater and Society in Asia" that thirty people attended.
At the Avignon Festival, Jack Ralite had organized a similar forum on
human rights and contemporary performing arts in Asia. This event, which

took place at the official Festival site Jardin Urbain V on July 25, drew several hundred people and resulted in a page-long article in the national daily *l'Humanité*.[10]

The Dutch publicity campaign peaked in October 1989. A total of 132 press items related to "Cry of Asia!" were eventually published, including twenty-three full-length articles, four interviews, and fifteen theater reviews. Radio and television also covered the project extensively. Posters, flyers, streamers, oversize billboards on theater facades, and announcements on electronic billboards further contributed to the numerical success of the caravan in the Netherlands. Lacking funds for commercial advertisements, we had opted to construct a life-size Styrofoam elephant on the roof of our blue Ford Transit van. A day after the arrival of our "elephant" on the streets of Utrecht, news of the tour hit the daily newspaper with a photograph and an interview. From then on, the "elephant" was parked in strategic spots of participating cities, and flyers were handed out to pedestrians. One direct result was an invitation to appear in one of the country's most popular radio talk shows. Twenty-four subsequent appearances on regional and national radio and five on national television ensued. The measurable result of the campaign was the recruitment of approximately five thousand theater spectators, workshop participants, and visitors to public forums on Asian human rights and the arts. The in-depth newspaper and magazine articles and long interviews reached an even larger audience.

Reception and Postevent Analysis

One of the aims of "Cry of Asia!" was to increase the respect for progressive Asia-Pacific performing arts by obtaining bookings for this work in prestigious Western theaters and by drawing in a broad cross-section of the European public. The Dutch leg of the project was reviewed by fifteen different theater critics, an unusually high number for what one critic called a "mere" Third World theater event. Despite two or three explicitly negative reviews, the majority of the critics reviewed the performances with respect and were mildly positive in their judgment. Alex van Hoof of the liberal national morning daily *Trouw* expressed admiration for the enthusiasm and professionalism of the artists, whom he called "a joy to watch" and "passionate" but regretted that much of the political message remained hidden behind foreign languages, traditional motions, and dance movements that were not easy to grasp for the average Dutchman. Max Arian of the progressive weekly *De Groene* highlighted the "attractive dances and stylized fighting scenes" and the "sympathetic" cultural collaboration between the

FIG. 9. Eugene van Erven and members of the "Cry of Asia!" tour with promotional elephant. *(Photo by Michael Kooren.)*

artists but found the political analysis extremely black and white: "good versus evil, women versus men, villagers versus oppressor, peace forces versus warmongers." Instead of the "big Asian porridge" he saw, Arian would have preferred to see more of the political and cultural differences between the Asian countries involved. Yet, Eric de Ruijter of the conservative *Telegraaf,* the country's largest morning daily, found the performance "accessible for everyone" and was not bothered by the political messages and the agitprop elements in the show. With a little flexibility in our rigid Western aesthetic standards, he suggested, a Dutch audience could appreciate it because "the artists offer a joyful and enthusiastic spectacle." Maarten Brakema of the Christian Democratic weekly *Hervormd Nederland* (21 October) stressed the "brilliant acting" and the "clear and convincing message" and called the show "an avalanche of dance, music, acting, painted faces, and symbols." Reviewing "Ahurangi," *Utrechts Nieuwsblad* music critic A. van der Kolk stated he could not care less about human rights abuses because "an artist has to be judged first and foremost by artistic standards." Finding Musadiq Sanwal an insecure and mediocre singer and Gusti Putu Alit Aryani unimpressive as a dancer, he detected some class only in Hemi Rurawhe's "wild mimicry and rawness." If van der Kolk represented the negative end of the Dutch critical spectrum vis-à-vis "Cry of Asia!" John Delemarre represented the other extreme. Reviewing the puppet show for *Poppenpodium,* a respected monthly specialty magazine on puppetry, he concluded that "Cry of Asia is really a refined gesture without bitterness or reproach. The unbearable lightness of puppetry."[11]

In Amsterdam, the participating theater managers were content with the amount of publicity the project had generated but observed that the country acts had received considerably less media attention than the big show. Bert Janssens of Theater De Balie regretted that Santos had left on a business trip to South America during the Dutch leg of the tour: "An artistic director should really be some kind of superman who keeps the whole cast together and motivated. He can't just disappear in the middle. A huge enterprise like this depends on one figure who oversees everything and who is capable of inspiring the artists again and again, even when they're dead tired." Hanneke Rudelsheim of Bellevue Theater summarized the opinion of her Amsterdam colleagues as follows: "The talent and enthusiasm were clearly there, but the structural concepts of the different shows were not well thought out. It leaves you with the need to apply special standards like 'oh well, those nice Asians are not all that bad.' But that undermines the kind of artistic respect for which they had come to Europe in the first place."[12]

On the positive side, Bart van Mossel of the Utrecht Municipal Theater and De Blauwe Zaal and Oscar Wibaut of the Royal Theatre in The Hague remarked that "Cry of Asia!" had attracted people to the theater they had never seen before. Van Mossel felt, however, that the shows had relied too heavily on the enthusiasm of the artists, which covered up intrinsic aesthetic and conceptual weaknesses. Wibaut had been fascinated by the big performance but had expected more integration of traditional oriental and avant-garde theater styles, as had been promised in the precampaign publicity. Voicing the opinions of several other managers, Van Mossel expressed understandable criticism of cast and technicians arriving too late: "Maybe it sounds tough, but we cannot be too concerned about fatigue and Asian habits of timekeeping. It simply is not professional. We pay good money for the show and are responsible to our own audience. In return, we expect the artists to be on time and the designer to bring a good light concept so that we can maximize our technical facilities to make the artists look as good as possible." Wibaut added a word of sensible advice to future European producers of similar events: "The Asian artists came to Europe to be taken seriously. Working efficiently, delivering on your promises, meeting deadlines, and maximizing the technical possibilities are also prerequisites for being taken seriously."[13]

Transparent financial agreements might well be added to Wibaut's set of recommendations. Money was a continuous worry throughout the project. Country budgets exceeded U.S. $100,000 and total revenues were uncertain until well after the caravan had left Europe.[14] Most participating artists ended up being paid only a fraction of what they were originally promised. In the early months of 1989, there was a frantic attempt on the part of ACPC to find as many European host countries for the tour as possible, not to broaden the sociopolitical and artistic impact of the caravan, but to increase the income for the skyrocketing production expenses. Italy, Ireland, Sweden, and Spain, who had all been serious candidates at one time, eventually fell by the wayside. At times, it seemed as if it were more important to acquire sufficient subsidies than to reach Europeans with compelling theater productions. Compared to Britain, West Germany, Austria, and the Netherlands, France got relatively little in return for the U.S. $14,000 it had to contribute like all the other countries: no workshops or murals, and only six unfinished, tryout performances. In many ways, the assessments of the French organizers mirrored that of Dutch theater managers. Mr. Perrot of the Christian Development Agency that funded the French leg and Mr. Roch, who had coordinated logistics in Avignon, had found the "Cry of Asia!" performances among the best of the entire festival but were critical of the communication with the Asian partners. Said Roch: "We didn't hear from them for months and suddenly we get this phone call, so we had to do things at the last moment. They should realize next time that when they come to the West they should also try to adapt to Western timekeeping and other customs of politeness, which, incidentally, vary from country to country here in Europe."[15] Roch's reaction should not be read as intolerance but as a sensible reminder to artists from the South (and their European producers) that they should prepare for different circumstances and expectations when performing in professional theaters in the North. Conversely, intercultural sensitivity and flexible adaptation to different circumstances (rather than an arrogant display of one's alleged professional superiority) is also appreciated from European artists and scholars when working in the South.

Despite the economic and psychological hardships caused by "Cry of Asia!" none of the Asian artists seem to have regretted their participation in the project. "But once was enough," remarked Thai actor Vitidnan Rojanaparnich. Describing the view of many artists involved, he notes,

> It was an incredible experience. I have the impression European audiences really appreciated our performances, and we, in turn, learned a great deal about European cultural and social diversity. I can't deny that we experienced severe difficulties in the creative process of putting the caravan components together and with the authoritarian attitude of the director. Half of us never got to maximize our talents, and we could have done much more with the technical facilities available in European theaters, but to perform here at all was a major accomplishment. In addition to meeting many Europeans, we also interacted with scores of Asians working in Europe who knew little about human rights issues in Asian countries other than their own. And I made friendships that will last a lifetime. Finally, I must say that I was never really bothered by the money. I don't think anyone gets involved in a project like this for the money. If I had, I should have stayed at home to work in Bangkok. It was long and exhausting and many of the frictions could have been avoided. But I have no reservation in saying that it was a very worthwhile thing to do. And should be done again. I am sure most of the other participants feel the same.[16]

From my perspective as a coproducer of the event, "Cry of Asia!" was trying and complex compared to the transparent simplicity and manageable scope of the New Zealand and Australia projects. No doubt, the fact that both the visiting artists and the target groups in the host countries were relatively homogeneous beneficially influenced the earlier initiatives. Extensive mutual cultural briefings and secure and transparent financing also helped. I had come to know the two Manila-based artists on the team very well; and the vast rural and tribal experience and the sensitive, unassuming personality of the third participant proved an invaluable additional asset. All three approached their overseas partners with humanitarian openness and seemed to harbor no preconceived notions about the behavior to expect from Westerners. Preproduction deadlines were met effortlessly, and, as a result, communications between the Philippine, New Zealand, Maori, and Australian partners ran relatively smoothly.

In "Cry of Asia!" intercultural dynamics operated on a Pan-Asia-Pacific as well as on an Asian-European level and were adversely affected by financial strains and unequal collaborative representation from early on in the project. These factors had a negative impact on the creative as well as on the production processes. A mutually supportive climate between the psychologically and culturally very diverse Asia-Pacific participants and the Filipino and European tour organizers thus never really got off the ground.

The Lessons to Be Learned

Even if lack of trust had not been such a detrimental factor, small-scale, low-cost, high-impact intercultural theater projects of the type that took place in New Zealand and Australia in 1987 seem ultimately preferable to complex, high-cost, high-profile enterprises like "Cry of Asia!" which place a heavy emotional and financial toll on volunteers. Professional tour organizers specializing in "Third World" shows are not a realistic option since they currently prefer to book more lucrative African and Latin American pop music and classical Asian performing arts to political theater. Due to across-the-board cuts of cultural and development aid budgets in Europe, funds and public interest for such events are now even harder to generate than a decade ago. And appreciation of people's theater aesthetics by mainstream audiences is difficult to obtain without adequate contextualization in the form of documentary films, workshops, printed information, and lectures, even full-fledged courses in university departments.

All of this is not to say that projects like "Cry of Asia!" should never be attempted again. But very few commercial theater production agencies in the West will get involved on the condition of paying U.S. $14,000 prior to a tour without having seen any visual documentation of the participants' artistic abilities, let alone paying an additional U.S. $19,000 afterward. Better to organize an experimental Pan-Asia-Pacific intercultural theater workshop first without attaching the prospect of a prestigious European tour. If something special does emerge, then document it professionally according to Western media standards, circulate this material among European theater managers and cultural support agencies, and thus generate sufficient interest to attract additional financial backers before deciding to further commit to a tour. The Dutch campaign proved that the public and the media can indeed be mobilized on a massive scale for such events. But even so, I am inclined to believe that it is preferable to travel like an actual caravan from village to village and town to town preceded by a small but effective publicity campaign and to work with local grassroots organizations rather than competing with well-financed operations in international mainstream venues and unavoidably raising unrealistic expectations (e.g., through flashy pictures in theater subscription brochures, which most mainstream theaters in Europe use to generate their audiences).

No doubt it is possible to find a group of skillful and talented performing artists in Asian grassroots organizations who, when provided with an egalitarian creative process, can produce a high-quality theater performance capable of appealing to sizable crowds in Europe. Whether the option is a small-scale or a large mainstream tour, however, (1) maintaining trust throughout the process, (2) securing firm financial backing early on, (3) not allowing the aesthetic demands of the main performance to take priority over other caravan components, and (4) thoroughly understanding the European sociocultural climate, as well as the expectations and codes of conduct in the European professional theater world, are absolute prerequisites. If met, the material and immaterial investments will return vast dividends for all partners at both ends of the intercultural divide.

NOTES

1. In the context of this article, North-South relations refer to relations between the First World (Europe, North America, South Pacific) and the Third World (Asia, Africa, Latin America). For examples of such discussions on intercultural theater, see Bonnie Marranca and Gautam Dasgupta, eds., *Interculturalism and Performance* (New York: PAJ, 1991), or J. Ellen Gainor, ed., *Imperialism and Theatre* (London: Routledge, 1996).

2. See Eugene van Erven, "Theatre of Liberation of India, Indonesia, and the Philippines," *Australasian Drama Studies* 10 (April 1987): 5–21; "Theatre of Liberation in Action: The People's Theatre Network of the Philippines," *New Theatre Quarterly* 3, no. 10 (May 1987): 131–50; and "Philippine Political Theatre and the Fall of Ferdinand Marcos," *The Drama Review* 31, no. 2 (summer 1987): 57–79.

3. See Russell Campbell, "Hakas and Jasmins," *Illusions* 6 (November 1987): 9–17.

4. See van Erven, "Philippine People's Theatre Down Under," *New Theatre Australia* (September 1987): 34–37.

5. With the exception of Nakko Kiritani and Grace Amilbangsa, none of the "Cry of Asia!" artists had ever heard of or worked with ACPC before. Back in 1989, ACPC had a paper board composed of Hotta Masahiko, Kiritani's ex-husband and a cultural worker of the Japanese Philippine solidarity group; Dr. Felix Sugirtharaj, head of a sociocultural action network in Madras (India); Fr. Ed de la Torre, an exiled Filipino activist-priest; and Al Santos himself. In practice, Santos did most of the fund-raising and policymaking on his own. Apart from Santos, the organization employed several Filipinos on a part-time basis, most of whom came from PETA circles, so that a certain level of cliquishness seemed unavoidable.

6. See the section on *Panata Sa Kalayaan* in my *Playful Revolution* (Bloomington: Indiana University Press, 1992), 56–59.

7. Thai puppeteer Ornanong Vongasawathepchai died in a car crash on 17 April 1996. I wish to dedicate this essay to her.

8. In the Netherlands, "Ahurangi" was performed twice in De Balie in Amsterdam, and once in Vredenburg in Utrecht, Korzo in The Hague, De Evenaar in Rotterdam, and the Muzisch Centrum in Emmeloord.

9. See *Playful Revolution*, 112–13. Kim Myung Gon's formidable acting skills can be seen in the Korean feature film *Soponye,* which also received acclaim in the western European and American art cinema circuit.

10. Claudine Galéa, "Un Cri d'Asie Chez les Papes," *l'Humanité,* 27 July 1989, 20.

11. Alex van Hoof, "Boeiend Aziatisch spel: Boodschap over misstanden komt niet over," *Trouw,* 17 Oct. 1989, 9; Max Arian, "Van heel ver," *De Groene Amsterdammer,* 18 Oct. 1989, 21; Eric de Ruijter, "'Cry of Asia' biedt universeel volkstheater," *Telegraaf,* 20 Oct. 1989, 33; Maarten Brakema, "Een lawine van symboliek," *Hervormd Nederland,* 21 Oct. 1989, 34; A. van der Kolk, "Cry of Asia blijkt in 'Ahurangi' een onzuiver gilletje," *Utrechts Nieuwsblad,* 27 Oct. 1989, 29; John Delemarre, "Maya Theater: De Schreeuw van Azië," *Poppenpodium,* Dec. 1989, 34.

12. Personal interview with Janssens and Rudelsheim, Amsterdam, 14 Dec. 1989.

13. Personal interview with Van Mossel, Utrecht, 18 Dec. 1989. Wibaut's remarks were recorded during a personal interview in The Hague, 20 Dec. 1989.

14. The Dutch budget was Dfl 190,000. We eventually received subsidies from the Ministry of Development Aid (Dfl 30,000), Amnesty International (Dfl 2,000), the European Human Rights Foundation (Dfl 2,000), the Dutch Embassy in the Philippines (Dfl 15,000), Development Agency NOVIB (Dfl 10,000), the Elise Mathilde Foundation (Dfl 3,000), the Provincial government of Utrecht (Dfl 5,500), the Municipality of Utrecht (Dfl5,500), the Provincial government of Zuid-Holland (Dfl 7,500), and Utrecht University (Dfl 18,000). The remaining income was generated through ticket sales, workshop fees, and donations in kind.

15. Telephone interviews with Roch and Perrot, 11 Jan. 1990.

16. Personal interview with Vitidnan Rojanaparnich, Utrecht, 20 June 1995.

Gender and National Politics

Marcia Blumberg

Re-Staging Resistance, Re-Viewing Women: 1990s Productions of Fugard's *Hello and Goodbye* and *Boesman and Lena*

The drama of Athol Fugard, South Africa's most prominent playwright, has long been considered synonymous with staging resistance against oppressive structures, culturally intervening when censorship, bannings, house arrest, and detention without trial occurred routinely for individuals or groups who defied state policies or were even suspected of oppositional activities. Although Fugard's plays are usually set in recognizable South African locales and emanate from a specific historical context, they have often successfully traveled from local to international stages with South African and other casts. The transcultural as well as the South African remountings raise complicated issues of interpretation and reception, and yet the very notion of resistance, as Rosemary Jolly has remarked, "is not a quality inherent in a cultural product but rather an effect of the process of that product's creation and reception."[1] Here I will examine the process of staging resistance in two recent productions of early Fugardian theater: *Hello and Goodbye,* directed by the playwright with American actors at Princeton (1994), and *Boesman and Lena,* produced in Johannesburg (1993) with a South African cast and director, who are "coloured" (so-called mixed race) and black.[2] While the Princeton production spans continents, the South African staging emanates from an imminent postapartheid time-space. The question is how Fugard's texts have altered in almost three decades. In what way do new spatiotemporal contexts propel the productions into what Marvin Carlson terms "a new local semiosis?"[3] How do 1990s spectators reassess plays that apparently resisted and certainly exposed systemic oppression when those very structures are being destroyed, reformed, and replaced? The representation of the

women, Hester and Lena, foregrounds the necessity of addressing the inex-
tricability of gender issues with those of class and race despite decades of
emphasis in South Africa on racial liberation and little attention in the main
to gender.

Together with *The Blood Knot* (1961), *Hello and Goodbye* (1965) and
Boesman and Lena (1969) form a trilogy termed "Port Elizabeth plays," since
this city provides the locale. Also called Fugard's "family" plays, *The Blood
Knot* explores the relationship between two brothers and their linkage to
absent women; *Hello and Goodbye* depicts ties between a brother and sister
in a complex intertwinement with their deceased parents; and *Boesman and
Lena* focuses on the bonds between spouses. Written and first produced at
the height of apartheid, the plays dramatize oppressive structures and their
effects on the voiceless and dispossessed of South Africa. At the same time,
the engendering of voice in the latter two plays draws attention to the
potential for resistance, albeit limited. Without naming the onerous laws or
speaking the word *apartheid*,[4] the plays explore marginalization. In particular, both *Hello and Goodbye* and *Boesman and Lena* offer strong women's roles
that exemplify Chandra Mohanty's caveat: "There is an urgent need for us
to appreciate . . . the complex relationality that shapes our lives. . . . Systems
of racial, class, and gender domination do not have identical effects on
women."[5] The plays not only emphasize differing effects of race on class and
gender but also problematize the construction of women as victims. Despite
their status as apparent survivors, the women possess limited agency and
unwittingly preserve the status quo. Notwithstanding their loud voicing of
existential angst, both women embody the silence of an unpoliticized materiality, especially since survival ultimately signifies the containment of resistance and denial of transformative potential.

In foregrounding the networks of power inscribed in these plays, I
examine their self-conscious staging of resistance and interrogate their
efficacy as political theater, a term that Fugard has consistently resisted over
the years: "I find myself frustrated by the label 'political playwright.' . . . I
am a story teller, not a political pamphleteer."[6] Yet, he invariably also
acknowledges the contradiction in his situation.

> [I]n the South African context the two are inseparable. I think of
> myself essentially as a story-teller. . . . an apolitical South African story
> is a contradiction in terms. . . . There is no area of my life, from that
> public identity as a man of the theatre, down to my most personal and
> private relationships, where the political realities and pressures of this
> society do not have consequences.[7]

Fugard associates his prodigious output with the imperative of exposing injustice: "my life's work was possibly just to witness as truthfully as I could the nameless and destitute (desperate) of this one little corner of the world"; he also articulates "the genuine desire to shatter white complacency and its conspiracy of silence."[8] Professed objectives, however, do not automatically translate into equivalent values in a script or onstage, where the material effects of the performance of words and gestures within a chosen setting provide a context whose ramifications merit careful analysis. This opportunity to review Fugard's early plays in new spatiotemporal contexts also assesses claims in the light of more complex structures of signification.

In addition, any analysis of the construction of women and their stagings in Athol Fugard's plays must acknowledge the contribution of Yvonne Bryceland, whose name is synonymous with portrayals of Fugardian women for over two decades. Bryceland's untimely death in January 1992 elicited Fugard's unequivocal praise.

> I would not be the writer I am today . . . had Yvonne Bryceland not come into my life at one of the most critical and formative periods of my writing career. My debt of gratitude to her as an artist, as human being, as comrade, as friend, is beyond words.[9]

He documented the collaborative nature of their working relationship as follows: "Y. and I embarked on a long dialogue as to why she as actress and myself as writer and director were turning our backs on the securities and orthodoxies of our past work" (*Notebooks,* 189). She encapsulated her commitment to Fugard's work thus: "It's what my life is about."[10] Dennis Walder's assertion, echoed by Fugard in many interviews, that "Bryceland [gives] the Fugard characters whom she plays their *definitive* form"[11] (emphasis added) adds another dimension to my reviewing of the two female characters from Fugard's 1960s plays. I question the concept of a definitive staging since rather than conveying the notion of a memorable performance, the phrase's implied fixity negates the very creativity and changeability associated with performance. Such a phrase also elides the vital problem of context and the impossibility of a particular staging, however effective, being the yardstick to measure all productions at various times and places. While recalling facets of Bryceland's portrayals of Hester and Lena, I shift the spotlight to two recent restagings of the plays.

In the two-hander *Hello and Goodbye,* a working-class white brother and sister, Johnnie and Hester, "the second-hand Smits of Valley Road"(165), renew their uneasy relationship when the sister unexpectedly appears after more than a decade of absence. The palpable presence of their biological father, whose recent death is Johnnie's closely guarded secret, as well as that of their heavenly Father, who is imbricated in their strong Calvinist roots, pervades the dialogue. If Johnnie's initial and closing actions envelop the play in the anguish of living, the ironic curtain line, "resurrection," facilitates his performance of the stance and story of his crippled, newly deceased father: the final tableau emphasizes lack of power and pessimistically denies future potential. The dynamism of the play, however, resides in the main action that is framed by Hester's voice, her "hello" a few minutes into act 1 and her "goodbye" in the penultimate moments of act 2. The construction of Hester as "evil daughter" in a motherless household results in her being rejected and expelled by her father, as well as her "choice" of prostitution as a mechanism for economic survival.

Hester's hatred for family and social structures discloses her intense desire to institute change. The play poignantly renders her need to wrest from her unhappy past good childhood memories after her mother's death robbed her of the potential of a loving relationship. Hester rummages through boxes for her father's compensation money but finds instead papers, photographs, and old clothes; her mother's dress affects her most: "It's Mommie's smell. . . . Hell man it hurts"(160). As she enacts the multiple subject positions of a lonely, poor woman, prostitute, family outcast, fighter, and schemer, the play makes visible societal structures and concomitantly marks audience members as partially complicit in their positioning, in this theater context, as silent spectators.

At the 1965 premiere of *Hello and Goodbye* at the Library Theatre, Johannesburg, critics acclaimed the acting of Molly Seftel and Athol Fugard but gave the play mixed reviews. Reacting to their expectations of conventional plays, critics and spectators resisted the spareness of the stage, the drabness of the circumscribed world, as well as the "poverty" of theatrical values. What Stephen Gray calls "the definitive production" was directed by Fugard with Bryceland and Bill Flynn at The Space, Cape Town, in July 1974.[12] It toured throughout South Africa and was also staged in London and filmed by the BBC. British critic Michael Coveney compared Janet Suzman and Ben Kingsley's 1973 performances, where the "play seemed over-long," with Fugard's "riveting" 1978 production, noting it was "thrilling to see Yvonne Bryceland—surely one of the great actresses of our time."[13]

The 1994 revival of *Hello and Goodbye,* which Fugard accords "favourite [play]" status, was directed by the playwright with Maria Tucci and Zeljko Ivanek at the McCarter Theater, Princeton. How does this production compare with the so-called definitive staging also directed by Fugard? Local and international acclaim greeted Bryceland's Hester; her nuanced diction and poor-white Afrikaner body language was uncannily mimetic, particularly for the South African spectator. Moreover, she invested Hester with a vitality no matter how desperate the situation: "I think Hester's a marvelous lady. I think she's got guts. She looks life in the face."[14] In the 1994 production Maria Tucci's Hester, while less convincingly South African in diction, still provided a powerful portrayal, juxtaposing hilarity and hatred, the futile and the funny, to relieve a painful present. Tucci applied these voicings to Hester's search for anything to redeem the past that involves her father's compensation and that would facilitate change; this inextricable linkage between money and empowerment emphasizes the difficulties that exist for a working-class Afrikaner woman. As all hope of finding the money vanishes, she realizes the terrible certainty of future hardship.

Fugard's categorization of Hester as "my feminist" stresses the apparent boldness of his 1965 construction of a woman who rebels against entrapment in oppressive patriarchal structures and resists the stifling rigidity of the church.[15] For Fugard these form "cornerstones of Afrikaner culture. . . . God in Heaven, Daddy's at the head of the table, the Bible at his right-hand, and the women are in the kitchen."[16] Hester resists the Smit's familial and societal "norms" and employs her mother's life and demise and the examples of other women as a caveat.

> Marriage! One man's slave all your life. . . . She fell into her grave the way they all do tired. . . . They live in hell, but they're too frightened to do anything about it because there's always somebody around shouting God and Judgement. Mommie should have taken what she wanted and then kicked him out. (176)

Hester escapes the strictures imposed by her father and the church and rejects the option of marital slavery. Nevertheless, her voice operates within the interstices of a substantial silencing, and her apparent empowerment ultimately signifies a survival mechanism that foregrounds her situation within different oppressions that control and contain her potential for fulfillment.

How does the construction of Hester in an American production speak to the material reality of the complex issues of women in South Africa? Jeanne Colleran's cogent analysis of Fugard's recent plays *My Children! My Africa!* (1990) and *Playland* (1992) and the implications of their reception in the United States, "where his plays are performed more than anywhere else in the world," highlights the potential for a reductive appraisal of the complexity of local historical and sociopolitical issues if specific differences between American and South African contexts are elided.[17] This problem of a reductive reading is not limited to international audiences, since many spectators in South Africa, especially in the 1960s and early 1970s, were either ignorant of the diverse ramifications of oppressive structures or lived in denial. Joseph Lelyveld's observation that "apartheid is no longer a concept. . . . it is the screen that hides the vast reality of black South Africa from the vision of most whites"[18] foregrounds the potential for a severe truncation of political awareness. This tunnel view, combined with Fugard's elevated status both in South Africa and the United States as well as the playwright's obvious sincerity and apparently widely acceptable moderate liberal inclinations, has resulted in what Nicholas Visser terms "South African reviews that adopted the eulogizing manner."[19]

Theater reviews in the popular press, especially in South Africa, have routinely hailed Fugardian productions with superlatives and approached them by insisting on emotional identification with the individual characters. Susan Hilferty, who has designed Fugard's sets since 1980 and collaborates with him as an associate director, concurs: "the emotions of the play should go directly into the viewer's system, *intravenously* almost. You should just be flat-out connected to what you are watching, without interference" (emphasis added).[20] Hilferty's organic metaphor connotes a palpable infusion of feeling that the spectator absorbs directly; does this approach valorize the emotions to such an extent that it devalues the exercise of rational processes? Spectators, who empathically identify with characters and engage in a cathartic process, operate differently from those who thoughtfully analyze the drama at the same time as they feel the joys and pain of the sites of struggle. In the latter case, the potential for a productive engagement with the stage increases. Until the past decade, few critics internationally, and even fewer South African reviewers, have read against the Fugardian grain or scrutinized the plays in terms of dramatic *as well as* ideological structures, practices that raise more complex questions about the engendering of voice and the effects of staging resistance.

In *Hello and Goodbye,* a thoughtful reading of Hester requires first of all some contextualizing of the position of women in South Africa. Although women have made their mark at definitive moments in South African history, gender oppression per se was strongly protested by South African women's groups only in the 1980s. This late mobilization is, for the writer Zoe Wiccomb, "the orthodox position," which "whilst celebrating the political activism of women" presumes that "the gender issue ought to be subsumed by the national liberation struggle."[21] Yet some South African feminists explore a middle ground between Wiccomb's position, which emphasizes racial inequities and insists that people of colour fight for liberation across gender lines despite the power differential, and the women's movement, which foregrounds the issue of gender domination. Fugard's designation of Hester as "my feminist" also requires further scrutiny since she merely substitutes oppressions when she replaces paternal control with lack of empowerment as male clients pay to use her body at their behest. Her final speech posits the future as a reiteration of the past: "There's always jobs. And I got my room. That's me—a woman in a room" (188). In the light of Fugard's categorization, Hester's self-naming resonates ironically with Virginia Woolf's significant feminist text *A Room of One's Own*. Decades later Hester's anticipation of her father's compensation package— "Five hundred pounds is a lot of money" (167)—names the exact sum that would set Woolf's female writer on a firm footing. Importantly, Woolf's room evokes a space conducive to creative work and self-fulfillment as well as a refuge from domestic demands and the spiritual depletion associated with a crowded family existence. In contrast, Hester's small, dark, rented room is the only place she calls her own. At the same time, her work conducted in this room inscribes it as a societally unsanctioned place even for economic survival and thereby makes her continuing occupation of the room tenuous.

Nuances of difference in Bryceland's and Tucci's potent portrayals of Hester seem less urgent than issues arising from the spatiotemporal shift and variations in the reception and discursive constructs. Fugard claims that the play offers "no message . . . [rather] a rich emotional experience."[22] Instead he accords a debt: "Camus helped me understand my Hester. . . . 'courageous pessimism'—a world without hope but you've got to have courage . . . you carry on, you live."[23] In the 1990s, audiences may observe Hester's tribulations as an existential predicament but are more likely to be attuned to the political factors of race, class, and gender in the embodiment of Hester's voice. Moreover, while Fugard uses the possessive adjective "my" with obvious affection for his creation, the hint of a proprietary tone adopted toward a female character provides a linguistic replication of the oppressive gendered structures that entrap Hester in the play as well as many women in South African society.

If middle- and upper-class women in South Africa in the 1960s often focused on other pursuits, Hester's prime concern is work: "You want a sin, well there's one. I *Hoer*. I've *hoered* all the brothers and fathers and sons and sweethearts in this world into one thing . . . Man" (158). In addition to the reduction of diverse men into an essentialist category, Man, Fugard yokes Hester's self-construction as whore with her insertion into a punitive theological discourse, reinforcing a stereotype of women as evil. A view of Hester as "itinerant tart"[24] reinforces Fugard's unedited notebook entries: "common prostitute . . . one reality—her bruises, her physical flesh. Flesh that has said fuck-you to the spirit."[25] Hester's rebellion in leaving her familial home is subjected to the limited opportunities available to an unskilled working-class woman; escape from paternal oppression embodies a "choice" that further commodifies her as sexual object. The humiliation imposed by married women provokes her anger: "Who the hell do they think they are? Laughing at us like we're a dirty joke or something" (168). Hester also interrogates the double standard of class privilege as it affects marriage: "happy families is fat men crawling on to frightened women. . . . I've washed more of your husbands out of me than ever gave you babies" (168). Hester points out that her profession involves dynamics significantly similar to that of married women—only the status and terms of payment differ. Hester's juxtaposition of the entrapment of prostitutes and wives also contests one current view that prostitutes practice a chosen profession and exert control over their bodies. She reinforces the notion of prostitutes as those who tolerate the violation of their bodies in situations that, often dangerous to their health and physical well-being, are brought about not through choice but in contexts of exploitation, abuse, or economic necessity. For Gail Phetersen,

> [a] profile of psychological propensity, economic need, and coercion is not all wrong. What is wrong with it is the assumption that prostitutes are more neurotic . . . more financially needy . . . and more coerced in life choices than other women. One reason such comparisons are invalid is that they ignore the wide diversity among prostitutes.[26]

The central difference of the restaging pertains to discourse. The high moral tone and individual blame previously ascribed to Hester is superseded in most 1990s readings by an emphasis on material societal conditions, here especially the effect of class on gender. Spectators perhaps less easily adopt the judgmental stance of deeming her "other," an object of ridicule or abjection, if they concede their implication in the very societal structures that fail to change those conditions.

The intersection of issues of race and class is also vital in the play. This 1965 construction of poor-white Afrikaners exposed conditions for a small group of whites whose situation, although onerous, was still better than that of many blacks by virtue of the apartheid regime with its job-protection laws that privileged whites. Unlike the devastation suffered by many white Afrikaner farmers, who were financially ruined during the depression, the plight of this marginal group of working-class Afrikaners was erased on the assumption that all "whites in South Africa, for decades wallowing in affluence . . . used to enjoy one of the highest living standards in the world."[27] Fugard's 1994 production evokes a new awareness of the working-class Afrikaner family in relation to the nation-state: "that family is not just mine but a metaphor for South Africa—the decaying patriarchy, the despairing youth, the woman rooted in carnality and common sense with a huge, heroic heart."[28] In a complex set of displacements—boycotts, recession, and the dismantling of apartheid—South African society at the time of the Princeton production in February 1994 reels in a state of upheaval. Political divisions are rife, and Afrikaners can no longer rely on racial privilege and job protection. A democratic regime under President Nelson Mandela and a government of national unity comprise a majority of black parliamentarians. They promise equality of race and gender, and we can be assured that much redistribution of electoral power will occur, although little redistribution of wealth. A 1993 article in *New African* reports on

a new reality . . . the emergence of a class of poor unemployed whites. . . . [Some] are joining their black brothers on the streets where they beg . . . hundreds of whites have become squatters. (26)

Since systemic oppression can no longer go unheeded, *Hello and Goodbye* takes on new urgency. Spectators at this production who historicize the play find a changing backdrop that marks the difficult journey of the Afrikaner from outcast to ruler and recently to a minority power holder or a member of a growing group uprooted from decades of racial privilege and economic stability.

In Fugard's third family play, *Boesman and Lena* (1969), the eponymous pair of homeless "coloureds" (mixed race in apartheid terminology) share the same racially motivated poverty and discrimination but not the same power in the dynamics of gender relations. Albie Sachs analyzes this issue, now that "gender is on the agenda of the new South Africa":

one of the few profoundly non-racial institutions in South Africa is patriarchy . . . [which] brutalizes men and neutralizes women across the colour line. *At the same time, gender inequality takes on a specifically apartheid-related character; there is inequality within inequality . . . some are more unequal than others.* (emphasis added)[29]

In *Boesman and Lena* this hierarchy of gender is apparent from the opening tableau. As in *Hello and Goodbye,* arrivals and departures demarcate an interval where monumental conflict is enacted, only here these actions frame the entire play. Exhausted and heavily burdened by their few worn-out possessions, Boesman leads and Lena blindly follows him onto an empty stage that offers a temporary locale for two characters in search of an abode. Displaced and homeless after their squatter shack has been bulldozed by men and machinery sanctioned by apartheid, Lena encapsulates their plight: "The right time on the wrong road, the right road leading to the wrong place" (219). Lena's utterances here and throughout the play disclose a ventriloquized voice; history has demarcated her status and has subjected her to various oppressive positionings. While she recognizes and articulates her lot in life, she directs her attention to perfecting different modes of survival; this reactive stance promotes strategies for continuing existence but precludes any attempt to institute meaningful change.

Lena's opening monologue performs the verbal and gestural fury of a cycle of violence rendered concrete as repression, submission, never-to-be-attained freedom, and objectification as garbage. Mired in mud, Lena bares her victimhood: "This piece of world is rotten. Put down your foot and you're in it up to your knee. . . . Another day gone. Other people lived it. We tramped it into the ground" (196). Ontological violence associated with the equation of certain racial categories with trash infects personal relationships yet nonetheless operates according to gender differentials. Lena is Boesman's property: "it's *me,* that thing you *sleep* [drag] along the roads. My life . . . been used too long. . . . Time to throw it away. How do you do that when it's yourself?" (198). The play comes full circle in the final tableau, but unlike the entrance (when Lena follows Boesman), their departure together marks altered dynamics of power. Despite the shared exit, the interrogatives Lena has voiced throughout the play may provoke spectators to attend to her concerns.

The relationship between the couple is enacted through Boesman's violent self-hatred, which he inflicts on the only person more powerless than himself. Lena's response to Boesman's silence is self-expression. Unlike the loquacity of some Pinter and Mamet characters, who dominate their adversaries with vocal bombardment, Lena's survival mechanism stems from a verbalization and self-interrogation of her very existence. She regards silence as tantamount to annihilation. She also performs metatheatrical moments of song and dance to confirm that she is alive or to rejoice for an instant despite her onerous circumstances; this fleeting release epitomizes Frantz Fanon's argument that "violence is canalised, transformed and conjured away. . . . the circle of dance is a permissive circle."[30] Boesman situates himself within patriarchal structures and racial classification so that he ironically dominates Lena and concomitantly acts subserviently within the system.

The catalytic intrusion of a dying black man, Outa, changes the dynamics and complicates the enactment of racial oppression. Boesman's vilification of the stranger as "vuilgoed" (rubbish) (231) emphasizes the specifics of positionality in South Africa and foregrounds hierarchies of oppression: "He's not brown people, he's black people." Lena simultaneously designates him "other" and tries to bridge the racial divide: "They got feelings too" (212). Her response signifies a desperate desire for nonabusive communication with anyone who will listen. The play explores the enactment of voice and embodiment of silence in the triad. Outa speaks Xhosa, which Lena in dire frustration terms "baboon language" (212), yet his repetition of her name, as well as his mere presence, constitute the act of bearing witness—a partial antidote to what Fugard terms Lena's "ontological insecurity" (Notebooks, 173). Outa embodies silence in death as well as in the "babble" of words that are neither comprehended by Lena nor by spectators, even at local productions (unless they are conversant with Xhosa). The image metonymically conveys the political silencing of the black South African majority (almost thirty million people), who effectively gained legitimate voice with their first votes in April 1994. Boesman, however, is either sullenly silent, refusing to listen, or uses language as a weapon. Lena's bruised body, a visual mark of racial and gender oppression and evidence of Boesman's attempted silencing, can be read as a text that powerfully voices her subjugation as a coloured woman who is abused by a man, himself emasculated by societal structures.

The changing contexts of this play provoke even more complex questions than those of Hello and Goodbye. The first production in Grahamstown in July 1969 (with Fugard directing and acting) praised Bryceland's portrayal of Lena as "stunning" and a "tour de force." Dennis Walder examines the choice of Bryceland as Lena.

Nobody [was] available from Lena's submerged class. . . . brought up in the Cape, [Bryceland] was able to draw on a lifetime of unconscious absorption of the way of speaking and moving of "people like Lena."[31]

In performing Lena, Bryceland, a white actor, spoke for a destitute woman who was voiceless and extremely marginalized. Foregrounding multiple oppressions, this production apparently resisted the apartheid status quo and, in the context of the late 1960s, was critically acclaimed for memorable portrayals and a searing comment on racial and gender inequality. In the decades since this first production, critics have become more attentive to problems of representation in theater stagings and drama texts—who represents whom, who speaks for whom, and how representations are rendered concrete in political and aesthetic senses. For example, Gayatri Spivak differentiates between representation as

> *Vertretung* . . . to tread in someone's shoes . . . political representation [and] *Darstellung*. . . . *Representing:* proxy and portrait. . . . Unless the complicity between these two things is kept in mind, there can be a great deal of political harm.[32]

There is a greater awareness of this complicity in the implications of issues such as cross-racial casting, historical context, appropriation of voice, and positionality, which are considered relevant and yet completely intertwined with the structural and dramatic aspects of the staging. Many critics are reappraising stagings in a more theorized interrogation of the embodiment of voice. Moreover, they as well as spectators who read both with and against texts refuse to lionize Fugard's drama. Whilst praising the power of dramatic images and the poetry of pain in the playing out of agonizing human predicaments, it is also possible to critique the effects of words and gestures performed by actors whose corporeal presence on a stage realizes a multiplicity of issues constructed by the playwright. The chosen parameters for each character in their very distinctive locale first demands contextualization; rather than eliding specificity in a universalizing gesture, the attempt to understand and value differences also emphasizes power differentials and reminds us of work that still needs to be done.

Although *Boesman and Lena* powerfully exposes the effects of apartheid, the play has engendered diverse critical reactions. Dennis Walder gauges Janet Suzman's portrayal of Lena in London in 1984 according to Bryceland's portrayal:

> What Bryceland conveyed, and what is missing [here]. . . is a dimension of extremity: an intensity of suffering and, at the same time, defiance, which transcends the circumstances of everyday life.[33]

Suffering and defiance combine most acutely in the finale. Boesman's imperative, "Come" (244) elicits Lena's "No," the most vital word in a play punctuated with monosyllables. Her refusal signifies a shift in power, yet her departure from the stage together with Boesman, albeit as a supposed equal, contains and subsumes the defiance and performs an endless vicious cycle.

British critic Michael Billington probes the political ramifications of the dramatic conflict in *Boesman and Lena* in an insightful reading that no local reviewer had yet voiced.

> Fugard presents us with a memorable image of the human degradation engendered by a racist regime. . . . it seems to me not quite enough for the white liberal dramatist to offer his coloured contemporaries his pity, his compassion, and his despair. What surely is needed . . . is an affirmation of the fact that the country's tragedy is man-made and therefore capable of change. . . . while deploring the status quo, [the play] also unwittingly helps to reinforce it.[34]

The playwright had, however, raised these concerns in then unpublished notebook entries of December 1968: "Our hell (history) is man-made, to that extent it can be unmade by men" (*Notebooks*, 179). This statement clearly advocates changing conditions that are untenable, yet the play evades that aspect and demonstrates instead Lena's indomitable will to survive. Fugard identifies another problem.

> The "social" content of *Boesman and Lena*. Nagging doubts that I am opting out on this score, that I am not saying enough. At one level their predicament is an indictment of this society which makes people "rubbish." Is this explicit enough? (179)

Fugard's question prompts another: if the quality of theatrical intervention is one of exposure, is this disruption an effective and explicit enough "coming between" the oppressive societal conditions and the audience of mainly white middle-class South Africans? In the 1990s, it is also useful to heed Nadine Gordimer's reminder: "We whites in South Africa present an updated version of the tale of the Emperor's clothes; we are not aware of our nakedness—ethical, moral, and fatal—clothed as we are in our own skin."[35] Since the invisibility of whiteness as well as the passing references to white culpability place all the stress on the oppressed, it may encourage some spectators to avoid confrontation with ethical and moral issues associated with support for or complicity with the system of oppression.

Hester's claim in *Hello and Goodbye,* "Life in here was second-hand . . . used up and old before we even got it" (172), and her depiction of their possessions as "second-hand poor-white junk" (181) make no attempt to hide the Smit's poverty and underclass status, but *Boesman and Lena* offers neither a home nor enough possessions to store in boxes and call junk. Instead, the nexus of race and class elicits Boesman's realization: "We're whiteman's rubbish. . . . His rubbish is people" (231). Although this image is patently clear, the emphasis on verbalization of existential angst and philosophical voicing of pain in the context of survival as the acme of existence emphasizes a lacuna of resistance; it therefore shifts attention away from the notion of agency as it could be applied to material conditions of society, the ideological structures, and strategies of power on many levels that have specific significance in South Africa.

In confronting Boesman's reaction to forced removal and the destruction of their shack, Lena conflates their oppressor and the instrument of violence: "Blame the whiteman. Bulldozer!" (194). Yet with the demise of apartheid, easy solutions are unclear. Mantoa Nompikazi explains,

> As a black woman . . . I've had my fair share of suffering. . . . One of the . . . fights has been with myself. Centuries of women's oppression, African traditions and prejudices against women too, had left their indelible mark on me, resulting in an inferiority complex that needed a bulldozer to move.[36]

She evokes the systemic ventriloquizing inherent in patriarchal structures, both Eurocentric institutions and customary laws, that muzzle those who are subjected into a state of silence.

Fugard constructs Lena as a poor "coloured" woman at a particular intersection of race, class, and gender that is triply devalued in this South African context. Despite her constant metaphysical inquiry, what Boesman calls "All your bloody nonsense questions" (208), this construction allows her to resist Boesman but also denies her the ability to understand the ramifications of her material condition as an effect of an egregious political process. Many black South African theater practitioners have acknowledged Fugard's contribution to South African theater in general and their work in particular; yet concerns expressed about the representation of black or "coloured" people in the theater and in Fugard's plays should be heeded. John Kani's complaint that "imposters jumping on the bandwagon" had lowered the quality of protest theater—*"No one wants to sit back and be told that we are black and we are suffering. We know that"* (emphasis added)[37]—may apply here, despite differences between the protest genre and Fugard's dramas. While Kani respects Fugard and has acted in many of his plays, he has also voiced concern about the political implications of the construction of characters and agonized over some portrayals since they are often antithetical to his views and can be detrimental to future liberation and democratic processes. Zakes Mda, a black South African playwright, director, and academic is quite specific about Fugardian representations of people of colour in the articulation of his unease.

> [The play] clearly protests against racial segregation by depicting its inhuman nature. . . . The oppressed suffer in silence and are not involved in any struggle against the oppression. Instead they are endowed with endless reservoirs of stoic endurance. The spirit of defiance . . . in the real life situation is non-existent. When one has seen a play like *Boesman and Lena* . . . [if unaware of the struggles] against oppression . . . one is left with the impression that the blacks really deserve to be oppressed, for they let oppression happen to them.[38]

The critics draw attention to Fugard's construction of Lena as self-reflexive in ontological terms, yet she never completes the trajectory from the immediate dilemma to interpellation in the material conditions and networks of power; instead, her voice is stunted and politically silenced. These critics refuse to view the play solely as existentialist drama, adopting an approach that views the specifics of the stage against the wider historical and political milieu.

In a recent analysis of the play Craig McLuckie contends that "Boesman fails to take an independent or even a skeptical view of the white perspective that is privileged by raw power." More puzzling is his endnote.

> For whatever reasons Fugard's characters are rarely aware of the mass movements of their time: black consciousness, the African National Congress, the Communist Party of South Africa, the Pan Africanist Congress, Fanonian psychiatry, etc. Either Fugard believes that his characters would not come into contact with these movements or Fugard himself has not, so the question of their inclusion is a moot point for him.[39]

McLuckie raises an important question but provides strange answers. That Fugard refuses to utilize his characters as a vehicle to ventriloquize the voices and agendas of political organizations, many of which have only recently been unbanned, is hardly surprising. I presume McLuckie's suggestion that Fugard has not come into contact with the movements is jocular since while Fugard, a self-declared liberal, may never have attended a meeting of any of the listed organizations, his notebooks attest to him being well read. Perhaps a more helpful discussion is raised in the *Notebooks* when Fugard discusses the limitations of his characters.

> Terrible things like bigotry and prejudice—I never (consciously) seem to get past the fact that they "are"—the reality is sufficient. I do ask questions of course, but always in the context of a Hester or a Morrie—*their* reality. Never in my own life. And if that reality—no matter how superficially limited it may seem . . . is seen with enough Truth, all the other questions will be there. (131)

Fugard's conviction that the portrayal of societal reality as "Truth" will take care of all the other questions seems to raise its own problems: the feasibility of portraying Truth rather than truths, the demand that "superficially limited" portrayals of reality can bear the weight of the complexities of the conditions, and the continued choice of characters who, being restricted in their situation in society, can only communicate in limited ways. After years of adulatory reviews, some critics more frequently raise these questions and point out the discrepancies between Fugard's statements about the plays, intended claims made for them, and the ways that the texts sometimes work in apparent support of his declarations and at other times perhaps foreground issues and processes that seem antithetical to his stance.

What his downtrodden characters in the main depict (with the exception of *My Children! My Africa!*) is a preoccupation with a present crisis that is related to, or is a reiteration of, situations from the past. Apparently for Fugard, the characters' immersion in human suffering necessitates strategies of survival but offers limited modes of perception rather than any accounting of the effects of gross inequities in power distribution in specific material conditions; a more significant lacuna is the noncomprehension and the concomitant lack of impulse to alter these processes. An emphasis on the universalizing of suffering foregrounds characters as individuals representative of humankind at large rather than characters situated in a specific place and space at the nexus of complex sociopolitical coordinates. This so-called absence of political awareness is in and of itself a political stance, that of liberal humanism, which Catherine Belsey argues assumes a world of non-contradictory (and therefore fundamentally unalterable) individuals whose unfettered consciousness is the origin of meaning, knowledge and action. It is in the interest of this ideology above all to suppress the role of language in the construction of the subject . . . and to present the individual as a free, unified, autonomous subjectivity.[40]

The supposedly "unpoliticized" stance of liberal humanism, therefore, evades the implications of different subject positions and the engendering of voice in networks of power.

The July 1993 production of *Boesman and Lena,* directed by Jerry Mofokeng at the Market Theatre, Johannesburg, raises questions about Lena's portrayal by a black actor, Nomhle Nkonyeni. An original member of the Serpent Players founded by Fugard in the 1960s, Nkonyeni, in Barry Ronge's estimation, gave an "unforgettable" rendition of Lena in this production.[41] Speaking to me after the performance, she maintained that her experience as a black woman who had lived in the Eastern Cape translated into a different portrayal of Lena than that so powerfully acted by Bryceland. Robert Greig has also noted that Nkonyeni

plays a coloured woman with more conviction than any white could. . . . [It is] one of the great performances in our theatre . . . because of its emotional range and insight; because of its technical skill; and finally, it seems weighted with experience.[42]

Nkonyeni and Greig privilege the authority of experience, a term that Foucault defines as the "correlation between fields of knowledge, types of normativity, and forms of subjectivity in a particular culture."[43] Based on the biological attribute of a dark skin encoding a commonality of identity, the performance of a coloured character by a black actor is considered more authentic than that of a white actor; in this instance, the South African racial designation, "nonwhite," apparently assumes comparable victimization of coloured and black under oppressive structures. Sandra Harding reminds us that "[f]or women and other marginalized groups, subjectivity and its possibility of legitimated 'experience' must be achieved; subjectivity and experience are made, not born."[44] On stage clad in broken old clothes, Nkonyeni's corporeal presence instantaneously signifies material deprivation in the South African socius, but the differences in experience between a "coloured" and a black woman should be appraised. Terry Goldie's exam-

ination of verisimilitude and other issues relevant to the representation of
the indigene in Canadian, Australian, and New Zealand literatures is
instructive here too.

> Stage conventions play an important part in the response to that signi-
> fying power, particularly that of the actors' bodies. Suspension of dis-
> belief does not imply that the audience forget that they are watching
> actors. . . . [At the same time] each stage indigene is perceivable as
> generic.[45]

While Nkonyeni is perceived as the generic class called "nonwhite,"
Goldie's injunction that the audience should not "forget that they are
watching actors" points to the subtle and complex nuances of South African
society, all of which have effects on real lives and material worlds. The
specific situations of individuals within racial groups require analysis at multiple sites of conflict. In fact, the play itself marks a racial hierarchy as
demonstrated by the "coloured" man's superior stance in relation to the old
black stranger. Outa's putative silence, the so-called mere prattling of Xhosa
words, unintelligible to the two "coloured" characters and most audience
members, marks the juridical silencing of the majority of black South
Africans, who, like Outa, have until recently existed under an oppressive
silence and erasure of subjecthood.

Queries about the appropriation of voice in *Boesman and Lena* also
require scrutiny. As a black woman, Nkonyeni embodies Lena's voice to
speak *as* a coloured woman albeit in a text engendered by a white male,
who therefore in a sense speaks *for* Lena. Barry Ronge's assessment that
Fugard's language makes this one of his best plays locates what I find problematic; he writes that "within the pithiness and uneducated speech of these
two derelicts he has embedded speeches of pure, rich poetry." The poetry,
however, also foregrounds Fugard's construction of a character whose language forms an important strategy for survival rather than a staging of resistance. In the 1960s, this play gave voice to some South Africans who were
politically stifled, but during the past two decades, many black men and
women have expressed themselves in fiction, memoirs, poetry, and theater.
It is imperative that their constructions are realized on stage; the making
vocal of voices that have long been silenced will expose diversity, help dis-
pel stereotypes, and assist audiences in valuing difference.

Greig also suggests that the 1993 Market Theatre production of *Boesman and Lena*

FIG. 10. Nomhle Nkonyeni in the Market Theatre production of
Athol Fugard's *Boesman and Lena*, July 1993. *(Photo by Ruphin
Coudyzer, courtesy of The Market Theatre Foundation.)*

deserves to be seen as a new play, not a revival. . . . [As] the looming
presence of apartheid has moved a distance from our theatre walls [it]
gains a new expansiveness. We don't watch victims: we watch people.
. . . it allows us to laugh with recognition not embarrassment. . . . The
play is funnier now; it makes one aware that its genealogy was music
hall via Beckett.

Certainly Beckettian resonances evoke the exchanges of Didi and Gogo,
but *Waiting for Godot* emphasizes the metaphysical and eschews the distinct
spatiotemporal context of *Boesman and Lena* that Fugard concedes cannot
evade its political consequences. While Beckett's play is set on a road in a

nameless, timeless place, Fugard's play utilizes the very naming of the places from which they have been evicted or to which they move their belongings as a way for Lena to continue to exist. Boesman and Lena are also waiting, but spectators are informed in detail about the process as well as some of the aspects that would inform or change the process.

Greig's insistence that the 1990s production of *Boesman and Lena* is a new play, that we do not watch victims but people, is utopian but faulty on two accounts. Although Lena defies Boesman, she is in Mda's terms a victim who "lets oppression happen to her" without resistance and with seemingly no potential for future empowerment. Notwithstanding the demise of apartheid and the repeal of laws such as the Group Areas Act, which legalized forced removals, many Lenas existed in South Africa at the time of this production. Moreover, despite the momentous changes in South Africa since April 1994, little has occurred in material terms to change their desperate economic plight, though now they are constitutionally empowered. This initial postelection era so redolent with the miraculous is nevertheless associated with a government of national unity operating for a five-year term within new structures that bespeak the multiple compromises and tensions bred in a formulaic consensus. Reviewed against this backdrop and in light of the performance history, the play's initially powerful representation of issues that exposed systemic violence can no longer be the central criterion if we accept Greig's "new play" status; moreover, such categorization only exacerbates the characters' ultimate refusal to stage resistance and institute any change.

The embodiment of articulate, politically self-conscious women and men on South African stages in a range of dramatic situations and formats is timely. In early 1994, Fugard conceded that he was "going through an extraordinary identity crisis in terms of being a South African playwright." He termed himself "the New South Africa's literary redundancy."[46] Since that time Fugard has constructed *My Life* (1994), *Valley Song* (1995), and his latest play, *The Captain's Tiger* (1997). These and other Fugardian stagings provide rich material for answering Walder's questions: "Which voices are heard, and which have been silenced? And does the passage of time and history change the answers?"[47] As Fugard's drama shares the limelight with voices of other South African playwrights, spectators can appreciate the cultural diversity of South Africa as a rainbow nation. In a revitalized theater, surely the construction of new stories and the performance of voices that embody difference will stage resistance in continually changing ways. Will we listen attentively and act to intervene?

NOTES

1. Rosemary Jolly, "Rehearsals of Liberation: Contemporary Postcolonial Discourse and the New South Africa," *PMLA* 110.1 (1995): 19

2. Thanks to Dan Bauer at the McCarter Theatre, Princeton, and to the Market Theatre, Johannesburg, for sending diverse materials pertaining to the respective productions. My gratitude to Ian Sowton and Stephen Oldenburg Barber for their constructive readings of this article and to Dennis Walder for the opportunity of devoting special time to South African Theatre. Sincere thanks to Jenny Spencer for insightful editorial comments.

3. Marvin Carlson, *Theatre Semiotics* (Bloomington: Indiana University Press, 1990), 112.

4. One exception is Lena's use of this word to the dying black stranger:

No, Outa not us. [*Shaking him*]

Listen to me. You'll never sleep long enough.

Sit close. *Ja! Hotnot* and a *Kaffir* got no time for apartheid on a night like this. (233)

Although Lena refers both to the sense of apartness and the political system that has designated them in different racial groups, she is silent about the oppressiveness of apartheid structures and the need to challenge them. All pagination for *Boesman and Lena* and *Hello and Goodbye* refers to Athol Fugard, *Selected Plays,* ed. Dennis Walder (Oxford: Oxford University Press, 1987).

5. Chandra Mohanty, "Cartographies of Struggle: Third World Women and the Politics of Feminism," in *Third World Women and the Politics of Feminism,* ed. Chandra Talpade Mohanty, Ann Russo, and Lourdes Torres (Bloomington: Indiana University Press, 1991), 13.

6. Athol Fugard, *Playland . . . and Other Words* (Wits: Witwatersrand University Press, 1992), 72, 73.

7. Fugard, *Playland,* 66.

8. Fugard, *Notebooks 1960/1977,* ed. Mary Benson (London: Faber, 1983), 172, 142. Hereafter cited in the text.

9. Qtd. in Malcolm Hacksley, "A Tribute," *Lantern* 42, no. 1 (1993): 6.

10. Yvonne Bryceland, qtd. in Jack Kroll, "The Lady from Cape Town: Bryceland on Broadway," *Newsweek,* 2 May 1988, 49.

11. Qtd. in Hacksley, "A Tribute," 6.

12. Stephen Gray, *File on Fugard* (London: Methuen Drama, 1991), 25.

13. Michael Coveney, "*Hello and Goodbye,*" *Financial Times,* 1 Mar. 1978, 15.

14. Yvonne Bryceland in Robert Greig, "Paired 200 Times in Fugard Play—Now for Europe," *Star Tonight,* 30 May 1977, 7. Subsequent references are from this review.

15. Maria Tucci offered Fugard's categorization of Hester in a dialogue with the audience following the performance on 13 Feb. 1994.

16. Fugard, qtd. in Jane Huth, "Athol Fugard," *Home News,* 23 Jan. 1994, F2.

17. See Jeanne Colleran, "Athol Fugard and the Problematics of Liberal Critique," *Modern Drama* 38, no. 1 (fall 1995): 389–407 for a detailed analysis of the reception of his plays in the United States. My thanks to Jeanne Colleran for providing me with the manuscript of her article and for her generosity in sharing material and ideas.

18. Joseph Lelyveld, *Move Your Shadow* (New York: Times Books, 1985), 28.

19. Nicholas Visser, "Drama and Politics in a State of Emergency: Athol Fugard's *My Children! My Africa!*" *Twentieth Century Literature* 39:4 (Winter 1993): 486.

20. Susan Hilferty, "Realizing Fugard," *Twentieth Century Literature* 39:4 (Winter 1993): 481.

21. Zoe Wiccomb, "To Hear the Variety of Discourses," *Current Writing* 2:1 (1990): 37.

22. Fugard, qtd. in Andy Seiler, "Say 'Hello' to Searing, Forceful Family Drama," *Courier News,* 7 Feb.1994, n.p.

23. Fugard, interview by Robert (Buzz) McLaughlin, *Dialogue on Drama* (McCarter Theater, Princeton, 6 Feb. 1994.)

24. Michael Billington, "*Hello and Goodbye,*" *Guardian,* 23 Mar. 1973, n.p.

25. Athol Fugard, introduction to *Three Port Elizabeth Plays* (New York: Viking, 1980), xiv.

26. Gail Phetersen, "The Whore Stigma: Female Dishonor and Male Unworthiness," *Social Text* 37 (winter 1993): 53.

27. "A White Beggar in South Africa," *New African* 307 (April 1993): 26.

28. Fugard, qtd. in William A. Henry III, "Home Is Where the Art Is," *Time,* 8 Feb. 1994, 67.

29. Albie Sachs, *Protecting Human Rights in a New South Africa* (Cape Town: Oxford UP, 1990), 53.

30. Frantz Fanon, *The Wretched of the Earth,* trans. Constance Farrington (New York: Grove, 1963), 45.

31. Dennis Walder, "Resituating Fugard: South African Drama as Witness," *New Theatre Quarterly* 32 (Nov. 1992): 361.

32. Gayatri Spivak, "Practical Politics of the Open End," in *The Post-colonial Critic,* ed. Sarah Harasym (New York: Routledge, 1990), 108, 109.

33. Dennis Walder, "To Be Witnessed," *Times Literary Supplement,* 2 Mar. 1984, 221.

34. Michael Billington, "Review of *Boesman and Lena,*" *Plays and Players* 18 (1971): 49.

35. Nadine Gordimer, "Letter from Johannesburg, 1985," in *The Essential Gesture,* ed. Stephen Clingman (New York: Alfred A. Knopf, 1988), 303.

36. Mantoa Nompikazi, qtd. in Shireen Hassim, "Where Have All the Women Gone? Gender and Politics in South African Debates," paper presented at the Women and Gender in Southern Africa Conference, 30 Jan.–2 Feb. 1991.

37. John Kani, qtd. in Frank Meintjies, "Albie Sachs and the Art of Protest," in *Spring Is Rebellious,* ed. Ingrid de Kok and Karen Press (Cape Town: Buchu Books, 1990), 34.

38. Zakes Mda, "Politics and the Theater: Current Trends in South Africa," in *Theatre and Change in South Africa,* ed. Geoffrey V. Davis and Anne Fuchs (London: Harwood Academic Press, 1996), 201. My thanks to Zakes Mda for providing the manuscript of his article before publication.

39. Craig W. McLuckie, "Power, Self, and Other: The Absurd in *Boesman and Lena,*" *Twentieth Century Literature* 39, no. 4 (winter 1993): 426, 429.

40. Catherine Belsey, *Critical Practice* (London: Methuen, 1980), 67.

41. Barry Ronge, "Sound Problems Can't Dull Fugard at His Best," *Sunday Times,* 25 July 1993, 18. Subsequent citations refer to this review.

42. Robert Greig, "Lena Learns a New Language," *Weekly Mail and Guardian,* 30 July–5 Aug. 1993, 48.

43. Michel Foucault, *The Use of Pleasure,* trans. Robert Hurley (New York: Vintage, 1990), 4.

44. Sandra Harding, "Subjectivity, Experience, and Knowledge: An Epistemology from/for Rainbow Coalition Politics," in *Who Can Speak? Authority and Critical Identity,* ed. Judith Roof and Robyn Wiegman (Urbana: University of Illinois Press, 1995), 128.

45. Terry Goldie, *Fear and Temptation: The Image of the Indigene in Canadian, Australian, and New Zealand Literatures* (Montreal: McGill-Queens University Press, 1989), 171.

46. Fugard, interview.

47. Walder, "Resituating Fugard," 350.

Tracy C. Davis

A Feminist Boomerang:
Eve Merriam's *The Club* (1976)

Algy. You know, there's something not quite masculine about
   that little Johnny.
Freddie. Well, maybe it's because half his ancestors were male
   and the other half female.
Algy. Point well taken. Think I'll sing. To Cissy! Who's like the
   Venus de Milo—beautiful, but not all there.

—THE CLUB

The language isn't obscene but mild. Indeed, they're exactly
the jokes which still live in spirit on TV, at a family reunion—that's what's
not funny.

—ERIKA MUNK ON THE CLUB

Publicity materials for George Griffin's 1975 short film *The Club* describe
the setting as a place "attended solely by that other kind of member. As ani-
mated phalluses drift absent-mindedly about, Griffin's panning camera
catches them in characteristically clubby activities: reading newspapers,
slurping on pipes, matching their pitches for an impromptu barbershop sing.
The Club plays with accessible, stereotypical images of the male through
humor and plain visual shock" (fig. 11).[1] Making a pitch for appropriate
audiences, the publicity proclaims: "This hilarious spoof on male bonding is
a favorite with women's groups and men with a well-developed sense of
humor!" Eve Merriam's 1976 play of the same name uses a similar premise,
though instead of featuring disembodied genitalia, it relies on vaudeville
routines and turn-of-the-century joke books for dialogue, cross-casting
women for the all-male dramatis personae. Set in a gentlemen's club circa
1903, it documents fraternal conviviality in a revue format focused on
drinking, anxiety over the stock market, billiards, and a rehearsal for the
club's annual Spring Frolic by five gentlemen, a page, and a servant.[2]

   The Club plays in a single act as a collage of "found" historical dialogue
and songs accompanied by a pianist (the maestro). The gentlemen span a
wide age range: some are more accustomed to the routines of clubland and

FIG. 11. Advertisement for George Griffin's *The Club* found among papers in the collection of Eve Merriam.

fraternity than others, but all perfectly understand the power of masculine privilege. In a succession of musical vignettes culminating in a rehearsal for the Spring Frolic (to which ladies will be admitted), the gentlemen performers archetypically represent kinds of domestic relationships, ranging from promiscuous bachelorhood, to the newly wedded, to the sour containment of a man whose life is dominated by a wealthy mother-in-law. Their reflections on the female sex switch from the vacuously sentimental intoning of sweethearts' names to raunchy innuendo, with imperceptible transition, as likely to exchange misogynist one-line banter as to fixate on the stock quotations off the ticker tape and turn it into a ritualistic ballet. Even with virtuoso singers and dancers, it might easily be misperceived as a naive, apolitical revue inexplicably successful in its time but of no historical consequence.

Alternately, *The Club* may supply a cogent demonstration of the constructedness of gender, be the first feminist play to experiment extensively with cross-gender casting, and ironicize the antifeminist neo-Right that was burgeoning in the midst of the sexual and gender revolutions at a turning point in the feminist Second Wave. Today, Merriam's play is little read, rarely performed, and completely unhistoricized. In the light of Judith Butler's articulations of gender identity, Madonna's reclamation of female clothing as a sign of sexual power, and a sophisticated debate on camp theory, this 1976 experiment with masking and role play may seem naive; but is this because the play is inappropriately neglected or because *ex post* arguments have deflected attention onto other matters? The play is the closest feminists got to Broadway during the extended International Women's Year celebrations (it opened at the Circle in the Square), instigating a slew of productions in London, Amsterdam, Tokyo, Sydney, Melbourne, Toronto, and elsewhere. The enthusiasm with which it is remembered by the generation who saw it suggests that historical reconsideration is warranted on *ex ante* lines. While this essay is primarily concerned with identifying the play's topical referentiality to a 1976 New York audience through a sampling of Geertzian thick descriptions, there is also much that explains its interest to international spectators in the 1970s, who coined it "a musical Rorschach test."[3] By restoring some of the historical signs, reception can be (hypothetically) reconstructed.

At a point when feminist theaters—especially during the U.S. bicentennial—were often concerned with reconceptualizing the Great Stories in order to make myths with feminist meaning,[4] *The Club* focused on banal songs, misogynist jokes, limericks, and performance shticks lifted from turn-of-the-century sources to challenge audiences' assurance about the correlation between appearance, sex, and gender. Much of the response— positive from female and negative from male critics—focused on the device of reverse-gender casting. Neither the social nor the theatrical precedents for women so thoroughly impersonating men as to be mistaken for them predisposed audiences to being comfortable: women passing as men implied usurpation of male privilege and/or lesbianism practiced with the sanction of an overt appearance of heterosexuality. The cross-dressers not only confirmed right-wing fears that "Americans taken in the aggregate do not demonstrate the clarity in sexual identity differentiation that they did in the past," but also recalled nineteenth-century unease with the masculine female capitalized upon by male impersonators in vaudeville and everyday life.[5] Such women could, as with Vesta Tilley, be a superb impersonator yet also a Conservative scion; alternately, as with Sarah Bernhardt or Isabelle Eberhardt, she could represent the decadent movement deeply feared by conservatives. This anxiety shows up in the "sanitizing" of gender impersonation in music hall, proof beyond doubt that sex was absolute and gender was built on its foundation.

In order for *The Club* to be successful, virtuosity had to make the impersonation convincing without eradicating the perceptibility that this was reverse-gender casting. The illogic of women knowing these horrible misogynist jokes had to register. As Alisa Solomon noted:

How much easier it would be to take the satire if spectators couldn't tell that the performers were women. But then, what would be the point? The all-woman cast creates a guilty, or at least embarrassing, tension as the targets of such jokes aren't supposed to know about them—much less throw them back in the tellers' faces.[6]

The play requires that the transvestitism be opaque and that it be enjoyed as part of the unisex "power" fashion of masculine-cut suits, which women were sporting in the early 1970s. This fashion was not limited to any one type of feminist politic yet tended to iterate the claim for equal access and treatment.[7] The uniform of male evening wear worn by the clubmen in the play reinforced the idea that the club is a closed upper-class community, subjugating individuality and distinct identity except through minor generation-based nonconformities.[8] The conformity that signals masculine communities could be mistaken for a conservative endorsement of male enclaves; however, any such orthodoxy wobbles noticeably as an endorsement of the Right's agenda in that the club life is not compatible with family life and is pursued by members engaging in nonprocreative sex. During the 1976 season, white-collar women realized that dressing like men was not investing them with the power of men; the pseudomale look was being abandoned in favor of figure-concealing, comfortable, layered ensembles.[9] Thus, with a historical pretext, Merriam investigates the possibility of androgyny, rejecting it in favor of aiding the impersonator of gender to comment pointedly on the customs of the impersonated. As Nancy Scott observed, the cast appeared "not male, not female. Not gay either. Androgynous? Yes, but no abstract label quite defines the subtle, strange and comical experience of watching these women turn men's jokes about women into one superb joke on men. A feminist boomerang."[10]

As far as I can discern, *The Club* was the first play of the Second Wave to employ this device.[11] As the first of many, it is worth historicizing what Merriam and her cast thought they were doing and how cross-gender dressing was perceived as a feminist aesthetic invention. According to Moe Meyer's definition (contra Susan Sontag, who prevailed in 1976), *The Club* seems to be a perfect candidate for camp: "Camp appears, on the one hand, to offer a transgressive vehicle yet, on the other, simultaneously invokes the specter of dominant ideology within its practice, appearing, in many instances, to actually reinforce the dominant order."[12] Implicit in this view is the expectation that camp is always and unavoidably queer; when it is no longer queer and has been appropriated by the mainstream, then it is no longer camp. Notes given by the director, Tommy Tune, explicitly eschew camp. In one such note pertaining to the back-up trio for the number "Miranda," a paean to a woman introduced with the quip "To Miranda, who's nicely-reared . . . and not bad from the front either" (14), Tune scolds: "dont do the Andrews sisters gestures—thats camp and there shall be no camp in this show" (rehearsal notes, 22 June 1976). The director's notes consistently encourage the cast to simulate men's gestures (bold, direct, and sparing), confident bearing, and supreme enjoyment of their own jokes.

The difficulty of aesthetically categorizing the play arose from the novelty, three-quarters of the way into the twentieth century, of women impersonating men. Erika Munk could not liken it to a direct reversal of hitherto male aesthetics.

> All of this is done in drag. But the effect is very different from male homosexual impersonations of women. There was little attempt at deception; nor could there be, given the singing voices. Instead of the transvestite combination of contempt and identification, there was a lighter mockery, a more modest imitation, no loss of self. If those songs had been sung by men, *then* they'd have been camp.[13]

As the feminist historian Gerda Lerner observed, "your mind says one thing and your eyesight shifts—all seems absurd that you once took for granted."[14] But what Lerner saw and questioned was not necessarily a universal spectatorial experience. Alisa Solomon argues that the reason some critics were unenthusiastic about *The Club* was because the women didn't convince them that they were men.[15] Rex Reed even likened it to whites in a minstrel show.

> Of course, if Reed couldn't recognize that women impersonating men are not analogous to whites in blackface for the obvious reason that their relative social positions are reversed, one could hardly expect him to understand that the show would not only be laughed out of town if performed by men, it wouldn't *exist* if performed by men.[16]

Marilyn Stasio, reviewing for *Penthouse,* points to women's thorough amusement and liberation at seeing other women perform material preserved for men, while "male faces . . . light up with interest and then rear back in dismay when their brains caught up with their groins."[17] Merriam's rehearsal log indicates that it took months for the actresses to become acclimated to their roles, weeping at having to cut their long hair, and defiantly wearing obtrusive jewelry to rehearsals.[18] But by the New York opening, she writes in all capitals, "they are on POWER TRIP AS MEN, LOVING THEIR SUITS OF ARMOR AS TIE AND TAILS AND TOPHATS. MEN FIND "SOUP AND FISH" UNCOMFORTABLE BUT MEMRIE [Innerarity, playing the maestro] CLAIMS ITS COMFORTABLE AND FROLIC [Taylor, an understudy] SAYS SHE WANTS TO WEAR IT ALL THE TIME. THIS IS REALLY WANTING TO HAVE MALE PERKS OF POWER AND POSITION. NEED THIS ATTITUDE FOR SHOW TO WORK" (rehearsal notes, 17 June 1976). Elsewhere, she writes: "I'd put down on the front page, 'This must *not* be camp, this must not be "Nudge, nudge" "wink, wink."' It will be *death* if we get women who are up there and just think they're too cute for words."[19]

Claiming this as camp by Meyer's definition is misleading, for as I will detail, there is empirical evidence that *The Club* did invoke lesbian desire and foreground alternatives to heterosexual viewing. In that sense, particularly considering that we are talking about 1976, *The Club* was probably queer. Sontag allowed a broader range of phenomena under the heading of camp: almost anything highlighting artifice and style and bearing any trace of the ineffable sensibility of being out of proportion, parodic, or extravagant.[20] This accords with Tune's and Merriam's concept of camp, but I do not think Sontag's concept takes account of the political pointedness of the plot or queered aesthetic. In the Spring Frolic rehearsal scene, for example, a woman plays a man playing a woman. Bertie, the handsome ladies' man, plays Mrs. Blanche Sterling in an outtake from Clyde Fitch's 1901 melodrama *The Climbers*.[21] In this speech, she is admonishing her husband for neglecting her love.

> *Bertie.* Life to me was like a glorious staircase, and I mounted happy step after step after step, led by your hand till everything culminated in our wedding. You men don't realize, *can't* realize, what that service means to a girl. In those few moments she parts from all that have cherished her, and gives her whole self, her body and even her soul—for love often overwhelms us women. I tell you, a *man* can't understand! *(Getting entangled in skirt, finally drops it.)* You treated this gift of mine, Dick, like a Santa Claus plaything—for a while you were never happy away from it, then you broke it, and now you have even lost the broken pieces! Adieu! *(Exits.)*
> *Algy.* I *will* find them, Peg!
> *Bobby. (As prompter.) Blanche.*

(31)

Edith Oliver noted that in this passage, Gloria Hodes, playing Bertie, signaled that managing the hyperinflated speech *and* her female drag (on top of the male drag) was too much, so in frustration she threw the ensemble over her arm.[22] The artificiality of the femininity registers against the artificiality of the masculinity, neither of which are naturalized for this performer at this moment. Is this camp? In a play about the constructedness of gender and the injustice of gender inequality, it is the moment closest to androgyny. Yet the insult of the character's husband mistaking her name (an allusion to an earlier lengthy sequence of sappy songs built around rhymable female names) recaptures the politic of who is telling the joke and upon whom it is, in this manifestation, supposed to register. The *point* is not queered, but it registers precisely when artifice (or "camp" in Sontag's sense) is dropped. Fitting neither Sontag's nor later theorizations, perhaps it is "not not" camp.

The efficacy of the turn-of-the-century jokes within their original misogynistic realm depends on their being reiterated simulacra of the infantilization, objectification, disparagement, violence, exploitation, and privilege exerted by men as a class over women. They call upon collective experience and stimulate collective covert enjoyment of power. Within the play, however, the concealment of the sentiments behind the jokes, limericks, and lyrics no longer operates, for their historicity and biologism are disclosed. In Judith Butler's terminology, the tropes are performative when displayed by men; however, in Merriam's play, the casting calls attention to the discursive practice and what it names, so it is somehow derailed and exposed. Merriam made her name as a poet in the 1940s while she made her living in the fashion industry, editing *Deb* and associate-editing *Glamour*.

> I've worked inside this fantastic world as a salesgirl, buyer, copywriter, fashion magazine editor, and lecturer. I've seen it move from a carny side show to the big main tent. This mysterious world of fashion that men are not supposed to know anything about has now grown into one of the greatest con games ever devised. (Draft for fashion article)

Maintaining the key to this discourse is what maintains masculinity, but *The Club* pointedly disrupts the realist plane of the characters' gender. Butler argues:

> Performativity cannot be understood outside of a process of iterability, a regularized and constrained repetition of norms. And this repetition is not performed *by* a subject; this repetition is what enables a subject and constitutes the temporal condition for the subject. This iterability implies that "performance" is not a singular "act" or event, but a ritualized production, a ritual reiterated under and through constraint,

under and through the force of prohibition and taboo, with the threat of ostracism and even death controlling and compelling the shape of the production, but not, I will insist, determining it fully in advance.[23]

The latter claim—"the threat of ostracism and even death"—may seem extreme for what is in essence a parody enjoyable largely because of implied realism. However, one of the later sequences overlays *I Pagliacci* (Leoncarallo's 1897 opera in which the Punchinello, Canio, is compelled to perform while in the throes of despair over his wife's infidelity) with the almost identical scene from *The Climbers* (in which a husband confronts his best friend for philandering with his wife), culminating in a scene with the club's president, Algy, throttling Freddie, a bachelor gynecologist, who has just been insinuated as Algy's wife's lover. The maestro sings a refrain that reminds the audience of the intertextuality: "The husband, the home, the wife and the lover / 'Twas his story repeated that night at the play." A reconciliation between Algy/Canio/Mr. Dick Sterling and Freddie/Silvio/Ned is enacted.

> *(Lights up as we see Freddie rubbing his neck. . . . Algy at piano, smoking as if in a trance. He is in the same stance that Freddie* [the club's middle-aged treasurer] *was in for his "Miranda" routine. Bertie sings Vesti la Giubba from* I Pagliacci [as a coloratura, not a tenor].[24] *He embraces Algy and they go offstage together.)* (32)

Many observers emphasized the significance of this moment. Bertie sings "Bah, se' tu forse un uom? Tu se' Pagliaccio! / Vesti la giubba e la faccia infarina. / La gente paga e rider vuole quá (Be strong! Are you not a man? You are Pagliacci the clown. / Put on the costume and the make-up. The people pay, and want to laugh). The opera's "on with the show" motif wrings with pathos, but in Merriam's hands it refutes the arbitrariness of assigning roles. Rather than giving the aria to the character representing Canio, it is sung by the actress representing his wife, romantically involved with the dashing Silvio. In the opera it is Canio who must persevere despite heartbreak, whereas in Merriam's play the artifice of comedy is maintained by women, especially the audience, who are told, "Ridi del duol che t'avvelena il cor!" (Laugh, for the sorrow that is eating thy heart). In the jokes, ditties, and now high opera, *The Club* enables women to perform material preserved for males. As Dorothy Bryant noted, "the idea of make-up & dress masking agony is transformed" (letter, 13 July 1980). What is a man's agony compared to what compounds women's lot?

Duly instructed, the "show" goes on: the constructed nature of gender is emphasized through the drag-upon-drag procession of "The American Beauty Rose" pageant and songspiel, which in turn segues into a refrain of a drinking song as the gentlemen characters mime relieving themselves at urinals. For the umpteenth time in the show, Merriam invites her audience to see the pleasure to be found in the performers' virtuosity, then disrupts the narrative with a reminder of the inability of the actresses themselves as social agents or biological entities to truly do what they are presenting. Masculinity is inscribed upon them, but privilege is not. These ritual acts serve to underline the gender dissonance in the bodies.

Eventually, the other characters depart in the early dawn, and Algy is left alone. In the New York production, Joanne Beretta was the only performer whose coif was not illusionistically masculine: her long tresses were stuffed down her costume, and a wig placed over top. Facing upstage, Algy lets down his hair. Still with his back to the audience, he sings:

> IN THIS SAFE RETREAT WHERE NO PETTICOATS DARE
> TO DISTURB OUR SEX SUPREME . . .
> ALL THE ROUNDERS MEET FOR A MIDNIGHT TEAR
> AND A MORNING AFTER DREAM . . . [ellipses in original]

Then, turning full front, Beretta delivered the epilogue.

> Illusion now is at an end,
> it's time our curtain must descend.
> We need no epilogue to show
> the real world, since full well we know
> that he and she do equal share,
> that both our sexes are judged fair,
> and there's true justice—everywhere.
> Depend upon it, that you can:
> *upon my honor, as a man.*
> The curtain now, with no more pause;
> we welcome her—and his—applause.

(35)

Beretta does not lose her "footing" or "cultural gravity," in Butler's terms, destabilizing the intelligibility of sex (139). Instead, she takes the true position of her gendered and sexed social and biological allotment and allows irony between body and speech to deliver the political referent. It was not universally welcome. A designer for NBC wrote to Merriam,

> I was profoundly moved at the almost total effects created by the cast of "The Club," which I saw on Sunday matinee. I wondered then why the character let his hair down, and really have not gotten over the confusion it caused me.
>
> At the beginning I saw the hair was stuffed down the back of the neck, in contrast to the gor[g]eously treated other male heads. . . .
>
> The cigar smoke, everything was a testimony of the exclusion of the role of women in the "active" world, made absolutely powerful by the acting. . . .
>
> The hair came down, I couldn't believe. Would you have Octavian step out of his role? or roles? . . . I almost plead with you to change it. (Warfield, letter, November 1976)

For the out-of-town tryout (at the Lenox Art Centre, Connecticut, July 1976) Merriam used another ending in which Johnny (the page) delivers a Puck-like salutation in pastoral rhyming couplets, which concludes:

> May we with joy and will and heart
> Do justice to each manly part.
>
> *(As Johnny finishes his epilogue, Algy takes off his hat and lets down his hair.)*[25]

The deconstructive gesture was retained intact, though in the final version the upstage posture added emphasis. Explicitly signifying, once and once only, that this was not just ironic virtuosity and gender parody, but also sexual transvestitism, Merriam pointedly constructed the moment for an allusion to the contentious Equal Rights Amendment (ERA) cause and the lethal immediacy of this "bygone" era of the club.

The struggle for ratification of the ERA particularly occupied liberal feminists in coalitions of religious, professional, unionized, and civic-based groups from 1972 to 1982. When the ERA was written in 1923—and still when it was revived in the 1970s—the only right guaranteed to women under the Constitution was the right to vote. Women called the ERA "the blanket amendment," believing it would invalidate all laws with differential treatment. Feminists of the 1970s wanted to enter the labor market on an

equal footing, receive equal pay for equal work and equal treatment under
the law. The ERA relied on assimilationist politics, favoring the women
who were willing to play by men's rules and be treated like men, but also
threatened divorced women's "right" to alimony and other compensation. In 1972, both houses of Congress approved the amendment in
Washington; by 1975, thirty-three of the necessary thirty-eight states had
ratified it. Organizing was most intense from 1974 to 1978, when the
deadline for ratification was pushed back four more years due to pressure
exerted by one hundred thousand marchers on Capitol Hill. Feminists
took time off from college and jobs to campaign for the ERA, yet the
opposition was widespread, well organized, and all too effective as a
minority view. The New Right borrowed the "personal is political" slogan, and leaders like Phyllis Schlafly rallied sentiment around campaigns of
misinformation: pregnant women would be forced onto battlefields, rape
laws would be abolished, homosexual marriage would be legalized,
mother-daughter and father-son events would be banned, and all public
toilets would be made unisex. Such "potty politics" entrenched opposition. By 1977, only thirty-five states had ratified, and despite all the
efforts, three more could not be persuaded to join. The Republican Party
had supported the ERA for forty years, yet in 1980, Ronald Reagan
dropped it from his campaign; with his election the measure was doomed,
and the deadline passed mournfully in 1982.[26]

Postmortems of the ERA movement identify a range of causes leading
to defeat, but during *The Club*'s New York run the goal still seemed attain-
able: the National Organization of Women (NOW) was gaining momentum, and thirty-three women's magazines endorsed equal rights in their
Fourth of July bicentennial issues. Though feminists recognized schisms in
the movement, it cohered around the ERA. There was cause for optimism
but not confidence. Feminists had been targeting beauty contests since
1968, so *The Club*'s penultimate sketch, the "American Beauty Rose"
pageant between "Vesti la Guibba" and the epilogue, was an excellent
choice for carrying cautionary meanings, but by means that are unpredictable in feminist tradition. Each character enters in turn, conspicuously
sporting a white hat with red roses, sings a "rose" song, and holds a pose.
When Henry (the black servant) enters, he is wearing a gigantic picture hat
with "red file satin base completely covered in brilliant red plumed and
fringed feathers [and] red 'bird in flight' wings perched at tip of front
brim." His ensemble is completed by a "large satin bow, 2 or 3 red roses
[and] red gloves." He sings "My Dusky Rose," superficially instilling an
African American presence in the pageant;[27] the pointed class disparity is

complemented by the dissonant assimilationist symbolism of roses as political implements. Representing passionate love and the prime of womanhood, roses were a mainstay of right-wing sentimentality. At the same time, feminists played on the sappy connotations for postcards that read "Send me no Roses on Mother's Day / Ratify the ERA" and in 1978 declared "Housewives for Roses Day," encouraging women to deliver roses to their recalcitrant Illinois legislators in the same way that Americans sent tea bags to register opposition to taxation measures.[28]

The pageant's colors were as topically suggestive as the event itself. The white hats symbolized unsullied femininity but also recalled the suffragists' chief color, consciously borrowed for marches by ERA activists. Red was even more loaded. At the time, Phyllis Schlafly's forces were pushing "Stop ERA" buttons utilizing red stoplight symbolism, itself a co-optation of the 1975 International Women's Year "Why Not!" campaign.[29] Green, the ERA supporters' symbol of "Go," was nowhere to be seen in the play. The pageant culminates with Johnny, in an American flag toga, enshrined atop Henry's shoulders in the apotheosis of red-white-and-blue feminized patriotism (on the back of an oppressed race). Both feminists and antifeminists borrowed Old Glory's colors, especially in this bicentennial year, so the point about form matched to variable content was clear. Accentuating a different kind of overlap, and suggesting the antecedent for the Illinois Roses Day, the pink roses on Bobby's hat and Johnny's crown may be a reference to the outrageous Pink Ladies who emerged in 1975 in efforts to get the Texas legislature to rescind its endorsement of the federal ERA. According to *Mother Jones:*

> The ladies would swarm into the state's pink granite capitol in long pink party dresses, short pink mini-dresses, polyester pink maternity outfits, pink hats, pink shoes, [and] pink plastic purses setting off their blue-rinse perms. They came bearing the fresh-baked cakes they are renowned for and begged their hometown reps to save Texas children from unisex toilets, homosexual marriages and the destruction of the divine family structure.[30]

These "pinkos" were allied with the John Birch Society, the Ku Klux Klan, and other far-right organizations. Their activism against the federally financed International Women's Year state-by-state conferences was so successful that in Texas they clinched 25 percent of the delegates' seats. To make the resonance with *The Club* complete, it turned out that the Pink Ladies were an inspiration to antifeminist men who subsequently tried to capitalize on their momentum and may even have impersonated them. When a measure to rescind the ERA came up a second time in Texas in 1976, it was sponsored in the House by Clay Smothers, a black Democrat.

Feminists and anti-ERA activists were locked in conflict, often waving the same banners, battling to register ownership of the same icons, and unsure of their allies. Thus, the "American Beauty Rose" pageant could be comical in *The Club* if the real stakes were not so high. The ERA would have overturned states' rights to enforce differential laws on women and men. Algy's concluding invocation that we trust his word—"as a man"— that equality is universal is a cogent allusion to the Constitution and the realpolitik as it stood. This is the sorrowful "comedy" that Bertie's aria launches us into: a high-culture moment of tremendous consequence amid all this low joke book material.

As a community-building tool, Merriam's play works in harmony with contemporaneous consciousness-raising projects to enhance women's understanding of themselves in relation to society, recognizing the personal implications of living in a patriarchal culture that oppresses them. Two very significant conflicts simmered in the feminist movement at this historical juncture: race privilege and lesbian identification. Like the populist technique of consciousness-raising, which was geared to middle-class straight white women, the play is evidence of how white middle-class feminists nodded at issues of racial and sexual privilege but prioritized others.[31]

The servant role, Henry, was played by an African American in New York. Merriam's goal was as much realism as racial commentary. In her instructions for foreign productions, she wrote: "If black servants would not have been employed in a turn-of-the-century club for men, then concentrate on class relations: a peasant type or a country yokel imported into the city. The key is authenticity" (memo to Audrey Wood [agent]). I regard this as a conscious choice on Merriam's part, for one of her earlier plays, *Inner City: A Street Cantata* (1972), was predicated on ghetto conditions and the social consequences for African Americans. Otherwise, race is not foregrounded in *The Club,* though this casting insures that the differential status of Johnny the page and Henry the servant, resulting in generous tips for one and barely any for the other, is motivated by bigotry. Feminist theater of the time offered more far-reaching critiques. Spiderwoman's *Women in Violence* (1976) cast Lisa Mayo (a Native American) as "the perfect woman in white face with blue eyes, blonde ringlets and a silhouette of the perfect [woman in] a long black dress. 'At the end she took everything off and was in a beige leotard outfit. People were absolutely shocked.'"[32] On Joyce Aaron's suggestion, the effect was underscored with violent racist jokes from popular culture. According to Muriel Miguel,

> it started with "Why do Puerto Ricans wear pointy shoes? To kill cockroaches in corners." "How can you tell an Arab at the airport? He's feeding bread to the plane." Finally as the audience was still laughing the performers would deliver the final blow "What's the difference between a Jew and a pizza? The pizza doesn't scream when you put it in the oven." We kept smiling, it got worse, we slaughtered them.[33]

But to deliver this kind of satire it was necessary to have a company of women of color, which was decidedly not the profile present in *The Club* or other mainstream middle-class feminist ventures. *The Club* appealed to middle-class feminists because it was largely about them.[34] The Association of Women Business Owners and National Organization of Women chapters took prominent block bookings.

The Club also attracted the gay community.[35] While the gay/straight split was being battled in feminist organizations, female spectators found themselves shocked by being attracted to the actresses. Male critics hated the show and pronounced it banal, possibly because they did not participate in this sexual aspect. The earliest Second Wave lesbian play was produced in the United States in 1974, so while *The Club* may not have been breaking new ground, it was breaking it closer to Broadway than any feminist group had so far ventured.[36] Simone Benmussa's *The Singular Life of Albert Nobbs* was produced in France in 1976. If Jill Dolan's contention about Albert's costuming is correct, it too has implications for *The Club*. She writes:

> When Albert intends to vacation with Helen Dawes, she buys a new suit and silk ties for her impersonation of a male lover courting his potential fiancée. This costume resonates not only with the masculine gender role, but with lesbians' assumption of "butch" roles as sexual symbols, particularly in the 1920s through the 1950s. The allusion to lesbian desire, however, is subsumed by Albert's position as male, and she is unable to situate her desire via her male—as opposed to lesbian—role.[37]

The Club likely capitalizes on the butch connotation of cross-dressing that Dolan identifies in *The Singular Life of Albert Nobbs*, but unlike Albert

Nobbs its characters are not complicated by maintaining a pretext of being male. This means that lesbian attraction felt by the audience could, potentially, be consummated in fan logic. The *Penthouse* review quotes Merriam as saying: "Generally, straight women seem surprised at their strong sexual reactions to other women. At first, they start talking about the politics of the show; but after a while they bring up the sex. It shocks them. They weren't prepared to respond sexually."[38] Rehearsal notes emphasize Freddie's desire for Algy (the two who compete for the woman in *The Climbers/I Pagliacci*), and though this is latent homosexuality, it is, in a sense, exercised through the adultery (rehearsal notes, 20 July 1976): for in any permutation of the triangle, what is implicated is sex between two biological women. Like so much in the production, this covert lesbianism served to articulate ideas that were of concern and interest to feminists but had not yet found *theoretical* expression.

Michelene Wandor argues that "cross-dressing or transvestite theatre has flourished during historical periods when attitudes to sexuality and the position of women have been challenged," which is certainly borne out by the turmoil of the mid-1970s.[39] It might be argued, following Norbert Elias, that the theater is depoliticizing because, by ordering and regulating experience and fantasy, "civilization" is promoted, passive spectatorship is achieved, and the senses mediate experiences that are at best vicarious.[40] Feminist critics and historians, however, argue that feminist performance exists on a rhetorical model of spectator involvement as implicated community, sharing and reinforcing mutual values and objectives.[41] The latter position best accounts for reports of the play's audiences, though if the former position prevailed, it could explain the play's historicization. *The Club* has longevity in oral histories but not, with the sole exceptions of Erika Munk and Alisa Solomon, as part of the intellectual capital of feminist theater, let alone as a defining moment of lesbian theater that played on polymorphous desire and attempted to give gestural, auditory, and conceptual language to drag performance by women in a mainstream venue. Like Benmussa, Merriam can be said to use "drag for women among women, making gender a quality of social behavior, not a biological fact."[42] This, in turn, served not to reinforce but to disclose the ideology in the spectators' position and in the narrative.

Gender inversions typically reflect a dynamic rather than static world.[43] In 1976, the difficulties of the ERA's ratification were all too apparent, but an impasse had not yet been reached. The ERA was known as "the ultimate gender-neutral statement," but of course its intent was to improve women's status, not to neutralize it. In the historical window of the 1970s, *The Club* theatricalized the stakes, parodying both sides in ways that facilitated feminists' agendas. At the same time, however, the folly of settling on equality as a goal when so many reparations were necessary was also becoming evident. In the ensuing decades, performance scholars have theorized how aesthetics like those in *The Club* operate, referring back and forth between social theory, philosophy, and theater, to reiterate the basic theme of social constructivism. In Solomon's terms, *The Club* depicts women "crossing toward power" not so much by embodying it as by demonstrating the dissonance between male social power and female visibility.[44] Taking this stance, in the first feminist drag play, was a deeply comic subversion of gendered, sexual, and racial norms achieved principally by casting choices and montage of existing songs, dance steps, and well-known performance motifs that were not—until this time—the purview of women.

NOTES

1. Ron Epple, *Filmmakers Newsletter,* quoted on a publicity blurb for George Griffin's *The Club* (1975). A copy of this was found in Eve Merriam's papers, included among the transcriptions of turn-of-the-century joke books, passages on the etiquette and dress of gentlemen, and a photograph of a gentlemen's dinner transpiring on horseback at Sherry's Restaurant (New York City, 1903). Merriam delved into the culture ca. 1900 but evidently was also informed by images around her and what they conveyed about the temporal transcendence of sexism.

2. Before her death in 1993, Eve Merriam granted me access to rehearsal notes, working scripts, and private letters relating to the play and her career. I gratefully acknowledge her generosity. All quotations from the collection of Eve Merriam will be cited parenthetically in the text.

3. David McCaughna, "(Fe)Male Schauvinist Pigs," *The City. Toronto Star Sunday Magazine,* 5 Mar. 1978, sec. 11, p. 6.

4. For example, see the Rhode Island Feminist Theatre's *Persephone's Return* (1974). The concept of Great Stories was expanding to include feminist foremothers, e.g., Elisabeth Jenkins Dresser's *The Story of Abigail Adams* (1976); Tuhs McCall's *What Every Woman Knows* (New York, 1982), featuring Victoria Woodhull; and Merriam's *Out of Our Fathers' House* (published 1975, first produced 1977) and *We the Women* on CBS (1974). Merriam's interest in historical reclamation spanned her career: her first historical revue was *Singing with Women,* dating from the late 1940s, and she served on the board of the Women's History Research Center (Berkeley, CA) in the 1970s. See Schlesinger Library, Radcliffe College, Vertical Files.

5. Harold M. Voth, *The Family and the Future of America* (Alton, IL: Phyllis Schlafly Report, 1977), 4. Originally delivered as an Eagle Council Address, 23 Oct. 1977.

6. Alisa Solomon, "It's Never Too Late to Switch," in *Crossing the Stage: Controversies on Cross-Dressing,* ed. Lesley Ferris (London: Routledge, 1993), 148.

7. Sociologists of dress write about the period, "In a kind of natural experiment, women working in white-collar jobs began to choose tailored business suits with a jacket similar to a man's suit jacket, worn with either trousers or skirt. Such dress was adopted by women maintaining ideologies from relatively conservative feminist to radical feminist. Somehow this ensemble stood, in the ideology of the time, as a claim for equal opportunity for women and men, particularly in the economic arena. As time went by, masculine properties in colors, texture, garment shape, and even the suit itself, gave way to more feminine-distinct features in dress, such as bright colors and surface designs in fabric. . . . The suit as a political statement had yielded to fashion. . . . This takeover in no way rules out that dress functions as a powerful though often underestimated system of visual communication that expresses gender role, which is usually intertwined with age, kinship, occupational, and other social roles throughout a person's life. From womb to tomb, the body is a dressed body." Joanne B. Eicher and Mary Ellen Roach-Higgins, "Definition and Classification of Dress: Implications of Gender Roles," in *Dress and Gender: Making and Meaning in Cultural Contexts,* ed. Ruth Barnes and Joanne B. Eicher (Providence: Berg, 1992), 22–23. See also Anne Hollander, *Sex and Suits* (New York: Alfred A. Knopf, 1994), 168–70.

8. Malcolm Young, "Dress and Modes of Address: Structural Forms for Police-women," in Barnes and Eicher, *Dress and Gender,* 273. Compare to the costume plot of Eve Merriam, *The Club: A Music Diversion* (New York: Samuel French, 1977), 37. Hereafter cited in the text.

9. Jane Mulvagh, *Vogue History of Twentieth Century Fashion* (London: Viking, 1988), 342.

10. Nancy Scott, "When a Woman's a Man for All That," *San Francisco Examiner,* 23 June 1980, E5.

11. Susan Carlson traces the tradition of this device in Britain, skipping from Vesta Tilley directly to Caryl Churchill's *A Light Shining in Buckinghamshire* (1976), which is in no sense as broad an experiment as *The Club*. See *Women and Comedy: Rewriting the British Theatrical Tradition* (Ann Arbor: University of Michigan Press, 1991), 213–21. Charlotte Canning in *Feminist Theaters in the U.S.A.: Staging Women's Experience* (London: Routledge, 1996) provides no earlier examples from the United States.

12. Moe Meyer, ed., *The Politics and Poetics of Camp* (London: Routledge, 1994), 11. See also n. 23 below.

13. Erika Munk, "Only the Uncomfortable Few Don't Laugh," *Village Voice,* 25 Oct. 1976, 96.

14. Merriam's typescript, including notes from Gerda [Lerner]. Collection of Eve Merriam.

15. A good example of this is provided by Elenore Lester in a negative review: "The women aren't in the least androgynous. They are simply women in men's clothing—evening clothing at that. When men put on tails and top hat and carry a cane, they are just as much in drag as women. The ideological point of the stagey arrogant gestures is lost in the sheer theatricality of the costumes." *Soho Weekly News,* 28 Oct. 1976, 28.

16. Solomon, "It's Never Too Late," 147.

17. Marilyn Stasio, "Scenes," *Penthouse,* Apr. 1977, 43.

18. The Toronto cast also found cutting their tresses traumatic. Linda Thorson, playing the womanizer Freddie, was famed for playing a femme fatale on the television series *The Avengers.* "The hairdresser's scissors was just the first step. 'The heavy stuff

came later,' Monica Parker [playing the page] reports. . . . Pam Brighton [the director] recalls catching Thorson putting on lipstick along with her moustache during a rehearsal, and she ordered it removed. The actress burst into the dressing-room in tears" (McCaughna, "[Fe]Male Schauvinist Pigs," 12).

19. Patricia McLaughlin, "Found: Eve Merriam," *Pennsylvania Gazette,* Apr. 1978, 18.

20. "Notes on Camp" (1963), in *A Susan Sontag Reader* (New York: Vintage, 1983), 105–19.

21. In *The Climbers,* which Brander Matthews predicted would become a social document of its time, Richard Sterling illegally speculates with others' money (first his wife's, then her treasured aunt's), losing everything. His embezzlement is about to be exposed when his friend, Ned Warden, restores Sterling for the sake of the woman he loves (Sterling's wife Blanche). In act 3, Sterling walks in on Blanche and Ned the moment after they have recognized their passions and opted not to act upon them. Sterling makes a big scene, things are explained, and (on the verge of suicide) he is calmed by news that Mason (another friend) will cover his debts. The "glorious staircase" scene follows the moment in act 4 when Blanche says she will give her husband one more chance before divorcing him.

> Blanche. *(Smiles sadly and shakes her head; the smile dies away.)* Life to me then was like a glorious staircase, and I mounted happy step after step led by your hand till everything *seemed* to culminate on the day of our wedding. You men don't, *can't* realize, what that service means to a girl. In those few moments she parts from all that have cherished her, made her life, and gives her whole self, her love, her body, and even her soul sometimes—for love often overwhelms us women—to the *man* who, she believes, wants, *starves,* for her gifts. All that a woman who marries for love feels at the altar I tell you a *man* can't understand! You treated this gift of mine, Dick, like a child does a Santa Claus plaything—for a while you were never happy away from it, then you grew accustomed to it, then you broke it, and now you have even lost the broken pieces! (694–95)

The play ends enigmatically with Sterling taking an overdose and Blanche and Ned, *thinking* he has only fallen asleep, planning their elopement. See *The Climbers. Plays by Clyde Fitch,* vol. 2 (Boston: Little Brown, 1915).

22. Edith Oliver, "Off Broadway," *New Yorker,* 25 Oct. 1976, 64.

23. Judith Butler, *Bodies That Matter: On the Discursive Limits of "Sex"* (London: Routledge, 1993), 95. Hereafter cited in the text.

24. R. Leoncavallo, *I Pagliacci* (Chicago: Fred Rullman, n.d.). The relevant lyrics of "Vesti la Giubba":

> Recitar! . . . mentre preso dal delirio
> Non so più quel che dico e quel che faccio!
> Eppur . . . è d'uopo . . . sforzati!
> Bah, se' tu forse un uom? Tu se' Pagliaccio!
> Vesti la giubba e la faccia infarina.
> La gente paga e rider vuole quà. [ellipses in original]

[To act, with my heart maddened with sorrow.
I know not what I'm saying or what I'm doing.
Yet I must face it. Courage, my heart!
Thou art not a man; thou'rt but a jester!
On with the motley, the paint and the powder,
The people pay thee, and want their laugh, you know.]

25. Two versions of the text exist in Merriam's files. One includes the final stage direction, the other does not. A third typescript version of the epilogue (without character attribution) retains some of the phrasing in the published version and its liberal feminist stance, but without quite the political bite:

Tonight you've watched our sportive play,
We trust our pranks do not dismay;
Our means should justify our ends
That men and women should be friends.
Our moral is, yes, there is one,
That where two sexes are, there's fun.
Our moral's double, let it be
That he and she may each be free.
A bright tomorrow let us share
And both our sexes be judged fair.

26. Flora Davis, *Moving the Mountain: The Women's Movement in America since 1960* (New York: Simon and Schuster, 1991), 385–411.

27. Vanessa Williams, the first African American to become Miss America, won her title in 1984. Even then, such a break with racial prerogative was noteworthy.

28. ERA files, Northwestern University Library, Special Collections.

29. Carol Burbank, "The Master's Tools: Phyllis Schlafly and Her Parodic Mirror Ladies against Women," Association for Theatre in Higher Education, 1994. See also Barbara Ryan, *Feminism and the Women's Movement: Dynamics of Change in Social Movement, Ideology, and Activism* (London: Routledge, 1992), 73–74.

30. Kaye Norcott, "At War with the Pink Ladies," *Mother Jones,* Nov. 1977, 22.

31. See "Guidelines for Consciousness-Raising Drawn up by the Women's Collective," c/o Eileen Sarkissian, Stratford CT, Schlesinger Library, Radcliffe College.

32. Muriel Miguel, qtd. in Canning, *Feminist Theaters,* 168.

33. Ibid.

34. Merriam claimed: "We get very mixed audiences. I think there are a lot of middle-class women who are housewives who enjoy it a lot because they can't really laugh at their husbands, and [yet] they can laugh at these replicas of them." Interview with Eve Merriam, cassette tape T-72, Schlesinger Library, Radcliffe College.

35. Ibid.

36. I have in mind the Lesbian Science Fiction Liberation Theatre, performing in Boston in 1974: "Songs, poetry, prose, skits as conceived and delivered by the five-woman company . . . koans, intellectual riddles and mundane situations experienced by lesbians." Debra Weiner, "Lesbian Theater Arrives," *Boston Globe,* 3 July 1974, 17.

37. Jill Dolan, *The Feminist Spectator as Critic* (Ann Arbor: UMI Research Press, 1988), 105.

38. Stasio, "Scenes," 43.

39. Michelene Wandor, *Carry On, Understudies: Theatre and Sexual Politics* (London: Routledge and Kegan Paul, 1981), 25.

40. Chris Shilling, *The Body and Social Theory* (London: Sage, 1993), 165.

41. See Charlotte Canning and Elizabeth J. Natalle, *Feminist Theatre: A Study in Persuasion* (Metuchen, NJ: Scarecrow, 1985).

42. Sue-Ellen Case, "Gender as Play: Simone Benmussa's *The Singular Life of Albert Nobbs,*" *Women and Performance* 1, no. 2 (winter 1984): 24.

43. John Emigh and Jamer Hunt, "Gender Bending in Balinese Performance," in *Gender in Performance: The Presentation of Difference in the Performing Arts,* ed. Laurence Senelick (Hanover, NH: University Press of New England, 1992), 196.

44. Solomon, "It's Never Too Late," 145.

Josephine Lee

Pity and Terror as Public Acts: Reading Feminist Politics in the Plays of Maria Irene Fornes

Georgia (rapidly). I'm not talking about being nice. But just to know that others exist. To be curious about someone. To want to know someone other than yourself. Not to be nice. But to be curious. "Oh, look at him. I wonder what he's doing. Oh, he's picking up something. I wonder what it is. Oh, that woman is leaning over him. She's telling him something. What is she saying?" Just that. You don't have to weep over anyone. Just be curious. That's how you know other people exist and that they're a part of you. If you are not curious, you are alone. What do you think bliss is? To go outside yourself. That's all. If you only experience yourself you feel no relief. And you can't feel tranquillity. To get lost outside yourself is bliss. Not always thinking, "I think." "I enter." "I exit." "I wear this." "I wear that." "Do you like this?" . . . You go around in circles. . . . If you look outside yourself, you feel a natural person. You see and you wonder, and you identify. And you learn. And you love and that's how you feel a natural person. If you only think of yourself you get mean crazy and tight and frustrated and wild and mean and cruel.

—Maria Irene Fornes, libretto for *Terra Incognita*

Although several recent theoretical studies of drama, theater, and performance have carefully outlined the differences between liberal, radical, and materialist approaches to feminist critical practice,[1] there is another, and perhaps more subtle, way of envisioning the schisms within feminist theories of performance. Along one divide, some feminist critics embrace Brecht's principles of dramaturgy: a choice that formulates political agency in terms of a conscious subject who is able to articulate and resist the repressive ideologies around her. Such an approach locates resistance in a "self" distanced from experience and emotion, thus implicitly privileging the rational as the locus of effective action. Significantly, this prescription is incompatible with assumptions informing other theoretical practices—also self-identified as political and feminist—that rely on notions of empathy and identification for their models of political action.

I begin this essay by reflecting upon how these differences affect the way in which we view the plays of Maria Irene Fornes. Though sometimes praised for using alienation effects, Fornes's work does not fully conform to "Brechtian" principles of dramaturgy. Considered within certain paradigms for a feminist dramaturgy, the intensely emotional dynamics and the use of audience identification in her plays might arouse suspicion. I will suggest that a more probing consideration of her plays *as* feminist and political becomes possible if we surrender a notion of agency as something manifested only through an apparent objectivity or mastery over a situation. By doing so, we can consider not only how Fornes's work creates complex theatrical moments, but also how other contemporary plays might complicate the interpretative politics critics bring to them.

Janelle Reinelt has articulated the need for feminist critics to reformulate drama and dramatic theory in terms of "political acts" that resonate not only with "a keen awareness of exclusion from male cultural, social, sexual, political, and intellectual discourse," but also with "a resolve to radically change these circumstances."[2] Reinelt, Jill Dolan, and others have focused their feminist critiques not only on the subject matter of dramatization, but also on particular forms of representation; they suggest that certain kinds of dramaturgy, such as the naturalistic stage, reinforce still-dominant patriarchies by coercing, however subtly, the spectator's eye.[3] Their strategies for the feminist theorizing of theater take cues from Brecht's suspicion of the empathic and identificatory relations of "dramatic" theater: how spectators are affected by and recognize themselves in the drama.

Brecht's distrust of theatergoers' empathy is more than mere suspicion of self-indulgent sentimentality. It suggests that empathy is deeply tied to the very nature of theatrical perception through bodily imitation, what Francis Fergusson has described as "a basic, or primary, or primitive virtue of the human mind."[4] This "histrionic sensibility" posits that the spectator experiences stage events as a felt response, that bodies respond to other bodies in a process of instantaneous imprinting: a "mimetic perception of action" that fuses the audience member with the action she sees performed (Fergusson, 236). If empathy is intimately linked to theatrical mimesis—both in the actor's performance and in the audience's felt perception of that imitation— then Brecht's politics seem even more radical. Not only must the superficial pleasure of the unthinking spectator be ruined; on a deeper level, the histrionic perception itself must be interrupted and subverted. As Brecht writes,

> [t]he spectator was no longer in any way allowed to submit to an experience uncritically (and without practical consequences) by means of

simple empathy with the characters in a play. The production took the subject-matter and the incidents shown and put them through a process of alienation: the alienation that is necessary to all understanding.[5]

Brecht's writings on political theater demonstrate a deep suspicion of theater as a medium for propagating what is already freely replicated. Brecht reads theatrical mimesis, the theater's power to imitate and to inspire imitation through perception, as one of the most powerful apparatuses for reproducing ideological patterns: "it is precisely theatre, art, and literature which have to form the 'ideological superstructure' for a solid, practical arrangement of our age's way of life" (23). Epic theater's political purpose is thus to interrupt the dominant ideology's replication of itself as "natural," to interrupt the process of ideological propagation through its effects of alienation and distancing.

Theater potentially produces mimetic effects in more than one way. First, the spectator might feel stage events as well as observe them, and second, the spectator might herself repeat such actions, either in her psychological response or in her actual behavior. Brecht's theater both employs and tries to stand outside such processes of mimesis. Using the alienation effects of Brecht's epic theater interrupts the illusion of reality and prevents the spectator's being "carried away." Instead, the spectator is positioned outside the action, and by extension, outside or "beyond" ideology—at worst, in the interstices of a fluid, mutable ideology, caught in, as Reinelt suggests, "the contradictions of competing practices" and at best, in a conscious resistance and reconstruction, "surpassing a given ideological grid."[6] Brecht's formulation, according to Reinelt, escapes the "overdeterminism" of Marxists such as Althusser. Formulations of ideology as inescapable and pervasive can be met with assurances of individual agency, a "subject capable of grasping and struggling with this knowledge"; political drama can only be successful when "characters do possess knowledge of their own positioning . . . able to make or fail to make their own limited interventions" (103). Reinelt thus postulates a "tension between social construction and a self who wishes it were otherwise" as necessary to the feminist political project (105).

But recognizing the subversive potential in Brecht's theories should not preclude a more careful investigation of how "epic" theater *uses* its power. In particular, Brecht prefers, and formulates as ideal, a seemingly disaffected critical response, as opposed to a naive, unthinking mimesis of the body. A feminist embrace of Brecht sometimes plays off fears that contemporary feminism will, as Alice Jardine puts it, "revert to a more 'natural' view of things: reality is what I see, hear, and touch."[7] The danger is, of course, in the opposite extreme—wholeheartedly embracing a supposedly "objective" perspective that operates in favor of "abstraction" (Brecht, 109) and thus further discounting an admittedly partial perspective that already finds itself marginalized. Historically, observations that can pass themselves off as "objective" have held greater authority than more "experiential" modes of knowing. To celebrate a theater in which Brechtian technique and feminist enterprise are perfectly wedded may in fact be premature.[8]

In Brecht's terms, those who fall prey to the illusion of the stage action experience a loss of agency. Although Brecht allows for emotion, he speaks of it in terms of a necessary mastery of response.

> A considerable sacrifice of the spectator's empathy does not mean sacrificing all right to influence him. The representation of human behavior from a social point of view is meant indeed to have a decisive effect on the spectator's own social behavior. This sort of intervention is bound to release emotional effects; they are deliberate and have to be controlled. A creation that more or less renounces empathy need not by any means be an "unfeeling" creation, or one which leaves the spectator's feelings out of account. But it has to adopt a critical approach to his emotions, just as it does to his ideas. (100–101)

Emotions, when used by the actor, must be "brought clearly and critically to the conscious level." Agency might be conceived of as control over empathic identifications, a movement to seize control over instincts and impulses that, Brecht insists, are "neither infallible nor independent of the reason . . . neither uncontrollable nor spontaneously engendered" (101). The combination of emotion and rational mastery produces what Reinelt calls a "flicker effect" that allows, borrowing Fredric Jameson's terms, first a "naive 'belief' and then a later 'bracketing' of that experience" (106). Thus representation without empathy implies a twofold mediation and a corresponding twofold pattern of dominance. The active, suffering body of the character becomes the instrument first of the actor whose alienation remains evident, then of the spectator who—through a process of "bracketing"—remains in control.

To build paradigms of feminist dramaturgy on these models is to rely on several assumptions: that the theatrical spectator can gain some further measure of objectivity through highlighting and questioning the terms of theatrical representation and that critical freedom can only be gained through throwing off the shackles of emotional affect. Just as Brecht worried about the deceptive power of the empathic, we might well worry about the power of a theatrical perspective that would destroy empathy completely. The theater as "laboratory" might become a theater subject to the same dangers as science, where particular kinds of "knowledge" are discounted as supported by "feeling" rather than "thinking." In the 1992 trial of four Los Angeles police officers accused of brutalizing Rodney King, the videotape of the beating as used by the defense became "alienated," transformed by a frame-by-frame deconstruction, repeated viewings, and commentary that successfully distanced the jury from the immediacy of the events displayed. So bereft of its immediate impact, the videotape became a tool for the defense to construct its own critical perspective. The result was an acquittal, in part influenced by a dissection of videotaped evidence to show a more "objective" view of a large black man threatening white police officers and their various techniques of "legitimate" police restraint.[9] The example invites us to question whether "objectivity" is itself an empowering "agency," or simply the illusion of mastery through intellect.

The use of alienation effects to produce a more "objective" gaze does not necessarily make for escape from ideology. How, then, do we avoid a construction of agency as only the ability to move *outside* ideology, avoid imagining self as essentially constituted outside the social field and thus able to "step out of role"? Judith Butler's writings on gender performativity as repetitive mimesis may help. Butler insists on subjectivity not as a manifestation of an independent "self," but as constituted within the complex repetitions that make up ideological performance:

> performativity cannot be understood outside of a process of iterability, a regularized and constrained repetition of norms. And this repetition is not performed *by* a subject; this repetition is what enables a subject and constitutes the temporal condition for the subject. This iterability implies that "performance" is not a singular "act" or event, but a ritualized production, a ritual reiterated under and through constraint, under and through the force of prohibition and taboo, with the threat of ostracism and even death controlling and compelling the shape of the production, but not, I will insist, determining it fully in advance.[10]

For Butler, agency does not stand outside the repetition of ideology, but rather is constituted from *inside* these performances. If agency exists, it does so through that repetition, in the "range of *disobedience* that an interpellating law might produce" (122). Butler's idea of political agency is generated from within the instability of performance—the possibility of signifying through repetition and excess, what she calls the "hyperbolic": "the parodic inhabiting of conformity that subtly calls into question the legitimacy of the command, a repetition of the law into hyperbole, a rearticulation of the law against authority of the one who delivers it" (122). Such agency neither requires nor implicitly privileges an enlightened, knowledgeable, critical "self" that can know truth or perform actions outside the deceptions of ideology.

Butler's formulation is useful in thinking about a politics of performance that does not necessarily put the empathic and the critical at odds with one another. Such a model avoids reinforcing the traditional split between mind and body, thinking and doing, analyzing and experiencing, and prompts a move toward interpretive readings of plays in which a notion of critical consciousness need not be split from the body: where sensations, desires, fantasies, and impulses become inseparable from the critical judgments we make. These more flexible paradigms are indispensable in considering the works of Maria Irene Fornes.

The works of Fornes invite a variety of opinions and, with them, a range of suggestions for the ways in which her plays can be read as "political" or "feminist." While some critics emphasize the subversive potential of Fornes's dramaturgical innovations, others find in her a more "experiential" approach that emphasizes the process of emotional and psychological identification. Dolan reads Fornes as calling for "violence as social *gestus*" and finds *Mud* particularly "Brechtian" in its brief, episodic scenes.[11] W. B. Worthen praises Fornes's experimentation with dramatic forms such as realism in a way that allows for different ideological perspectives. For instance, *The Danube* uses language recordings and puppetry in combination with actors' scenes, to open "a dissonance between speech and language, between the bodies of the performers and the gestures of their enactment, between life and the codes with which we conduct it."[12] In contrast, Gayle Austin lauds Fornes for her presentation of characters who represent voices and presences hitherto suppressed.[13] Austin concentrates on the figure of the madwoman, whom Fornes has allowed "to speak for herself." This, according to Austin, is

a radical act. On the stage we see her, and other women, escape confinement in various ways. And by placing her women in the spotlight, Fornes helps the audience, as well as future women playwrights, escape restriction by form, society, and themselves. (85)

However different, each of these critics reads the plays in terms of their value for feminist audiences. (Compare, for example, Susan Sontag's characterization of Fornes's "imagination" as "profoundly Cuban," a comment that, despite all its nationalistic and political resonance, is intended to describe certain aspects of the plays' aesthetic form.)[14] However, the feminist value springs from different, even contradictory sources. Dolan clearly links Fornes with both Brechtian theory and contemporary experimental theater practice. Worthen agrees with Fornes by suggesting that the plays cannot be firmly identified as "feminist" (180). But by insisting that Fornes continually disrupts the "ideological field" set up by dramatic forms, Worthen does suggest that Fornes's "games" have radically subversive principles: "a delicate, sometimes rueful, occasionally explosive irony, a witty moral toughness replacing the 'heavy slow, laborious and pedestrian' didacticism we may expect of 'ideological' drama" (181). In both cases, Fornes's plays lend themselves to feminist awareness because they subvert traditional forms of representation. In contrast, Austin praises Fornes for using the emotional power of a more straightforward identification and mimesis, in which the energy of Fornes's female characters is felt to empower female spectators.

The problem of "placing" Fornes as a political and feminist playwright is more than just a question of finding the right critical labels for a set of works. More importantly, it raises the need to explore how critics too quickly assume the political value or danger of particular dramatic forms and modes of reception. Dolan and Worthen understand Fornes as informed by the desire to read certain traditional genres and devices of representation as coercive. For them, Fornes is successful insofar as she introduces through formal experimentation a Brechtian subversion of the traditional empathic relations between spectator and performance. A necessary critical distance allows the spectator to understand, rather than be carried away by the emotional effects of the drama. But Austin's insistence on reading Fornes precisely in terms of empathy and identification ("we see her") reintroduces not only a different sense of feminist politics—the politics of experience, identification, and solidarity, which may be founded on dangerously essentialistic assumptions—but also disturbing questions about Brecht's viability for feminist politics. Is Fornes's formal "game-playing" (Worthen) or emphasis on the "visual sign" as historicized moment (Dolan) then undercut by the emotional impact of her plays, as Brecht's plays themselves are often thought to be? If so, and such conclusions lead to a judgment of Fornes's plays as less effective in their mixed messages, then perhaps the problem is not in the plays themselves, but in the tools with which we explicate them.

What I have shown here is the propensity of critical models to lead us into binary or oppositional thinking. The challenge is how not to think of Fornes's work as empathic rather than critical, or more "alienated" than visceral. Fornes complicates such an opposition in a number of ways. First, she illustrates the attempts of characters to rationalize their own situations, highlighting the difficulty in achieving critical distance from performance. In doing so, she questions whether or not "objectivity" is really a position of knowledge, mastery, and power—and whether or not it really constitutes agency, an ability to stand outside the "ideological grid." Furthermore, her plays suggest that empathic identification and rational thinking are not mutually exclusive responses; in her plays, what might be marked as moments of critical consciousness or self-reflection are not necessarily separable from those actions that can be attributed to "instinct" or "feeling." Finally, Fornes's work forces us to reconsider the assumption that the dramatic theater's uninterrupted action automatically results in a simple mimetic process, with the spectator compelled to repeat ideological patterns imprinted on her by the events she witnesses. Her works question outright any notion that identification takes place in one fashion, that characters or spectators will automatically identify on the basis of race, class, gender, or any other category of identity.

Interestingly enough, in accounts of her own writing process, Fornes emphasizes her feeling *with* characters: "As I'm writing the play, I suffer with the characters and I share their joys—or else I can't write." At the same time, she insists "I don't romanticize pain. In my work people are always trying to find a way out, rather than feeling a romantic attachment to their prison."[15] An important aspect of that "way out" might be how characters attempt to read their own actions and to articulate their own situations. *The Conduct of Life* provides us with numerous instances of a character's ability to consider his or her situation self-consciously, yet these instances deny either a purely "objective" or "empathic" stance. At the opening of the play, Orlando expresses disgust with his sexual desire as "detrimental to my ideals"; his inability to control and contain such desires prompts him to rationalize his behavior even during the act of rape (68). The chilling spectacle of his repeated abuse of twelve-year-old Nena is intensified by Orlando's accompanying attempts to explain his own behavior; Orlando's speech both provides his own explanation for his actions and denies them the quality of rational choice: "It is a desire to destroy and to see things destroyed and to see the inside of them.—It's my nature" (82). What is striking is how Orlando tries to articulate his own "nature," even as his speeches fail to encompass the situation fully. Such a moment is perhaps Brechtian insofar as empathy is denied him despite his earnest disclosure and attempt at self-analysis.

Orlando is implicated as "dangerous" precisely in his inability to experience empathy, in his troubled relation to human feeling. Orlando, as Leticia describes him from the beginning, cannot truly feel with another: "Nothing touches him except sensuality. . . . He is romantic, but he is not aware of what you are feeling" (70). In fact, he converts empathy into violence; in him, desire for contact with others becomes a desire to know and destroy. For Orlando, the mastery of emotion is accomplished by blaming the pain he inflicts on the victim's own capacity for feeling.

> *Leticia.* Don't make her cry. *(He looks at her.)* I can't stand it. *(Pause.)*
>   Why do you make her scream?
> *Orlando.* I don't make her scream.
> *Leticia.* She screams.
> *Orlando.* I can't help it. *(Pause.)*
>
>   (82)

When accused of mishandling a political prisoner, Orlando denies having killed one of his victims; he projects onto his victim an excess of feeling, claiming that the man literally died of empathic suggestion: "There are people who have the nerves right on their skins. . . . I didn't even touch this one and he died. He died of fear" (80). Orlando repeatedly translates the function of affect into political oppression as it is used in the service of intimidation, torture, and coercion. Still, Orlando himself cannot fully escape into a world that denies the perception of feeling. The horrors of his violence against others are manifest in the nightmares he experiences; his body enacts these horrors as he sleeps on the dining room table.

In stark contrast, Nena's litany ("I want to conduct each day of my life in the best possible way") suggests a martyrdom that denies her the relief of either intense feeling or distance: "And if someone should treat me unkindly, I should not blind myself with rage, but I should see them and receive them, since maybe they are in worse pain than me" (85). Her only means of response to sustained suffering is to translate her victimization into terms that allow her a more active role. Thus she refigures Orlando's cruelty into a violence she herself has deserved (he beats her because she is "dirty") and transforms her situation into one over which she has some control. Ironically, this control is in fact not just a prohibition against respond-ing to violence with violent feeling—the empathic "I should not blind myself with rage" (85)—but also the imagining of a voluntary, allowed state of contact ("to receive them"). Unable to protect herself from further abuse, Nena expresses a painful charity, one that allows her no mastery of her sit-uation.

At the play's end, Leticia shoots Orlando and then places the gun into Nena's terrified and acquiescent hand. Her successive acts can be read once again as impulsive, even automatic responses to her situation. Letitica responds to Orlando's threat "emotionally" rather than in a carefully planned strategy: "She kills Orlando. Not because he has betrayed her, but because he attacks her physically. When he does, she shoots him" (Savran, 69). But in placing the guilty evidence in Nena's hand and stepping "away from her," Leticia also distances herself from her earlier act of shooting her husband. Though perhaps neither act is premeditated, the second act enacts a complex, ambiguous displacement of the first: responsibility for the firing of the gun becomes projected onto the helpless Nena. In this sense Nena's unarticulated "rage," as well as Leticia's response to Orlando's attacking her, becomes inseparable from the murder.

Whether any of these characters demonstrates political agency is difficult to determine because moments of critical consciousness seem inseparable from acts of pure instinct. This makes us question whether a strict division can be drawn between "agency" and action driven by blind adherence to ideology. How to interpret the frequent repetitions of acts in Fornes's plays is not always obvious. It is tempting to look at repeated action in these plays as indicative of a pervasive ideological patterning that enslaves the characters. Scenes where female characters learn by rote sug-gest the ways in which they are "hailed" into their situations, trapped by their desire to conform to impossible standards of feminine behavior. Julia's recitation of her "prayer" in *Fefu and Her Friends* and Marion's opening speech in *Abingdon Square,* uttered "as if in an emotional trance," are mantras of good conduct, self-negation, and penance.[16] Such characters are punished when they deviate from norms. In its most extreme forms, the dictates of patriarchy are exemplified by Nena, who believes she is being continually raped as a punishment for her own bad behavior. Female char-acters in particular seem to enact their submission to patriarchy in a series of patterned behaviors. In *Sarita,* the main character tries several times to leave her shiftless lover Julio; she can only escape her desire for him by murdering him. In *The Conduct of Life,* Olympia's description of her daily routine illustrates the oppression of class as well as gender. Certainly Fornes herself sees these characters as having choices limited by their social situations; as she puts it, the question for many of these characters is not "individual freedom and happiness, but survival" (Savran, 53). In their emphasis on limited degrees of human freedom, the later plays reflect the writing process Fornes used for her earlier *Promenade,* working from a set of cards to generate a set of predetermined situations.

Yet we cannot always read the repetition of action in Fornes's plays as only indicative of entrapment within an "ideological grid," where repetitive behavior indicates a loss of agency or habit becomes the great deadener. Some uses of repetition are less frightening, as suggested in Fornes's reaction to a particular production of *The Danube.* Fornes contests the interpretation of the play's taped dialogue and puppet mimicry as representing psychological entrapment in a linguistic prisonhouse. Instead, Fornes says she finds, "such tenderness in those little scenes" and sadness in "the bygone era of that record, and how sorrowful it would be to lose the simple pleasures of our own."[17] Her sense that "this play is about life and the destruction of life" contradicts a reading of the play's repetitions as wholly oppressive. In the reading that Fornes suggests, the language tape evokes bygone days; the dialogues' gentle routines contrast with the profound disjunction caused by radiation and the bomb's explosion; the puppets provide tender and nostalgic reenactment rather than a fully parodic mockery. Repetition becomes an attachment to patterns of being and doing necessary to emotional life, evoking the rhythm of ongoing communal relationship rather than the deadening monotony of individual existence. Characters find in repeated actions a ritual of shared experience, familiar enactments with positive as well as negative overtones.

The performance of song and dance in some of Fornes's work can likewise be differentiated from Brecht's use of music. Rather than satiric commentary, songs in *Sarita* and other musicals are performed in character within the fiction of the plot, providing a sense of emotional closeness (a feeling-with) rather than distance. In *Fefu and Her Friends,* Christina and Cindy's rendition of "Winter Wonderland" soothes after a highly emotional discussion; the performance of "Angry" in *Abingdon Square* is both ironic and poignant. Emotional empathy—the recognition experienced in familiar, repeated action—is emphasized as pleasurable as well as necessary.

The repetitive actions of Fornes's characters do not only indicate the systemic oppression imposed upon thought and behavior. Nor does the spectator's response to characters' actions necessarily follow any set fashion. Both in the ways characters respond to one another and in the ways we respond to them, Fornes's plays are far from providing the "simple empathy" Brecht describes. As Judith Butler has argued, arguments made by feminist antipornography groups often presume that pornographic representation spurs a subsequent mimetic action within its viewers.[18] Yet, as Butler argues, such immediate connections are by no means certain; nor, if they were, would they necessarily disallow interpretive distance, critical analysis, or the possibility of cross-identifications. In this same vein, Fornes contests readings of her plays that define their impact in simple mimetic terms. For her, the power of the presentation does not preclude a more critical stance.

> We have the potential to learn by example or by demonstration. If you're trying to teach people to be careful when they cross the street and not just trust the light, and you show them a film where someone doesn't look and a drunk driver comes by and kills him, you're not saying, "You're going to get killed." You're saying, "Look what happened to this person. You look and don't get killed." That is a classic way of teaching. (Savran, 57)

Similarly, she contests those who take her characters as positive or negative role models, such as women who lament Mae's inability to escape death at the end of *Mud:* "I feel terrible that I have made them lose hope. The work that has most inspired me to action or to freedom is not work that's saying, 'Look, I'm going to show you how you too can do it'" (56). Fornes admits she has no control over women who do leave the play without hope: "I don't know what my work inspires, because I'm never the spectator" (56). But she insists,

> Some people complain that my work doesn't offer the solution. But the reason for that is that I feel that the characters don't have to get out, it's you who has to get out. Characters are not real people. If characters were real people, I would have opened the door for them at the top of it—there would be no play. (56–57)

Likewise, Fornes describes the "hell" she went through to create Orlando's speeches in *The Conduct of Life:* "I worked very hard to try to imagine the experience of a sadist. . . . It was so difficult. It was so ugly." Yet, she concludes, "I hope that I didn't write them too convincingly. If I did, I would eliminate them from the play" (63).

   To acknowledge that in the theater "the spectator" is not restricted to one possibility of identification, but in fact might have multiple, even contradictory, responses to the characters' actions, makes the surety of transmission through empathy more difficult to support. Both the assumption that the characters might serve as "role models" for particular spectators and that identifications are made solely on the basis of gender distinctions can be contested. Fornes is a playwright for whom questions of empathy are of immediate importance: the playwright feels with the characters, the characters with one another, the audience with them. Yet what distinguishes her writing is that such empathy is not posited as a simple set of identifications. The complexity of empathetic relationships is played out in an early scene in *Abingdon Square,* in which Marion and Mary gossip about an incestuous sexual triangle. In this scene, it is not clear to the girls whose sin it is: the man, the wife, or the sister, all of whom they describe as looking at one another "with passion." But they are fascinated by the story's "perverse" and "horrible" inclusion of all three parties as both participants and voyeurs. At the end of it, "terrified and thrilled," the girls conclude that they, too, have sinned in imagining the scenario, and fall on their knees in repentance (3). Although their furtive sexual desires are revealed by their interest in the story, it is never made clear with whose desire the two girls find themselves identifying or identified.

The endings of *Sarita, Abingdon Square,* and *The Conduct of Life* set up similarly complex, though less playful, moments. The traumatic and violent events at the endings of these plays are immediately reframed within a shared experience. After having symbolically or literally murdered the character who acts as both lover and oppressor, the female character shares gazes with, and appeals for help from, an intimate third party. After having murdered her lover Julio, Sarita asks the ever-faithful Mark: "What do you think will happen? What will they do to me?" Marion sobs over Juster after he has suffered from a stroke, and desperately tells her stepson and confidante Michael that "he mustn't die!" Leticia's tentative "Please . . ." appeals not only for understanding of, but also complicity in, the transference of guilt to Nena. In the fear and consequences of these acts, now shared between the two characters, is a kind of ambivalence. The third party's suspension of judgment is key: Mark locks hands with Sarita; Michael gazes compassionately upon Marion and the incapacitated Juster; Nena, terrified and helpless, holds the gun and looks heavenward.

The endings here arouse different responses, but the same pattern—the third character's refusal to pronounce a critical judgment and an ambivalent, empathic bond between the two survivors—appears in each. The reappearance of such an ending suggests that Fornes's interest in the triangular relationships of many of her plays lies not only in the rivalries that can develop, but also in the complicities—in the multiple and tentative identifications that each can allow. Moreover, in each play empathy is evoked not as some universal feeling, but as an ambiguous understanding across barriers. To have empathy take place across what might seem to be unlikely boundaries confounds both easy notions of oppressor and oppressed. It also confounds easy assumptions about feminine sympathy and identification that we might otherwise read into the play.

Because Brecht's theories are so often described in terms of binary oppositions, they can tempt the construction of totalizing categories—dramatic versus epic, empathic versus critical, masculine and ideological versus feminist and subversive. Such oppositions tend to fall back into old patterns: the construction of what is positively female only in terms of a male opposite. Such thinking reinforces the erasure of diversity and differences of power within gender categories. This is a danger whether one sides with those who adapt Brecht for feminist purposes or those who defend "dramatic theater" against these charges. The latter may naively presume a necessary moment of unqualified emotional identification between the female spectator with the female character ("her") onstage. Yet a similar danger exists in the former strategy, insofar as it assumes that alienation from this image necessarily leads to empowerment, or that "objectivity" rescues women from positions of helplessness through critical enlightenment.

Fornes neither cultivates the sense that women are provided access to their true selves through uncomplicated empathic identifications with female characters; nor does she encourage a sense of mastery through "objective" distancing. As evidenced by the pointed lack of understanding that Marion gets from both Mary and Minnie, and the further victimization of Nena at the hands of Leticia, her social superior, Fornes's plays do not encourage a sense of "natural" solidarity or compassion among female characters. What complicated bonds do exist are explored most fully in *Fefu and Her Friends,* the play perhaps most resonant for those considering the terms of a feminist theater practice. On the one hand, Fefu reminds the audience that not all women are the same, nor are all identifications made on the basis of some totalizing state of womanhood. On the other hand, the play presents women as able to share experience through a complex process of empathy and identification. In doing so, *Fefu* offers insight into the challenges of how to present the pervasive and pernicious effects of patriarchy without losing a sense of difference among women.

Fefu specifically constructs itself as a play about women's experience, yet its lack of unifying action makes it difficult to empathize fully with any one character. The play includes numerous reminders that the characters differ—in personality (as manifested in the contrast between Fefu's pain and the seemingly unshakable confidence of Emma), sexuality (as shown in the lesbian relationship between Cecilia and Paula that offsets the heterosexual bonds dominant in the rest of the play), and class (as suggested in Paula's speech: "I had been so deprived in my childhood that I believed the rich were all happy," 38). Such reminders undermine homogeneity even in a circle of women who share similar interests, education, and concerns. In the third act, Cecilia's description states outright that "we cannot survive in a vacuum. We must be part of a community." But she goes on to qualify the need for community with the dangers of letting the need to "identify" obscure differences: "Well, we each have our own system of receiving information, placing it, responding to it. That system can function with such a bias that it could take any situation and translate it into one formula" (29). The purpose of the educator, according to Cecilia, is to be "sensitive to the differences . . . not to supervise the memorization of facts." Obviously, such "differences" refer to the gendered oppositions of male and female, constructed both as social and biological, and hinted at in Fefu's playful line: "Plumbing is more important than you think" (13). But her words also more subtly insist on differences among women.

As well as illustrating a range of female characterization, the play suggests various ways in which characters identify or empathize with one another. Fefu's extravagant acts, and the degree of empathy that characters feel for her situation, become the touchstones by which "women's bonds" are measured. In the first act, Cindy and Christina both witness Fefu "shooting" her husband. While Cindy understands Fefu's unconventional behavior and how it suits her marriage ("If I didn't shoot him with blanks, I might shoot him for real," 12), Christina is frightened by Fefu's extravagant words and actions, calling her "outrageous" and "crazy." That Christina remains resistant to Fefu's way of life, finding it "dangerous to me," even though she comes to like Fefu, is significant. Christina has a similarly guarded response to the frightening dream Cindy describes in act 2, a dream in which Cindy is sexually molested and verbally abused by a doctor and two policemen, then tries to escape with her sister. Christina's literal interpretation of the dream undercuts the repetitive and excessive symbolism of the dangerous and authoritarian male figures: "I think it means you should go to a different doctor . . . I'm sure he's not a good doctor" (23).

That identifications can remain uneasy and impartial without suggesting some natural allegiance allows Fornes to wrestle playfully with the notion of instantaneous empathy among those who are presumably the same.

Fefu. Cindy, I'm not talking about anyone in particular. I'm talking about . . .

Cindy. No one in particular, just women.

Fefu. Yes.

Cindy. In that case I'm relieved. I thought you were referring to us.

(8)

Though Fornes's stage interrupts the illusion of homogeneity with reminders that women can be divided among themselves, she nevertheless relies on a complex notion of empathy among women, one that does distinguish them from men. In *Fefu,* any reciprocal empathy between women and men is noticeably absent. Fefu feels the lack of a "spiritual lubricant" visibly registered in her fearful and antagonistic relationship with male figures, notably with the malevolent cat and her husband Philip ("his body is here but the rest is gone," 39). Whatever is "felt" between men and women seems oppressive, violent, and even murderous. Julia's speech, her paralysis, and torture from the imaginary "judges" illustrate the connection in its most extreme form. In Julia's tortured "prayer," the stated division into two genders (man as "human being" and woman as "another species") necessarily erases differences among women; her uniqueness and fearlessness are turned into something that must be controlled and eradicated through punishment: "They say when I believe the prayer I will forget the judges. And when I forget the judges I will believe the prayer. They say both happen at once. And all women have done it. Why can't I?" (25). Significantly, Julia finds herself "contagious," as if contact, and the processes of witnessing and imprinting, would transmit her physical infirmity to other women. The controlling "judges" are associated with figures of male authority throughout the play, those whose presence is felt through the curbing of any overt displays of sexual, intellectual, or emotional energy. In act 3, the characters recall the "difficult times" at school, when, as Julia notes, "everybody ended up going to the psychiatrist" (38).

In contrast to the rigid relationship with the absent male, a more flexible, more ambiguous sharing of experience is present between female characters. What is shared is precisely their awareness of subordination within the patriarchy that forms them—through their common exclusion from power—into an uneasy group. Though she is disconcerted and angered by Fefu's behavior, Christina does agree with Fefu's distinctions between men and women ("They are well together. Women are not," 13); she shares her sense of exclusion ("I too have wished for the trust men have for each other. The faith the world puts in them and they in turn put in the world. I know I don't have it," 13). Fefu mischievously plays on the idea of women as "loathsome" to both Philip and herself, associating femaleness with that which is deeply buried, repulsive, and fascinating. The ability to empathize, to recognize aspects of one's own situation in those of others through emotional identification—to feel, through the intimacy of attraction or revulsion "another life that is parallel to the one we manifest" (9)—challenges rather than concedes to this dominant ideology. Fefu suggests that a dangerous, potentially subversive, energy is at the heart of empathy between women.

> Women are restless with each other. They are like live wires . . . either chattering to keep themselves from making contact, or else, if they don't chatter, they avert their eyes . . . like Orpheus . . . as if a god once said "and if they shall recognize each other, the world will be blown apart." (13)

In keeping with her words, the play emphasizes the difficult relations among women in instances ranging from intimate to distanced, domestic to professional, organized to disorderly. The careful rehearsal of their professional presentations, the civilized drinking of coffee and doing of dishes, disintegrates into a riotous water fight that directly displays this "restless" energy.

The breaking of stage space in act 2 suggests the same combination. Breaking into different groups demarcates various perspectives on the action, and the audience is reminded that they each experience the stage action differently. At the same time, the division encourages a sense of empathy and connection, insofar as the scenes share thematic and structural links. Although the scenes unfold in separate spaces, they each end with the mention or appearance of a character in another scene, thus establishing simultaneous action in adjacent space. Moreover, the proximity of spectator to performer not only creates different experiences for various spectators, but insures a more intimate theater experience between spectator and performer. Like the characters' croquet game, the play's structure allows for close and intimate contact within a more flexible framework.

Lest such activities be construed as unabashedly celebrating female solidarity, however, Fornes provides an ending that reinforces the ambivalent, unpredictable nature of empathy among female characters. The highly evocative death of Julia at the end of the play remains ambiguous in its meaning. Julia's situation suggests a deeply felt empathy between Julia and the other characters, especially Fefu, and a larger symbolic scapegoating, insofar as Julia suffers externally the psychic trauma that patriarchy inflicts on women. Julia empathically feels the death of the innocent deer, registering the symbolic wounding of male-inflicted violence on her body. What is significant is not only Julia's punishment by her unseen oppressors, but also the identification with Fefu that both sustains and threatens her. Julia has been "punished" through paralysis and hallucination for being "afraid of nothing"; Fefu is similarly independent and unconventional. Fefu is frightened when Julia looks at her ("I lose my courage when you look at me," 40), troubled by the same fears that have crippled Julia.

Paradoxically, it is not a male hunter, but Fefu who fires the final shot that "kills" Julia, in a literal embodiment of her earlier statement that "the world shall be blown apart" when women—she and Julia—"recognize each other" (13). Once again Fornes presents us with a complex action, as Fefu's desire to kill her husband is displaced onto the rabbit and its violent murder is enacted on Julia's body. The most positive reading of the scene, as Worthen suggests, is a mercy killing in which Fefu finally frees Julia from her pain and the watchful eyes of her oppressors (180). But Fefu also acts in the capacity of the symbolic masculine "judges" who have sentenced Julia to death for telling another woman of her torment. In her shooting games, Fefu vents her frustration with Philip; but her aggression succeeds only, as Julia points out, in "hurting herself." Trying to escape her own pain, Fefu kills an innocent animal and enacts a final, fatal punishment on Julia.

Significant to both these interpretations is the failure of Fefu's previous attempts to incite Julia toward united and open rebellion against the fears that possess them both. Immediately prior to the final shooting, Fefu and Julia enact a ritual of identification: Fefu tries to rouse Julia ("Fight with me!" 40) while Julia, whether from fear or weakness, can only pronounce a prayer of protection over Fefu. Though they share a common torment, neither can save the other. Within this dynamic of tragic events, the role of the other women is uncertain. Women remain potentially dangerous to each other because their relationship is more ambiguous—they act as allies, helpless witnesses, or sources of pain.

Instead of the shared gazes of two characters over the murdered victim in Fornes's other plays, Fefu ends with a circle of women surrounding Julia. This ambiguous end suggests that the empathic connection might be more complex and the need for solidarity stronger than we might think. In considering Fefu and other of Fornes's plays in light of their "feminist" politics, we are forced to reconsider the act of theatrical "identification" in looser terms. In the Brechtian model, the look of the spectator is marked by compulsion. Within the empathic response, the "feeling-with," the spectator runs the risk of being imprinted mimetically by the drama she watches. As Brecht notes,

Everyone (including every spectator) is then carried away by the momentum of the events portrayed, so that in a performance of *Oedipus* one has for all practical purposes an auditorium full of little Oedipuses, an auditorium full of Emperor Joneses for a performance of *The Emperor Jones*. (87)

But Fornes's theater suggests another view of the spectator's identification—a more open, fluid, and unpredictable interaction. Following Elin Diamond, a Freudian idea of identification might in fact be an apt description for this theatrical process. Diamond writes that

identification in Freud always works both ways: it is an assimilative or appropriative act, making the other the same as me or me the same as the other, but at the same time it causes the I/ego to be transformed by the other. What this suggests is that the borders of identity, the wholeness and consistency of identity, is transgressed by every act of identification.[19]

As Fornes's characters are themselves empathic with one another, so do they deeply involve us in such transformation. In Fornes, understanding a difficult and new situation fully does not involve distancing oneself, but finding empathy, sometimes despite vast differences. While her plays might manifest the difficulty or even impossibility of insuring full identification, nonetheless they suggest the need for empathy as at least a partially redemptive force and a reason for theatrical action.

Fornes's work forces us to reassess not only our responses to her plays, but also how we theorize such responses. While her didacticism is undeniable ("The play is there as a lesson, because I feel that art ultimately is a teacher" [Savran, 56]), it is nonetheless a humbling task to account for the complex ways in which her theater "teaches" us what is feminist and political.

NOTES

1. See Jill Dolan, "In Defense of the Discourse: Materialist Feminism, Postmodernism, Poststructuralism . . . and Theory," *The Drama Review* 33 (fall 1989): 58–71. See also Janelle Reinelt, introduction to "Feminism(s)," in *Critical Theory and Performance,* ed. Joseph Roach and Janelle Reinelt (Ann Arbor: University of Michigan Press, 1992), 225–30; Lizbeth Goodman, "Contemporary Feminist Theatres," in *Contemporary Feminist Theatres: To Each Her Own* (London: Routledge, 1993), 14–37.

2. Reinelt, introduction, 225.

3. See Jill Dolan, "'Lesbian' Subjectivity in Realism: Dragging at the Margins of Structure and Ideology," in *Performing Feminism: Feminist Critical Theory and Theatre,* ed. Sue-Ellen Case (Baltimore: Johns Hopkins University Press, 1990), 40–53.

4. Francis Fergusson, *The Idea of a Theater* (Princeton: University of Princeton Press, 1949), 238. Hereafter cited in the text.

5. Bertolt Brecht, *Brecht on Theatre,* ed. and trans. John Willett (New York: Hill and Wang, 1964), 71. Hereafter cited in the text.

6. Janelle Reinelt, "Rethinking Brecht: Deconstruction, Feminism, and the Politics of Form," in *Essays on Brecht/Versuche Uber Brecht, The Brecht Yearbook/Das Brecht Jahrbuch* 15, ed. Marc Silberman et al. (Madison, WI: International Brecht Society), 105. Hereafter cited in the text.

7. Alice Jardine, *Gynesis: Configurations of Women and Modernity* (Ithaca: Cornell University Press, 1985), 155.

8. As Reinelt describes this marriage, Brecht and feminism "share the subversive agenda of deconstruction, but in refusing the endless play of signifiers in an ever-suspended production of meaning, both affirm the reconstructive possibility on the laboratory of the stage" ("Rethinking Brecht," 795).

9. See Oliver Gerland, "Brecht and the Courtroom: Alienating Evidence in the 'Rodney King' Trials," *Text and Performance Quarterly* 14 (1994): 305–18; and Robert Gooding-Williams, *Reading Rodney King/Reading Urban Uprising* (New York: Routledge, 1993).

10. Judith Butler, *Bodies That Matter: On the Discursive Limits of "Sex"* (New York: Routledge, 1993), 95. Hereafter cited in the text.

11. Jill Dolan, *The Feminist Spectator as Critic* (Ann Arbor: University of Michigan Press, 1991), 108, 109.

12. W. B. Worthen, "Still Playing Games: Ideology and Performance in the Theater of Maria Irene Fornes," in *Feminine Focus: The New Woman Playwrights,* ed. Enoch Brater (New York: Oxford, 1989), 173. Hereafter cited in the text.

13. Gayle Austin, "The Madwoman in the Spotlight: Plays of Maria Irene Fornes," in *Making a Spectacle: Feminist Essays on Contemporary Women's Theatre,* ed. Lynda Hart (Ann Arbor: University of Michigan Press, 1989). Hereafter cited in the text.

14. Susan Sontag, introduction to Maria Irene Fornes, *Plays* (New York: PAJ, 1986), 7. All quotations from *Conduct of Life,* hereafter cited in the text, come from this edition of the play.

15. Fornes, qtd. in David Savran, *In Their Own Words: Contemporary American Playwrights* (New York: Theatre Communications Group, 1988), 55–56. Unless otherwise noted, all Fornes quotes come from Savran's interview, hereafter cited in the text.

16. *Abingdon Square* is reprinted in *American Theatre,* Feb. 1988, *Fefu and Her Friends* in *Wordplays: An Anthology of New American Drama* (New York: Performing Arts Journal Publications, 1980). *Mud, The Danube, The Conduct of Life,* and *Sarita* appear in Fornes, *Plays.* References to these plays hereafter cited in the text.

17. Ross Wetzsteon, "Irene Fornes: The Elements of Style," *Village Voice,* 29 Apr. 1986, 43.

18. Judith Butler, "The Force of Fantasy," *Difference* 2, no. 2 (summer 1990): 113.

19. Elin Diamond, "The Violence of 'We': Politicizing Identification," in Roach and Reinelt, *Critical Theory and Performance,* 396.

Linda Kintz

Chained to the Bed: Violence and Abortion in *Keely and Du*

In Gwendolyn Brooks's poem "The Mother," a woman addresses the following words to the fetus she has aborted: "Believe that even in my deliberateness I was not deliberate." The complexity of this line is produced by the status not only of the fetus but of the mother, as Barbara Johnson shows in her gloss of the mother's words: "Believe that the agent is not entirely autonomous, believe that I can be subject and object of violence at the same time, believe that I have not chosen the conditions under which I must choose."[1] Johnson argues that the poem attempts the impossible by trying to humanize—to turn into a human agent—both the mother and the fetus at one and the same time. The failure of that attempt reveals not only the impossibility of a "good" choice but "the inadequacy of language to resolve the dilemma without violence." Condensed in this linguistic impasse is the impossibility of the simultaneous double agency of fetus and mother, that impossibility a matter of personal, legal, religious, and political import, where "the uncertainty of the speaker's control as subject mirrors the uncertainty of the children's status as object" (33).

An ostensibly realist drama, *Keely and Du* edges up to this deepest of questions about identity in contemporary America, not because the play is able to show us reality but because its use of the conventions of dramatic realism, along with their inevitable failure, can be analogized to the impossibility of defining life in the abortion debate.[2] Rather than merely recognizing the linguistic impasse, however, the play also situates it within a specific cultural context about which a number of questions have to be asked. First, what institutions exploit the inevitability of signification's impasses by claiming that meaning is grounded in a narrow version of natural law based on the traditional family? Conversely, which institutions deny that language has any access whatsoever to materiality and the body and in whose interests do they do so, leaving us locked within an unproductive, even dangerous binary opposition? Finally, we need to ask with Johnson: how is "the collusion between deviousness in language and accuracy in violence" maximized (29), and what does it have to do with women and abortion?

These questions touch on the issue of aggression, and they do so in a number of ways. First, aggression refers to the destructiveness of the death drive, its negativity theorized by Melanie Klein and Freud as the very "ground" upon which the ego rests, where the ego perceives the undoing of its Being. And more concretely, the process of naming the fetus shows the aggressive resistance of the social order to the recognition of non-Being and, in particular, to what reveals it, women's agency. That resistance is reflected in a double taboo on women's violence. First, violence committed by mothers is tabooed, in particular when it has to do with "speaking about the death of a child in any sense other than pure loss" (Johnson, 38). And second, the taboo on women's violence codes lesbians as "fatal women," to use Lynda Hart's term; in right-wing rhetoric, the militant feminist, characterized by the "unnatural" aggressiveness of an abnormal, nonprocreative woman, becomes the murderous dyke.[3] The two then come together: "Butch" Reno is the woman at the center of the bull's-eye for America's Freikorps militia, and at a workshop for some of these same militia groups, Randall Terry teaches that "abortionists should be put to death; they are murderers."[4]

It is strange that abortion, an intensely private and intimate matter fought over in the most public and violent ways, should not have made its way more frequently onto the public space of the stage, particularly in light of the fact that another public space, the street in front of abortion clinics, has been the site of militantly theatricalized activism. *Keely and Du* was first presented and directed by Jon Jory at the 1993 Humana Festival of New American Plays. It was written by the pseudonymous Jane Martin, who has been rumored to represent the collective authorship of Jon Jory and Marsha Norman of the Actors Theatre of Louisville, or more recently, to be the pseudonym of Jon Jory alone. If this latter speculation proves to be true, it suggests the possibility of a rich dialogue about what it means for a man to write about abortion through the lens of two female characters, or whether such a question really matters. And while the play deals with a conversation between two women isolated in an interior space that suggests both a womb and a prison, it undercuts any comforting promise of a common female understanding of abortion.

The setting could not be simpler—and simultaneously more complex. The entire play, at least until the final scene, takes place in a dark, windowless basement in which there is an iron bed bolted to the cement floor, a rocking chair, a small refrigerator, and a water heater; sealing the room is a heavy, security-locked door. A fundamentalist pro-life group, Operation Retrieval, modeled on Operation Rescue, has kidnapped four women in different regions of the country as each attempted to get an abortion. One of these women is Keely, a young working-class woman who had been raped by her ex-husband. Anesthetized and carried into this fortressed basement located in an anonymous city, she is gently put to bed, then handcuffed to it, to be watched over by Du, an older, motherly woman. Keely is to be kept here until her seventh month of pregnancy, at which time she will be released and given financial support for either of two decisions she might make—to raise the child or to give it up for adoption.

The plot at first seems to follow a fairly straightforward, linear narrative carried forward by a series of asymmetrical episodes, some short, some long, some intense, some banal, with minimal prop changes, at least until the very end, which is marked by two explosive, stark changes; all are punctuated by the darkness and silence that separates them. But time only gratingly lurches forward in this hell or limbo of unease and vulnerability, while it also paradoxically seems to stretch out, as several months go by unmarked. Neither of the two women has the power to make decisions and enforce them, as plot and dialogue mimic a grammatical sentence that cannot quite get itself said. Depending on the view one has of abortion, the unease about this passage of time is different. For the one who wants the fetus to come to term, time passing is good; for the one who seeks an abortion, bad.

While pro-life logic and personal reasons for the choice of abortion clash throughout the play, it is only within the women's exchanges that anything resembling communication takes place, even though it is only oblique and indirect. When each woman makes her most powerful statement to the other, she does so in the stammering, almost animal inarticulateness of a moan, communicating only a kind of sympathy conveyed through affective, though not irrational, signifiers—they are not the words of the social contract's winners but the sediments of its sacrifices.

Two issues are important to the historical debates about abortion framed by *Keely and Du*—particularly those concerning the cultural weight of conception, as both a biological and a metaphysical term. One issue has to do with the opposition between religious and secular definitions of abortion, the other with an economic agenda that exploits this issue in its own interests. In terms of the first, the debate about abortion has since *Roe v. Wade* been locked into an artificially rigid binary opposition, as if religious and secular arguments could be kept cleanly distinct from each other. In *The Politics of Virtue: Is Abortion Debatable?* Elizabeth Mensch and Alan Freeman describe the way pro-choice discourse drew on the language of the secular Enlightenment in claiming choice as a right.[5] But as Horkheimer and Adorno had earlier pointed out, the instrumental rationality of utilitarian capitalism—that is, the form of reason in which things are evaluated primarily according to their usefulness for profit—deformed the dialectical, nuanced critical discourse of Enlightenment thought, which recognized that thought is always engaged in a dialectical negotiation with nature, not simply an instrumental domination of it.[6] The discourse of rights was uneasily limited by a utilitarian, truncated form of Enlightenment rationality.

In a related way, Mensch and Freeman argue, the rights discourse of a secularized Enlightenment tradition also undialectically repressed the history of its own concepts, in particular its relation to religion. That is, it repressed the recognition that the ethical positions it espoused and universalized as rights had themselves been developed out of the *relation* between secular and religious traditions, just as conservative religious arguments against choice repressed their own dialectic with secular culture. Having lost a rhetorical framework for more nuanced dialectical arguments, the voices of such religious leaders as Dietrich Bonhoeffer and Karl Barth, who had theorized with great care the impossibility of ethical absolutes, were lost to contemporary discussions of abortion.[7]

Added to this rhetorical and logical impasse have been the abstractions of conservative political economy, which has returned to its utilitarian roots to posit the market as the template of reality. This political economy also exhibits, in spite of its disclaimers, an inherently supremacist logic in which nonprocreative sexuality for white women and a mythologized dangerously procreative sexuality for women of color are condemned. In many ways, this recalls Theodore Roosevelt's concern in 1905 that white women were bearing too few children. Warning that "race purity must be maintained," he called white women's "willful sterility–the one sin for which the penalty is national death, race suicide."[8] Of course, arguments in favor of reproductive rights, too, often overlooked the way their proposals presumed a middle-class lifestyle and impacted women of color, who faced the dangers of sterilization. As Angela Davis writes: "What was demanded as a 'right' for the privileged came to be interpreted as a 'duty' for the poor" (210). Many of these themes can still be heard when pro-choice proponents uncritically echo racist arguments about the dangers of overpopulation.

In contemporary America, a narrative of apocalyptic warnings, both religious and secular, frames subtexts of racism, homophobia, and misogyny with warnings about cultural disintegration. Before returning to the play itself, I want to make the cultural context for the play more specific by means of an excursus through the work of an influential secular political spokesman, George Gilder, whose sociobiological texts have influenced much contemporary public policy. Though progressives and academics don't often read the popularized texts of secular conservatives, they show very clearly how fundamentalist religion and conservative economic policy come together around gender. Religious fundamentalism based on the traditional family shares a key element with the fundamentalism of the market, where the traditional family provides the disciplined social context in which the market can flourish. In both, as Allen Hunter writes, "the organic unity of the family resolves male egoism and female selflessness into a smoothly functioning expression of divine intent." And in both, the "inherent tension between cultural traditionalism and economic dynamism is metaphorically resolved with a systematically gendered view of the world encapsulated in the 'traditional family.' "[9]

While George Gilder may sound like someone from the far right fringe, he is in fact a Harvard graduate and editor of *Forbes* magazine's technology supplement; a founder of a Seattle techno-utopian think tank that helps develop conservative public policy; an influential voice in matters of cyberspace who merited a cover story in *Wired* magazine; and a contributor to Newt Gingrich's textbook *Renewing American Civilization*. The textbook was part of a college course partially funded by GOPAC, the conservative PAC that helped organize the Republican takeover of Congress in 1994 and framed the Contract with America. Gilder's articles also appear regularly in *National Review, Wall Street Journal, American Spectator,* and *Harper's;* Rush Limbaugh contributes the bookjacket blurb to the recent edition: "Timely when originally published, [it] is essential now given the warlike climate of male-female relationships, unfortunately fostered by radical feminism."[10]

Gilder's book *Men and Marriage* (its 1974 title was *Sexual Suicide*) blames a demonized feminism, or the ideology of unnatural aggression on the part of women, for everything from crime in the inner-city to the breakdown of the work ethic to impotence. In a broadly symbolic way, nonprocreative sexuality and unnaturally aggressive women, including not only radical feminists and lesbians but overly procreative and "parasitic" welfare mothers, threaten the species with suicide. According to Gilder, only a certain kind of proper, preferably religious, woman can save us, even though in another of Gilder's essays, he admits that you need not necessarily believe in God, but you do have to believe in religious *culture.*[11]

Linking apocalyptic religious rhetoric to secular warnings about the cultural crisis caused by feminist activism, Gilder reminds us that it was Phyllis Schlafly who brought the personal and the political together and joined national defense to the defense of the family:

> [She was able to tap] the energies that spring from the eloquent asser-
> tion of any long suppressed, evaded, and fragmented set of primal
> truths. All politics is on one level sexual politics. Defending the sexual
> constitution, she is clearly America's leading exponent and protector of
> democracy and capitalism. (*Men,* 112)

Her defense of "the sexual constitution may be even more important to the social order than preservation of the legal constitution" (*Men,* 105). For Gilder, as for Schlafly, the most important political goal is to reconstruct culture so that it once again reflects the true nature of masculinity, rebuilding institutions to help adjust masculine sexual rhythm to the cyclical, long-term nature of women's sexuality and to honor man's essential warrior nature. Because, as Gilder tells us, masculine sexuality, or erection, is so much more precarious and less dependable than female sexuality, civilization must devise ways to recognize men's sexual vulnerabilities and protect them from the humiliations that might render them impotent. The principal sources of such humiliations are, of course, aggressive women.

In Gilder's reading, it is feminist critiques of male behavior that most dangerously threaten society by alienating men and turning them back into the violent adventurers and hunters they really are beneath civilization's veneer:

> The imperious power and meaning of male sexuality remains a para-
> mount fact of life and the chief challenge to civilized society and
> democratic politics. Failing to come to terms with masculinity, a soci-
> ety risks tearing its very ligaments, the marriage and family ties that
> bond men to the social order. For it is only their masculinity, their sex-
> ual nature, that draws men into marriages and family responsibilities.
> (x)

That is, they must be seduced into carrying out their productive roles in society by being seduced into marriage, the lure being their legal claim of paternity, which cannot be guaranteed any other way; a man "becomes law-abiding and productive, in essence, because he discovers it is the only way he can get sex from the women he wants, or marriage from the one he loves" (39). Gilder continues: "When our social institutions deny or disrespect the basic terms of male nature, masculinity makes men enemies of family and society" (x).

Gilder's arguments bear on abortion in a very particular way. Because masculine sexuality and psychology are so delicate, women's call for "control over their own bodies," a phrase thought to be unobjectionable, in fact struck at the most vulnerable aspect of masculinity because men cannot psychologically grapple with the fact that reproductive technologies have, in Gilder's words, "shifted the balance of sexual power further in favor of women" (107). And even more radically, "a man quite simply cannot now father a baby unless his wife is fully and deliberately agreeable. . . . Male procreativity is now dependent, to a degree unprecedented in history, on the active pleasure of women" (107). Gilder finds this development to be catastrophic, for historically men could imagine that their sexual organs were "profoundly powerful instruments" and male potency was "a fell weapon of procreation. Women viewed male potency with some awe, and males were affirmed by this response" (107). They could, in other words, dependably get it up.

However, masculine identity, he argues, has been almost completely destroyed in contemporary culture: "The male penis is no longer a decisive organ in itself. Thus the feminist demand that women have control over their own bodies accentuated an unconscious recognition that males have almost completely lost control of procreative activity," which Gilder sees as the very ground of all human identity (107). Women (even "unnatural" lesbians) can now conceive without a man, and in a description of the current situation that sounds remarkably nostalgic for the good old days of forced sex, Gilder argues that a man "cannot validate his procreative powers, his role in the chain of nature, without the active, deliberate, and now revocable cooperation of a woman. A man's penis becomes an empty plaything unless a woman deliberately decides to admit a man's paternity" (107). Two people cooperating in the decision rather than one, or the insistence on agency by women, seems to be the radical demand that will shatter the coherence of the "family values" social contract.

In a remarkably unself-conscious way, Gilder here overtly states what we feminists long thought we had to tease out in our analyses of conservatism. He goes on to connect the anxieties aroused by gun control to anxiety about impotence in a frightening description of the paranoid logic of a certain American masculinity:

The obstinate refusal of many males to support gun control is not chiefly a product of conditioning by the weapons industry. Rather, millions of men fear gun control because they are losing life-control; they are losing the sense of a defined male identity and role in the family. They cling to these weapons and persist in their hunts as totems of masculinity, as rites and symbols of their continuing role as protector and provider in the family. In this sense, the guns have a virtually religious import, and gun restrictions pose a serious psychological threat [except, it seems, when those guns are in the hands of African American males]. Unless this erosion of the sexual constitution is recognized as a major social problem—gun control, however desirable, will remain politically difficult and practically unenforceable outside a police state. (106)

Thus at the highest levels of conservative political discourse, in the very frame of the language of public policy at the national level, is a determined and intense attack on women's equality, with Gilder's secular arguments indistinguishable from those of many religious conservatives.

The context in which fetus and woman are defined is thus overdetermined from every direction. Given the spare simplicity of *Keely and Du,* the use of Brechtian projection might help open the play out to simultaneous images of these other stories that circle around and haunt it. But the play's simplicity reveals with blinding clarity the way the violent control of naming the fetus is less about the life of that fetus than it is about the force that must be applied to control the behavior of white women. Gilder's warrior male and entrepreneurial economy; the masculine leadership of Operation Rescue head Randall Terry; and the absolutist God of the Christian Coalition's Pat Robertson all depend on that control.

The Portland performance of *Keely and Du* drew attention to several problems that are both thematized and encountered in the actual staging of the play. One is the near impossibility of dialogue when religious arguments originate from an absolutist perspective that elides the complicated history of different religious arguments about abortion. Local pro-life groups in Portland refused John Kretzu's invitation to read the play, see it, or engage in postperformance discussions. As a result, the audience at the performance I saw was clearly pro-choice, and there was very little disagreement or engagement with conflicting views. Yet Kretzu's strategy of playing down the fanaticism of the pro-life characters in an attempt to allow an audience to analyze these arguments meant that the characters could not be played in a way that resembled the street behavior of the most militant activists. Randall Terry, for example, is never subtle but is consistently histrionic, his language always aggressive and radical. Speaking to a militia group, he exhorts the audience to make fathers the Godly leaders of the family, with

> the woman in submission, raising kids for the glory of God. . . . My friends, America is going to enter the next millennium in convulsions. We are going to see turmoil and disruption that will make the civil war look civil. It's going to be a horrifying time and it's the judgment of God.[12]

To present this kind of fanaticism seriously, Kretzu had to translate it into the language of middle-class civility for his audience, the spectators who go to theater, for whom the real may look more like caricature than the representation does.[13]

The play opens as Du, an older woman in a housedress, enters, then puts on a mask. Walter, a very ordinary looking middle-class man in suit and tie, is a fundamentalist minister and leader of Operation Retrieval; he enters already wearing a mask. Two orderlies then bring in the unconscious Keely, whom Du gently handcuffs to the bed, before smoothing the sheets and pillow to make her more comfortable. After Keely and Du are left alone, the silence is shattered by one of the play's most powerful scenes. Keely slowly wakes up to find herself handcuffed to the bed in an unfamiliar place, and her response is practically unbearable both for her character and for the audience. When she realizes she is chained to the bed, she turns into a desperate, hunted animal. Such animality might be described in the terms Walter Benjamin used to refer to the excess or residue left over from the domination of nature by instrumental reason: "the obscure impulse of the animal . . . detects, as danger approaches, a way of escape that still seems invisible."[14] Keely represents that residue of nature, its sorrowing, grieving, rage expressed without words. But though Benjamin calls sorrowing nature mute, Keely is not silent. Brilliantly played by Valerie Stevens in the Portland production, her mournful rage and anguish seem interminable, before she finally "declines into a beaten, exhausted silence that leaves her staring at Du, who sits in a rocker" (13). The awful terror of this scene essentially hemorrhages over the rest of the play, putting the woman within the pregnant body at the play's symbolic center. Keely's sheer physicality as the missing woman around whom public debate circulates thus contextualizes the pro-life arguments about abortion that are to come. Even if her body is

absent from the rhetoric of the pro-life arguments, it is never absent from
our vision.

After that devastating scene, it is hard to imagine a second more perfectly symbolic encounter, as Keely's dominated body, chained to the bed,
is juxtaposed to the "nice" motherly figure of Du, sitting in a rocking chair.
Du provides the motherly face of conservative women, who deny any
responsibility for violence because they honestly do not intend it. But this is
postmodernity; effects as well as intentions must be considered, and here the
effects are violent. This scene also emphasizes the multiple configurations of
the domestic space in which things that are mythologized in terms of the
sheltering home and family are metaphorized by Du's rocking chair. That
chair, however, now also signifies the force latent in home and family.
Keely's anguished emotional reaction to the discovery of her entrapment is
followed by the unintentional cruelty of Du's cheery domestic banter:
"Rise and shine. The British are coming" (14). Then, in the dark we hear a
crash, as a breakfast tray is thrown to the floor.

Barbara Ehrenreich describes a similar juxtaposition of family images in
relation to the media fixation on celebrity trials like those of the Menendez
brothers and O. J. Simpson at a time when the dominant discourse is one of
traditional family values.

> A disturbing subtext runs through [the trials] . . . The family as personal
> hell. . . . Only with the occasional celebrity crime do we allow our-
> selves to think the nearly unthinkable: that the family may not be the
> ideal and perfect living arrangement after all—that it can also be a nest
> of pathology and a cradle of gruesome violence.[15]

Walter tells Keely that Operation Retrieval is a group of "like-minded
Christians motivated by a belief in the sanctity of life and the rights of
unborn children" in opposition to those groups that have been promoting
death since the turn of the century (17). The predictability of his language
undercuts the play's attempts to present the complexity of pro-life arguments to an audience of outsiders, for no matter how ordinary the activists
are made to appear, no matter how determinedly their fanaticism is down-
played, the mechanically repetitious phrases we have heard so many times
before rob the characters of their individuality:

> We are one nation, under God. And the moral law of our God is all
> that makes us a nation . . . but when we transgress or ignore Christ's
> commandments we no longer have democracy, we have anarchy, we

no longer have free speech, we have provocation, and this anarchy begins in the family which is a nation within the nation . . . and when that family sunders, and turns on itself, and its children make their own laws and speak only anger, then will the nation founder and become an obscenity that eats its young. (44)

Try as I might to enter the world of these activists, I found myself shutting it out; I was clearly outside its logic. Yet when I later taught the play, encouraging discussion of both sides, I discovered that while most students were pro-choice and deeply angered by the treatment of Keely, some were very resentful of what they considered to be an unfair picture of activists and Christians. However, they refused to speak up in class and turned to angrily written response papers and individual conferences to express themselves and their own religious beliefs. These interpretations of abortion resembled Gombrich's example of a drawing that is simultaneously a rabbit and a duck. Though there is only one image, there are two pictures. Looking from one perspective gives you a duck, from another a rabbit, but, like the fetus and the mother as human agents, the two can only be seen one at a time, not simultaneously. In terms of the arguments here, we are in the terrain, not simply of ideology, which we can read from the outside, but of deeply held belief, which requires that we try to feel it from the inside. As Lawrence Grossberg argues, belief is not so much about what can be said as about what can matter, in the sense of matter as both materiality and emotion.[16]

One has only to enter the world of pro-life believers to begin to understand the power and seductiveness of that world. At the national convention of Concerned Women for America (CWA) in Washington, D.C., the largest pro-life, conservative women's organization in the country, which claims six hundred thousand members, I was present at an evening memorial service for all the fetuses aborted in America since *Roe v. Wade*. Presuming that I could evaluate this manipulative propaganda from my stance as outsider and expecting to find the ceremony repugnant, I very quickly understood, as I watched Beverly LaHaye and other leaders of CWA walk out one by one to lay roses in an empty crib, that these kinds of rituals, with their repetitious language, are precisely where the emotional power of pro-life belief is generated and grounded. The members of the large audience of CWA members and their families were soon in tears, which were both sincere and a part of the emotional climate of charismatic religious rituals in general. The twelve-year-old girl sitting beside me was limp from the emotional impact of the ceremony, a reaction reflected in her deep sobs.

This CWA memorial could not be understood at all if it is only viewed cynically; it somehow has to be evaluated, at least for a moment, on its own terms. The impact of the ceremony would define the humanity of the fetus for that twelve-year-old girl in a way that would never again have to be articulated; the "fact" would be felt in terms of a belief that fully engaged her body. Such experiences are also intimately linked to daily Bible readings within a close community in which everyone knows the same interpretations, part of the construction of a powerful belief grounded in what might be called sacred intimacy. This is also a specific and historical form of the semiotic, or preoedipal strata of signification (which is not by any means precultural), in which the bodily ego is first organized through the practices of childrearing.[17] Here the body is intimately trained within the framework of absolutist theology, where it finds sensual power for the denial of difference in the service of an absolutist God.

That sensual training also conceals the threat of violence and the connection between this version of sacred intimacy and violence—the connection between deviousness in language and accuracy in violence, as Johnson phrased it—is overtly staged by *Keely and Du*. Raped by her ex-husband and now three-months pregnant, Keely was selected precisely because of that rape, for rape, says Walter, "has always been understood as the extreme edge of abortion policy, and we must make clear that infant rights extend even into this catastrophic area" (18). While the rape victim must be cared for and supported, "the fact of the child is critical" (18). "Your unborn child is separate from [the issue of rape]. . . . It's a separate life which may not be taken to solve your very real problems," to which Keely replies, "Hey, it's cells, little cells" (17). No, it is a separate life, as their exchange becomes an allegory of institutional power: "And what about my life?" His answer: "I need to clarify the situation for you." "Oh," she says, yanking on the handcuff, "it's clarified" (17).

The interchanges between Walter and Keely identify the two participants in this debate; it is clearly not Du who makes the decisions or sets the terms of the activism, though like the women of Concerned Women for America, her motherly image provides the kindly face that inadvertently makes Operation Retrieval's force more acceptable. Walter assures Keely that she will be able to return home to give birth after her seventh month of pregnancy, where the birth will be paid for and she will be given a childcare subsidy and an education fund for the child, if she decides to keep it. Her paralyzed father, a former policeman shot on duty and now dependent on her two jobs and care, is already being supported by Operation Retrieval. Walter seems to have godlike knowledge of her (as well as of the cultural conditioning of women in general): "Everything I know about

you, Keely, and I know considerable, leads me to believe you will fall in
love with your baby" (19). But Keely knows something else about women:
"My sister-in-law, she threw her baby on the floor. You think 'in love with
your baby' . . . is all that's out there?" (19).

Like CWA's memorial, the pro-life strategy of anthropomorphizing
the fetus begins here in earnest. In its third month, Walter tells her, "Your
baby is sensitive to the touch. If you stroke its palm, it will make a fist" (19).
And from there, he moves to the overly familiar rhetoric of pro-life pam-
phlets and *The Silent Scream* video, describing yet again suction curettage:
"A powerful suction tube is inserted through the cervix into the womb.
The baby's body and the placenta are torn to pieces and sucked into a jar.
The baby's head is crushed and then extracted" (19). Paradoxically, these
constant and impassioned descriptions tend to inoculate the audience, make
us stop listening; rather than draw attention to the human being Walter sees
at the center of this violence, his words unintentionally trivialize it. Increasingly displacing our attention from violence exacted on the fetus to himself,
Walter takes over the space that should be carefully and even mournfully
reserved to respect this very difficult question of fetal life. Instead, he gets in
the way. Keely's response: "Screw off."

In a later scene, Walter tells Keely exactly what happens in the stages of
fetal development, while she sits with her hands over her ears. Sexual difference is already established at three months, he says; the "baby" sleeps,
wakes, excretes, has vocal cords, and at four months, it has "eyelashes and
expressions you could recognize from your grandmother" (22). In a later
scene, she responds again to this verbal violence: "Little hands, little faces,
you make me sick. . . . Jesus, can you listen to yourself? All this crap about
babies. You don't care about this baby, you just want it to be your little
. . . I don't know . . . your little political something, right, God's little visual
aid you can hold up at abortion clinics instead of those pickled miscarriages
you usually tote around" (38). To counter this image, the staging provides
its own visual aid—a woman chained to a bed. Reading between the lines
here, trying to imagine how the twelve-year-old who sat next to me might
react, I can see her mentally focus on the baby booties and the descriptions
of eyelashes and tiny fingers. But what would she make of Keely, whom she
has perhaps never had to watch?

Walter's visits make his need for control more and more overt, a fact
that the staging, handcuffs, prison-like room already signify: "We need people to tell us what to do when we act out of panic or confusion. I have limited your options and taken control to give you the chance to step outside
your runaway emotions. I will return your options to you when you are
thinking clearly and ready for them" (20). His demand for control takes the

form of verbal violence, the control of language providing an allegory of social power: "The baby isn't rape, Keely, the baby is a baby" (23). As she starts to cry, he verbally bludgeons her: "Last year there were 700,000 people wanting babies who couldn't get them . . . I know carrying this baby is difficult and emotional . . . but, after abortion there are frightening side effects . . . serious depression, terrible guilt, mental illness, self-destructiveness. . . . Spare yourself, Keely, finish this in a life-giving way so you can respect yourself" (23). After pleading with him to stop, she finally yells in his face, "Screw you!" He grabs her face in his hand and forcibly turns her face to his, this resort to force all the more powerful because it is so near the otherwise highly controlled surface.

In another scene, Walter hurls biblical verses at Keely, who, with her hands over her ears, unable to interrupt or to leave, finally spits in his face. This time, after Walter again apologizes, she says, "Fuck you," to which he replies, "Thank you for accepting my apology." By then, however, this strict control of the situation has begun to break down, and both women break into uncontrollable laughter, a shift that follows scenes in which sheer boredom had led the two women to share stories. Du becomes a sympathetic figure here, even though she soon begins to use her own story as a way to blame Keely for the selfishness of her abortion decision: "You are better than that, you know you are, and how you feel or what trouble you might have is not so important as a life" (25). The born-again belief that provides, with its certainty of salvation, such a powerful sense of self-worth also has another side: doubting that belief can mean doubting one's very identity.

Thus the chess game is stalemated because for Keely that gift of fetal life will eliminate her own.

> *Keely.* Hey, I didn't choose to have this baby.
> *Du.* And the baby didn't choose, honey, but the baby's there.
> *Keely.* And I'm here . . . I could get messed up, who knows, killed by who impregnated me, not to mention I might, I don't know, hate this baby, hurt this baby, throw the baby or something like that, I'm not kidding, what's inside me. Now, do you have some Bible quotes for that, or am I just beside the point, handcuffed to this bed, carrying the results of being fucked by my ex-husband while he banged my head off a hardwood floor to shut me up.
>
> (27)

By this time, it is not Keely who seems to be the missing woman, but Du: "What the hell happened to you, Du? Do you see where we are? Look at this where you got to. Look at me. You used to be a person sometime, right? You look like one. You sound like one. You see the movie 'Alien' where they end up with snakes in their chests? What happened to you?" (39). One asks similar questions about women like Beverly LaHaye, who writes: "We want the power to be meek, not weak."[18] Du's recitation of her pro-life lines, however, gently turns into her own very personal mourning about something other than abortion.

> They tear apart the babies, they poison them with chemicals, and burn them to death with salt solution, they take them out by Cesarean alive and let them die of neglect or strangulation, and then later on these poor women, they cut their wrists or swallow lye, and then they bring them to me because I'm the nurse. Over and over. Over and over. Little hands. Little feet. Little babies. I've lost babies. I took my own baby through three heart operations and lost that baby. (40)

The action here comes to a momentary halt in soft, sad mourning balanced with extraordinary fragility over many kinds of deaths: Du's baby, the fetus, and Keely and Du themselves as people unable to control their own lives. The sadness between them is a still center that counters the more overt levels of violence; the faint outlines of a different and very deep, sad rage is barely perceptible, though its quietness suggests how powerfully it has to be controlled. Keely gently says to Du:

> I can't raise this baby, Du. . . . I'd be angry at the baby, I think so. I'd hurt the baby sometime and might not even know it, that could happen. . . . I have such black moods, it frightens me. The baby would come out of being chained to a bed, you know what I mean. It's not my baby, it's the people's who made me have it, and I couldn't treat it as my baby, not even if I loved it, I couldn't. He'd come around, see. He wouldn't stay off if I had his baby. He would never, ever in the world leave off me, and I think sometime he'll kill me, that's all I can think. Or hurt the baby, whatever, however in his head he could get me, he would do . . . would do it. Really. And I can't have his baby . . . uh . . . it's just not something I can do . . . because I'm about this far, you know . . . right up to the edge of it . . . right there . . . right there. So I guess it's me or the baby, so I guess that's crazy, but you don't . . . I don't show you . . . just how . . . how angry I really am. I don't. I don't. (40)

The collaboration between the two eventually builds to a celebration of Keely's birthday, when Du sneaks in a six-pack of beer and a dress for Keely. As they get a bit tipsy, Du puts Keely's hair up in flannel rags, and the two sit on the bed like family. While Du makes the essentialist claim that women are inherently concerned with relationships, Keely disputes it. For Du, it is impossible to imagine being "perfectly alone" because she seeks "perfect union and powerful life-giving connection" (52). A mother can "be together with a child in a perfect way, in a union that surpasses any wish you ever wished for yourself. If you haven't felt it, you can't imagine it, and it's within your power to feel it. There is union, they say, with a higher power. The baby though, that's a sure thing" (50). For Keely, however, it is that very union that constitutes a fatal threat:

> I would give all the babies and Gods just to be alone with myself now, I'm sorry but I would. I don't want to be in another box where something else is more important than I am . . . Maybe when I get healthy, but not now. They say an animal will go off by herself to heal. That's what I want . . . I haven't ever been alone! (53)

The dialogue reveals a deep unarticulated sympathy between them. When Keely tells her more about the rape, Du holds her like her own lost child; the scene again becomes excruciatingly still and quiet as it honors the mourning that structures the relationship: "I kind of drifted off while he pumped. Yeah, I was out of there for sure" (54). As Du consoles her, the two fall asleep like mother and daughter.

The next morning, when they hear Walter coming in, they hide the dress, the hanger, and the plastic bag it came in under the mattress and stash the beer bottles away, but their misbehavior is overshadowed by Walter's surprise for Keely: he has brought Cole, an apparently clean-cut, respectable-looking young man in suit and tie. As Walter says, Cole has now accepted Christ into his life, kicked his alcoholism, and found a job: "This man who has been cleansed is not the man who attacked you" (58). Coming just after the deep sadness of the previous scene, the appearance of Cole could not be more offensive and brutal, and she reacts accordingly: "Goddamn it! Are you, crazy, you're all crazy, do you know that? You think I care about rapists who find Jesus? . . . Let him hold you down and do it and you might have some idea" (58). When Du steps forward to intervene, it is clear that she knew about the plan all along, and the betrayal is devastating after the intimacy of the night before.

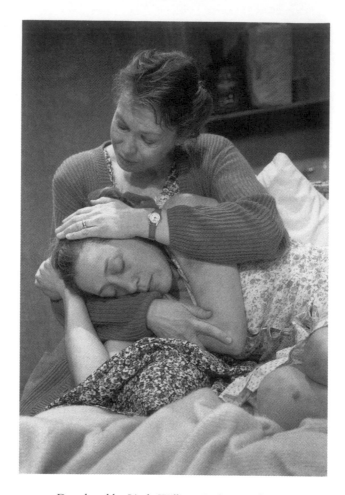

FIG. 12. Du, played by Linda Williams Janke, comforts Keely, played by Valerie Stevens, in a 1995 Artists Repertory Theatre (Portland, Oregon) production directed by Jon Kretzu. *(Photo by Owen Carey.)*

Du. I knew he was saved . . . They found him and worked with him.
Keely. They?
Du. We.
Keely. So you knew?
Du. *(a pause).* Yes.
Keely. He was always going to come here?
Du. It was always possible. *(pause)* Let me brush your hair.
Keely. No, thank you.

(59)

Their separation is conveyed in this slight but complete refusal of the offer of a now-tainted intimacy, for it has been circulated through Cole, and by way of him, Walter and an absolutist God.

The play has marshaled every possible means to repair the things that might justify an abortion: her lack of money, her father's dependence on her, and her violent marriage. Cole is their final offering, for his own salvation seems to depend on her. During a long monologue in which he sits opposite her on the bed, edging slowly closer and closer, he extends a hand that excruciatingly focuses the audience's attention on the question of whether or not she will take it. This scene presents the most horrific violence of the play. In a domestic context, with both of them sitting on the bed to which she is handcuffed, Walter has completely negated the importance of the rape and by extension of Keely, except in her role as the glue of civilization. Walter's complete control of language now means that he can enforce Cole's right to make her listen. Cole describes the changes he has gone through. After finding Jesus, he now wants to "dedicate my life to you, because it's owed, it's owed to you. . . . I hurt you so bad you would kill a baby!" (63). He tells her how he dreams of her and of her body: "What am I without you? I'm only what I did to you. I can't demand. What could I demand? Choose to lift me up" (63).

The knowledge of the rape, the force represented by Walter watching all this from behind, are focused with overdetermined intensity on a struggle against the expectations an audience has learned from the generic conventions of romance. An ending should be happy; here is the solution if she will only forgive him, save the baby, save her soul. Depending on how he is played, his humility and earnestness can carry all the signs of the sincere, reformed hero, the prodigal son with whom we are trained to sympathize. His sweetness threatens to seduce us to his side, just as it happens in the movies; the form threatens to produce the content. This is a frightening moment because it makes the spectator aware of that conventional temptation. That temptation is momentarily activated, showing how fickle one's convictions can be in the face of the cultural formations through which we interpret. The outstretched hand moves closer to her: "One gesture, you could save me. We could raise a child. With one gesture we could do that. Come on, Keely" (64). As the tension is drawn out and prolonged, we are also essentially observing Cole make Gilder's argument about women's responsibility for civilization.

But the outstretched hand also works like the buzzsaw toward which the heroine is drawn by the conveyor belt. It activates the fear that she might, in fact, take it. Finally, to our great relief, and without a word, she sinks her teeth into his hand, refusing to release it. He draws back, yanks his hand away, and hits her. The explosive reaction releases the tension that the latent violence had threatened. And the audience sags. Looking around at the faces of the audience, I realized that many others in this liberal audience had like me been intensely worried that she was going to give in. Or even worse, worried that we might have been wanting her to, which is a much more terrible suspicion. Walter grabs Cole, calls him an idiot, advises him to walk with Jesus, then forces him out of the room; Du follows. But there is a second catharsis that has to do with another one of culture's conventional romances, the happy ending between mother and child. Keely yanks the hanger that was stashed earlier under the mattress, pulls the sheet over her head, and aborts herself. The lights go out. The next scene reveals her in a bed soaked with blood.

In the final scene (Walter and Cole fled, but Du decided to stay until medical help arrives), we discover Keely and Du in a completely reversed situation. The end of the stage is now partitioned off by huge metal prison bars, whose clanging noise we hear when Keely is let in to visit Du, now the one imprisoned. Having suffered a stroke, she sits in a wheelchair while Keely gives her the McDonald's breakfast she has brought and reverses the pattern of who chats to whom. She tells Du about taking care of her irascible and ungrateful father, about her job as a waitress, about the new guy she met, who happens to be married. Du occasionally nods or shakes her head, obviously listening, the visits obviously frequent. This ending does not give us Keely as the romantic heroine who conquers all and lives happily ever after: "Listen, he swears he's separated. Listen, he's paying. I should get out. I don't get out. Take my mind off" (69).

The last words of the play draw on the pattern set earlier in which what is inarticulate yet understandable makes the most powerful statement.

(*The conversation burns out. They sit. Du looks directly at her. They lock eyes.
The pause lengthens.*)

Du. Why? [As Linda Williams Janke played Du, this "why" was barely understandable because it was spoken with agonizing difficulty, like someone whose speech had been impaired by a stroke. Its wrenching, almost primal resonance made it a match for Keely's screams at the beginning, not so much a word as a moan.]
Keely. (*Looks at her. A pause.*) Why?

(70)

The play does not end with a period, but with the dialectical punctuation of the question mark.

Though realist in its conventions and intent, *Keely and Du* intervenes more radically in the abortion debate if interpreted not as realism but as allegory, or rather, if realism itself is shown to be a form of dialectical allegory. The definition of allegory, a narrative in which a superficial meaning parallels or refers to a deeper, more profound one, paradoxically describes the way realism's generic conventions work. That is, realism posits a match between two different narratives: a superficial one, language, and a deeper one, the real. Curiously, contemporary conservative discourse also provides a powerful allegory of the real in their claim that the culture of traditional conservatism is the superficial narrative that matches a more profound one, the tenets of a divinely sanctioned, rigidly narrow interpretation of natural law. Thus in similar ways, both dramatic realism and traditionalist conservatism reflect a belief in the transparent nature of language, in the match between signifier (allegorical narrative) and referent (profound meaning).

But as Walter Benjamin argued in relation to German baroque drama, allegory cannot verify an exact match between two homologous systems on its own. Instead it requires a theological or transcendent meaning to hold those layers together so that they will match. Thus rather than simply doubling an "original" narrative by a secondary one, traditional allegory inevitably adds to or supplements the antecedent, or "original" meaning. And it does so by introducing signification that is in excess of the layers that are supposed to match. In other words, each new reading to locate the allegorical meaning proves to be site-specific and inevitably different from the reading that preceded it. The recognition of these constantly changing interpretations (which reveal the way forms are always undone by time and death) is thus more closely related to the real than are those interpretations that insist on a literal match.[19] Benjamin's revised notion of allegory is, in fact, a form of dialectical reading; as Susan Buck-Morss describes it: "To read reality like a text is to recognize their difference . . . Humanity's historical responsibility is an interpretive task, 'naming' both the socialist potential of the new nature (now synonymous with nature's 'redemption') and the failure of history to realize [that potential]."[20] Owens quotes Benjamin in this regard.

> At one stroke the profound vision of allegory transforms things and works into stirring writing. . . . Written language and sound confront each other in tense polarity. . . . The division between signifying writ-

ten language and intoxicating spoken language opens up a gulf in the solid massif of verbal meaning and forces the gaze into the depths of language.[21]

A careful extrapolation from Benjamin's concept of allegory as dialectical script makes it possible to talk about the plot of *Keely and Du* as an allegorical sentence. That is, its plot can be analogized to a grammatical sentence, with the permutations of that sentence described in relation to historical change, just as one does with generic conventions or the formal structures of plot, all part of a historical typology of signifying forms. Focusing on the sentence—and in particular on the difficulties of speaking it—makes it possible to decipher the changing status of the speaking subject over time. Julia Kristeva calls such an interpretive practice, which recognizes the history that is sedimented in poetic and linguistic forms, the "direct successor of the dialectical method." She also suggests that it might avoid the limitations of the Hegelian dialectic, which did not account for the materialist component of negativity, and the Marxist one, which reduced negativity to an economic externality without accounting for the individual subject.[22] The heterogeneous dialectic of negativity she develops draws on Freud's notion of the psychic apparatus and reconfigures it historically by conceptualizing subjective identity as the soul.

> [The soul is] a theoretical construction that is irreducible to the body, subject to biological influences, yet primarily observable in linguistic structures. Fixed firmly in biology by the drives yet contingent upon an autonomous logic, the soul, as a "psychic apparatus," gives rise to psychological and somatic symptoms and is modified during transference.[23]

While the soul, or this "network of signifying relations that characterize symptoms, discourse, transference, and subjects is a theoretical construction, it is nevertheless the only reality in which psychic life can be manifested and developed" (*Maladies,* 34). Heterogeneous, it is "formed from the first years of our lives, grows and develops alongside us, and ultimately determines our symbolic destiny" (the symbolic capacities a culture makes available). It is our "being of language" that governs our psychic life. As Kristeva argues, you are alive if and only if you have a psychic life.

> However distressing, unbearable, deadly, or exhilarating it may be, this psychic life—which combines different systems of representation that

involve language—allows you access to your body and to other people. Because of the soul, you are capable of action. Your psychic life is a discourse that acts. Whether it harms you or saves you, you are its subject. (*Maladies,* 32)

Like Benjamin's dialectical allegory, identity here is posited, then infinitely reinterpreted in ways that are site-specific and undone by the negativity through which materiality makes itself known. Both historical and infinite, its play of meaning is both free and constrained in a coherence that depends on momentary stability before reflecting on that stability and revising it— infinitely.

The psycholinguistic concept of the soul might help work our way out of the impasse between the secular and the religious binary opposition that blocks the abortion debate, where the repressed returns with such violence. Appropriating the resources of the religious concept of the soul while attempting to write against its grain, as Benjamin does in using the concept of redemption, also makes it possible to conceptualize the embodied human subject: "Enriched by the Judaic pluralism of its interpretations, the soul has evolved into a multifaceted and polyphonic psyche that is better equipped to serve the 'transubstantiation' of the living body" (*Maladies,* 6).

At the center of the discontents of postmodernity, Kristeva argues, are new maladies of the soul that cross secular and religious borders: "Everyday experience points to a spectacular reduction of private life. These days, who still has a soul? . . . As for the renewed interest in religion, we have reason to wonder if it stems from a legitimate quest, or from a psychological poverty that requires that faith give it an artificial soul that might replace an amputated subjectivity" (*Maladies,* 7). Not only the fundamentalist believer but also the secular postmodern citizen is left stranded in a society of the spectacle that conquers "the invisible territory of the soul."

> You are overwhelmed with images. They carry you away, they replace you, you are dreaming. The rapture of the hallucination originates in the absence of boundaries between pleasure and reality, between truth and falsehood. The spectacle is life as a dream. . . . If drugs [or alcohol] do not take over your life, your wounds are "healed" with images, and before you can speak about your states of the soul, you drown them in the world of mass media. The image has an extraordinary power to harness your anxieties and desires, to take on their intensity and to suspend their meaning . . . the psychic life of modern individuals wavers between somatic symptoms. . . . and the visual depiction of their

desires (daydreaming in front of the TV). In such a situation, psychic life is blocked, inhibited, and destroyed. (*Maladies,* 8)

Media's imagination, within which the religious Right and its closed world of biblical references are also powerfully situated, makes available an imaginary that is the "artificial replacement for the autistically-shrunken ego," as Hans Magnus Enzensberger describes it.[24] The autistic postmodern subject and the pro-life militant are "actor[s] or consumer[s] of the society of the spectacle who [have] run out of imagination" (*Maladies,* 10). Because these actors cannot symbolize their "unbearable traumas," the inability to work through and mediate those traumas implodes in depression or explodes in violence.

But what unbearable traumas? In an uncanny doubling, the figure that haunts the impoverished soul is that of the aborted fetus, which Barbara Johnson finds a particularly unstable figure: "There is something about the connection between motherhood and death that refuses to remain comfortably and conventionally figurative" (38). As one observer of an abortion, quoted in a pro-life text, puts it:

> [The doctor] pulls out something, which he slaps on the instrument table. "Here," he says. "A leg" . . . He points to the instrument table, where there is a perfectly formed, slightly bent leg, about three inches long. It consists of a ripped thigh, a knee, a lower leg, a foot, and five toes . . . My vision and my hearing though disengaged, continue, I note, to function with exceptional clarity. The rest of me is mercifully gone.[25]

This "literal" description of the fragmented body parts of the aborted fetus eerily mirror the psychoanalytic language Lacan, drawing on the work of Melanie Klein, uses to describe the psychic images that occur at the outer limits of the ego, what he calls the *corps morcele,* or fragmented body. These are "the images of castration, mutilation, dismemberment, dislocation, evisceration, devouring, bursting open of the body, in short, the imagos that I have grouped together under the apparently structural term of imagos of the fragmented body."[26] Lacan argues that such images resemble those painted by Hieronymus Bosch, whose paintings provided "an atlas of all the aggressive images that torment mankind" and mark birth as "the gates of the abyss through which they thrust the damned" (11–12). These kinds of images "crop up constantly in dreams, especially at the point when analysis appears to be turning its attention on the most fundamental, most archaic fixations"

(12). They also resemble the familiar images of the Book of Revelation and contemporary apocalyptic prophecies.

In making a much more direct link between these images, birth, death, and the mother, Kristeva argues that such apocalyptic images reflect a terrified reaction to the horror of non-Being associated with the phantasmatic scene of birth: "something horrible to see at the impossible doors of the invisible—the mother's body. . . . Giving birth: the height of bloodshed and life, scorching moment of hesitation (between inside and outside, ego and other, life and death), horror and beauty, sexuality and the blunt negation of the sexual."[27] It is here, perhaps, in the terrors of the symbolic abortion of the normative subject himself, of the coherence of his psychic identity, that we might find much of the impetus of the pro-life militant and the reactionary conservative responding to the challenges to paternal authority that mark the historical era of postmodernity. For that authority is increasingly, phobically, unable to guard the borders of sexual difference. This psychic anguish might, in fact, be the historical marker of the historical emergence of other forms of subjectivity.

Keely and Du's simple allegorical sentence circles around the anxieties of collective unease, as the social order experiences an identity crisis marked not only by the possibility of new forms of subjectivity but by fears exacerbated by the dizzying fragmentations of an information society and the economic assaults of a postindustrial, globalized economy. In its attempt to appease that anxiety by refusing to work through the inevitability of feminism's continuing struggle for women's equality, contemporary conservatism gives us an allegory of natural law that is the very opposite of the one proposed by Benjamin. While his dialectical script revealed the impossibility of a literal match between two narratives, conservatism is engaged in an intense reconstruction of a culture that will link traditional morality, family, and market together—absolutely.

But this is an absolutist allegory that cannot hold without force. *Keely and Du*'s incomplete sentence, like the undecidable name of the fetus, is situated in the gap between these two versions of allegory: the dialectical one and the doubled fundamentalist one. It is a sentence, in both the linguistic and penal sense of the word, that is interrupted, halting, stumbling, spoken neither in a public space nor in a domestic one, but in a strange limbo-like basement. Though both women are sentenced, they cannot share a sentence. A dialogic sentence between women is jammed; it can be neither refused nor spoken, even if its sounds and its mournfulness communicate a mute sympathy, a kind of keening.

Such an incomplete sentence reveals the historically specific typology of possibilities for the speaking subject as woman, its lurches and violence symptomatic of the unsymbolizable trauma whose effects now convulse the real. With determined simplicity (which takes the risk simplicity always does of turning into banality), *Keely and Du* pulls back the curtain to trace a dialectical allegory that shows both the symbolic meaning of a social order whose coherence rests on the exchange of representations of women by male agents as well as the historically specific way groups like Operation Retrieval require that women enact the violence of that sacrifice on and in their bodies. While the play foregrounds the terms of that social contract, it also reveals resistances to it, keeping the physicality of the body upon which that violence is to be enacted directly in front of the audience.

In the Oedipal narrative of an earlier *socius,* woman and bed were indistinguishable in terms of their function within the male plot, as Page du Bois has argued in terms of classical Greece.[28] But in this postmodern moment, the woman has differentiated herself from the bed and walked out of the bedroom. The only way to bring her back now, the only way to maximize what Johnson called the "collusion between deviousness in language and accuracy in violence" (70), is to handcuff her to the bed.

NOTES

1. Barbara Johnson, "Apostrophe, Animation, and Abortion," *Diacritics* 16, no. 1 (1986): 24–39. Hereafter cited in the text.

2. Jane Martin, *Keely and Du* (New York: Samuel French, 1993). Hereafter cited in the text.

3. Lynda Hart, *Fatal Women: Lesbian Sexuality and the Mark of Aggression* (Princeton: Princeton University Press, 1994).

4. *US Taxpayers Party Wisconsin Convention, May 27–28,* videotape, Public Policy Institute, Planned Parenthood Federation of America, 1994. See James William Gibson, *Warrior Dreams: Paramilitary Culture in Post-Vietnam America* (New York: Hill and Wang, 1994) for an important discussion of American popular culture and paramilitary groups.

5. Elizabeth Mensch and Alan Freeman, *The Politics of Virtue: Is Abortion Debatable?* (Durham, NC: Duke University Press, 1993), 12.

6. Max Horkheimer and Theodor Adorno make this argument in *Dialectic of Enlightenment,* trans. John Cumming (New York: Seabury, 1972).

7. See in particular chapter 3, "Protestant Ethics: The Legacy of Barth and Bonhoeffer," Mensch and Freeman, *The Politics of Virtue,* 48–65.

8. Qtd. in Angela Davis, *Women, Race, and Class* (New York: Vintage, 1983), 209.

9. Allen Hunter, "Children in the Service of Conservatism: Parent-Child Relations in the New Right's Pro-Family Rhetoric," *Legal History Program: Working Papers,* series 2 (Madison, WI: Institute for Legal Studies, 1988), 2–8.

10. George Gilder, *Men and Marriage* (Gretna, LA: Pelican, 1993). Unless otherwise noted, all subsequent page citations refer to this edition.

11. George Gilder, "America's Entrepreneurial Spirit," in *Readings in Renewing*

American Civilization, ed. Jeffrey A. Eisenach and Albert Stephen Hanser (New York: McGraw-Hill, 1993), 59–79. His arguments have influenced articles like David W. Murray's in *Policy Review* entitled "Poor Suffering Bastards: An Anthropologist Looks at Illegitimacy," influential in policy discussions of welfare reform that targets, in particular, African-American fatherless families. *Policy Review* is the organ of the influential Heritage Foundation, the corporate and privately funded think tank started by Joseph Coors and Paul Weyrich; the foundation was in charge of the initiation workshop for freshmen Republicans elected to Congress in 1994.

12. Randall Terry, qtd. in Karen Branan and Frederick Clarkson, "Extremism in Sheep's Clothing: A Special Report on Human Life International," *Front Lines Research* 1, no. 1 (1994): 1–3.

13. Frederick Clarkson describes an example of extremism in the research journal of Planned Parenthood. Just after Paul Hill was charged with double murder in Pensacola, a sixty-page article by Michael Hirsh about to be published in *Regent Law Review,* the journal of Pat Robertson's Regent University Law School, was pulled from circulation. Hirsh is a graduate of Regent's law school and argued that "the murder of Dr. Gunn was 'consistent with Biblical truth' and under a Florida law justifiable, if one 'reasonably believes that such force is necessary to prevent imminent death or great bodily harm to himself or another.'" Hirsh, a former director of Operation Rescue in Atlanta, also wrote a 1990 paper "The Ethics of Operation Rescue," arguing that "Christians who rescue innocents from child slaughter houses are simply extending mercy." *Front Lines Research* 1, no. 1: 2.

14. Walter Benjamin, "One-Way Street," in *Reflections: Essays, Aphorisms, Autobiographical Writings,* trans. Edmund Jephcott (New York: Harcourt Brace Jovanovich, 1978), 71.

15. Barbara Ehrenreich, "Oh, *Those* Family Values," in *The Snarling Citizen* (New York: Farrar, Straus and Giroux, 1995), 45.

16. Lawrence Grossberg, *We Gotta Get Outa This Place: Popular Conservatism and Postmodern Culture* (New York: Routledge, 1992), 162.

17. Kristeva describes the semiotic in this way: "Discrete quantities of energy move through the body of the subject who is not yet constituted as such and, in the course of [its] development, [these quantities of energy] are arranged according to the various constraints imposed on this body—always already involved in a semiotic process—by family and social structures: it is already regulated, its vocal and gestural organization is subject to what we shall call an objective ordering . . . dictated by natural or socio-historical constraints such as the biological difference between the sexes or family structure." Julia Kristeva, *Revolution in Poetic Language,* trans. Margaret Waller (New York: Columbia University Press, 1984), 27.

18. Beverly LaHaye, *The Desires of a Woman's Heart* (Wheaton, IL: Tyndale House Publishers, 1993), 65.

19. Craig Owens, "The Allegorical Impulse: Toward a Theory of Postmodernism," in *Art after Modernism: Rethinking Representation,* ed. Brian Wallis (Boston: D. R. Godine, 1984), 203–35.

20. Susan Buck-Morss, *Dialectics of Seeing: Walter Benjamin and the Arcades Project* (Cambridge: MIT Press, 1989), 240.

21. Owens, "The Allegorical Impulse," 217.

22. Julia Kristeva, "The System and the Speaking Subject," in *The Kristeva Reader,* ed. Toril Moi (New York: Columbia University Press, 1986), 24–33.

23. Julia Kristeva, *New Maladies of the Soul,* trans. Ross Guberman (New York: Columbia University Press, 1995), 4. Hereafter cited in the text.

24. Hans Magnus Enzensberger, *Civil Wars: From L.A. to Bosnia* (New York: New Press, 1993), 55.

25. Randy Alcorn, *Pro-Life Answers to Pro-Choice Arguments* (Portland, OR: Multnomah Press, 1992), 148.

26. Jacques Lacan, "Aggressivity in Psychoanalysis," in *Ecrits: A Selection,* trans. Alan Sheridan (New York: W. W. Norton, 1977), 11. Hereafter cited in the text.

27. Julia Kristeva, *Powers of Horror: An Essay on Abjection,* trans. Leon S. Roudiez (New York: Columbia University Press, 1982), 155.

28. Letter to the author, n.d.

Esther Beth Sullivan

What Is "Left to a Woman of the House" When the Irish Situation Is Staged?

If there was more respect for Irish things among the learned men that live in the college at Dublin, where so many of these old writings are stored, this work would not have been left to a woman of the house, that has to be minding [*sic*] the place, and listening to complaints, and dividing her share of food.

— Lady Gregory, introducing *Cuchulain of Muirthemme*

Christina Reid's play *Did You Hear the One about the Irishman?* dramatizes a Romeo-and-Juliet-like tragedy set in the context of contemporary Northern Ireland.[1] A Catholic woman and Protestant man fall in love, try to manage the differences of their respective Republican and Unionist family ties, and end up dead—possibly by suicides, possibly at the hands of their "tribes." The tragedy of this story is scripted in earnest, but the narrative is broken up by interjections from a stand-up comedian who rattles off trite and politically incorrect "Mick and Paddy" jokes. As the play begins, the comedian takes the stage saying, "Good morning everyone. This is your captain speaking. We are now approaching the city of Belfast. Will all passengers please fasten their seatbelts and turn their watches back three hundred years. . . . Did you hear the one about the Irishman who. . . ?" (66).

Reid's comedian makes clear the distinguishing characteristic of the play's context—Northern Ireland is a "situation" haunted by three hundred years of history relating to the larger nationalist context of Ireland and inextricable from the colonialist context of Great Britain. Whether in tragedy or comedy, *Did You Hear the One about the Irishman?* dramatically emphasizes the impossibility of referring to Ireland, Northern Ireland, Ulster, the South, the Free State, the Six Counties, or any other related namesake, without re-presenting the history, or histories, that have produced this "situation." Reid is not alone in stressing this impossibility. Gerald Fitzgibbon argues that attention to events such as the Troubles, partition, and ascendancy are nothing short of "historical obsessions in recent Irish drama."[2] Moreover, other critics have observed that Irish playwrights seem to garner recognition only inasmuch as their plays realize this obsession. According to Ian Hill, "There is an international expectation that Irish playwrights should write about The Troubles, directly or indirectly."[3]

Certainly the theaters of Ireland and Northern Ireland are alive with productions that have little, if any, overt reference to the Troubles. However, whether by obligation, lived experience, or obsession, the Troubles and its centuries of haunting prehistory strongly inform the focus and reception of much recent Irish, Northern Irish, Anglo-Irish, and even British drama. This obsession in the theater was made evident to me when I traveled to Ireland and England in the spring of 1993. Frank McGuinness's *Someone Who'll Watch over Me* had its Irish premiere at the Abbey that season. While the play dealt with hostages in Lebanon, two of the three characters were distinctively an Englishman and an Irishman—for the audience of the Abbey, there was no mistaking *that* history. Across town, Charabanc, a Northern Irish company begun by actresses devoted to finding theater work for women, performed its touring production of *The House of Bernarda Alba*. Federico García Lorca's drama had been reimagined to recall the members of a wealthy Catholic family "somewhere in the middle of Ireland"[4] plagued by the way in which they had come to lord over the land—in other words, plagued by the sense of becoming like ascendant Protestant landlords before them. Again, even for an uninformed visitor, there was no escaping the Irish/English history overlaid on Lorca's drama. As I traveled that spring through Northern Ireland, Ireland, and England, the politics of the Irish situation was characterized again and again by one word—intractability. The theater's obsession with history, or the critics' expectation of finding history onstage, appeared related to this sense of intractability. With no compelling evidence that thought and action could produce political rapprochement, the culture of the present seemed overwhelmed by the presence of past events.

Three years later, I write almost "historically" about this obsession with history. Between 1993 and 1996, significant political developments occurred. A relatively long IRA cease-fire accompanied by promising political negotiations produced optimism for the future. One could even find U.S. news headlines touting the tourist appeal of Northern Ireland. But the cease-fire eventually faltered, and hard-line wrangling over the criteria for all-party talks has continued. Current reports indicate that the "situation" is still troubled by intractable ideologies.

Writing from afar, it's difficult to discern whether or not the current sense of intractability is producing the same kind of representational obsessions that I witnessed in 1993. However, despite geographical distance, I remain critically connected to, if not obsessed with, the Troubles and their stage representations. More specifically, my interest concerns a subgroup within the larger phenomenon of recent Irish history plays. As Anthony Roche notes, "the Northern situation has brought several women playwrights to the fore."[5] According to Roche, while "women playwrights [in the Republic] have been markedly absent from the main stages," Northern dramatists such as Anne Devlin, Christina Reid, and Charabanc Theatre have produced an impressive bulk of work "questioning the inherited norms of identity and relationships" directly or indirectly associated with the Troubles.[6] Ironically, the very opening that has been forged by playwrights who deal with the specificity of their situation may ultimately limit their appeal; such historical specificity may lead audiences to condemn their plays as too particularized, or worse, time-bound. Unapologetic and proud of their work's time-bound quality, Eleanor Methven of Charabanc nevertheless acquiesces that plays like those produced by her company in the 1980s "will be a footnote in Irish theatre history."[7]

A footnote? Perhaps. But I would argue that such a footnote merits further appraisal. Collectively, the plays written in the late 1980s by Reid, Devlin, and other women of the North resist a certain kind of historicism. Where the "political" crisis takes center stage and becomes History, "personal" crises are usually cast as quotidian. History turned toward political events aims at movement or change; it can be marked with a beginning and (temporarily) an end. The quotidian seems to be ever present, ongoing, forever the same—in short, undramatic. Without arguing about the nature of the quotidian, women playwrights have resisted its erasure through their plays. I felt the distinctiveness of this resistance when, in the spring of 1993, I witnessed Peter Shaffer's *The Gift of the Gorgon,* read the works of Reid and Devlin, and followed the performances of Charabanc in Ireland. The sum of these experiences produced an understanding of how an obsession with history might bring the feminist playwright and/or critic to the footnote: to a notation about surviving the quotidian, to a notation about the ongoing, seemingly never-ending nature of patriarchy, to the documentation of how resistance is found in daily acts rather than in monumental occurrences. A play like Shaffer's *The Gift of the Gorgon* (1993) takes its audience beyond the specific historical moment to history and its discourses. In contrast, many Northern women dramatists have resisted going beyond the particularized history of their personal situation. The footnote provided by their work is the focus of this reflection.

The History

My spring in England and Ireland was filled with Warrington. In March 1993, an IRA bomb exploded in the market of this Western English town. Two children were killed, many people were wounded, and the event took "center stage" on the newstands for weeks to come. During that period, Peter Shaffer's new play *The Gift of the Gorgon* opened in the West End, and shortly thereafter, in Dublin. The play is basically an argument between two characters over the ethics of meting out, or even representing, unmitigated revenge. On one side, the lead character, a playwright, argues that if violence is met with immediate and uncompromising retribution, history will be saved from incremental, torturous, and debilitating resentment. On the other side, the playwright's wife argues that civilization is forgiveness. She maintains that civilization is doomed if it is subject to its lowest common denominator. In the midst of this debate, Northern Ireland, the IRA, and terrorist violence are interjected as examples and evidence for both sides of the argument. While *Gorgon* was hailed as an aesthetic achievement for the actors, director, and designers, its abstraction and rhetoric were not so warmly received by critics and audiences; the play's ideas were unquestionably upstaged by the real events at Warrington. One Irish reviewer critiqued *Gorgon*'s reasonable approach to understanding violence, claiming that the play was "de-Warringtonized" and asking how artists like Shaffer could take a position "above politics . . . above Warrington."[8]

Shaffer, of course, could not have foreseen the coincidence of *Gorgon* sharing a historical moment with Warrington. On the other hand, Irish, English, and Anglo-Irish theater exists in the context of another theater— the "theater" of operations, the "theater of war," the particular region or regions in which a war is being fought. A recent anthology of plays produced at the Royal Court is entitled *Frontline Intelligence*, as if to reckon with the relationship between the theater of plays and the theater of war. While Shaffer's play doesn't situate itself on the "front line," it nevertheless dramatizes this reckoning. The turning point in Shaffer's play comes as Damson, the playwright, writes a play dealing with an IRA bombing. In Damson's play, the IRA instigator does not escape retribution. Rather, the English mother of the bomb's victim secretly searches out the bomber and ritualistically kills him. Damson hopes this act of revenge will function ritualistically, causing his audience to endorse swift "eye-for-an-eye" vengeance as just punishment, as hope against the "perpetual acceptance of obscenity" that seems to arise from perpetual forgiveness for crimes against humanity.[9]

But his hopes are dashed, as some of his spectators laugh nervously at his ending and others boo. Damson's wife notes in understated terms, "The reception was dreadful" (64). In Shaffer's play, Damson then becomes a sunken, sullen man who drowns his bitterness in wine and womanizing.

In *Gorgon,* Shaffer certainly struggles with the reckoning that "war" and "drama" are etymologically linked by "theater," but he casts this struggle in the terms of a cultural representation, which, I would argue, solidifies a sense of political intractability rather than providing any grounds upon which to act or think through the circumstances of stalemate. Shaffer envisions arguments for and against vengeful retribution in concretely gendered terms. Damson—the central male figure—wants to act; he wants to live out his bloody thoughts on the stage and wants theater to "reclaim its moral power" (58) by ritualizing the necessity for revenge. Learned—the central female character—constantly tempers her husband's passions, arbitrating between his most deadly inclinations and the practicalities of marketplace theater. While he acts, she reacts. While he lives passionately, she lives pragmatically. While he makes war, she makes peace. The play certainly doesn't condone "an eye for an eye"; on the contrary, it is a play about the power of argumentation. As Hugh Leonard notes in his review, "Mr. Shaffer should be . . . given brownie points . . . for bringing argument into the West End."[10] However, the play represents the rhetorical positions of that argument in essentially irresolvable polar extremes—as naturally opposite, as, say, "man and woman"; as naturally connected or balanced, as, say, "husband and wife."

The use of gender as a metaphor for absolute, essential difference is not new, nor is the feminist critique of that signifying process. So, in the spring of 1993, I was quite taken aback to see such blatant deployment of the former and to hear so little criticism launched to recall the latter. A possible explanation of this gendered state of affairs presented itself once again in relation to Warrington. The Uncommon People of Ireland—an organization striving for peaceful resolution to the situation and led by working women in Ireland—called for a demonstration to protest the Warrington bombing. In response, fifty thousand people, including the president, Mrs. Mary Robinson, gathered in Trinity University's commons (across the street from the site of the 1916 Dublin uprising), and presented themselves as Irish persons against violence. It is a fact that the history of the Irish situation includes numerous peace organizations "manned" by women. Documenting the history of women in Ireland, Roger Sawyer goes so far as to claim, in light of the remarkable contribution of some women as peacemakers and stabilizers of society, it may not be straining things too far to suggest that the pacification of Ireland may depend on them. Women's organizations are the most potent force for peace in Northern Ireland today.[11]

The representation of woman as peacemaker, a representation that Shaffer uses unquestioningly in *Gorgon,* seems to have historical referents, and therefore the weight of actuality or material truth, in groups such as Peace Women and Women Together. In the reverse, paramilitary organizations such as the IRA and Ulster Defense Force (UDF) are "family" groups, "tribes" that maintain some of the most rigid patriarchal ideology in the world. Hence, not surprisingly, the paramilitary activity appears populated by men, by the heads of the family, by the inheritors of patriarchal power. So it seems that Shaffer's deployment of man-aggressor/woman-peacemaker is shorn up by the actuality, reality, and history of the Irish situation.

But if an obsession with history produces anything, it is the realization that history is not so neat, discrete, nor easily represented in tidy dualisms that can be generalized and subsequently universalized. Women Together is a women's peace organization, but it is not a women-only group. Also, depending upon one's perspective, the British Army is sometimes referred to as a colonizing force inducing war, but just as often regarded as a peace force sent to keep the situation from deteriorating. An easy sexual identification of gendered war/peace makers is also complicated by the reality within paramilitary organizations. A popular representation of a female terrorist is the femme fatale, devoid of feminine vulnerability, harder at heart than any man. The "truth" is that paramilitary factions deal out of homes—where mothers, wives, and sisters are reported to have a hand in everything from hiding armaments to building bombs and executing the most grievous kinds of terrorist plans and attacks. As Sawyer notes, "The feminine/female dimension of 'the armed struggle' and of resistance to it is a complex one," but nevertheless part and parcel of the "situation" (xv). The dualism that aligns man/war/action as opposed to woman/peace/pacification presents a contradiction: while such representations may be based on reality, the "simple truths" conveyed by them are also complexly inaccurate.

Writing for the Field Day Theatre Company of Northern Ireland, Terry Eagleton has addressed this kind of contradiction as it relates to the Irish situation and to feminist critiques of gendered dualisms. Rather than dismissing such contradictions as untruths to be corrected, he speaks of "try-

ing to live" the contradictions posed by dualisms.[12] Here his particular
emphasis is on the aporia of oppositional politics—the contradiction that,
like any dualist phenomenon, "as political radicals our identity stands and
falls with those we oppose" (27). In light of this aporia, his prescription
highlights methodology and form rather than topic and content. He argues,

> A radical politics can prescribe what must be done [to lift the repres-
> sion, so that dialogism can actually take place]; but it cannot prescribe
> the content of what will then be lived, for the content as Marx says,
> goes beyond the phrase. All radical politics are thus in a profound sense
> formalistic. (29)

Noting the "dis-ease" of that dynamic, he testifies that his understanding of
such a process comes by way of feminism and feminist critiques of gender
construction:

> If the binary opposition between "man" and "woman" can always be
> deconstructed—if each term can always be shown to inhere parasiti-
> cally within the other—then just the same is true of the opposition
> between those other virulently metaphysical forms of identity,
> Catholic and Protestant. (24)

The form, then, that Eagleton assumes in order to understand the contradictions of identity and the process of constructing identity in dualistic
representations is a combination of feminism and deconstruction—a marriage, if you will, of two discourses, performed in the spirit of materialist
beliefs.

It's interesting to me that in Eagleton's analysis, feminism is championed on account of its method, question, and form—but as to its content,
nothing is mentioned. Except to say that feminism, like all radical politics,
must learn from the "other," no specifics of women's experience and no
particulars of gender critique are found in the article. Perhaps such content
goes beyond Eagleton's phrase, but in the context of nationalist and colonialist critiques regarding Ireland, the absence of feminist content is a particularly loud silence. According to Sawyer, "For half a century Ireland's
two principle cultures were prized apart by a succession of laws concerning,
directly or indirectly, women's rights" (176). He notes, for example, that

> the permissibility or otherwise of divorce and contraception, and the
> general approach to the concept of the family, were issues which drove

a series of wedges between the independent state and the separated counties of Ulster. (xiv)

Sawyer concludes, "'A woman's place' has always been at the heart of the Irish question" (177).

"A woman's place" is central to Irish and Northern Irish politics. As such, it's not surprising that the man/woman dualism can be so useful to Shaffer in structuring a drama that directly and indirectly refers to the Irish situation. It's also not surprising that the feminist project of critiquing the man/woman binary can be of use to Eagleton in understanding dualistic forms of opposition like those that exist in Northern Ireland. But in both cases, the "form" of argumentation takes precedence, and the old-fashioned "content" of women's experience seems almost provincial, too narrow for attention, a matter to be dealt with after, in Eagleton's words, we learn to "live the dialectic passionately" (38).

The Footnote

While in Ireland and feeling the obsession of history that marks theater in that context, I was struck by a certain content dealing with "women's experience" that may or may not have anything to do with "dialectic passion," but that does indeed have to do with what was described as the intractability of the Irish political situation. Reading the plays of Reid and Devlin and tracing the developments of Charabanc, an "other" historical obsession held me—the experiences of women surviving in the political crisis of the Troubles.

Anne Devlin's *Ourselves Alone* (1985) "hails" a feminist reader by making its audience aware that the theater of war that is the Irish situation has its front lines in people's homes. That's where the camps are, that's where the guns are, that's where the violence is. However, in these homes, war is only one example of violence. Set in the onslaught of the recent Troubles, *Ourselves Alone* is a melodramatic telling of three Catholic women dealing with the havoc of paramilitary politics in their kitchens, parlors, and bedrooms. These women are variously involved or not with the "struggle"—Josie serving in the high ranks of her unit, Donna "keeping the homefires burning" in order to hide and support the soldiers of her life, and Frieda trying to disavow any and all political activity. Outside the home, authorities chase down political adversaries on account of their war crimes. Inside the home, other crimes occur: women are beaten. Inasmuch as the latter crime has no "historic significance," no power structure exists to chase down the perpetrators. In relation to this kind of nonhistorical violence that is deprioritized by the very historic Troubles, small daily acts are the mode of resistance. This is highlighted in the opening scene when Frieda is rehearsing for her show. She refuses to sing a "patriot" song, saying, "I don't want to sing this anymore. . . . I'm fed up with songs where the women are doormats."[13] Her resistance stops the song.

A feminist audience is likewise "hailed" by the attention to women's lived experience in the work of Charabanc. Like *Ourselves Alone, Somewhere over the Balcony* (1988), a play commissioned and produced by Charabanc, focuses on three Catholic women living their lives in what others might refer to as the "encampment" of Divis Flats, a Catholic ghetto in Belfast. Like Devlin's play, *Somewhere* reiterates the message about warring "tribes": homefronts produce violence specifically targeted at "ourselves." In documenting a kind of American disinterest regarding news of the Irish situation, David Remnick makes an important point. When U.S. media attention is turned to the Irish question, it is usually on account of some terrorist act that affects people in England. But the majority of violent acts committed by the various paramilitary organizations of Northern Ireland are acts that establish the organizations' power within their own "families" or "tribes." Remnick writes, "Paramilitaries on both sides . . . act brutally in their own communities, taking on the role of judge and jury and meting out punishment: kneecapping, beatings, exile."[14] In the "black comedy" of *Somewhere over the Balcony,* the women sit on a balcony overlooking their territory; they fade in and out of memories; and their stories focus on the violence aimed at them, or people like them, in their family units. As Maria DiCenzo notes,

> [t]he violent nature of domestic life is generally denied the political value assigned to acts of military or terrorist violence. By focusing on women, Charabanc's plays foreground trench warfare in the domestic sphere and highlight the role played by working-class women in day to day survival.[15]

Christina Reid's play *The Belle of Belfast City* (1989) again provided for me a message specific to Irish homes. Here the storyline is made up of scenes from the life of a now-older woman, Dolly—a life filled with real and threatened violence inside, outside, past, and present, in a Protestant ghetto of Belfast. A part of this plot includes her granddaughter, Belle, who was born illegitimate and then raised in London. When she returns to Belfast, Belle is viewed as absolutely different because of her "blackness"— her father is African American. The events that make up this aspect of the plot point out the prevalence of racist thinking in fundamentalist organizations like the Ulster Defense Association (UDA) and its subsets of the Ulster Volunteer Force (UVF) and UDF, as well as the perhaps better-known opposition organization, the Irish Republican Army. In Belfast, *race* is a word that means "Protestant" or "Catholic." However, "racism" is sustained as much by ideologically maintaining those dual identities as it is by identifying those two categories as "pure" and "balanced" in their opposition. Belle's presence is unnerving in the situation—exotic to some, gossip to others, a reminder of other colonies or worlds. This play minces no words: fundamental organizations such as the UDF are dependent upon the image of a "pure" Protestant; as Belle's mother states, the UDF, IRA, and all related factions are alike in fostering an image of "all God's children" who are "blue-eyed, blond-haired, and white" (40). It is in Irish homes, in the alignments of families, that racism starts—when children like those in *The Belle of Belfast* are taught that Catholics, or is it Protestants, have "close-set eyes." In this ideological indoctrination, the deeper lesson is driven home: even if Ireland is backward and common, it is nonetheless pure and made so by the enforced "purifying" of women. So as Jack, an ultraunionist will advise, "Guard our women . . . Lest they succumb to the insidious evil that festers and grows in our land. . . . Guard your mothers. Guard your daughters. Guard your sisters and your wives" (55). In Reid's play, the audience sees the guarded existence produced by racism and patriarchy—two forces that the playwright represents as having developed a specific historical conjoining in the Troubles.

As I was to learn later, it is not unusual for critics to read across these plays, as if together they form a kind of collective perspective regarding "other" aspects of the Troubles. Roche and McMullan both speak of women's contributions to Northern theater by grouping the aforementioned dramatists. While Maxwell doesn't offer any analysis of their work in his examination of political drama, he mentions *Ourselves Alone* as being "directly political" and Reid and Charabanc as having produced "plays where the brutalities of the warring factions are not directly the issue, [but] their assumptions pervade the daily run of domestic and social discourse"[16] Charabanc is hardly ever mentioned without attention to its entire chronology, which spans many productions. In fact, criticism that would focus singularly on any one of these plays, without making reference to any other feminist or "women's" plays, seems almost nonexistent. It would appear that the critical reception of this "footnote in Northern Irish theatre" will be distinguished by generalized attention to a bulk of work by many diverse writers. Since my own method here reflects this "bulkanization," I hope the dynamic is not necessarily dismissive. It does, though, demonstrate the way in which these plays must be argued into importance—the common method to date being to argue substance by amassing numbers.

When trying to establish the significance of this group of plays, the method that proves most problematic to critics is one that attends to the plays' form. Roche goes a long way to assess the merits of the formal features of these plays alongside Julia Kristeva's theory of "women's time."[17] But, like mine, his analysis remains primarily focused on content rather than form. In other analyses, the form is characterized quickly as a "largely naturalistic mode."[18] Some critics mention briefly that Reid's plays are augmented by "use of songs and other anti-illusionistic devices."[19] Always, Charabanc's early working process is mentioned: "The majority of their shows involve careful research and interviews with local people. Their form remains within a broad framework of community theatre."[20] Otherwise, form gets little critical attention in relation to these plays. Behind much analysis of this work is a criticism that Helen Lojek articulates in regards to *Ourselves Alone:* "Devlin's [play] has a feminist orientation, [but] it mounts none of the challenges to theatrical realism frequently associated with feminist plays."[21] In an age of "advanced" forms, the "largely naturalistic" quality of these plays seems to diminish their worth.

The merits or demerits of realism have been debated for some time among feminist scholars, but it would be erroneous to say that "we" have arrived at consensus in this debate. However, at least one issue has a degree of support. Realism, like any other phenomenon, cannot be generalized as to its purpose or effects. In certain contexts, it reinscribes bourgeois ideology; in others, it is the strategy par excellence for making the "quotidian" significant enough to garner focus and to underscore its "historical" dimensions. Nuala O'Faolain makes this kind of argument as she endeavors to understand why so few Irish women have become writers:

> We inherit a country, modern Ireland, where the single imaginative construct we might admire—what Irish men did with words—is utterly at variance, in respect of images of women, with what the men who have power over us want us to be. . . . Our exemplars are socially impossible.[22]

O'Faolain is speaking of the discrepancy between mythic images of women in Ireland and the legalistic paternalism of the Republic's constitution, which in effect guards against women's rights. As a corrective, she lays claim to an absent tradition:

> it is the absence of realism from our great literary tradition which oblit-
> erates women. . . . that whole area of realism, above the shared mater-
> ial facts of furniture—the area where the structures of life, economic,
> political, are determinants of human potential—is the area which con-
> scious women believe is tainted. . . . We know no other world than
> this we are in, but we deeply suspect it.[23]

Realism, naturalism, or perhaps "the quotidian" is championed by at least
this one Irish woman as the formal difference through which her "suspicions" might be voiced. These sentiments might also characterize women
writers of the North who, as the Troubles persist, have employed a suspi-
ciously naturalistic mode—or perhaps, a naturalistic mode that harbors deep
suspicions. Relatively speaking, it is a mode that resists the metaphorization
of Woman—whether that metaphor be launched by Yeats, Beckett, or
Shaffer. Out of its context, this mode may, as Lojek argues, "pose problems" and fail "to reassess conventional categories."[24] In context, though,
both myth and modernity have formalized "Woman" to such a degree that
many Irish women desire to be seen in their "quotidian" best.

The Postscript

The *Gift of the Gorgon* was an eye-opening experience for me. Its focus on
rhetoric as a perfectly balanced state of mutually contested oppositions
reminded me of a kind of "reasonable" historical account where there are
always "two sides to every question." That said, though, for decades, the
maintenance of balance in the Irish situation has equaled intractability and
stalemate. As evidenced in Shaffer's play, traditionally drawn representations
of gender make an excellent home for such stasis. Deconstruction seems to
offer the form with which to analyze that kind of epistemological bind. In
the closing moments of Anne Devlin's *The Long March,* Helen reminisces,
"I still remember that time when we thought we were beginning a new
journey. . . .What we didn't see was that it had begun a long time ago
before with someone else's journey; we were simply getting through the
steps in our own time" (155). Certainly, deconstruction is the exercise of
seeing the transparent inscriptions of history, signification, and ideology just
as Helen begins to do at the end of Devlin's script. But from within the context of the Irish situation, and with or without any "advanced" artistic
forms, feminist dramatists have obsessed about a very particular history—
Irish women's lived experiences that, past and present, do not show evidence of a balance between two sides, and that, despite being repeatedly

called upon to mythologize the political stalemate, cannot be understood by any metaphor of Woman. I experienced their particular obsession as highly contextualized resistance. This essay, then, records my own attention to, and interest in, an essential "footnote" to the "history" of the Irish situation and its Troubles. The work of women dramatists across Ireland and Northern Ireland deserves more critical attention as they continue to question the notions of balanced opposition, mythologized women, and seemingly intractable situations.

NOTES

I wish to acknowledge Ohio State University's College of the Arts Research Fund and the Elizabeth D. Gee Fund for Research on Women for their support of this project.

1. Christina Reid, *The Belle of Belfast City* and *Did You Hear the One about the Irishman: Two Plays* (London: Methuen, 1989). Page numbers hereafter cited in the text.

2. Gerald Fitzgibbon, "Historical Obsessions in Recent Irish Drama," in *The Crows behind the Plough: History and Violence in Anglo-Irish Poetry and Drama,* ed. Geert Lernout (Atlanta: Rodopi, 1991), 42.

3. Ian Hill, "Staging the Troubles," *Theatre Ireland* 31 (1993): 42.

4. *The House of Bernarda Alba* was produced in Dublin at the Project Arts Centre. As described in the production program, "The play takes place somewhere in the middle of Ireland, at some time in the not too distant past."

5. Anthony Roche, *Contemporary Irish Drama: From Beckett to McGuinness* (New York: St. Martin's, 1995), 229.

6. Roche, *Contempory Irish Drama,* 229.

7. Jane Coyle, "Now We Are 10," *Theatre Ireland* 30 (1993): 17.

8. Hugh Leonard, "In Praise of Revenge," *Irish Sunday Independent,* 11 Apr. 1993, 9L.

9. Peter Shaffer, *The Gift of the Gorgon* (London: Viking, 1993), 58. Page numbers hereafter cited in the text.

10. Leonard, "In Praise of Revenge," 9L.

11. Roger Sawyer, *"We Are but Women": Women in Ireland's History* (London: Routledge, 1993), xv. Page numbers hereafter cited in the text.

12. Terry Eagleton, "Nationalism: Irony and Commitment," in *Nationalism, Colonialism, and Literature,* ed. Terry Eagleton, Edward Said, and Fredric Jameson (Minneapolis: University of Minneapolis Press, 1990), 38. Page numbers hereafter cited in the text.

13. Anne Devlin, *Ourselves Alone* with *The Long March* and *A Woman Calling* (London: Faber and Faber, 1986), 13. Page numbers hereafter cited in the text.

14. David Remnick, "Belfast Confetti," *New Yorker* 25 Apr. 1994, 61.

15. Maria DiCenzo, "Charabanc Theatre Company: Placing Women Center-Stage in Northern Ireland," *Theatre Journal* 45, no. 2 (1993): 182.

16. D. E. S. Maxwell, "Northern Ireland's Political Drama," *Modern Drama* 33, no. 1 (1990): 1–2.

17. See Roche, *Contempory Irish Drama,* 231–42.

18. Susanne Greenhalgh, "The Bomb in the Baby Carriage: Women and Terrorism in Contempory Drama," in *Terrorism and Modern Drama,* ed. John Orr and Dragan Klaic (Edinburgh: Edinburgh University Press, 1990), 166.

19. Anna McMullan, "Irish Women Playwrights since 1958," in *British and Irish Women Dramatists since 1958: A Critical Handbook,* ed. Trevor Griffiths and Margaret Llewellyn-Jones (Buckingham: Open University Press, 1993), 121.

20. McMullan, "Irish Women Playwrights," 121.

21. Helen Lojek, "Difference *without* Indifference: The Drama of Frank McGuinness and Anne Devlin," *Eire-Ireland* 25, no. 2 (1990): 65.

22. Nuala O'Faolain, "Irish Women and Writing in Modern Ireland," in *Irish Women: Image and Achievement,* ed. Eiléan Ní Chuilleanáin (Dublin: Arlen House, 1985), 130.

23. O'Faolain, "Irish Women and Writing," 131.

24. Lojek, "Difference *without* Indifference," 64–65.

Toward a Civic Theater

Tom Burvill

Playing the Fault Lines: Two Political Theater Interventions in the Australian Bicentenary Year 1988

The two performance pieces I discuss in this paper were made and performed during the 1988 Australian Bicentenary Year. In both cases, their significance as political theater events derives from their implicit challenge to dominant narratives of nationhood foregrounded during the Bicentenary celebrations. In Sydney, Sidetrack Theatre's *Whispers in the Heart* was a deliberate intervention: the project was intended to contribute to the wave of critiques and countercelebrations generated by the Bicentenary.[1] In the Northern Territory, the refugee Timorese Association and the Darwin Theatre Group, making *Death at Balibo, the Killing, by Indonesian Forces, of Five Australian T.V. Newsmen during an Attack on Balibo, East Timor, on October 16th 1975*, took similar strategic advantage of the Bicentenary rhetoric of diversity to make both a cultural and a political statement.[2] However, the latter production sparked a diplomatic protest from Indonesia that gave the show, via national television coverage, an additional level of political significance highlighted by its occurrence in this year of self-congratulatory national self-construction.[3]

Like most nation-founding celebrations, the 1988 Bicentenary sought to construct the *present* Australian "nation" as imagined community in specific ways. Insistent media images of inclusiveness, equality, and affluence projected the nation as a colorful spectacle of multicultural consensus.[4] Television advertising centered around the key image of a smiling representative crowd all joining in to sing the Bicentenary theme song "Celebration of a Nation": "Let's make it great, in '88, / C'mon and give us a hand" with the outback icon Ayers Rock in the background. The image of Australia as an identity of interests and values—a classless democracy united by an unproblematic bond to a unique continent—was rein-

229

forced as sentimental common sense.[5] The assertion of an already achieved multicultural equality appears particularly ideological when images of the land are appropriated, given that Aboriginal and Torres Strait Islander peo-ple[6] are the most disadvantaged group in the population, and land rights are, for them, a central political issue.[7]

There are several reasons for discussing these two theater pieces together. First, each addresses an important problem of cultural representa-tion of minority or oppressed groups. Specifically, how can the destructive-ness of oppression be registered while preserving a sense of the agency of those subjected—how, in short, to avoid both "victim narratives" and sim-ply speaking for the "other"? This concern is inscribed in the performance-making strategies of both theater events, where the "victim" becomes active as a speaking subject both in process and performance. Both shows were based on research with written documents and by interactive community research, involving discussion with a wider local group with a stake in the representations of themselves that were emerging. Although the shows con-trast markedly in their political theater strategies—in the aesthetic choices and performance styles employed to address their very different respective audiences—both performance groups worked as a devising collective with cross-cultural membership and similar political concerns.

Second, both performances work on fault lines of the national imagi-nary. They bring to mind situations that are like guilty (open) secrets, aspects of the political repressed, issues that, when they surface culturally, usually do so in displaced and unacknowledged ways. Hodge and Mishra argue that unresolved guilt at the dispossession of the Aboriginal people cre-ates an underlying anxiety of legitimacy for white Australia, what they call the "bastard complex."[8] East Timor is a matter for guilt and anxiety not only because of the failure of Australia, as an influential regional power, effectively to defend the rights of the Timorese at the time of the Indone-sian takeover and subsequently, but also because majority Australians—as a largely European population geographically located in the Asia-Pacific— have ongoing identity problems and other insecurities about their current relation to postcolonial "Asia." Indonesia is the closest Asian nation to Australia, with a population of almost 188 million people (compared to Australia's 17.2 million) and a population density on the main island of Java approaching ten thousand people per square kilometer, compared to two per square kilometer on the Australian continent. Aggressive question-ing of such obviously "un-Australian" behavior as the invasion of East Timor and the continuing abuses there may not only be risky—it may also be inappropriate, disrespectful of Asian cultural difference, or so we tell ourselves.[9] One of the ways political theater can work is by opening up these issues, by speaking some of the otherwise unspoken. In their differing ways, both theater events effectively dealt with the political repressed of Australian national identity.

Death at Balibo

Death at Balibo explicitly refers to a 1975 incident during the invasion of what was previously Portuguese East Timor and is now effectively the 27th province of the Republic of Indonesia. Five Australian journalists and an unknown number of Timorese were killed; television film of the journalists' last hours and personal greetings to family have survived, but the incident itself has never been conclusively investigated. The project that resulted in Death at Balibo was initiated by the Timorese Association in Darwin, the capital of the Northern Territory and five hundred miles closer to Timor than to any major population center in Australia. Hoping to produce a work that would communicate with the majority English-speaking population, the association hired Anglo-Australian writer Graham Pitts, cofounder of Sidetrack Theatre and well known for his collaborative work with nonmainstream companies and minority or subordinated communities. Pitts, in turn, worked closely as coauthor with two Timorese refugees: Maria Blanco and Jose Monteiro.[10] The Timorese had several explicit aims. The event would "build bridges" to the wider Australian community, gain visibility for exiles, and disseminate information concerning the continuing tragedy of their homeland in East Timor;[11] at the same time, it would strengthen the Timorese community's belief in itself and faith in the struggle by a communal activity celebrating the distinctiveness of their culture. In other words, the association had both "external" and "internal" hopes for this cultural-political event. A further aim was to help establish an ongoing theater group for their community. The latter was achieved by having Timorese "shadow" the Darwin Theatre Group sound operator, lighting operator, and other practitioners during rehearsal and production, as well as by having Maria Blanco actively codirect with Darwin Theatre Group director Mary Hickson.

The Timorese Association is a distinctive communal-political organization of a people in exile. Also known as the Lafaek (Crocodile) Club, it includes whole extended families and a range of activities that suggests more the translation of village communal life than what political organization normally implies in Western industrialized societies. Lafaek members of all ages participated as performers, as singers in the large onstage chorus, and in discussions of content and style. The association employed an Anglo-Australian writer but made sure he was one committed to a collaborative outcome. The show was valuable as a community-building and community-defining activity for a group with its own internal political debates in the context of the struggle continuing in East Timor.

The first act of *Death at Balibo* presents a picture of life in a small mountain village, or *povacao,* near the town of Balibo and presents its spirit in a time of impending crisis, as the Indonesian army approaches the area. The tension and horror of the invasion that is beginning is evoked through a mixture of song, choral poetry, and dialogue. A female character describes the massacre of her home village nearby. Toward the end of the act, the five Westerners arrive, are plied with copious quantities of tapioca, and asked what the world will do about what is happening. The Timorese believe that the presence of the journalists will mean the exposure of the truth of the invasion to the world, producing international outrage and direct intervention, particularly from their wartime allies the Australians. In the play, the journalists respond that they can only show what they see; they can't answer for what Australia will do. According to Graham Pitts, the wartime partnership of the Timorese with Australian soldiers during the Second World War makes the "unexplained" deaths of the Australian journalists even more sardonically emblematic of the Australian government's present relationship to the Indonesian state. The Timorese fought beside and succored Australian troops, with great danger to themselves, in the battles on Timor against Japanese forces threatening the Australian mainland. Australian Timor veterans reportedly feel ashamed at the "un-Australian" abandonment of people who were not only allies but friends—a betrayal of comrades-in-arms deeply at odds with the national mythology of masculine "mateship" and of solidarity with the underdog.

The village scenes in act 1 center on a battle for the soul of the Timorese people. The Buan, an ambiguous seer and part spirit, attempts to possess the young man Coa Tai, who symbolizes the future, with fatalism and belief in the necessity of submission. As the people of the village try to deal psychologically with the threat of invasion by a massive modern army in a situation of immense uncertainty and insecurity, the struggle within Coa Tai represents "the determination to be free and to resist oppression"[12] under severe strain. Coa Tai is aided by the spirit-form of his mother, Cai Fou, who represents the earth, the originating womb of the people. Cai Fou is defiant against pessimism and clear that resistance to tyranny is the only way to survive as a people. The struggle is physicalized on stage by a painfully writhing Coa Tai, fighting defeatism in the form of possession by a demon. The spirit of his mother wins and enables him to leave the village and accompany the journalists to Balibo. In performance, the overcoming of despair is foregrounded, rather than any Aristotelian tragic irony, even though as spectators we already know the fate of the journalists, the villagers, and of East Timor itself.

During act 1, and particularly during the prophetic speeches of the Tata Gassi—in this case an elder, "keeper of the sacred objects and a seer able at times to prophesy the future" (notes to playscript, 3)—an English paraphrase is provided from the stage by a narrator, giving the essence of the dialogue and major speeches, which are delivered in Portuguese. The Portuguese passages draw on the resources of that language in romantic anthropomorphism: the Timorese landscape is imaged poetically as in mourning while the soldiers of "Batavia"[13] with blood on their faces murder even mothers, children, and old people because they are part of a people that wishes to be free. The indigenous Timorese language Tetum is used largely in the choruses that introduce and close the act, incorporating traditional village songs and chants. The first act embodies in distinctive performance modes—the semichant of the choruses, the oratorical style of longer prophetic speeches, the *tebe* dance—the forms and styles of a unique culture. A distinctive worldview and spirituality is evident in the typology of semimythical characters involved and the allegorization of a struggle between fatalism and resistance, conceptualized within a framework of traditional Timorese belief. The stage set for act 1 consisted of three areas: an almost bare main playing area; a second area for villagers, as observers, chorus, and musicians; and a third, raised area to represent the *lulic* or sacred domain of the spirits. The texture of Timorese preinvasion daily life in a mountain village is also suggested in the traditional musical styles employed. The opening statement of the narrator emphasizes that the play does not claim to show every little thing, every little detail. "Every little detail is the subject of much argument. But the ending is true. What happened, did happen. . . . A war, an invasion, much killing. . . . And there is a truth that is greater than any argument. It is to be *a verdade da conscienca*—the truth of the heart" (2). The phrase *a verdade da conscienca* recurs as a choral refrain and appears prominently on the posters for the show. It is understood to mean that there is a truth beyond expedient politics in the East Timor situation; that there exists a distinct East Timorese people whose inhabitation of the island is basic to their culture, identity, and spirituality; and that the invasion and occupation by Indonesia can never be retrospectively justified on the pretext that some Timorese collaborators were in favor of "union" with Indonesia. It also signifies a persisting belief that this truth will emerge, will become irresistibly recognized.

Act 2, the shorter of the two, initially uses naturalistic, conversational dialogue as the newsmen chat, joke, play cards, wonder about the next day, and express various reactions to being in the path of an invasion force. They talk about their families and home, painting an Australian flag on the side of their hut and showing all possible signs of their foreign-journalist status. The evidence of the final videotape footage recorded by the group was used to supply character details. In a final, nonnaturalistic scene, the journalists in the play run onto the stage as their names are called in a litany of remembrance by the Timorese chorus and fall one by one to the sound of machine-gun fire.

Apparently it was the explicit reference to the still-unexplained killing of the five journalists on the advertising poster for the show that created the international incident. A poster for the show was displayed in the Darwin Journalists' Club. The poster features the full title of the show, the words *A Verdade da Conscienca* and a splattering of blood red splashes across the white background. A small group of Indonesian journalists, about to begin a tour of Australia, had arrived in Darwin and were taken as guests to the club, where they reportedly were offended by the display of the poster; they returned to Indonesia the next day, canceling their visit. The show became the subject of heated debate in the Northern Territory Assembly, and the funding of the show by the Australia Council's Community Cultural Development Unit was criticized. Suggestions were made to ban the performance or to prosecute those involved, and Graham Pitts and others were interviewed by Australian security intelligence organizations. The departure of the Indonesian journalists was widely reported as a difficult incident for Australian-Indonesian diplomatic relations and was featured on national news broadcasts. The national multicultural broadcaster SBS (Special Broadcasting Service) aired an intelligent and serious television documentary about the whole affair, which included shots of the live performance and interviews with the writers, directors, and representatives of the Journalists' Association in Darwin.[14]

I would not wish to privilege the "power" of the show's unexpected media exposure over its local meaning—its political effect in the local Darwin and Northern Territory context and its value for the Timorese community itself. The *furor* created, however, was an acute indication of the geopolitical sensitivities involved on both the Australian and Indonesian sides and indeed of the importance of issues of representation to both governments.[15] Instances of resistance or subversion of hegemonic ideologies are not disabled by having only a geographically local reach—live performance will almost always be restricted or particular to its audience in this sense. Such particularity is an aspect of the *specificity* of performance as a form of resistance—a *specificity* requiring a careful strategic fit between the forms of representation (and presentation) employed and the particular audience or constituency. Performance *as* performance requires the copresence of a live audience sharing the space of the event in order to achieve its distinctive semiosis. Performance as resistance must build on this necessity, avoiding the commodity relationship to exercise political agency in relation to an interpretive community very closely understood and addressed. While this community can be constructed by a commonality of needs or interests, it should never be thought of as a general or universal audience (terms that, in fact, usually disguise address to a particular interest and class fraction).

Whispers in the Heart

Sidetrack Theatre's *Whispers in the Heart* marked the beginning of the company's current emphasis on exploring the politics of the discourses of theater itself.[16] This has meant developing new performance modes to address a new audience. The company's community theater work of the early and mid-1980s emphasized "expression" of differences in social power with a strong attention to the foregrounding of cultural difference in the productions. This meant employing a multiethnic performance ensemble, using collaborative performance-making techniques, researching in the community, and incorporating community languages in the performances.[17] It also meant continuous company training in dance, acrobatics, and other theater skills to develop stage images that were fluid, vivid, and arresting. Sidetrack performances assumed the existence of distinctive cultural reference-fields, specific verbal and physical lexicons that at times only a particular community had the cultural competence to fully decode. Since 1988, the shift has been toward examining the social and discursive construction of meaning and difference in performances that encourage an interrogation of meaning systems. Such a "postmodern" political theater practice addresses a different audience: one made up of students, intellectuals, artists, cultural and educational workers, with oppositional interests across a range of contemporary issues.

Since *Whispers in the Heart* aims at "undoing" discursive constructions of Aboriginality, it will be useful to first outline the discursive situation it was aimed to undo. According to Hodge and Mishra, Aboriginality has been constructed by non-Aboriginal Australian culture, from first contact, within a dominant discursive regime they call "Aboriginalism," a construction parallel to Edward Said's "Orientalism." Within this discursive regime,

Aboriginal people are viewed as fearsome and dangerous, childlike and passive, or primitively attractive but not as capable of self-government or as equal civil or moral subjects. Essentially they will be spoken about or for but cannot speak themselves. Nineteenth-century anthropology participates in the Aboriginalist discursive regime, amassing a huge volume of written, photographic, and diagrammatic description, documentation, analysis, measurement, classification, and explanation. Stephen Muecke divides the normally available discourses on Aboriginality into three broad categories: the anthropological, the romantic, and the racist.[18] Muecke describes the anthropological, after Foucault, as a "transcendental-empirical" discourse. The collection and investigation of empirical (arti)facts of the colonized other is directed toward a furthering of knowledge of a "mankind" inscribed diversely across human races. Contemporary, postmodernist or poststructuralist anthropology is more self-conscious and attempts to foreground the constructed and discursive nature of anthropological narrative. Earlier "scientific" work was dominated by a Darwinian paradigm that resulted in the traffic in severed Aboriginal heads back to British collections as evidence for an evolutionary history of "man" with European, or British, "man" at its apex. Even mid-twentieth-century anthropology often participated in the "romantic" discourse of Aborigines as a primitive and vanishing people. Only some of the more virulent early racist discourses saw Aboriginals as powerful or as having agency, this becoming the excuse for racist aggression against them.

Sidetrack artistic director Don Mamouney explains the project of *Whispers* like this:

> the approach was to look at knowledge, to look at the ways in which knowledges of black Australians have been constructed—the ways in which anthropology and prior sciences like phrenology, to a certain extent history, and other social sciences . . . were implicated in the course of our knowing and (our) being able to construct Aborigines in such a way that we could not only rob them of their land two hundred years ago, but we could continue to justify that two hundred years later.[19]

The title *Whispers in the Heart* came from a book by the leading revisionist historian Henry Reynolds.[20] Mamouney explains:

> The title is based on the idea that we still, we white Australians still have these whispers in the heart. . . . A whisper in the heart in medical

terms is a presentiment of a heart attack, or of the body not working quite right, of a catastrophe. . . . We push to the back of our minds this knowledge that this land is actually a graveyard of genocide of Aboriginal people. . . . But you can't repress these things forever because they come out in other ways. Henry Reynolds as a white Australian has played a role in trying to bring to the surface those things, in a way that may enable a new future to be built. . . . *Whispers in the Heart,* the performance, continues that tradition. . . . The most important thing about Henry Reynolds's work for us was that reconstruction of Aboriginal identity, as not simply a people who lay down before the massive arms of the whites, but to suggest that they did maintain resistance, that they did attempt to negotiate, that their role was far from being passive . . . and bringing out the many complexities of that history.

Part of the strategy of theatrically deconstructing existing discourses of Aboriginality was to foreground in the style(s) of the piece the constructedness of performance itself as a staging of knowledges. Thus each scene in *Whispers* opened in a different surreal environment, keyed by its own music and sound treatment. These sound assemblages combined electronically composed music with sampled sounds, combining exaggerations of stock sound effects with blatantly "mood creating" musical themes, deliberately reminiscent of horror or action movies. In several sections the performers, most of whom took several roles, wore radio microphones, and their voices were radically pitch-shifted. The fictional English anthropologist Dr. Earnest Zarah was played initially by a recently arrived male Chilean actor with heavily accented English and later by a female actor. The staging visually quoted a museum exhibition with white ropes enclosing a long narrow playing area; the audience faced each other across the playing space, and two pseudoclassical columns stood at one end of the space. Lighting was obtrusive, changing markedly in color from scene to scene, along with the sound. Costumes were obviously fantastic, mixing various colonial periods of military and civilian dress. Dance and stylized movement were used, with some effects based on the Suzuki movement training of Malaysian-born company member (and company choreographer) Meme Thorne. In all the areas of costume, sound, movement, and lighting, there were clear signals that the stage images created were not to be taken as "neutral" or "documentary" historical re-creations. Like the museum, this was a writing of the past, but one emphasizing the mediated and already interpreted character of historical representations.

The scenes were arranged in a loosely narrative order, telling an obviously fantastic story of fictional British anthropologist, Dr. Earnest Zarah, who arrives in Tasmania sometime in the nineteenth century looking for wild Aborigines. In the opening scene, a Tasmanian Aboriginal dubbed "King Wudjella the last of the wild natives" is arbitrarily shot by the military commander of the colony while Wudjella and Zarah are watching the spectacular ritual flogging of a white convict. The word *wudjella* is a joke, suggesting the sound of the expression "white fella" in contemporary Aboriginal English. King Wudjella was played by Aboriginal performer of multiracial heritage Raymond Blanco, with patches of chalky white makeup in a visual pun on Frantz Fanon's "black face, white mask." Zarah heads off to the mainland, guided by a "part-Aboriginal" named Michael McHale, who promises, for large amounts of money, to find some "wild fellas" for Zarah to study. A gothic scene in the town morgue shows Zarah beaten to the body of Wudjella by another group of scientists, who dismember the corpse. Zarah manages to get the head to send back to London. In an outback desert scene, we see Zarah scientifically photographing an Aboriginal man. The fourth scene shows a reception for Zarah at Government House in Sydney, where Lola Montez and Florence Nightingale are guests. Finally, we see Zarah and McHale at Buckingham Palace, preparing for the presentation to Queen Victoria of an authentic, live Aboriginal collected in the wild.[21]

Whispers mixes events and images from different periods and aspects of Australian colonial history in an obviously "impossible" way. In the Government House grand reception and ball scene, for example, a figure representing Governor Lachlan Macquarie slavishly courts on his hands and knees a Lola Montez figure—an exotic "Latin" (although actually British) imported entertainer—who dances a tarantella. Meanwhile Florence Nightingale, representing the opposite Victorian stereotype of womanhood, weeps constantly, overcome by her own pity. Wishing to "smooth the pillow of a dying race," this Florence Nightingale represented the sentimental philanthropism that assumed the Aboriginal people were doomed to extinction—thus participating in the Romantic-tragic discourse of Aboriginality that has been so disabling of indigenous agency. The latter part of this "sequence" shifts emotional registers from an atmosphere of inauthenticity, posturing, and farce to positive cultural interaction. "Lola Montez" and the Aboriginal waiter, respectively the fetishized and the suppressed "other" of the grotesque colonial culture, gradually construct a dance together. The dance they make, and the music that now dominates the sound environment, quotes and hybridizes European and Aboriginal ele-

FIG. 13. Jai McHenry as Florence Nightingale in Sidetrack
Theatre Company's 1988 production *Whispers in the Heart.*
(Photo by Chooi Tan.)

ments in a bricolage that becomes emblematic of working freely and
actively *between* cultures.

   Whispers in the Heart, like other Sidetrack shows, uses comedy to avoid
locking an audience into a solemn "correctness" of response. Some of this
comedy comes from the grotesque exaggeration and gothic imagery, the
excess of the performance style. But another more thematic source of comedy is the continual contrast between the self-deluded pomposity of the
white colonial figures and their monocultural smugness, and the witty and
culturally adaptive tricks of the Aboriginal people, signified by the clever-

FIG. 14. Mémé Thorne as the ritual public flogger in Sidetrack Theatre
Company's 1988 production of *Whispers in the Heart*. *(Photo by Chooi Tan.)*

ness of Michael McHale. Company members report that the reception by
urban Aboriginal audiences was in terms of a sometimes hilarious entertainment. Aboriginal audiences appeared to laugh more freely at some of the
more anarchic, carnivalesque moments than their more "sophisticated,"
postmodern-literate (and historically compromised) "White" counterparts.
In this regard the involvement of the two Aboriginal performers, Raymond
Blanco and Allan Cohen, was crucial to the show. Raymond Blanco is by
training and profession a dancer and choreographer, now artistic director of
the national Aboriginal and Islander Dance Theatre. Beyond the technical
skills of these performers, their personal resources of "survival humor," the
subversive comedy of the colonial subaltern culture, enabled the company
to find a sardonic, unsentimental performance idiom. Another important
aspect pointed out by Don Mamouney was that urban Aboriginals like Raymond Blanco and Alan Cohen are conscious and adept at occupying multiple subject positions, multiple identities. Constantly constructed by the
dominant culture as Aboriginal in conventional ways, they are particularly

aware of the borders they actually cross, the hybrid identities they negotiate as political-theater performers, participants in inner city subcultures, and members of extended families with ties to traditional tribal "country."

The final scene of the show involves a carnival of reversals. Dr. Earnest Zarah returns to Britain to report to Queen Victoria, bringing a savage collected "in the wild" by his "native assistant," Michael McHale. In a scene of mayhem, a rash attempt by Zarah to clean up his living specimen for the grand occasion reveals that the "wild man" (carefully fitted out by McHale as an amalgam of "primitive" stereotypes with bones in the nose, animal skins, etc.) is in fact the Irish convict McKelvey we had seen being flogged in the first scene, now blacked up with boot polish. This discovery that the fruit of his scientific labors and hardships in the desert is "really" a "White man" drives Zarah into a frenzy. Meanwhile the Aboriginal assistant Michael McHale reblacks the white man and continues to train him in "primitiveness." The point here is not only the obvious one—the construction of Aboriginality as primitiveness by the anthropological gaze. The trickster sophistication of McHale, whom Zarah had rejected as an object of investigation because he was not "black" enough, plays with the idea that "natives" may at times have had surprising ways of dealing with their anthropological investigators. The scene gives an alternative reading of Aboriginal people and their possible forms of agency under colonial dominance, as well as suggesting that the "victim" narrative within which indigenous people are often inscribed is being rewritten. The constructed "through the looking glass" world is further emphasized when Queen Victoria totters forward on enormously high heels and turns out to be Raymond Blanco, in high drag as the great queen herself, come to look upon the exotic and to bestow honors on her eminent scientific servant Dr. Zarah.

In an earlier scene, however, the implicit violence of the empiricist-transcendental discourse of anthropology is imaged with a different theatrical rhythm. In "The Measure" sequence, a lone Aboriginal figure, forced to discard any European clothing or other signs of cultural contact and adaptive practice—a small cross on a chain for instance—stands in a pose instructed by the anthropologist. At a measured distance from him, Zarah has his special camera for making standard photographic records from which calculations and correlations can be made. Here, the minimal but obstinate subversive agency of the Aboriginal subject is figured by his refusal to maintain the required pose. Time after time he changes the angle of his head so as to look away from the camera, or down, or across its commanding line of vision. Each time, the anthropologist readjusts the head, walks back to the camera in a measured way, and looks through the view finder to find that his composition has been disrupted once again by this minimal act of dis-obedience. The action of walking up to the Aboriginal man, adjusting the head, walking back to the camera, seeing the disrupted image, walking back, adjusting again, is insistently repeated. Each time the Aboriginal varies his stance, the anthropologist returns to insist on the pose. This scene takes place in a harsh desert light with a sound environment that included the sounds of bush-flies, foreboding music, and the mundane murmuring sounds of a long, hot suburban summer afternoon with the cricket match on the radio. The repetition builds on and on, but gradually a group of riders appears at one end of the space, masked in white cloth, with the appearance of mounted soldiers wearing the iconic Anzac slouch hat. They move on the spot, like riders seen in the far distance. With sound suggesting a cavalry advance intensifying in volume and pitch, the effect is a nightmare image of bearing down in attack of pursuit. Finally, a climactic explosion from the camera as the photograph is taken fells the Aboriginal man as if with a bul-let. The imagery associates the mounted massacres of Aboriginal people, scarcely admitted into history until recently, with the iconography of the Light Horse Brigades of the First World War, part of the mythology of war-rior nationhood. The "scientific" activity of anthropological photography is metaphorically linked both to those quasi-military massacres and to the mil-itary character of traditional "Australian" images of identity. At the same time, the audience sees Aboriginal resistance—a constrained resistance, cer-tainly, but something other than simple passive victimhood—in the Abo-riginal's refusal to accept the imposed pose, to render himself compliantly to the scientific gaze.

The two shows discussed here addressed different audiences to differ-ent strategic ends. Sidetrack Theatre's interrogation of the dominant discur-sive constructions operating around "Aboriginality" in Australian culture led them to research its discursive "archaeology" and to develop a reflexive performance language with which to undertake a theatrical deconstruction of these discourses. The result was a "fantastic" (re)construction of the his-tory of anthropological contact, one that reinscribed Aboriginal agency into that story. This form of performance invited the audience's cocreation of the meaning of the piece, foregrounding the making of meaning in general as an intensely political process.

The events around *Death at Balibo* show the powerful vector that can develop through electronic media between a particular local event and an international regional issue along sensitive ideological fault lines—an important aspect of postmodern global-local relationships. One role for political theater is to "work" these fault lines, these contradictions that

FIG. 15. Raymond Blanco as the Aboriginal subject of
anthropological photography in Sidetrack Theatre Company's
1988 production of *Whispers in the Heart. (Photo by Chooi Tan.)*

societies structured around inequality necessarily produce. Political culture
can open up the ideological cracks and work against that suturing and
attempted erasure of the traces of contradiction, which is a major function
of hegemonic cultural production. Political theater practice can also—
more "positively"—provide spaces for the experimental construction of
new subject positions and intersubjectivities, new ways of constructing the

historically "other." This disconcerting of certainties, this unsettling coun-terimagining, may offer alternatives to ideology's "lived imaginary relation to the real," alternatives that provide necessary modeling on both cognitive and affective levels for the new understandings and new human relations involved in the process of progressive social change. This may be especially crucial in societies (like Australia and the United States) where a major political task is to build a genuinely equal and democratic multicultural society without effacing difference and without allowing the apparently benign "ethnicizing" of sections of the population to become a new cul-tural form of social segmentation.

NOTES

1. *Whispers in the Heart* was first performed in May 1988 at the Marrickville Com-munity Centre in Sydney, followed by university and high school performances. It had a season at the Sydney Performance Space in July 1989. A videotape adaptation, directed by Peter Knapp, was made available to school and college libraries accompanied by a teaching-resource package.

2. *Death at Balibo* was performed for three weeks indoors by the Darwin Theatre Group at Brown's Mart Community Arts Centre during May–June 1988; the SBS TV news-documentary program about the production broadcast on September 18. Graham Pitts was supported for this project by a grant to the Timorese Association from the Community Cultural Development Committee of the Australia Council.

3. In addition to the examination of available records, research for this essay has been based on direct interviews with key participants in the production process for both groups. Including the perspective of the practitioners involved, however, was easier in the case of the Sidetrack company, with whom I am in regular contact (and whose show I saw many times) than for the Timorese in Darwin, over twenty-five hundred miles away. For the latter, I have relied on the invaluable accounts and documents supplied by writer Graham Pitts, including the unpublished playscript of *Death at Balibo* (with trans-lations of the portions performed in Portuguese and Tetum) and invaluable videotape recordings of both the performance itself and the numerous media reports of the inter-national incident involved.

4. Australian official multiculturalism may appear to give state sanction to worthy values, but exhortations to harmony are all too easily substituted for policies and pro-grams to redress actual inequalities. Official multiculturalism too often concentrates on superficial aspects of lifestyle—"spaghetti and polka" multiculturalism—rather than on the more difficult and painful aspects of lived cultural difference in a complex, highly industrial, capitalist society. See Stephen Castles et. al., *Mistaken Identity: Multiculturalism and the Demise of Nationalism in Australia* (Sydney: Pluto Press, 1988), for a discussion of Australian state multiculturalism as public policy and contradictory to the theme of a "unified" national identity. Australian and U.S. multiculturalisms are compared in Jon Stratton and Ien Ang, "Multicultural Imagined Communities: Cultural Difference and National Identity in Australia and the USA," *Continuum: The Australian Journal of Media and Culture* 8, no. 2 (1994): 124–54.

5. On positive aspects of the Bicentenary and nationalism, see Graeme Turner, *Making It National: Nationalism and Australian Popular Culture* (Sydney: Allen and Unwin, 1994), and Meaghan Morris, "Panorama: The Live, the Dead, and the Living," in *Nation, Culture, Text: Australian Cultural and Media Studies,* ed. Graeme Turner (London: Routledge, 1993).

6. This is the usual collective term used to refer to Australia's indigenous peoples as recognized administratively. Torres Strait Islanders are a distinct group geographically, culturally, and ethnically. The term "Aboriginal people" is also used by indigenous spokespersons as a convenient abbreviation, although even the concept of a single Aboriginal people is a postinvasion one.

7. Until granted citizenship in 1967, Aboriginal and Torres Strait Islander people (approximately 1.6 percent of the Australian population) were considered "protected persons," something like children in their legal rights, including restricted movement from place to place. Aboriginal people are the most heavily imprisoned group in the world, have high rates of preventable diseases (including diabetes and blindness caused by diet and environmental factors), and high infant and adult mortality rates. A policy of removing young children from their families and bringing them up effectively as state wards, like orphans, was abandoned only in the 1970s. A Royal Commission into Aboriginal Deaths in Custody has failed to halt an appallingly high rate of deaths in prison and police custody, mainly young men on minor charges including drunkenness. The High Court in 1994 upheld, after many years, a claim for native title on part of a small Torres Strait island (the Mabo decision). This decision reversed the previous legal doctrine of *terra nullius,* with its implication of a land empty of habitation, or at least of legal subjects, before white settlement. The ensuing federal Native Title Act has failed so far to deliver any significant land back to traditional owners and is under heavy attack by farming and mining interests and their parliamentary representatives.

8. Bob Hodge and Vijay Mishra trace the effects of the not yet fully acknowledged, and certainly not compensated, colonial dispossession and near-genocide of Aboriginal people on white Australian invader-settler culture from first contact through to the mid–twentieth century in *Dark Side of the Dream: Australian Literature and the Postcolonial Mind* (Sydney: Allen and Unwin, 1990).

9. Potential aggression by this neighboring population giant has been at times a main preoccupation of Australian defense policy. Since the Whitlam Labor government of the early 1970s, a bipartisan policy of regional cooperation combined with mild diplomatic rebukes for the more outrageous cases of human rights abuse has prevailed. Even Gough Whitlam, the most adventurously reforming postwar prime minister, chose not to confront Indonesia over its invasion of East Timor in 1975. Under both Liberal-National (conservative) and Labor (social-democratic) administrations, Australia has not only defense cooperation arrangements with Indonesia that include training Indonesian troops in Australia and supplying military equipment but also has arrangements for joint exploitation of Timor Sea oil resources, in a region where the border between the territorial waters of the two nations have been specially negotiated.

10. Graham Pitts wrote Sidetrack Theatre's first production *Drink the Mercury—the Minamata Disaster.* The Timorese Association had sponsored earlier musical performances for the Timorese community audience before *Balibo.* Maria Alice Blanco and Jose Monteiro had written unpublished poetry and fiction in Portuguese before their work on *Balibo.*

11. Timorese resistance to the takeover continues to be suppressed with violence amounting to genocide by Indonesian military forces. Amnesty International has reported abuses including unjustified detention, torture, and "extra-judicial executions." Many Timorese have become refugees. Jose Ramos-Horta, East Timorese "foreign minister in exile," was recently awarded the Nobel Peace Prize for 1996 jointly with Carlos Belo, Catholic bishop of Dili, the capital of East Timor. On the continuing situation in Timor see Jose Ramos-Horta, *Funu: The Unfinished Saga of East Timor,* preface by Noam Chomsky (Trenton, NJ: Red Sea Press, 1987), and Matthew Jardine, *East Timor: Genocide in Paradise* (Tucson, AZ: Odonian Press, 1995).

12. All quotations from *Death at Balibo,* hereafter cited in the text, are from the unpublished playscript supplied to me by Graham Pitts. Graham's invaluable assistance is gratefully acknowledged.

13. "Batavia" refers to the Dutch colonial name for their "East Indies" colony, which became, after a resistance struggle, the Republic of Indonesia.

14. *Death at Balibo* had by the time of this incident already been filling the 140-seat Darwin Theatre Group venue six nights a week for two weeks, and it continued fully booked for a third week. Audiences included Anglo-Australians, Timorese, and others from the diverse Darwin community. Audience response was reported as powerfully emotional and appreciative. The Australian Journalists' Association is an active industrial union that strongly supported the show. Darwin journalists believe that the Indonesian journalists themselves were not personally offended so much as placed in a position where they were forced to react in defense of Indonesian national honor.

15. Compare the sensitivity of the Malaysian government to an ABC TV drama series, *Embassy,* set in the fictional nation of "Ragaan." See Suvendrini Perera, "Representation Wars: Malaysia, *Embassy,* and Australia's *Corps Diplomatique,*" in *Australian Cultural Studies: A Reader,* ed. John Frow and Meaghan Morris (Sydney: Allen and Unwin, 1993).

16. The company changed its name in early 1994 to Sidetrack Performance Group to signal further a change in the direction of the work. From 1979 to 1994, however, the company was Sidetrack Theatre Company.

17. I discuss this period of Sidetrack's work in my essay "Sidetrack: Discovering the Theatricality of Community," *New Theatre Quarterly* 11, no. 5 (1986): 80–89.

18. See chapter 1 of Stephen Muecke, *Textual Spaces: Aboriginality and Cultural Studies* (Sydney: New South Wales University Press, 1992).

19. All quotations from Don Mamouney are from a personal interview, 10 Feb. 1995.

20. Reynolds's work on the legal implications of prior black occupation and use of the Australian land helped prepare the ground for the recent landmark High Court Native Title decision, the Mabo decision. See Henry Reynolds, *The Law of the Land* (Ringwood, Vic.: Penguin, 1992). Reynolds's earlier research on black resistance was particularly important to the making of *Whispers.* See Henry Reynolds, *The Other Side of the Frontier: Aboriginal Resistance to the European Invasion of Australia* (Ringwood, Vic.: Penguin, 1982).

21. The scenes were given working titles—The Spectacle of Justice, The Morgue, The Measure, Government House, The Audience (With the Queen)—for use during devising and rehearsal but were not used in performance or referred to in the program.

Elaine Brousseau

Personalizing the Political in
The Noam Chomsky Lectures

It has long been a commonplace, popularized by late-1960s feminists, that the personal is political, that the experience, say, of being a single mother, or living in poverty, or being a corporate raider, is not just an individual experience but one very much connected to and determined by the distribution of power in political systems and in society. The late 1960s, the 1970s, and the 1980s have seen an outpouring of plays, many of them by women, in which the personal is represented as political. In *Wedding Band* (1966) by Alice Childress, for example, the interracial relationship between Julia and Herman in a South Carolina town in 1918 is played out against the prejudices of both whites and blacks and the cultural and legal restrictions that thwart their desire to marry. In Marsha Norman's *Getting Out* (1977), the ex-con Arlene Holsclaw, just released from prison, must deal with the ghosts of her past and make difficult choices about work and family as she faces the world outside of jail. But while these plays can certainly be read politically, they are not political in the way Graham Holderness defines the term *political theater*. Rather they are what he calls "political by accident," meaning that a play may "address political issues, in exactly the same way as a play can represent love, or old age, or poverty, or madness"—hence "political" without being "political theater." Political theater, on the other hand, is partisan, "lining up one particular political group, or cause, or ideology, and offering articulate opposition to another group, or cause, or ideology."[1] Holderness later goes on to suggest conflating this distinction between theater that is political and political theater by acknowledging "the kind of 'cultural materialism' that recognizes the essentially political nature of all drama."[2] But in postmodern theater practice, that is, theater informed by the conviction that there are no universal truths and that subject positions need to be foregrounded, political theater may take yet another turn. The feminist rediscovery of the political embedded in the personal seems now to reverse itself: the political becomes personal or, at least, personalized. Indeed, the more overtly political a dramatic "statement" is, the more intensely personal it may need to be. In a theater piece where the line between character and actor is virtually indistinguishable, the character/actor's political stand, if intended to change the way an audience thinks, can be convincing only to the extent that it becomes personalized. *The Noam Chomsky Lectures,* by Canadian actors and playwrights Daniel Brooks and Guillermo Verdecchia, is a brilliant and witty illustration of this paradigm. This dramatic work, which sets out to expose the "necessary illusions"[3] that citizens use as blinders in their dealings with government and social institutions, succeeds only because Brooks and Verdecchia reveal so much of themselves as well.

The Noam Chomsky Lectures can be viewed as a case study that raises a number of questions central to the discussion of political theater as an aesthetic experience. What does it mean to air political ideas—in this case, Chomsky's ideas—dramatically? Or, as Verdecchia put it when he explained the theatrical problem the two authors wanted the work to grapple with, "Can we speak overtly about politics in a theatrical context?"[4] If so, what makes this text emphatically a theater piece and not something else, not a lecture outlining a political agenda, nor what Chomsky himself identifies as "maybe a new genre . . . in the making"?[5] Is there a point at which political theater stops being theater and becomes the recital of a political agenda?

Indeed, there could hardly be a more self-consciously political play by any definition of political theater than *The Noam Chomsky Lectures,* an anti-illusionist dramatic piece described rather glibly by one critic as "a cross between *My Dinner with André* and *Rosencrantz and Guildenstern Are Dead.*"[6] The approximately one-hour play (different versions are of different duration) is, as the "characters" Brooks and Verdecchia explain at its start, "an attempt to bring to you some of the ideas present in the political writings of esteemed Professor Noam Chomsky, as well as some information you may not be familiar with. According to Chomsky, you are not familiar with it because the Western Press consistently caters to the interests of Big Business, because the Western Press *is* Big Business (14–15). *The Noam Chomsky Lectures* is structured basically as a dialogue between Brooks and Verdecchia about issues that have obsessed American linguist and public intellectual Noam Chomsky for years: namely, the "manufacturing of consent"[7] and the practice of "doublespeak" by U.S. media; U.S. imperialism in Latin America and other parts of the world; and state terrorism, among other issues. The play seeks to teach the audience how to read the information it receives from the media. As Verdecchia explains in the "Lecture" section of the play,

> Because we live in a democratic society, the information we have presented is available if one knows where to look, how to piece it together, and, most importantly, if one has the time to do so. The information does not appear in our mainstream press because of a combination of factors: pressures from advertisers, editorial pressures, inadequate information or directed misinformation from government sources, and the built-in ideological assumptions of the journalists themselves. These factors all contribute to historical engineering, or the manufacture of consent. (33–34)

The play is not narratively structured; rather the action consists of an onslaught of information about versions of history intended to get the audience to question its assumptions about the media, governmental policies, and the general goodwill of democratic states. Brooks's and Verdecchia's conversations and demonstrations are interspersed with slides and with occasional addresses to the audience. The dialogue is organized formally into nineteen "scenes" or sections: Introductions, Clarifications, Terms of the Show, History, A Play within the Play, History, Part Two, Universal Wit Factor, Intermission, Lecture, Manufacturing Consent, Response to Critics, The Auction, Audience Opinion Poll, Silence and Falling, Digression, Marketing Plan, Public Service Announcement, Dramaturgy, and Last Part. The set is a table on which Chomsky's books and a few other props, including a slide projector, are arranged;[8] the actors' conversations with each other are juxtaposed with the projection of slides displaying statistics, quotes from a number of sources, and examples of media coverage from then current events like the Gulf War. There are no "characters" as such; Brooks and Verdecchia "play" themselves, relating and interpreting history and current events and offering Noam Chomsky's views about how the world works.

In a real sense what the play does is present Chomsky—to dramatize his ideas—in an hour-long format for those without time, patience, or inclination to read his dozens of books. Although one reviewer rather dismissively characterized the play as "a quick and dirty reduction of Chomsky's systematic political and cultural analysis,"[9] it is hard for someone familiar with Chomsky's views to draw such a conclusion. The play brings to the forefront many of the political concerns Chomsky has spent a good part of his life lecturing and writing about, including his challenges to accepted thinking on terrorism and U.S. policies in Central America and the Middle East. Furthermore, the play succeeds in theatricalizing Chomsky's rhetorical method. Using their own words, Brooks and Verdecchia manage to convey the logic and rigor of Chomsky's positions on these issues, and to incorporate his distinctive rhetorical style: statement, followed by example after example, followed by overwhelming evidence, which often takes the form of copious footnotes. And yet the play's conversations also capture the flavor of the many interviews with David Barsamian in which Chomsky's sense of humor and his deep concern for democracy and for the future of humanity come across perhaps more clearly than they do in his densely argued books. In spite of his seemingly pessimistic views about corporate, media, and governmental control over American lives, Chomsky is passionately committed to the belief that informed citizens can effect change. In his conclusion to *Turning the Tide,* for example, a book that details the long and shameful history of the covert meddling by the United States in Central American internal affairs, particularly in Nicaragua, El Salvador, and Guatemala, Chomsky sounds a hopeful note, calling for the "honest search for understanding, education, organization . . . and the kind of commitment that will persist despite the temptations of disillusionment, despite many failures and only limited successes, inspired by the hope of a brighter future."[10] And, at the start of the Gulf War in 1991, Chomsky said that he was encouraged by the level of very early protests against the war, comparing these protests with the early years of the Vietnam conflict and the then almost total absence of opposition. Over the years, Chomsky's ideas and writings have demanded that Americans "have the integrity to look into the mirror without evasion."[11] As he told a Canadian interviewer in 1983,

> I'm not trying to convert, but to inform. I don't want people to believe me, any more than they should believe the party line I'm criticizing— academic authority, the media, the overt state propagandists, or whatever. In talks and in print, I try to stress what I think is true: that with a little willingness to explore and use one's mind, it is possible to discover a good deal about the social and political world that is generally hidden. I feel that I've achieved something if people are encouraged to take up this challenge and learn for themselves.[12]

The Noam Chomsky Lectures attempts to make the ideas and method of Noam Chomsky more widely known among Canadians. The play was developed as part of the Buddies in Bad Times Rhubarb! Festival at the

Annex Theatre in Toronto in February 1990, with the original version only twenty minutes long. To date, all performances of the play have been in Canada, specifically in Toronto and Ottawa. The published play is the version given during a two-week run at Theatre Passe Muraille in 1991.[13] This first performance was for an arts crowd, presumably not familiar with Chomsky's ideas. The two authors, in Verdecchia's words, wanted to "get a political discourse going in the theatre community," but audiences for subsequent performances came from a wide age range and also were drawn from different classes and backgrounds.[14]

In developing *The Noam Chomsky Lectures,* Brooks and Verdecchia were always highly conscious that they were writing and performing for Canadian audiences, that they needed to particularize the Chomsky material. The problem of how to contextualize Chomsky's ideas for a Canadian audience was a pressing one. As Brooks told Jason Sherman, "For years, I'd been struggling with how to do political theatre. I'd hated Canadian political theatre, hated it. It had no context."[15] Chomsky is, after all, an American intellectual whose principal concern is to awaken Americans to the activities, especially foreign-policy activities, of their own government and to expose the extent to which the media, under the guise of objectivity, actually presents only a very narrow spectrum of ideological opinion. Although Chomsky has lectured over Canadian radio, the authors could not assume his ideas were widely known.[16] What they did recognize was that Canadians had some "necessary illusions" as well. Verdecchia points out that Canadians have their own national myths, thinking of themselves falsely, for example, as a nation of peacekeepers. This point the play makes insistently: as the Verdecchia "character" says in the "Lecture" section of the play, "our [Canada's] reputation as a peacekeeper is still very strong. Our reputation as a peacekeeper, as a nation of quiet diplomats, is consistently reinforced by our mainstream press, and by our political leaders" (28). The "Lecture" section goes on to challenge this notion by examining Canadian policy during the Vietnam conflict, Canada's support of the Indonesian invasion of East Timor in 1975, and successive governments' nonaction in opposing apartheid in South Africa. The examples he cites "reveal that the real Canadian traditions are quiet complicity and hypocritical moral posturing" (33). Canadians generally don't see themselves as complicitous with U.S. policies—and Chomsky's methods of exposing these blind spots help them to understand themselves and their country's positions more clearly. As Brooks pointed out to interviewer Jason Sherman, the two authors weren't preaching to the converted with this theater piece: "I can't imagine that more than 10% of the Fringe audience, for example, had any idea of the details of American involvement in Central America or the false assumptions that the mass media makes."[17]

What makes the *Lectures* theater—and makes Chomsky's ideas work so well in a theatrical context—is the way theater affords these authors the opportunity to make them vivid, to give opportunities for what the text of *The Noam Chomsky Lectures* calls "demonstration." For example, the "Manufacturing Consent" section of the play (taken from the title of the 1988 book Chomsky wrote with Edward S. Herman) juxtaposes elements of Chomsky's ideas with "theatrical demonstration" of those ideas (34). To demonstrate the way placement of news items in the print media determines whether people even read them, the audience is shown a slide of a two-page spread from *The Toronto Star,* one page of which is a full-page ad for a retail chain. An article about the U.S. government illegally hiding documents from the lawyers of Panamanian dictator Manuel Noriega is placed at the very bottom of the page. In another example of how the media buries certain issues while making sure others are given play, Verdecchia puts his head in a trash can and speaks about the American invasion of Panama while Brooks drowns him out talking about, among other things, the ad publicizing a storewide sale. To demonstrate the use by the media of biased sources (for example, reliance by the media on the Pentagon information service and the media's presentation of this information as "truth" without questioning it), Verdecchia reads a comical, adulatory review of *The Noam Chomsky Lectures* that he wrote himself, comparing the work to Shakespeare and Zola and praising the actors as "consummate performers" as well as applauding their "exquisite haircuts" and costumes (40). To illustrate how the media encourages readers to make ideological assumptions—for example, the assumption made in mainstream press news stories that the American invasion of Panama was a defense of democracy—Brooks and Verdecchia demonstrate to the audience the falseness of its theatrical assumptions. The two actors throw paper balls and squirt water at the audience when the lights go out, because "we . . . will assume that you, the audience, will assume that we, the actors, won't throw anything at you or squirt water at you when we turn off the lights" (38). Clearly, politics is theatricalized in these demonstrations of how the media sets the limits of permitted discourse.

The Noam Chomsky Lectures is not only theatrical, but also highly conscious of itself as a theater piece. Playing with the definition of theater, it lurks along the boundaries—and challenges the very existence of those boundaries—between "art" and "propaganda." One of the props used in the play is the Artstick (described in the stage directions as "an elaborately decorated bamboo stick"), which Verdecchia explains "will be used by either Daniel or myself whenever one of the performers crosses that fine line between art and demagoguery" (13). But the Artstick "demonstration" that follows shows instead that the speaker is considered to cross the line into demagoguery whenever his political comments veer away from accepted mainstream opinion. The performers also occasionally resort to the Whistle of Indignation, which is blown to silence, as the Artstick does, emotionally charged political opinion. The performers metatheatrically incorporate audience comments and the reviews of Toronto theater critics, including the latter's criterion for good theater, into the work,[18] and they think aloud of making the play a more economically successful venture, coming up with a comical "marketing plan" that includes getting some big names on stage (including Wayne Gretzky to play Noam Chomsky) so that they can "increase the profile of the show" (60). Brooks also speculates about how they can profitably increase the "sexual content" of the show, getting Verdecchia to take off his shirt for starters. The two attempt definitions of theater during the course of the play as well: at one point Brooks offers "what is theatre but a bunch of people in a room together, some who pay, some who get paid" (60), while Verdecchia protests, "Some of you may be thinking that what we have embarked on here is not theatre. Well, that's too bad. I would like to say this: if the theatre is to survive, it must become something other than an expensive alternative to television" (59).

Descriptions of the play cannot convey the energetic pace of *The Noam Chomsky Lectures,* apparent even in a reading of the printed version, and a feature noted even by less than enthusiastic reviewers of the Toronto productions. Theater critic Liam Lacey observed that the creators try "to keep the information flowing at the lively pace of a TV news magazine," while Robert Cushman's generally favorable review in *The Globe and Mail* pointed out that *The Noam Chomsky Lectures* "is not the kind of piece that needs [an intermission]." Description and scattered quotes also fail to convey the play's humor. Brooks and Verdecchia comically attempt to analyze the worth of the play by using the Universal Wit Factor Chart and applying the "yucks-per-bucks quotient," a standard that one Toronto theater critic had developed to evaluate other theater productions.

As the previous discussion of theatrical demonstration and the play's metatheatrical musings has made clear, *The Noam Chomsky Lectures* is a play and not a lecture, but the authors, who have transformed their source material, still correctly invite the "lecture" comparison. To a certain extent, of course, *The Noam Chomsky Lectures is* like a lecture—prepared, controlled, rehearsed. As in a formal lecture, there is no room for audience participation or response (except for the very last moment of the play, when audience members are instructed to end the play by having one of their number call out "Light"). The questions that Brooks and Verdecchia pose to the audience are rhetorical, something Brooks even admits during the so-called "Audience Opinion Poll" section of the play. But while an actual lecture may be aware of itself as a lecture (i.e., the lecturer self-consciously performing), it generally doesn't convey that sense of aware-ness to its listeners. Comparing this play to a lecture does suggest a feature of both genres that a personal recollection will perhaps help illuminate. In January 1991, I saw Noam Chomsky lecture in Cambridge, Massachusetts, one week after the U.S.-led coalition forces commenced bombing missions against Iraq. Chomsky was scheduled to speak about Latin America, but the urgency of the Persian Gulf situation prompted him to change his topic. He spoke without notes but seemed to have a ready command of dates and statistics. His manner was highly engaged and yet calm and ratio-nal, never strident. I remember listening to him for well over an hour (he spoke for a time and then took questions from the audience) and leaving the auditorium exhilarated; I remarked to my companion that I felt as though someone had opened up my brain and blew fresh air through it. I felt this way even though I had been reading Chomsky's books for several years and so was already aware of his thinking on U.S. foreign policy and media manipulation. Yet, the military and political situation in the Gulf was a new topic, and nothing I had been reading or hearing about the Gulf War had cut through the government obfuscation the way Chomsky's talk did. His talk resulted in action as well: I traveled to Washington, D.C., that weekend to march in the protest against the Gulf War.

It seems to me that Brooks and Verdecchia are trying, within an artis-tic context, to give their audiences the sense of fresh air that can come from a direct contact with Chomsky's ideas in the context of urgent political issues. In *Lectures,* they create political theater that is not a narrative of injus-tice but something far more direct. This focus on theater as offering a direct experience invites comparison between what Brooks and Verdecchia try to do in *The Noam Chomsky Lectures* and what playwrights like Emily Mann and Anna Deavere Smith do with pieces like *Execution of Justice* and *Fires in the Mirror.* Mann, who thinks of herself as a political playwright, attempts a "theatre of testimony" in her plays *Still Life,* about Vietnam and domestic violence, and *Execution of Justice,* about the murder by Dan White of San Francisco mayor George Moscone and city supervisor Harvey Milk. Like *The Noam Chomsky Lectures, Still Life* is also a "table play," a self-described

FIG. 16. Guillermo Verdecchia *(left)* blows the Whistle of Indignation at the gesticulating Daniel Brooks in *The Noam Chomsky Lectures. (Photo courtesy of Guillermo Verdecchia.)*

documentary in which the three characters sit at a conference table and speak directly to the audience. In the "Author's Note" to her play, Mann says that, for the most part, she has used the words of three people she met in Minnesota, perhaps in much the same way that Brooks and Verdecchia use the words and analysis of Noam Chomsky.[19] She juxtaposes sections of monologues (except in a few instances, characters do not speak to each other) to make clear to the audience the connections she sees between different speakers' stories, just as Brooks and Verdecchia juxtapose Chomsky's ideas with examples from their own experiences to clarify the connections between government, media, and theater. But while Mann says that her plays "are about asking the audience to face [the information the play gives] and to actively question it," something that *The Noam Chomsky Lectures* also clearly does, she relies on narrative, insisting that the audience "must be sucked in by their emotions and love for story," that they "must experience the information in a visceral way so that they don't notice they are using their intellect."[20] So while Mann's "theater of testimony" does aim at giving the audience a direct experience with the event, it directs itself as much to the emotions (through its use of poetic language and imagery and juxta-position of voices) as to the intellect. The play by Brooks and Verdecchia, on the other hand, does not recognize the distinction between theater and agitprop that Mann makes when she explains why she didn't use the word *homophobic* in *Execution of Justice:* "I had a whole speech about it in an earlier draft, but I felt it was agitprop and decided to try to say something about it without naming it. That was a challenge I gave myself and I think the point is made stronger."[21]

Anna Deavere Smith's avowed aim in her one-woman performance pieces *Fires in the Mirror,* which delves beneath the surface of the Crown Heights conflict,[22] and *Twilight: Los Angeles, 1992,* which explores the after-math of the verdict in the Rodney King case, is "to develop a kind of the-ater that could be more sensitive to the events of my own time than tradi-tional theater could."[23] Although some have called her work journalism, Smith sees these pieces solidly as theater and in the tradition of social drama, although she doesn't use the term *political theater* to describe her work. Smith's method is to conduct extensive interviews with people connected to an event she is interested in exploring and then "perform[ing] the inter-viewees on stage using their own words" (*Twilight,* xvii). She does this by actually "inhabit[ing] the speech pattern of another, walk[ing] in the speech of another."[24] And, indeed, using the actual speech of others gives her per-formance texts "an authority they could never achieve as theatrical fictions."[25] While not tied to narrative the way Mann is in her political plays, Smith's work is character-focused in a way that *Lectures* isn't. Like Brooks and Verdecchia in *The Noam Chomsky Lectures,* Smith wants her work to make a difference—she wants people to talk about the work and perhaps be changed by it: "I performed it *[Twilight]* at a time when the community had not yet resolved the problems. I wanted to be a part of their examination of the problems" (*Twilight,* xxiv).

The Noam Chomsky Lectures also harks back to and invites comparison with Brecht's concept of epic theater, the appeal to reason instead of feel-ings in a kind of theater that sought to transform society. It could in fact be said that Brooks and Verdecchia have put together a dramatic work that cre-ates the kind of audience that Brecht imagined, an audience able to separate emotion from reason and to look critically at a play, not identifying with characters but seeing them as part of social and political situations that were capable of being changed. Epic theater "must report," Brecht insisted; in a statement that suggests an affinity with *The Noam Chomsky Lectures,* he con-tinued, "I give the incidents baldly so that the audience can think for itself. That's why I need a quick-witted audience that knows how to observe, and gets its enjoyment from setting its reason to work."[26] Brecht would also come to the rescue of a play grappling with the charge of didacticism: "Theatre remains theatre even while it is didactic," Brecht claimed, "and as long as it is good theatre it is also entertaining."[27]

If it is clear that *The Noam Chomsky Lectures* is an aesthetic experience, what about its political aim to make the members of the audience challenge their assumptions? Is it possible to calculate the political efficacy of a dramatic work? There was no attempt at any of the stagings of this play to chart audience reactions in any formal way: the authors simply talked to people after performances. According to Verdecchia, "the general response to the play [from audiences] was very positive, very positive." Some of those who had seen *Lectures* would send the authors material, which Brooks and Verdecchia would consider incorporating into future performances. Thus a kind of dialogue opened up between authors and members of the audience, some of whom chose to continue the conversation. That these exchanges took place frequently is evident from the authors' acknowledgment in the printed version of the play to "all the individuals who spoke to us after performances to correct facts and challenge our argument." Brooks is adamant that the work of theater needs to extend beyond the theater walls: "Alas, the most provocative ideas in the theatre tend to have a life span of two hours. Theatre should not happen only on the stage. It should happen in the lobby of the theatre, in the bars before and after, in kitchens and cars, in the physical and mental spaces of the world in which we live."[28] Emily Mann and Anna Deavere Smith also see their forms of political theater as contributing to a process of audience understanding or, as in the case of Smith's *Twilight*, reconciliation. Of *Twilight*, Smith says, "I see the work as a call. I played *Twilight* in Los Angeles as a call to the community" (xxiv).

In thinking about Brooks's and Verdecchia's play as a paradigm for politically efficacious theater, matters of audience and audience reaction are key. But while possible to gather audience reaction to the dramatic work, measuring political impact is far more complex. As Brooks points out, the political efficacy of the dramatic work is "impossible to measure." Anyone searching too hard for a yardstick to measure the effectiveness of political theater might do well to recall Brecht's remark that "it would be quite wrong to judge a play's relevance or lack of relevance by its current effectiveness. Theatres don't work that way."[29] While impossible to accurately gauge political efficacy, looking at the attention the play and its actor/authors garnered is one way to register political impact. In 1992, *The Noam Chomsky Lectures* won a Chalmers Outstanding New Play Award and was nominated for the Governor General's Award for Drama. Two years later, Guillermo Verdecchia, now living in Vancouver, received the Governor's General Award for his acclaimed one-man show *Fronteras Americanas (American Borders)*, a semiautobiographical theater piece in which the Argentinean-born Verdecchia struggles with the displacements that accompany emigration; he is currently at work on a new piece, *A Line in the Sand*, about Arab-West relations. Daniel Brooks, who continues as coartistic director of the Augusta Company in Toronto, was featured in a *Canadian Theatre Review* interview that focused in particular on his work on *The Noam Chomsky Lectures*. The play was reviewed in the *Toronto Star* and more than once in the *Globe and Mail*; the latter's Robert Cushman conceded that even the publicity for the play, which he initially thought was "pretentious garbage," turned out to be neither: "It [the publicity] is high-flown, yes, but it isn't pretentious; and, fairly far from being garbage, it is a good 70 per cent accurate"—this admission from the critic of a mainstream publication.[30] Although a play's popularity is not equivalent to its political efficacy, it is possible to chart a play's "notice," to chronicle the "attention-gettingness" of a dramatic work, and important to do so.

Verdecchia says that, in *The Noam Chomsky Lectures*, "We tried to deconstruct everything we could possibly deconstruct." For starters, this meant deconstructing expectations about the play's form. Early in the play, Daniel Brooks emphasizes its unfinished nature: "First let me state that *The Noam Chomsky Lectures* is a perpetual workshop, an unfinished play, a fourth draft, a work in progress; hence, you are a workshop audience, an audience in progress; hence, this is not a real play, you are not a real audience" (12). This conception of the play as unfinished, as constantly in progress, means that its content is always being changed. According to Verdecchia, the authors will "never run out of material." The piece will "be always more or less current, examining the necessary illusions at work in our media."[31] Although the show "doesn't date," says Verdecchia, "references become hazy." For example, the printed version of the play freezes in time a performance of the play that took place in March 1991, one that makes many references to the recently concluded Gulf War. A production today might still choose to include a section on coverage of the Gulf War, which illustrates very well Chomsky's point about how the media manipulates information. However, as Verdecchia explained, if they were to use that material in a production now, they would have to spend a fair amount of stage time contextualizing the Gulf War. At the time, no special contextualization was needed because the Gulf War was ever-present in the media; references were fresh in the minds of the audience. Brooks notes that a performance of the play today "would change fairly drastically in tone" as well. Although the political beliefs of the two authors have not changed, their lives in the theater world have. "We were obscure nobodies" when *The Noam Chomsky Lectures* was developed, Brooks admits, or, as he puts it in the play, "Guillermo Verdecchia and Daniel Brooks are not exactly household names" (60). Now "we're no longer [theatrical] underdogs," but the piece as it stands still "has the sensibility of the underdog."[32] Because the two have put so much of their theater lives into the piece, they would need to change the somewhat sour-grapes tone that conveyed their previous feelings of unimportance to accommodate their changed standing in the theater community.

Deconstructing everything means that the performance sets out to deconstruct even the information audiences receive during the performance by challenging the veracity of the deliverers of that information. The two actors do this by revealing information (secrets?) about each other—sexual, personal, theatrical. For example, in a hilarious parody of the Canadian corporation-media flow chart the two discuss earlier, Brooks reveals a "sexual flow chart" of his friends in the Toronto theater community: "The boxes on the chart represent people, and the lines connecting the boxes represent sexual linkages or corporal mergers between the people" (52). Brooks's friends are indicated on the chart only by their initials, although he indicates to the audience the position of GV (Guillermo Verdecchia): "Now let's trace the most direct route from me to Guillermo. As you can see, I slept with this person, this person slept with that person, that person slept with this person, and this person slept with Guillermo. . . . I think this gives us a hint of a rather strong inter-linkage between Guillermo and myself, a kind of shared corporal interest" (53). In its parody of the earlier flow chart demonstrating media-corporate linkages, the sexual flow chart suggests the who-is-sleeping-with-whom-ness of the corporation-media world while at the same time exposing the personal lives of the authors. The two expose their own hypocrisies as well—or, more precisely, Brooks exposes Verdecchia's. At one point, Brooks gets Verdecchia to admit if he "does drugs" and later reminds Verdecchia of his previous association with another play and opportunist remark, "I can't afford to be critical of a play when I am working on it" (85). In the printed version of the play, Brooks takes jabs at Verdecchia, but, as he told Jason Sherman, "There's lots about me for Guillermo to talk about. All he has to do is find out about it."[33]

The sexual flow chart and other personal disclosures have the power to undercut the more public political information in the text precisely because how much audience members accept of the Chomsky material is intimately bound up with how much they accept Brooks and Verdecchia, the deliverers of that information. In a postmodern world, revealing one's own agenda is crucial and necessary, because, as the play makes clear, "facts" are not neutral, and news-gathering organizations and persons are not objective; hence, Brooks and Verdecchia themselves are not automatically to be trusted. It is difficult, then, to see how Lisa Coulthard, in her recent essay about the play, can maintain that Brooks and Verdecchia do not apply "their own standards of critical reading and viewing to the reading and viewing of their own texts."[34] As I have shown above, Brooks and Verdecchia do precisely this—both theatrically, by undercutting themselves as deliverers of information, and directly through language, as when Verdecchia acknowledges in the "Response to Critics" section of the play, "We have . . . been told that we condemn Western, especially American, atrocities, but ignore Soviet crimes. We have been criticized for being one-sided" (51).

Because of the intimate connection between teller and tale, Verdecchia says that it would seem strange to have someone else perform the play: to have others doing the show, "they'll have to pretend they're us," he points out. "It's crucial that it's Daniel and I up there that have put our politics on the line. It's really us up there being implicated."[35] For this reason, although there have been inquiries from others who wanted to stage the play, the piece has never been done by anyone else. (Two Seattle linguists had one-time permission to perform parts of the play at a conference, and Brooks said that a friend of his gave a reading of sections of the piece in Paris.)

This bond between the dramatic work and the creators/performers raises questions about the actor and the role that have not really been explored in this essay. Why couldn't other actors take on the roles of "Brooks" and "Verdecchia"? On the one hand, this seems a possibility. After all, in the current version, the performers stress the forever unfinished nature of the play; their constant revisions and different versions of the play even for audiences within Canada suggest that the political play needs constant updating and revision, that there must be an interchange between what's current in the lives of the audience (e.g., the Gulf War, the Toronto theater scene) and the ideas that Chomsky puts forth. With this constant updating already under way for each performance of *The Noam Chomsky Lectures,* it might seem possible, then, to have other actors take on these "roles." But that's the difficulty. Although "Brooks" and "Verdecchia" in the play technically are roles, that is, characters with personae distinct from those of the actors themselves, the line between actor and role is so fine as to blur the normal distinction between actor and character.[36] Brooks and Verdecchia give the audience a mediated view of history and political events that problematizes their positions as characters. They project personalities more than they do personae, personalities for whom the political has become intensely personal—and needs to be, if the audience is to trust them and be moved to action. Because a person's political position is caught up with other subject positions, revealing a political stand necessarily requires disclosing one's personal agendas, like the career embarrassments and ambitions and the sexual-power connections that Brooks and Verdecchia reveal in this play.

It could be argued that Brooks and Verdecchia actually do not reveal that much about themselves during the course of the play, that what the audience sees of their personal selves is not really that personal—just complaining about their movements up and down the career ladder and exposing what could be interpreted as fictional or exaggerated sexual adventures. After all, the audience does not come to understand anything that could be considered truly "personal" about their lives, at least not in the sense that we've come to understand that word; there is nothing here about their relationships, their hopes and fears, their innermost thoughts. While perhaps the case, the objection itself shortsightedly genders the idea of the personal exclusively as female, associating the personal with the domestic, with the inner life. When Verdecchia says that he and Brooks have put "our politics on the line" in this play and that "it is really us up there being implicated," he is acknowledging his sense of having revealed himself in some way and the extent to which the political opinions themselves have become personalized ("our politics"). But the language is revelatory: the expression of putting something "on the line" connotes more of a laying down the gauntlet, a "male" willingness to argue one's position than it does baring one's soul or having a heart-to-heart talk. Indeed, throughout the play, there is a kind of "male" swagger to the revelations, a bravado that disguises the sense of the personal and masks insecurities.

Because it is imperative that the audience trust the givers of information in this play, it is a stretch to imagine how this work could be convincing if performed by others acting out "Brooks" and "Verdecchia" without sharing their characteristics, their foibles, their convictions.[37] Although Daniel Brooks can imagine someone taking the *idea* of this play and writing a different, but similar, play, it seems reasonable to conclude that, because of the interconnectedness between the dramatic work and the creators/performers in a politically committed play like *The Noam Chomsky Lectures,* the play performed by actors other than its creators would lose its power. Far from being a limiting notion, the idea is actually a liberating one because it allows the play to resist commodification as a script to be bought, sold, and performed in the theatrical marketplace. What Brooks says about *Indulgence,* a play he developed with other members of the Augusta Company, could also be said about *The Noam Chomsky Lectures:* "We don't trust the authority of a script. The written word has attained a kind of reverence in the theatre. We're interested in spreading authority around."[38] If *The Noam Chomsky Lectures* offers a different model for theatrical performances—openly political and ideological, popular and wittily entertaining, and requiring constant political analysis and revision—it also issues a challenge to those who would create meaningful political theater to develop alternative ways of structuring vision and stirring activism.

NOTES

1. Graham Holderness, *The Politics of Theatre and Drama* (New York: St. Martin's Press, 1992), 2.

2. Holderness, *Politics of Theatre,* 15.

3. The phrase is from Noam Chomsky's *Necessary Illusions: Thought Control in Democratic Societies* (Boston: South End Press, 1989) and refers to those false beliefs that sustain citizens in a democracy—for example, Americans' belief in the freedom of the press and in the objectivity of the media, or their belief that their government helps to promote democracy in the foreign countries in which it intervenes.

4. Guillermo Verdecchia, telephone interview, 17 Feb. 1995.

5. Daniel Brooks and Guillermo Verdecchia, *The Noam Chomsky Lectures: A Play* (Toronto: Coach House Press, 1991). Chomsky's quote appears on the back cover of this published version of the play, references to which are cited parenthetically within the text.

6. Robert Cushman, "Critics Hit with Tactical, Strategic Attacks," *Globe and Mail,* 22 Mar. 1991, C10.

7. The phrase "manufacturing consent" comes from *Manufacturing Consent: The Political Economy of the Mass Media* by Chomsky and Edward S. Herman (New York: Pantheon, 1988), which discusses how, in democratic societies where the government cannot control speech, the government attempts to use the media to bring about public consensus on policy. (The phrase was first used in 1921 by Walter Lippmann in *Public Opinion.*) As Chomsky says in *Language and Politics* (Montreal: Black Rose Books, 1988), "One of the ways you control what people think is by creating a debate so it looks like there's a debate going on, but making sure that debate stays within very narrow margins, namely you have to make sure that both sides in the debate accept certain assumptions, and those assumptions turn out to be the propaganda system. As long as everyone accepts the propaganda system, then you can have a debate" (672).

8. The actors are careful to distinguish themselves from the Wooster Group, which also does "table plays," and they say later that they "don't want *The Noam Chomsky Lectures* to turn into just another silly post-modern push-up" (14).

9. Liam Lacey, "Walking the Line of Childhood Fear," *Globe and Mail,* 25 Sept. 1991, C5.

10. Noam Chomsky, *Turning the Tide: US Intervention in Central America and the Struggle for Peace* (Boston: South End Press, 1985), 253.

11. Noam Chomsky, *The Culture of Terrorism* (Boston: South End Press, 1988), 3.

12. Noam Chomsky, *Language and Politics,* ed. C. P. Otero (Montreal: Black Rose Books, 1988), 389.

13. Toronto's Theatre Passe Muraille has had a reputation since the 1960s of developing alternative and especially improvisational theater pieces. See Denis W. Johnston, *Up the Mainstream: The Rise of Toronto's Alternative Theatres, 1968–1975* (Toronto: University of Toronto Press, 1991).

14. Unless otherwise indicated, my knowledge of the production history of the play and the reactions of audiences to it are drawn from my conversations with Guillermo Verdecchia in February 1995, and Daniel Brooks in February 1995 and July 1996; unless otherwise attributed, quotations from Brooks and Verdecchia are also from these conversations.

15. Jason Sherman, "The Daniel Brooks Lectures," *Canadian Theatre Review* 67 (summer 1991): 19.

16. For example, the five chapters that make up *Necessary Illusions* are versions of lectures Chomsky delivered in November 1988 over Canadian Broadcasting Corporation radio. Chomsky's relative obscurity may change now that he has become a favorite with some rock musicians; the group Bad Religion, for example, put a Chomsky lecture on the B-side of one of its singles. See R. J. Lambrose, "Chomsky Unplugged," *Lingua Franca,* May–June 1996, 10.

17. Sherman, "The Daniel Brooks Lectures," 21.

18. A slide that flashes on the screen during the performance quotes Robert Crew, drama critic for the *Toronto Star,* who refers to "some of the fundamentals of theatre, like communication, honest emotion, engagement, and commitment to the characters on the stage"—criteria that Verdecchia in the play describes as "Robert's Rules" (14).

19. Emily Mann, *Still Life: A Documentary* (New York: Dramatists Play Service, 1982), 7.

20. Kathleen Betsko and Rachel Koenig, eds., *Interviews with Contemporary Women Playwrights* (New York: William Morrow, 1987), 277–78.

21. Betsko and Koenig, *Interviews,* 279.

22. The Crown Heights incident involved the killing on 19 August 1991 in Crown Heights, Brooklyn, of Gavin Cato, a seven-year-old black boy from Guyana, by a car driven by a Lubavitcher Jew, and the subsequent fatal stabbing of a young Hasidic scholar, Yankel Rosenbaum, by a group of young black men.

23. Anna Deavere Smith, *Twilight: Los Angeles, 1992* (New York: Doubleday, 1994), xxii. References to the play and Smith's introduction hereafter cited in the text. It is interesting to note that Emily Mann directed the first performance of this piece, which took place in Los Angeles in May 1993.

24. Anna Deavere Smith, *Fires in the Mirror: Crown Heights, Brooklyn, and Other Identities* (New York: Doubleday, 1993), xxvii.

25. Charles R. Lyons and James C. Lyons, "Anna Deavere Smith: Perspectives on Her Performance within the Context of Critical Theory," *Journal of Dramatic Theory and Criticism* 9, no. 1 (1994): 54.

26. Bertolt Brecht, *Brecht on Theatre,* ed. and trans. John Willett (New York: Hill and Wang, 1964), 14. Willett points out that the interview this quotation is drawn from

is not in Brecht's own words, but that the interviewer translated very loosely to have Brecht speaking in what the interviewer called "normal language."

27. Brecht, *Brecht on Theatre,* 80.

28. Daniel Brooks, "De(CON)struction: A Provocation about the State of Canadian Theatre," *Theatrum Magazine,* June–July–August 1993, 7–8.

29. Brecht, *Brecht on Theatre,* 7.

30. In his review, Cushman says that the press handout for *The Noam Chomsky Lectures* "describes the show as 'a metatheatrical onslaught . . . unrelenting and sometimes rabid,' adding that it 'reaffirms the theatre as a place of dissent' and 'will radically alter your understanding of the theatre, the mainstream media, yourself and the world you live in'" ("Critics Hit," C10).

31. The two playwright-actors haven't done a performance of *The Noam Chomsky Lectures* in the last few years, but because the play's topicality can be easily altered, they don't think of the piece as dated.

32. For example, in the play *Verdecchia,* in discussing the connections between the media, business, and the banking communities, underscores his powerlessness when he considers exerting "some pressure on the CIBC [Canadian Imperial Bank of Commerce] by threatening to withdraw the remaining $47.26 from *The Noam Chomsky Lectures* account" (18–19). Continuing to discuss the corporations-media connections, he points out that the powerful Ken Thomson, president and chairman of Thomson Newspapers "and one of the richest men in the world," attended Upper Canada College, as did Daniel Brooks, but Brooks "is a director of an obscure Kensington Market Theatre company. . . . they're not on this chart" (20).

33. Daniel Brooks, qtd. in Sherman, "The Daniel Brooks Lectures," 21.

34. Lisa Coulthard, "'The Line's Getting Mighty Blurry': Politics, Polemics, and Performance in *The Noam Chomsky Lectures,*" *Studies in Canadian Literature* 20, no. 2 (1995): 54.

35. Verdecchia's one-man show *Fronteras Americanas* works in a way similar to *The Noam Chomsky Lectures,* except that the actor has two stage personae: himself (the "Verdecchia" character) and Wideload McKennah (Facundo Morales Segundo), an inflated stereotype of the Latino, who actually ends up deflating stereotypes. As he did with the Chomsky material, Verdecchia made changes to the piece nightly in performance, depending on location, audience, mood, etc. See Guillermo Verdecchia, *Fronteras Americanas* (Toronto: Coach House Press, 1993).

36. Xerxes Mehta's distinctions between actors and performers in performance art are somewhat useful, although Brooks and Verdecchia in *The Noam Chomsky Lectures* diverge from his definition of performers as much as they inhabit it. See Xerxes Mehta, "Performance Art: Problems of Description and Evaluation," *Journal of Dramatic Theory and Criticism* 5, no. 1 (1990): 187–99.

37. Smith's *Fires in the Mirror,* which was recently given a performance at Trinity Repertory Company in Providence, Rhode Island, by two actresses (one white, one African-American), *can* be done by performers other than Smith because she plays other people, not herself.

38. Qtd. in Sherman, "The Daniel Brooks Lectures," 18.

Harry J. Elam Jr. and Alice Rayner

Body Parts: Between Story and Spectacle in *Venus* by Suzan-Lori Parks

If there were ever a plot to evoke pity and fear, it would be the story of Saartje Baartman, the Khoikhoi woman who was brought from South Africa to England in 1810 by the trader Hendrik Ceza Boer, put on exhibition in a sideshow, arrested for prostitution, subjected to public medical analysis, and dismembered after her death. Advertised as the Hottentot Venus, she was known for her prodigious buttocks and her distended labia. Accounts tell of her being exhibited like an animal and paraded by her "keeper" in a public spectacle.

It was not uncommon to exhibit Hottentot women in Europe, but the Hottentot Venus stands as a singular emblem for figuring nineteenth-century colonial discourse on race and sexuality. The exhibitions reinforced the notions of pre-Victorian science that associated blackness with animality and deviant sexuality. The advertised image of the Venus combined the myth of the Roman goddess of love, the source of desire and seductress, with the myth of Hottentots, sign of primitive, promiscuous Africans. At once bizarre and exotic, the Venus Hottentot elicited desire and disgust; she fascinated science as much as prurient public curiosity. As Sander Gilman points out, "the figure of Sarah Baartman [*sic*] was reduced to her sexual parts. . . . her genitalia and buttocks serve as the central image of the black female throughout the nineteenth century."[1] Her body represented and reflected the common idea of a need to contain and control the barbaric, sexualized Other.[2] It is difficult to say which is more horrifying: the popular and scientific beliefs of the time or the public display.

Many details of her story are uncertain, conditioned as they are by nineteenth-century beliefs. It is not altogether clear, and was not even at the time, whether to consider Baartman a willing partner in her spectacle, or an exploited victim; whether to acknowledge her right to display herself or to

FIG. 17. Adina Porter as the Venus with the Chorus of the Spectators in Richard Foreman's 1996 production at the New York Public Theatre. *(Photo by T. Charles Erikson.)*

try to save her from herself. Apparently jailed for indecency and prostitution, it remains unclear whether she died of pneumonia, alcoholism, tuberculosis, or syphilis. Her death did not end the display or the controversy. After autopsies performed by Cuvier and Henri de Blainville, the preserved remains of her skeleton, brain, and genitalia were kept by the Musée de l'Homme in Paris, where they were exhibited as recently as 1994 as part of a documentation of "the harsh, racist portrayal of aboriginal peoples by nineteenth-century painters and sculptors."[3]

Even in death, in other words, Baartman's display shows how spectacle serves to confirm, as well as to constitute, a culture's beliefs. The use of her body as spectacle raises questions about the degree to which the body is a site of resistance to cultural discourse. The exhibitions in 1815 and 1994 encapsulate further questions about the meaning of her body, for they raise questions about the *rights* to both meaning and display. In 1996, the Griqua National Conference, descendants of the Khoikhoi, petitioned the Musée de l'Homme for the return of Baartman's dismembered body for burial. Spokesman for the Griquas, Mansell Upham, justified the demand by stating that Baartman is "a potent symbol of the dismemberment and dehu-

manization of the original people of South Africa. She's a human being who
has been denied the right to dignity after death."[4] It is not entirely certain,
however, that Baartman was an actual member of the Khoikhoi, so possession of her body continues to beg questions of ownership and meaning of
the body. Who has the right to her body? To represent the body? To view
the body? To possess the body? Whose body is it, anyway? Such questions
ask for an interrogation of the notion of political resistance in terms not only
of the body on display but of the roles of critic and audience.

With her play *Venus,* Suzan-Lori Parks brings the story of Saartje
Baartman to the stage and in doing so raises the same kinds of questions
raised by the display of Baartman during her life. There can hardly be a
more concrete example of how European beliefs about African nature were
created by self-fulfilling images and the complicity between prurient curiosity and science. What more, then, could Parks's play add to the obviously
objectionable racial and sexual exploitation of Baartman? Is it enough to
document her history on stage? What is the use of showing again the spectacle of her body? As Una Chaudhuri asks, "When working on this story is
there a danger of repeating the original violation?"[5] Parks theatrically resur-
rects the body of the Venus and doing so places her in the liminal space of
theater, neither live nor dead, caught between the texts of Baartman's life
and the illusions of theatrical representation. On the one hand, Parks's stage
presentation recuperates and refigures her body as a sign of opposition to
colonial exploitation and dehumanization. On the other hand, the play represents and reinscribes these same systems of oppression and degradation by
putting her once again on display before the gaze of an audience. Her body
and its parts are a site of contestation and ambivalence, complicity and
shame. The representation of the female black body in Western discourse
has long been a complex and ambivalent combination of fascination and
revulsion. As Kadiatu Kanneh points out, "The place of the body in analyses of gender or race has become so complicated and so fraught that words
like identity, subjectivity, and desire—all familiar words now—are anything
but simple."[6] In terms of resistance, Parks's play demonstrates that complicated problem and often raises more questions than it answers. What the
play does do, however, is situate the questions and contradictions in the performative space between narrative and spectacle, and in that space it is necessary to look for resistance. The play suggests that the truth of Baartman's
life has in fact fallen out in pieces between the contested narratives and the
contradictory effects of spectacle.

Venus continues Parks's dramaturgical concern with history and representation through the trope of showmanship. Within the paradigm of spec-

tacle, with riffs on the world of the theater, on show business, and the business of show business, *Venus* considers the politics of representation, how the "machineries and 'regimes' of representation . . . play a *constitutive* and not merely a reflexive, after-the-event role."[7] For the play does not just reflect the representation of the race and sex of the nineteenth-century Venus, but reconstitutes it in the present of performance.

In thirty-one scenes, the play chronicles the story of Baartman's life from her departure from South Africa to her death in Paris. It begins with the announcement of her death in an overture: "I regret to inform you that the Venus Hottentot iz dead. . . . There wont b inny show tonite."[8] The Spectators voice their disappointment. What a shame she will not be exhibited. The play proceeds, however, to do just that. The first stage direction says that the audience sees "Venus clothed and facing stage right. She revolves. Counter-clockwise. 270 degrees. She faces upstage. . . . Venus revolves 90 degrees. She faces stage right. . . . Venus revolves 180 degrees. She faces stage left" (41). The overture foregrounds the understanding that the audience will view a show about show business and theatricality. With the repetition of the phrase "There wont b inny show tonite" arises the irony that there is certainly a show, and the audience certainly will watch the display of an "aberrant" black body. Indeed, part of the attraction of the play is to see how the transformations of theater and design will reproduce the Hottentot Venus and her amazing steatopygia on stage.

Among the complications of Baartman's story represented in Parks's play is the fact that Baartman received money for her "show." She in fact testified in a courtroom case that she was a willing participant. There were vociferous protests against Baartman's show at the time. Sander Gilman notes that "in a London inflamed by the issues of the abolition of slavery, Baartman was exhibited 'to the public in a manner offensive to decency. She does exhibit all the shape and frame of her body as if naked.' The stated objection was as much to her lewdness as to her status as an indentured black."[9] The early-nineteenth-century complaints against her "indentured" status were, in other words, indistinguishable from the charges of indecency. Was sexuality or slavery the more offensive? The fascination and revulsion seem to have been of a single piece, but presented in terms of concern for the "human being." In the play, Parks quotes a letter from the *Morning Chronicle* from 12 October 1810.

I allude to that wretched object advertised and publicly shown for money—the "Hottentot Venus" who has been brought here as a subject for the curiosity of this country, for 2 cents a-head, not for her own advantage, but for the profit of her master. Her keeper is the only gainer. I am no advocate of these sights, on the contrary. I think it base in the extreme, that *any* human beings should be thus exposed.[10]

This liberal letter writer, with the best intentions, fails to recognize the erroneous, damaging, assumptions about the inferiority of race and female sexuality that are implied by the phrase "*any* human being." In the effort to show kindly concern, the letter implies that *even* Africans are human beings, thus continuing the assumption of inferiority. From a twentieth-century vantage point, this seems obvious. Even defending the humanity of the Venus, the letter betrays the paternalistic stance of a "romantic racialism" that retains the perception of the Venus as "a wretched object." An alternative view, even at the time, accords Baartman the "right" to self-display: "And pray, has she not as good a right to exhibit herself as the Famous Irish Giant or the renouned [*sic*] Dogfaced Dancing Dwarf?!?!" (56). A more recent version of that defense came from Kate Cloete, the secretary of the Griqua Conference: "She had to earn some money. She was a human being, not an animal."[11] It is not clear whether in watching the play now an audience can escape the same contradictory arguments over rightness and rights that were waged when Baartman was alive. Similar arguments can be made against Parks's own use and display of Baartman's story: for she too is making money from a repetition and spectacle of Baartman, exploiting her even as she tries to help. Parks has said, "I was trying to make it all all right somehow. . . . Sometimes telling the story is the only thing that makes it all right."[12] The audience does not escape the same dilemma. Can it ever be all right? Yet Saartje should not be forgotten, whatever the problems of "representation."

In trying to make it all right, Parks focuses on the issues of power and authority within and over representation of the body. The play reenacts the trial at which Baartman's right to autonomy was tested. Parks frames the trial scenes by the idea of habeas corpus, the law that requires the presence of the body. Baartman "has" the body and therefore has the right to represent herself. Yet the trial scenes in *Venus* reinforce the dubious nature of her rights. For even as she possesses her body, the "regimes," technologies, and "machineries" that control the meaning of representation rest with the dominant culture and inform even her self-perception. Though heavily marked by irony, Venus repeats the racist mythologies that emerge when a body is visually marked as black.

If I bear thuh bad mark what better way to cleanse it off? / Showing my sinful person as a caution to you all could, / in the Lords eyes / be a sort of / repentance / and I could wash off my dark mark. / I came here black. / Give me the chance to leave here white. (57)

During the trial scenes, the play points out, "The year was 1810, three years after the Bill for the Abolition of the Slave-Trade had been passed in Parliament. Among protests and denials, horror and fascination, the show went on" (57). After the verdict, the court congratulates itself that "it is very much to the credit of our great country / that even a female Hottentot can find a court to review her status" (57). The congratulatory liberalism of the court, as of the letter writer above, fails to account for its own complicity in the degradation of the Venus.

The contemporary lawsuit of the Griqua National Council concerns habeas corpus as well. Who has the body? Bartman's body certainly signals the history of colonial brutality long denied, but is being again torn apart. It is a collection of pieces in the same way that her story is a collection of fragments that are subject to the meanings designed by an owner. The Griquas want to own those pieces as part of a campaign to represent their own racial differences from others designated as "mixed coloured" by the old South African apartheid laws. The Griqua want to recapture a separate aboriginal identity in the context of the new South African government. At the same time the Musée de l'Homme claims that the body of Baartman remains an important link to the European past. The museum wants to maintain the bottled Venus as a sign of the constitutive role that race has played in the formulation of European modernity. Moreover, the museum fears that if they honor the claim of the Griquas, the floodgates will open for other dispossessed peoples to reclaim their ancestors and seek the return of valued art treasures and other preserved bodies now held in Western museums. The body of the Venus remains a powerful signifier even when there is no body at all.

Baartman never fully coincides with her multiple meanings, and in that sense is a sign as well as an instance of the loss that history entails. The disparities enable Parks to make her own claims on the Venus as a historic figure in order to show that loss. In her interview with Una Chaudhuri, Parks claims that "the butt is the past, the posterior; posterity."[13] The shifting symbolic and linguistic play on posterior/posterity is a typical way for Parks to connect language to questions of history and make a term carry multiple implications that are both literal and figurative. The idea that the "butt" is history suggests the very notions of biological determinism and racist pathology that correlated identity and anatomy where visual markers were taken to indicate intelligence, social position, gender roles. Gilman points out that in nineteenth-century European cultural expression, the association of fatty buttocks and promiscuity was not limited to the representation of black women. White prostitutes too were thought to have anomalies in their genitalia and larger-than-normal derrieres, indicative of deviant sexuality. For the Venus Hottentot, the derriere was indeed the cause and the sign of her history, and a case in which the part became the whole, while Saartje Baartman disappeared. Parks's method, clear in her statement above, is to find ways to embody language: here she moves from the body to the word *(posterior),* uses a cognate word *(posterity)* and traces from physical sense to a concept of history. Where biological determinism takes prejudice and applies it to bodies, Parks metonymically connects body, word, and concept, packing the figure with implication.

What then of the butt of the Venus in *Venus?* Her body represented in the play immediately conjures the ghosts of past representations of black women as well as the continued controversy surrounding the representations of the black female body.[14] The Venus on display in Parks's play indicts contemporary popular culture for its commodification of black women's sexuality even as it links the display of her body to a continuum of the exploitation of strangeness in freak shows, sideshows, novelty, and circus acts. In the New York Public Theater production of the play, Venus was costumed with enormously padded tights. The butt clearly did not belong to the actress, but it nonetheless gave the effect of total exposure. The vulnerability, shamefulness, and the shame of her exhibition are repeatedly enacted: in one scene the Mother Showman, played by a female, backs Venus up against a wall in mock rape; in another, the Spectators are encouraged to "Paw her folks. Hands on. Go on have yr pleasure. / Her heathen shame is real" (51) and proceed to grab her buttocks. When Venus stands alone in profile for the audience, the paying spectators of the Public Theater, no one can escape the discomforts of the Mother Showman saying "What a bucket! / What a bum! / What a spanker! / Never seen the likes of that, I'll bet. / Go on Sir, go on. / Feel her if you like" (50).

Throughout the production, the artificiality of this Venus struggles against the reality of the actress. Where does the costume end and the real body of the actress begin? Venus appears on stage as a construction, materially showing the imaginary concept of the black woman as "Venus." The artificiality of the costume cannot conceal the reality of the actress' body or the dismemberment of Saartje Baartman. In one sense, that theatrical construction, combining material and discursive elements, functions as a kind of postmodern aesthetic of resistance, quoting and criticizing but also rein-scribing the "regimes and machineries" of power that defined the Venus Hottentot. Her body now equals a body suit, but both an imaginary and a real body are on display. The lack of clear demarcation of the position from which to criticize that construction is a signal of the fact, as Philip Auslander has written, that "postmodern political art cannot place itself outside the object of its own critique. . . . Because postmodern political art must position itself within postmodern culture, it must use the same representational means as all other cultural expressions yet remain permanently suspicious of them."[15] The actress as Venus in *Venus* is not outside but literally inside the contested display of the body. The play accepts the forces of show business even as it reveals the abuses of that show business system enacted on the body of the Venus. As the Mother Showman counts her cash aloud, one might well wonder what the evening's box office take for *Venus* might be.

Two kinds of structure operate in *Venus,* and they too struggle against each other. One is the sideshow with scenes announced by the master of ceremonies called the Negro Resurrectionist. The play works here as a series of olios. In Richard Foreman's production the set was a combination of circus, sideshow, and pre-Victorian theater. At the same time, however, there is a narrative logic, tracing Baartman's story from South Africa, to the sideshow, to the laboratory and "love" of the Baron Docteur. The narrative unfolds within the circus scene to resurrect the Venus and calls for identification with her. Her story is told from the point after her death when "there wont b inny show tonite" and the coherence of its temporal sequence contradicts the olio form, which asks for an analytic perspective. These two opposing structures put the play in a precarious position between an apparently definitive version of Baartman's life and the fragmentation, ambiguities, uncertainties, and contradictions of her history. The narrative tends to offer the comfort of a whole story and threatens to obscure an audience's complicity in the spectacle. In many ways the story makes the racism and sexism seem too obvious; the circus sideshow aspect more subtly demonstrates our inevitable complicity in viewing the body. The immediacy of her display is not relegated to the nineteenth century but occurs in the present of performance.

The two structuring modes nevertheless have further complications. The spectacle of the body on stage is seductive even if it is only a costumed body. The coherence of the narrative, on the other hand, puts an audience in the position to make a judgment. The narrative gives Venus "character" in an Aristotelian sense, where character is a contingency of plot. Character is perhaps a necessary dimension for eliciting the sympathy that invites social and political change. Identification and sympathy, however, can easily obscure the implications of one's own participation in the spectacle. They tend to preclude analysis of the present conditions of the spectacle of racism that includes any viewing audience, in spite of best intentions. Because narrative tends toward the recapitulation of the past, it creates a kind of amnesia toward the here and now of performance and obscures the desires of an audience participating in the reinspection of the Venus. There is no *guarantee,* in other words, that the obvious artificiality of the Venus performance will make clear that the other Saartje Baartman was also constructed, theatrically and imaginatively, for a culture ready to confirm its biases. The olio sideshow features clearly foreground theatrical artifice, but the biographical narrative undermines this effect. Each of these modes offers a perspective on Saartje Baartman, but their contestation with each other insures that neither has the final word. Together, they suggest that it is possible for political judgments against colonial oppression and constructs of race and gender to coexist with the ambiguities and errors of performative fragments without canceling each other.

Parks goes to great lengths to insist on the continuum of theatricality in representations of the Venus. Foreman's production, furthermore, seemed to call for recognizing the ways in which the Venus is trapped within the words of her story. The borders of the flats were filled with lines of text. The story shaped the stage in words. The "real" Baartman had fallen between the cracks in textual representation, yet the borders of text contained and identified her. Both the spectacle and the narrative fail to produce the real Baartman, or the real story. She is built up artificially and rises out of the gaze of her spectators; narratives falsify and fragment her on stage, giving satisfaction only to an audience: between, Parks leaves a space for the real, if absent Baartman.

That absence is staged through a play-within-the-play, "For the Love of Venus: A Freak Show," which is part interlude, part romance. Like a medieval or Renaissance dumb show, it is an emblematic repetition of the core issues of the play, tracing a courtship of a young man and young woman in the stilted tones of rhymed couplets. In an early scene, the young man discusses the possibility of travel to Timbuktu, financed by his bride-to-be. He proclaims: "A Man to be a Man must know Unknowns! . . . before I wed, Uncle, I'd like you to procure for me an oddity. / I wanna love / Something Wild (51). Observing this play is the Baron Docteur, who similarly loves "something wild," the Hottentot Venus. This audience within the play doubles the dynamics between spectatorship, desire, and the exotic sexualized otherness of black women. The play and the play-within-the-play function as framing devices for each other. Each focuses on the spectacle of the desire for the unknown, the exotic oddity of the black woman. In "For the Love of Venus," the bride-to-be disguises herself as the Hottentot Venus but is invisible behind the wedding veil. The veil classically both protects from and inaugurates desire. The uncertainty of who is behind the veil (the actress playing Venus, another?) combines the two plays through concealment and indicates strongly the familiar awareness of how white male desires project onto an imaginary, blank Other, onto someone who is not there.[16]

The young man orbits around and stares as the bride-to-be is brought in: "Good god good god / She is so odd. / Love? / Youre Love?" (66). The veil hides the "something wild" desires, but the assumption of the veil identifies the Hottentot Venus again as a theatrically created sign for desire. In the spiral of masking between actress in a body suit and the images of the Hottentot Venus and the bride-to-be, any sense of a "real" Saartje Baartman is lost. Her absence is marked by the words of her autopsy, recited during the intermission by the Baron Docteur: "The height, measured after death, / was 4 feet 11 and 1/2 inches./ The total weight of the body was 98 pounds avoirdupois. / . . . The great amounts of subcutaneous fat were / quite surprising" (59). Saartje has disappeared between erotic desire and scientific interest.

The figure of the Negro Resurrectionist serves as showman, ringmaster, and narrator in the display of the Venus. He presents her to the audience, announces the number of each scene and at one point sings "A Song of The Hottentot ladie and her day in court and what the judges did therein" (54). But as a theatrical entity, he is complicit in the exploitation. As master of ceremonies, he is in part responsible for displaying and re-representing her body. As freak show impresario, he invites the audience to participate in the voyeurism acted out on stage. Then he also becomes voyeur as an audience-within-an-audience, echoing the dilemmas of a black audience on stage. He controls the regimes of representation as emcee. Yet as he condemns the dehumanization of the Venus he also indicts himself as a co-conspirator in the process.

> I used to dig up people / dead ones. You know, / after theyd been buried. / Doctors pay a lot for corpses / but "Resurrection" is illegal / And I was always this close to getting arrested. / This Jail-Watchman jobs much more carefree. (72)

These lines might be read as a self-reflective critique of Parks's own earlier work. Her methods for bringing bodies back to life, for making up history, and for challenging the foundations of that history have not always resulted in praise. Her craft has been vilified by some African Americans for being incomprehensible. Monte Williams acknowledges, "Some blacks have complained that Ms. Parks's work is too abstract to accurately capture the black experience."[17] Parks explicitly seeks to defy simple categorization. "That's just it," says Parks. "You get a reputation for being somebody, and you're categorized."[18] Her position as playwright echoes the positions of her characters in the sense that any kind of representation or category, performative or otherwise, will tend to imprison the truth of experience, or history, or resurrection by the very act of representation. Those who look for strictly realistic "accuracy" are unaware that such accuracy conceals the imaginary dimension of the story. It is easier to jail the truth than to resurrect it.

The notion of resurrection is consistent with much of Parks's work that points to how theatrical performance revivifies history, and how history is already performative. In the telling of Baartman's story, the Negro Resurrectionist is calling back a history lost and dismembered, created by a series of texts. Parks has elsewhere defined herself and her playwriting as a resurrection. "One of my tasks as playwright is to . . . locate the ancestral burial ground, dig for bones, find bones, hear the bones sing, write it down."[19] As she has done in *The America Play,* Parks relates her project to "digging" up the past. In this play, however, digging up the past connects to the cage in which Baartman was displayed and to the confining constructs of her story. The Negro Resurrectionist says he used to be a digger but left the profession to be a jailer. Spectacle and story comprise Venus's jail.

Shame and judgment are clear motifs in the text of *Venus.* The Negro Resurrectionist announces that "Venus, Black Goddess, was shameless, she sinned or else / completely unknowing of r godfearin ways she stood / totally naked in her iron cage" (43). But whose is the shame when the Baron Docteur takes Venus as both lover and object of scientific study?[20] Having taken charge of Baartman after the trial, he says, "Lets have a look. / Stand still stand still, sweetheart / I'll orbit. / Dont start Ive doctors eyes and hands. / Well. / Extraordinary. / (rest) / (rest) /" (58). In those rests, Foreman had the actor put his hands on her buttocks, with more salaciousness than medical disinterest. Later, he masturbates, turning his back on Venus because he is "polite." His masturbation reenacts what Homi Bhabha and others have termed the colonizer's ambivalence toward the black "native" in the recognition of Venus as both threat and object of desire. His shame goes public. The Grade School Chum scolds him for his affair. His "reputation is in shambles," his "wife is distraught." Through the play, the Venus is subjected to the narratives of spectacle, science, news, and law: all examining her and dismembering her. The display of the Venus is shameful, but the shame belongs more to the spectators than to her.

For a *Boston Globe* critic, Richard Foreman's trademark blinking red light is "a beacon, a warning that what happens to Miss Saartjie Baartman can happen again."[21] This idea about the light, or the play as a "warning," however, presumes an objective position from which to extract more or less correct or intended messages from a play. What it more significantly misses is that "what happens to Miss Saartjie Baartman" *does* happen again, in this performance. Even the approving reviewers miss, apparently, the fact that they too are audiences of the Hottentot Venus. It is easy to condemn the past abuses of spectatorship. That is what is obvious about the play. But that obviousness conceals the fact that even in a re-production we, the contemporary audience members, are still viewing the Hottentot Venus with an assumption of superiority over those earlier spectators, thus ignoring our own complicity in the sight.

The scientific and performative dismemberment of the Venus is particularly apparent in the intermission speech read by the Baron Docteur. He reads from Baartman's autopsy report by Georges Cuvier. In the time between acts, that is, the Venus has become nothing but a text. Her corpse is represented as a text, but the presence of the actress before and after intermission gives the palpable sense that the autopsy has been performed on a living being. Both the actress and the historical Baartman are missing, but both have been reduced to a diagram on display. The speech, furthermore, aims beyond the theater space to the world beyond: "Please take yourselves uh breather in thuh lobby. / My voice will surely carry beyond these walls and if not / my finds are published" (59).

The invitation to leave is reminiscent of the audience participation initiative enacted by black revolutionary theater of the 1960s and early 1970s, in which black performers encouraged their black audience members to join as a collective body in the symbolic overthrow of oppression. At the climax of Amiri Baraka's *Slave Ship,* for example, a play that details black history in America, actors shook hands with black audience members and escorted them onto the stage to the chant of "Rise, Rise, Black Man, Rise." At one particular performance in Baton Rouge, Louisiana, in 1970, doors had to be locked to keep the ready-to-riot audience from taking to the streets. Such participatory productions wavered between harmony and disharmony, chaos and containment. In this later work, Parks asks that the intermission similarly function as a moment that oscillates between the control of the script and the implication of the audience in the action. The audience actively interpenetrates the event. By standing up and leaving, the audience disrupts the Cuvier text and the performer's speech. And yet, the autopsy report in the intermission is far more ambiguous than the call to revolution in black theater of the 1960s. To stay to hear the report is almost obscene. The anatomical detail is horrific and fascinating. An audience, hungry for reality, is fed information about the "real" Baartman. But the information is what placed the Venus in a scientific taxonomy that served to confirm the belief that blacks were a primitive and inferior class of humans. To listen at all is in some measure to participate in the lie to the same degree that the gentlemen of the Royal College did so. While not every individual may have believed or accepted the conventional belief, the public nature of the discourse makes it a matter of public culture. In spite of the best intentions, the public nature of the theatrical discourse also dismembers and dissects the corpse of the Hottentot Venus.

To resist the lie of biological determinism and refuse to participate means leaving the theater. Whether out of political concern or need for a break, the audience that exits is to some degree staging a protest and resisting complicity. But leaving is also ignoring the fact of the textual reality that defined the meaning of her body. The speech "carries beyond these walls" of the theater space and cannot be denied, even if one is not present. The intermission puts the audience in a double bind: it is blind to complicity that is an inevitable part of performance, even if refusing to sanction Cuvier's report, and blind to the avoidance if trying not to listen. There is a measure of self-deception and duplicity in believing one can escape participation either by staying to listen or leaving.

Parks has compelled the audience, in short, to participate no matter which choice any individual may make. Like Baraka, she disrupts the frame of representation and brings the play out into the real. It is not clear, however, whether any audience can recognize its inevitable duplicity. The audience for *Slave Ship* could be consciously aware of their part in the call for revolutionary activism. In *Venus,* resistance to the obvious exploitation is complicated by the dynamics of voyeurism and consumption in which everyone takes part.

Significantly, the cycle of voyeurism and consumption breaks in those moments when the character and the actress looks back at her onlookers and refuses to feel shame. There is no moment, in fact, when Saartje really does seem to accept her circumstances or her treatment as shameful. Terrible, filthy, miserable, brutal, but never shameful. In the refusal of shame, she maintains an innocence that is not complicity; if it is still within the systems of oppression, it is nevertheless resistant. Even while she is the victim of others' desires and is the exploited commodity who is implicated in her own fate, her refusal is a negation from within the system. It defies the entire system of significations that oppresses and exploits her without escaping it. The defiance is, certainly, pragmatically ineffectual and does not change the horror of the situation. But it is an act that keeps Saartje from being only a pathetic victim who is caught unconsciously in the unconscious web of others.

Her refusal occurs most clearly in a series of moments that punctuate and interrupt the ongoing action of the narrative with the most egregious sign of her violation. They are those moments when the Hottentot Venus is called on to pose for the Spectators and the doctors, and, in effect, the audience. In terms of audience complicity, these are the most difficult images in the performance. On display, the focal point of both audiences, Saartje poses her naked body, in still life, on a podium for us to gaze at.

The notion of the "pose" has been considered by theorists from both the psychoanalytic and cultural standpoints. Craig Owens summarizes the social context of "posing" brought out by Homi Bhabha and Dick Hebdige. Homi Bhabha talks about "the look of surveillance [that] returns as the displacing gaze of the disciplined, where the observer becomes the observed"; similarly, Hebdige has said, "To strike a pose is to pose a threat . . . [transforming] the fact of surveillance into the pleasure of being watched."[22] The pose, in other words, is a sign of consciousness and knowledge. The object of surveillance knows the power that belongs to the focal point of the gaze; she accepts awareness of being watched and develops that awareness into a decisive pose or attitude that holds the spectator in its power. Owens points out that a viewer is transfixed by "the power of images to arrest us, take us into custody."[23]

From this viewpoint, Saartje's apparent complicity in posing her body for the spectacle is *also* (not instead of, or in actuality, but additionally) resistant to the desire of and projection by the spectators. This is to say far more than Saartje "chooses" to exhibit herself and is therefore exercising some kind of existential freedom. The pose is an act that paradoxically accepts and refracts the gaze of the spectator and turns the play itself into a test *of* the audience, not *for* the audience. It arrests the line of sight and transfixes the one who is looking. The immobilizing gaze that is returned by the pose to the spectators is "the figuration—the appropriation by the image as its own—of the gaze of the otherwise invisible photographer who framed and stilled this scene."[24] This return of the spectator's gaze, in other words, both refuses the desire of that gaze and mirrors back the absence of the object of the spectator's desire, as if to say that "it is not me (other) you are looking at; whatever you see is your own absence." And in this sense, the pose is, paradoxically, the "representation of the representation." The colonized, sexualized, dismembered other, that is, is a representation, and it is the *fact* of representation as much as its errors that needs revealing. The stillness of the actress marks the absence that is behind those representations. The pose holds our attention and paralyzes us. An actual audience at a performance, like the crowds and examining doctors on the stage, is held rapt, controlled by the still image. The figure posing is neither Hottentot nor Venus, and the actor embodies only the virtual Saartje. She is the blank mirror of desire. An exchange occurs between her desire for attention and our desire for possession. At the same time, her complicity, unlike ours, interrupts that exchange by freezing into the pose—the sign of absence and death as well as her conscious autonomy. The actress playing Saartje enacts the same representation of spectatorship presented by the other Saartje without duplicating or mimicking her. Her padded buttocks, furthermore, arrest attention no less than the flesh of the other Saartje. Both equally fake and represent the object of desire, and both equally enact the absence behind the representation of the "Venus," who is Eros. In this way, the pleasures of spectacle translate desire into the political unconscious.

Parks thus avoids portraying Venus as a simple victim. "I could have written a two-hour saga with Venus being the victim. . . . But she's multifaceted. . . . as black people we're encouraged to be narrow and simply address the race issue. We deserve much more."[25] By not making Venus simply a black victim, Parks complicates the position of both the oppressed and oppressor. Her Venus resists the reductions of racial essentialism and thereby recuperates Baartman as a complex subject, not a symbolic or figurative body. She was a woman who reputedly spoke four languages, fought against her own extradition, and understood the value of her commodification. And in this play, she is even a historian.

Near the conclusion, Venus relates the "history of chocolate." She explains that, in Western culture, chocolate has been both revered and reviled, detested and desired. Venus notes chocolate's evolution from being the food of the gods, to serving as the gift of love, to becoming a source of body fat and pleasure. The parallels between the story of her own chocolate-colored, fatty body and her treatise on the history of the cacao bean are obvious. And yet, within this obviousness exists the varied roles that both she and chocolate and, by extension, black women have occupied within Western cultural imagination. Each of these positions has depended upon the perceptions and authority of an external gaze. At the same time, Venus loves chocolate and herself. At the end, Venus turns to both the Baron Docteur and the audience and cries out, "*Kiss* me *Kiss* me *Kiss* me" (72). Her words act as both a challenge and enticement to further critical examination, to embrace her, and to perceive her as more than parts.

Venus the play, Saartje Baartman, the Venus Hottentot, the actor in body suit who reembodies the Venus—all evidence a problematic ambivalence. They are at once subject and object, present and absent, symbol and matter. The contradictions in Baartman as well as in her re-presentation and reembodiment in *Venus* are cause enough for critical equivocation. Yet, this equivocation is productive when it points to a site for resistance where spectators of the political and theatrical arenas recognize how we are implicated in the sight we abhor. Parks's representation of Venus actively embraces contradiction and complexity. This position by definition is not static but one that calls for rigorous and repeated interrogation of ourselves as well as the history of oppression. The equivocations and equivocating that have and continue to surround the Venus compel us to avoid simple analysis and to be referential and self-critical. The politics of equivocation lend support to the critical directions advocated by Kobena Mercer:

> If the "responsibility" of the artist lies in the quality of his or her response to what calls for thinking, criticism contributes to the conversation not by imposing the closure of its own conceptual system, but by entering into a critical, dialogical, relationship with the voices that do the calling.[26]

The replaying of the story of the Hottentot Venus places her not in the past, as a symbol of racist, sexist abuse, but in the present as a key figure within contemporary discourse. Her indeterminacy offers the potential for resistance and agency. To realize that potential it is crucial to avoid interpretive answers that would close off her meanings, and, rather, to continue negotiating those meanings as a way of keeping Saartje Baartman out of the cage.

NOTES

1. Sander L. Gilman, "Black Bodies, White Bodies: Toward an Iconography of Female Sexuality in Late Nineteenth-Century Art, Medicine, and Literature," in *Race, Writing, and Difference*, ed. Henry Louis Gates, Jr. (Chicago: University of Chicago Press, 1986), 235.

2. Gilman, "Black Bodies, White Bodies," 256.

3. Sudarsan Raghaven, "Body Becomes Symbol of Oppression," *Houston Chronicle*, 11 Feb. 1996, A33.

4. Raghaven, "Body Becomes Symbol," A33.

5. Suzan-Lori Parks, "For Posterior's Sake," interview by Una Chaudhuri, *Program of the Public Theater*, 2 Apr. 1996, 30.

6. Kadiatu Kanneh, "Feminism and the Colonial Body," in *Post-Colonial Studies Reader,* ed. Bill Ashcroft, Gareth Griffiths, and Helen Tiffin (London: Routledge, 1995), 348.

7. Stuart Hall, "New Ethnicities," in *Black Film—Black Cinema* (London: ICA Documents, 1992), 27.

8. Suzan-Lori Parks, *Venus, Theatre Forum* 9 (summer–fall 1996): 41. Pages hereafter cited in the text are from this first printing of the play.

9. Gilman, "Black Bodies, White Bodies," 232.

10. Qtd. in Ben MacIntyre, "Hottentots Demand the Return of Their Venus," *London Times,* 30 Dec. 1995, Overseas News, n.p. See also Parks, *Venus,* 56.

11. Parks, "For Posterior's Sake," 26.

12. Parks, "For Posterior's Sake," 32.

13. Parks, "For Posterior's Sake," 34.

14. The black butt is not simply in "posterior" history but in the present. It has been repeatedly valorized, fetishized, and commercialized. Josephine Baker as an expatriate in France in the 1920s and 1930s exploited an exotic, primitive image of blackness "symbolized by the extraordinary life and power of her undulating buttocks." Jill Matos, "Blonde, Black, and Hottentot Venus: Context and Critique in Angela Carter's 'Black Venus,'" *Studies in Short Fiction* 28, no. 4 (fall 1991): 468. More recently, in 1987, the Washington, D.C.-based Go-Go group scored a rhythm-and-blues hit and started a black dance craze with a song that was featured in Spike Lee's film *School Daze:* "The Butt." In 1992, rapper Sir Mix-a-Lot found space on the Top 40 with a song called "My Baby's Got Back," celebrating black women's posteriors. These popular cultural examples may recuperate the butt as a site of black beauty. But at the same time these and other black cultural practices continue to objectify and commodify black women through this rear-end view. They reinscribe the butt as a symbol of black sexual difference, exoticism, and desire.

15. Philip Auslander, *Presence and Resistance* (Ann Arbor: University of Michigan Press, 1992), 23.

16. The notion of the veil figures prominently in postcolonial criticism. Fanon writes, "It is the white man who creates the Negro. But it is the Negro who creates negritude. To the colonialist offensive against the veil, the colonized opposes the cult of the veil." Frantz Fanon, *A Dying Colonialism,* trans. Haakon Chevalier (New York: Grove, 1967), 47. For Fanon, "Algerian women are placed in a metonymic process where both veil and woman become interchangeable, scopic signifiers of colonized Algeria itself" (Kanneh, "Feminism and Colonial Body," 346). Translating Fanon's analysis to "For the Love of Venus" then, the unveiling of the bride-to-be serves as another example of her exposure, her exploitation, and her rape. Her veiled presence is a symbol of native resistance against incursions of the young man. However, here again the bride-to-be is complicit in her fate. Her desire to be taken by the young man on the one hand demonstrates this complicity, but on the other hand allows that she has agency. Yet even that agency is determined by the dominant culture. As a subject, she is in another double bind.

17. Monte Williams, "From a Planet Closer to the Sun," *New York Times* 17 Apr. 1996, C1, 14.

18. Suzan-Lori Parks, *The America Play and Other Works* (New York: Theater Communications Group, 1995), 1.

19. Parks, *The America Play,* 13.

20. The love story of the Baron and Venus recalls Angela Carter's story "Black Venus," in which she reconstructs the affair between Charles Baudelaire and his mulatto mistress, Jeanne Duval, the subject of a series of his poems. For Baudelaire, like the Baron Docteur, his black Venus is both bestial and divine, the subject of his lust and his poetry. Carter's work challenges the shameful and racist perceptions of Duval as "dark, diseased, corrupting." See Matos, "Blond, Black," 468.

21. Patti Hartigan, *Boston Globe,* 27 Mar. 1996, Arts and Film, 79.

22. Craig Owens, *Beyond Recognition: Representation, Power, and Culture* (Berkeley and Los Angeles: University of California Press, 1992), 202.

23. Owens, *Beyond Recognition,* 211.

24. Owens, *Beyond Recognition,* 206.

25. Williams, "From a Planet Closer," 14.

26. Kobena Mercer, *Welcome to the Jungle* (London: Routledge, 1994), 258.

Janelle Reinelt

Notes for a Radical Democratic Theater: Productive Crises and the Challenge of Indeterminacy

Politics is the activity of attending to the general arrangements of a collection of people who, in respect of their common recognition of their manner of attending to its arrangements, compose a single community. . . . This activity, then, springs neither from instant desires, nor from general principles, but from the existing traditions of behavior themselves. And the form it takes, because it can take no other, is the amendment of existing arrangements by exploring and pursuing what is intimated in them.
—Michael Oakeshott, *Rationalism in Politics*

I begin with the assumption that the optimal relationship between theater and society is one in which theater, as a cultural practice, has an active role to play in the discovery, construction, maintenance, and critique of forms of sociality appropriate to that society. When the goal is a radical democracy, this involves intervening in the imaginative life of the society by producing meditations on its current balance of equality with liberty, staging contradictions between democratic principles and the material conditions they purport to describe, or creating images of possible alternative configurations, other worlds. Radical democratic theory poses questions about the nature of membership in the political community—what does such citizenship mean and what does it entail?

The notion of a "radical democracy" itself is taken from political theorists and cultural critics who are attempting to rethink an understanding of the democratic tradition in light of the collapse of Cold War dualisms and the subsequent disintegration of any unified position that might be called Left. The recent work of Chantal Mouffe, Ernesto Laclau, Slavoj Žižek, Quentin Skinner, Michael Walzer, and others revisits liberal democracy to acknowledge the positive aspects of that heritage while attempting to radicalize its principles.[1] Chantal Mouffe provides the rationale for this project.

The problem . . . is not the ideals of modern democracy, but the fact that its political principles are a long way from being implemented, even in those societies that lay claim to them. Because of the wide gap between those professed democratic ideals and their realization, the general tendency on the Left has been to denounce them as a sham and aim at the construction of a completely different society. This radical alternative is precisely what has been shown to be disastrous by the tragic experience of Soviet-style socialism, and it needs to be discarded. . . . Instead of proclaiming the ideological and illusory character of so-called "formal bourgeois democracy," why not take its declared principles literally and force liberal democratic societies to be accountable for their professed ideals.[2]

Western theater, as an institution and as a social practice, is already deeply implicated in the heritage of Western democracy. The arts occupy a space in culture associated with the "free" expression of gifted individuals, the "enhancement" of national life, the production of entertainment for leisure consumption, the public representation of American (or British, or French) national character. Each of these functions is linked to an implicit set of values (liberty, equality, pluralism, sovereignty, individual rights) and presumes a group of "citizens" who form a symbolic community when they gather as an audience. This list of functions is not offered cynically; each has positive and creative aspects concomitant with its more deadly ones. Even "entertainment" has a positive dimension if the notion is understood as pleasure coupled with community rather than escapism coupled with homogeneity. My task in the remainder of this essay is to extend the struggle to radicalize democratic principles by including and foregrounding theater's possible role or function in that struggle.

In Western societies the decade of the 1990s offers specific opportunities for rethinking our fundamental beliefs and commitments; indeed, at this century's end, a crisis of political and social institutions is apparent to observers of all political persuasions and of diverse identity affiliations. Rather than dwelling on "crisis" in its negative and apocalyptic mode, I want to stress "crisis" as an enabling state of acute tension, opening a space of indeterminacy in conceptions, institutions, and practices formerly regarded as viable or at least entrenched. Crisis threatens to destabilize these social structures, often leading to the experience of anomie and disintegration, but also to a creative uncertainty.

This present indeterminacy emerged as the result of three specific challenges. At the most general level, postmodern and poststructural critiques have discredited Enlightenment discourses of rationality, teleology, and unified subjectivity (the bedrock of left as well as liberal political theory) producing an epistemological crisis of major proportion, which leaves no academic discipline, or for that matter, civil institution untouched—as the current debate in the United States about how to compile census data on race amply shows.[3] Second, the end of the Cold War and the collapse of really-existing socialism has destabilized an East/West binary that has organized the rhetorical tropes of many civil and cultural institutions, including theater. In the absence of distinct oppositional categories, confusion and fuzzy thinking have created on the one hand, the ambiguous discourse of a "new world order" and on the other, a neoromanticism for local, homogeneous communities that has taken both fascist and progressive forms (e.g., the militia movement, as it has come to be called, or alternatively, strong identity-group-based organizing against the AIDS epidemic). Third, a combination of global capitalism, total mediatization, and the cyborg revolution have made "nation" and "subject" seemingly obsolete categories, while daily life requires and indeed continues to inscribe bodies with codes of both subjectivity and nationality, even if these inscriptions are multiple and contradictory.[4]

Theater in the United States and the rest of the West has tended to reflect these tensions, contributing to a perception of crisis by staging it. Postmodern dramaturgy has decentered the subject, fragmented narrative, refused closure, and foregrounded the instability of its own signifying processes. Politically committed and engaged theaters have staged race, ethnicity, gender, and sexuality as foci for social struggles and possible community in the midst of difference, but concurrently the Right has attacked oppositional theater in the name of a "moral majority" culture, staging nostalgia for universal and nonplural principles (e.g., anti–affirmative action legislation in the first case and anti-immigration legislation in the second). Theater audiences are changing, due, in part, to a proliferation of local communities—most medium cities have a wide variety of performance venues, from regional repertory and touring sites to community centers, equity waiver houses, university and school productions, and small clubs and "off-spaces." In addition, new technologies and virtual realities are changing the way people engage in spectatorship, performance, even subjectivity itself. The question, "Is the theater transforming itself beyond recognition?" is closely related to similar questions about the nation and the subject—soon, it may all be screen(ed). As Sue-Ellen Case has written, "the body [is] poised in performance between its appearance within national and kinship systems and its disappearance among multiple screens."[5] What this screening means is as yet indeterminate: some argue it maximizes democratic participation; others think it forecloses it. Present reality is thus experienced as a diffuse field of social forces rather than a codified and stable system of structures.

While it comes as no surprise that theater is reflecting the conditions and future of political/ontological/social/cultural crises, it still seems worth realizing the myriad instances when theater becomes a site where these tensions in politics and society can be experienced and perhaps parsed. Could theater go further to contribute to producing radical democracy by actively seeking out opportunities for imaginative mimesis, simulation, or transformation of these contemporary crises?

In casting my comments within the discourse of what might be called "democratic civics," I am attempting to theorize a theatrical space patronized by a consensual community of citizen-spectators who come together at stagings of the social imaginary in order to consider and experience affirmation, contestation, and reworking of various material and discursive practices pertinent to the constitution of a democratic society. While this may sound idealistic, live stage performances often still mark a site where basically liberal-minded people asking liberal humanist questions gather together in a social ritual that makes little sense without this baseline interpretation. In a sense, live theater enacts one of the last available forms of direct democracy, gathering an assembly of "citizens" in the tradition of civic republicanism, related to the small assembly, town meeting, church social, school board meeting, or neighborhood block party. Spectators are, at the least, an implied community for the time of performance—even if riven with antagonisms and contradictions that make *community* a weak signifier. Moving beyond this minimal baseline to a truly radical form of civic spectatorship involves negotiation and contestation, and a fundamental transformation of the traditional "spectator" function from consumer to agent.

This model authorizes neither any permanent social formation nor any fixed notion of the common good. Rather it invokes the rhetoric of civic participation as a way to insist on the political character of performance. Spectators may be said to embrace equality and liberty as principles of democracy—this is the normative or ethicopolitical base of the specific historical community in question—but not any particular articulation of these values. Thus persons affiliated with a variety of identity positions, rather than a universal point of view, develop as many forms of citizenship as there are interpretations of those democratic principles. Likewise, performers will also produce this variety in competing imaginative stagings, which will both conserve and subvert aspects of received discourses, sometimes performing both functions of the social imagination, the ideological and the utopian, within one strategic performance frame.

These ideas about the citizen/spectator and the performance site as scene of democratic engagement entail two aspects of the political-theory discussion to which I have been alluding. Radical democratic critique stresses that bourgeois democracies have privileged individual liberty to the detriment of considerations of equality and justice, yoking this individualism to economic freedom and property ownership. Imagining radical democracy thus involves an appeal to communitarian thinking (usually associated with conservative and moral points of view) while simultaneously retaining an emphasis on individual freedom unhooked from laissez-faire economics. In fact, the first task must help provide support for the second.

A great deal of ink has been wasted in the recent discussions of radical democracy that contrast communitarianism to libertarianism only to argue that their characterization as mutually exclusive is simply false.[6] Nevertheless, it is useful to see what values are at stake in a quick sketchlike fashion (rather like Brecht's similarly inadequate but useful opposition of dramatic to epic theater):

Communitarian	Libertarian
common good	personal freedom
responsibilities	rights
civic virtues	incentives
community(ies)	individual
human nature	human will

The communitarian "correction" to liberalism involves rethinking community, civic virtue, and citizenship without the conservative baggage of ultranationalism, homogeneity, moral prescription, or "majoritarian" rule.[7] It seems easily apparent from this list what the appeal of communitarian principles brings to an attempt to reconceptualize the Left; but it should also be apparent that conservative religious and nationalistic interests are also represented here: Catholics against abortion, white supremacists, and fiscal conservatives opposed to the "welfare state" can invoke communitarian principles to support the sanctity of life, exclusionary racial definitions of community, and human nature against "unnatural" sexual acts. The indeterminacy of any particular configuration of these values is part of the risk and the challenge of the communitarian correction.

Radical democracy must retain an emphasis on pluralism and personal liberty, which means that an inevitable struggle between competing versions of identities as citizens will always accompany civil life. It recognizes that if existing rights have been established through the exclusion or subordination of the rights of others, the identities of all parties must be renegotiated. The permanent presence of conflict is indispensable to a radical democratic society because it is through the articulation and negotiation of plural notions of citizenry that democracy does its work.

I came to appreciate Michael Oakeshott, a conservative political theorist whose epigram opens the essay, through the work of Chantal Mouffe, only to find other radical thinkers were engaging with him as well: Homi Bhabha, for example, cites Oakeshott's "brilliant conservative account of the equivocal nature of the modern nation."[8] Mouffe wishes to appropriate Oakeshott's notion of a shared and consensual citizenship, which is not a legal status so much as a form of identification, a type of political identity: something to be constructed, not empirically given. Since there will always be competing interpretations of the democratic principles of equality and liberty," she writes, "there will therefore be competing interpretations of democratic citizenship.[9] Oakeshott offers a practical definition of community—a group of people who recognize that they are "attending" to their ongoing social arrangements, where the recognition makes them a community, not some particular bonds or common goals. This always-already existing activity can only be modified by following up on "what is intimated" in these arrangements in the first place. This version of politics can accommodate wide divergence (or even social antagonisms) between members of the community and explain why even in crisis, it still makes sense to use the term *community*.

This model of a consensual if conflictual affirmation of democratic citizenship, always under construction and negotiation, suits a theatrical space in which the imaginative possibilities for alternative social and political relations can offer up positions for spectator identification and critique. Critique, in fact, is the cultural practice that links theater and crisis. Rosemary Hennessy, interrogating feminist standpoint theory, argues,

> Critique is bound to crisis and to ideology in a definitive way. In that the dominant ideology continually works to seal over the cracks in the social imaginary generated by the contradictions of patriarchal and capitalist social arrangements, it is continually engaged in crisis management. As an ideological practice, critique issues from these cracks, historicizes them, and claims them as the basis for alternative narratives. . . . critique is "crisis diagnosis" which enables future social change.[10]

Theater and performance, seen as an institution whose chief function is the production of the social imaginary, can play a potentially vital role in shaping social change. In a time when much theater practice, especially in commercial and regional venues, seems anemic or irrelevant to public life, the affirmation of this constitutive function of theater is essential. It means that we will have to reconceive of our theaters as a place of democratic struggle where antagonisms are aired and considered, and where the voluntary citizenry, the audience, deliberates on matters of state in an aesthetic mode. While there have been times in U.S. history when theater functioned this way—arguably the colonial period for example—it is difficult to claim that it functions this way at century's end.

This deliberative attitude that will, indeed must, be adversarial does not mean that the theater, pace Brecht, is like a courtroom. Aesthetics does have its own realm insofar as aesthetic modalities appeal to a range of experiential and epistemological resources other than conceptual argumentation. Processes of imagination, identification, and subjunctive contemplation go beyond the straightforward discursive prose of other avenues of public life. Attacking what he considers to be "the romanticization of deliberation," Amatai Etzioni unknowingly charts a course for theater in the new communitarian theory. Viewing as a general fallacy the belief that individuals are rational and can be appealed to for reasoned, logical decision-making, he stresses that

> the less discussed question is how do members of community work out their different value commitments, presumptions about the nature of the world, favored public policies, and so on through processes that are only in part deliberative. Grassroots leadership, influence of opinion leaders, expression of affect, and mobilization of power all play a key role in community decisions, and not via cognitive channels.[11]

A range of aesthetic modes of knowing can contribute to this process by providing alternatives to traditional political modes of deliberation (political parties and activities, news coverage analysis, or the courts). Social theorists need to understand the productive role of the arts in culture just as theater critics and practitioners need to understand how their art articulates with other political processes.

In particular "communities," theater in the United States has been performing the work of radical democracy for some time. A rich array of texts and performances have come from the "new social movements"—from feminism, gay and lesbian rights activism, racial and ethnic cultural struggles. These have, for the most part, played in regional theaters and local venues where audiences associated with the identity formation of these performances have had financial and geographic access to suitable performance spaces. From the Asian American Theatre in San Francisco to the Highways Performance Space in Santa Monica; from the WOW cafe in the East Village of New York to the Mexican Fine Arts Center of Chicago; and in many less well-known venues all over the nation, audiences have gathered together to see work by and about Chicano/a, African American, Asian American peoples, women, and those claiming the appellation "queer." These audiences have not always *identified* with the subject positions of these representations; indeed they are not always *affiliates*. The word *associated* signifies the combination of loose connection with free choice that might describe the meaning of a "community" of spectators at these events within the definition offered by Oakeshott. These performances, whether Cherríe Moraga's *Heros and Saints,* Roger Williams's *Huey,* Split Britches's *Lesbians Who Kill,* or Philip Kan Gotanda's *The Wash* have provided foci in performance for negotiating our national diversities, and not always, maybe even not usually, to like-minded spectators.

In an article specifically addressed to countering the "preaching to the converted dismissive," Tim Miller and David Román argue forcefully against homogenizing spectators.

> The idea of "the converted" assumes an inert mass of people which absorbs a performance uncritically and passively, without explicit interaction, and with immediate approval of the representation imbedded in the performance. The charge that queer artists are preaching to the converted reveals an arrogance on the part of the accuser, who assumes a knowledge of the people gathered in the space of performance. This charge assumes that a stable and static mass has arrived fully into an imagined state of conversion—a state that, though not articulated, is both assumed and belittled. To claim that artists are only preaching to the converted implies a fixed position for the audience assembled that trivializes the ever-changing and never immediately apparent needs and desires of queer spectators.[12]

In addition to suggesting that even those who are identified with a particular group do not form a uniform and homogeneous mass, Miller and Román further point out that the activity of performing and spectating is itself an aspect of community formation, and that "these very marginalized communities are themselves subject to the continuous rhetorical and material practices of a naturalized hegemonic norm."[13] So even the performance event itself constitutes a form of radical democratic activity as people choose to participate in an event that recognizes the marginality of some members of the society and strengthens that group by force of taking place.

I have wanted to argue strongly for the efficacy of seeing these obviously politicized performances in venues that draw a sympathetic target audience as local sites of resistance to dominant culture. Some of these artists do also perform in mainstream venues and achieve wide national exposure. Tony Kushner and Anna Deavere Smith have had this kind of widespread attention in the last few years, and their work embodies both the possibility and the practice of mainstream theater as radical democratic critique. Their work has as its subject the deep racial, class, and sexual divisions in American society and simultaneously displays a negotiation of those differences. Insofar as audiences across the country have seen Kushner's *Angels in America* and Smith's *Fires in the Mirror* and *Twilight—Los Angeles, 1992,* these works have had as wide a reception as any play (except musicals) is likely to get. Both Kushner and Smith have been treated as media celebrities and are often summoned as lecturers to college campuses and universities. As I have remarked elsewhere, when young black students in Oakland, California, laughed and disrupted a screening of *Schindler's List,* Anna Deavere Smith was asked to come to the students' school to speak about race and the Holocaust.[14] One could say that Smith and Kushner, as a result of their work, have been constructed by the media as "authorities" on the tensions in American life, but I would prefer to see them as citizens who take seriously their role in the democratic struggle to produce a just and free society.

Smith's performances have been created under the title "A Search for American Character," which foregrounds her activity as an investigator in producing her work. Both *Fires in the Mirror* and *Twilight* have been based on events of extreme national importance involving race. One event took place on the East Coast, the other on the West Coast, and her first performances of the respective plays opened within a year of the events in the geographic location where they happened. Thus Smith's work has contributed to a local as well as to a national dialogue and reflection on race relations in the troubled present.[15]

Beyond the sociopolitical thematics of her work, Smith has been incorporated into public discourses on race because her dramaturgical techniques have aligned her with other types of public discourses such as oral histories, documentary reportage, television talk shows, and network news broadcasts. Smith constructs her plays from interviews with persons directly or indirectly involved in the historical events in question and delivers, verbatim, their words and the essence of their physical beings in characterizations that fall somewhere between caricature, Brechtian epic gestus, and mimicry. This imbrication in the cultural codes of news and history has magnified the authority of Smith's work beyond representation toward an always elusive horizon of "Truth" and has constructed her as a privileged voice who may speak for others across race, class, and gender boundaries.

Smith is herself acutely aware of the problems of representing race and other differences. In the introduction to the printed text of *Fires in the Mirror,* Smith writes,

> "Who has the right to see what?" "Who has the right to say what?" "Who has the right to speak for whom?" These questions have plagued the contemporary theater. These questions address both issues of employment equity and issues of *who is portrayed.* These questions are the questions that unsettle and prohibit a democratic theater in America. If only a man can speak for a man, a woman for a woman, a Black person for all Black people, then we, once again, inhibit the *spirit* of the theater, which lives in the *bridge* that makes unlikely aspects *seem* connected. The bridge doesn't make them the same, it merely *displays* how two unlikely *aspects* are *related.*[16]

I have quoted Smith at length because I think this passage characterizes Smith's performance technique as such a bridge that makes unlikely things seem connected. She ghosts her portraits with her own persona, signifying sympathy, fairness, and also her own subject position as a specific black woman with specific identity markers (class, education, style, etc.) of her own. She is able to "get away with" criticizing others because she also criticizes members of her own groups, and she is not a member of the dominant group, that is, white.[17] This kind of reasoning, however, goes only so far.

If we agree with Smith that people are not completely trapped by their differences, then this quid pro quo isn't enough. It is the bridging of difference that must be enacted, displayed, performed in order to make visible the possibility of replicating it in ordinary life. In order to produce this bridging, Smith needs the authority of the discourses of news and documentary combined with the liberal humanist view of the artist's empathetic capacities. Describing her performative technique, Charles and James Lyons write, "While the performance is verbally polyphonic, it is acoustically and materially unified in the presence of Anna Deavere Smith whose voice assumes the characters of the other figures but retains her own unmistakable individuality and, blends, curiously the idiosyncrasies of her own voice and speech with that of the person interviewed."[18] Smith must have it both ways in order to produce this effect of oscillating between identification and difference; she needs to be identified as both journalist and artist. In a sense, Smith dares to speak for the Hasidim, or the Koreans, as well as for her own ethnic group *not* because she is objective, fair minded, and even-handed, but because she demonstrates the process of bridging difference, seeking information and understanding, and finessing questions of identity. The relationship between interviewer and speaker is mobile—it changes—and since the audience is positioned in the direct address sequences to "be" Smith, they are positioned to experience the activity of bridging, working with difference. This effect is the most important element of Smith's work—it engages the spectator in radical political activity to the extent that the spectator grapples with this epistemological process.

Smith's work enables people, glossing Oakeshott, to attend to their arrangements and to explore what is intimated in them. Smith does not attempt solutions to the national dilemmas she stages; she provokes the "community" witnessing her performance to undertake the search and negotiate the solutions. The subtitle of Tony Kushner's *Angels in America, A Gay Fantasia on National Themes,* already announces itself as a radical democratic text. In performance, it is certainly possible, as David Savran has recently written in a brilliant essay, to realize just another form of liberal pluralism at its political core.[19] However, it is to the "communitarian correction" implicit in the text, and available in some productions, that I would turn.[20]

The pluralism of *Angels in America* is, of course, in its gesture toward inclusiveness and healing. If Ethel Rosenberg can say a kaddish for Roy Cohn, there is a utopian horizon in this play that stretches ideas of justice. The closing image of the "imagined community" of the new (queer) nation is composed of harmonious diversity—across region, class, and even gender, although as Savran points out, "the celestial 'sexual politics'. . . of the play guarantee that the feminine remains Other."[21] In contrast to the stasis of this final image, the contestatory nature of real democracy ensures that this is a false image, or rather more importantly, a *fantastical* image, an always elusive horizon of possibility or perhaps of only momentary achievement. Chantal Mouffe has argued that antagonisms can never be abolished from democracies, and that while we must work toward the goal of harmonious pluralism, this will never be achieved. The blast through the continuum of history figured by the angel in Walter Benjamin's terms is both utopic and apocalyptic in its associations.[22] Yet the work of utopia is precisely to offer a horizon of possibility, a negative or empty space, an imaginary no-where, as a provocation to desire. Indeed, from Fredric Jameson to Donna Haraway, the question of utopia, its meaning and its usefulness as a concept in this moment, has generated widespread attention.[23] In *Heterotopia: Postmodern Utopia and the Body Politic,* Tobin Siebers identifies an "aesthetic community—an imaginary republic of citizens—that rivals any worldly republic and that can be realized on the strength of the desire for community inspired by its very imagination."[24] In its structural and dramaturgical relations between spectators and performing subjects, something quite like an aesthetic community is constructed in the theater, and such a community is also thematized in *Angels in America.*

The work of social imagination that cultural practices perform involves two different but related modalities. Paul Ricoeur links them to projects of ideology and utopia.

> On the one hand, imagination may function to preserve an order. In this case the function of the imagination is to stage a process of identification that mirrors the order. Imagination has the appearance here of a picture. On the other hand, imagination may have a disruptive function; it may work as a breakthrough. Its image in this case is productive, an imagining of something else, the elsewhere. . . . Ideology represents the first kind of imagination; it has a function of preservation, of conservation. Utopia, in contrast, presents the second kind of imagination; it is always the glance from nowhere.[25]

Ricoeur wants to argue for the necessity of both ideology and utopia, in their positive aspects as well as their negative ones. Ideology's negative attribute of distortion complements the positive attribute of integration and stabilization; utopia's negative attribute of escape complements the positive attribute of social subversion, what Ricoeur calls "the function of the nowhere in the constitution of social or symbolic action."[26]

I would, therefore, disagree with David Savran about the ultimate conservatism of the politics of *Angels in America.* For Savran, discussing a scene of argument between Louis and Belize in which "their conflict is suddenly overrun by an outbreak of lyricism," antagonisms are not resolved but transcended in a false promise: "Like the ending of *Perestroika,* in which another dispute between Louis and Belize fades out behind Prior's benediction, this scene enacts a movement of transcendence whereby the political is not so much resolved as left trailing in the dust. In the American way, contradiction is less disentangled than immobilized."²⁷ But I would offer a different reading, one in which an ongoing set of adversarial relations are precisely *not* overcome, but rather temporarily set aside for a vision of utopic possibility that holds onto what is best and useful in tradition (this is the ideology part) while gesturing toward something beyond, something impossible, but something worthy of desire and of action—a national community of diverse enfranchised citizens. In the very next moment, the conversation, nay, the haggling, will resume again. Louis and Belize have not resolved their antagonisms, but for a moment the continuum of history is ruptured by a millennial desire.

I have been waxing lyrical, perhaps, over the recent possibilities for representing and also producing struggle for radical democracy on the nation's stages. Lest I myself seem to be suffering from a brand of messianic utopianism, let me end this essay with what I think are the difficulties of the communitarian correction for left artists and intellectuals. The serious assertion that rights should sometimes be superseded by an appeal to the social good not only applies to free-market economism; it also applies to free speech and censorship issues. The notion that social antagonisms are necessary and productive for democracy means that the debates around NEA funding may be necessary, and that Arlene Croce's scathing and vicious attack on Bill T. Jones's choreography is part of democratic process. Before completely discrediting my feminist and leftist credentials, let me explain what I mean.

Interpretation of the First Amendment in its libertarian versions insists that "government must maintain a hands-off laissez-faire approach to speaking and publishing, leaving the market free to determine who speaks and how loudly. In this view individuals have a right to choose for themselves what ideas are worth saying or hearing." In contrast, the communitarian view "insists that the crucial democratic value is not an unregulated press but an accessible one. Of course, the public interest means that the press must be guaranteed the independence from government it takes to be an adversary and critic of the government."²⁸ Thus the Supreme Court, under libertarian interpretations of the First Amendment, has refused to restrict campaign expenditures by PACs (*Buckley v. Valeo,* 1976). It has also been unwilling to regulate public-access requirements for broadcasters, even in the face of significant deficiencies in the people's "collective right . . . to receive suitable access to social, political, esthetic, moral and other ideas and experiences" (*Red Lion Broadcasting Co. v. F.C.C.,* 1969). But noninterference has not promoted wide market competition and thriving public access programming because the "top ten cable systems . . . account for 41 percent of all cable subscribers," and they are owned by media conglomerates such as Time Warner and General Electric.[29]

Nevertheless, when the National Endowment for the Arts cancels funding for radical artists under the sham excuse of poor quality, the arts community (that word again) largely responds by invoking First Amendment rights as its chief defense. Although a more difficult argument, the appropriate course from a communitarian view would be to engage in a serious debate about the relationship between what is represented and the social needs and goals of the society. While recognizing the importance of the protections of free expression, the criterion of social good must also be considered. In addition to arguments about free expression, the ideologically saturated targeting of homosexuals (three of the NEA four were gay or lesbian), of sexually explicit materials (nudity), and of national critique would become the major grounds of the debate—not negatively by those on the right, but by our own side, arguing this bias is not serving the public good.[30] As the country consolidates two decades of movement to the right, winning these arguments may become harder to do because persuading other citizens of the social necessity of such representations will be an uphill battle. But the First Amendment argument has certain limits, indicated by the unwillingness of many courts to prohibit "hate speech" under a rationale of not limiting individual free expression. Artists have long identified with that part of the libertarian interpretation that has protected them as individuals seeking self-expression, but it is a two-edged sword that may not always serve the best interests of democracy. Jeffrey Abramson and Elizabeth Bussiere remind us of the conservative side of this view: "It is important to note that a full communitarian interpretation of the First Amendment ultimately must balk at the reigning notion that communities are virtually powerless to make moral judgments about what individuals wish to say."[31] This language of morality has always been a flash point for artists' battles with censorship. However, if we think about an involved, diverse, and wide-ranging citizenry participating in this decision making, and see these judgments as historical and contextually bound and limited, there is perhaps not quite so much to fear.

Besides a reconsideration of the First Amendment defense, the other difficult task required in radical democracy is to embrace the opportunity for wide-ranging and adversarial debate about issues of art and culture. As hateful as the NEA controversy was to artists who believed that the actions of the agency were completely unfounded and politically motivated, a healthy national debate sprang up in the country beginning with the controversy about Mapplethorpe and Serrano. Along with the slanted and polemical writing on these topics, artists and critics were also able to make significant arguments about the relationship of performance to society. Holly Hughes, Karen Finley, John Fleck, and Tim Miller suffered under the unfair and vicious charges made against them, and for that there is no justification. But the process of the argument itself may be at the heart of democratic discussion of the arts. At least the relationship between politics and art, government and its cultural institutions, became very clear for anyone willing to follow the debate. Similarly, Arlene Croce's attack on Bill T. Jones's *Still/Here* has been the occasion for Jones's work to come to national prominence among people who never see dance and has occasioned eloquent and passionate responses in letters to the editor in a subsequent issue of the *New Yorker* (including a letter from Tony Kushner), in the *Village Voice* and the *New York Times,* and in many other less formal venues, including the Performance Discussion Group at Stanford University.[32] Maybe this is how democracy works, when it works.

If one were to attack Croce from within the perspective I have been sketching out here, there would be plenty to say. "I have not seen Bill T. Jones's 'Still/Here' and have no plans to review it," she begins. Well then she should shut up. One of the major requirements of participating as a citizen in radical democracy is that you inform yourself and engage in dialogue. But Croce is ignorant and engages in monologue. She claims she "feels excluded by reason of its express intentions, which are unintelligible as theatre. . . . my approach has been cut off" (54). Invoking the passive victim's role she is at such pains to castigate, she removes herself from democratic debate by refusing to participate in the "community" in attendance at the event of performance while making use of her access to "community" channels (her role as dance critic presumes such membership in the dance community, and at the *New Yorker* in the national democratic one). She claims such work is undiscussable but of course discusses it, travestying the notion of a free and open discourse by trying to foreclose it. Not having seen the work, Croce is forced to rely on the media "blitz" about Jones's work, thus contributing to the media's commodification of "news" in ways that foster only the illusion of community and that, through the news media's gaps and omissions, in turn produces her own inaccurate account of Jones's work, its tone (actually upbeat instead of self-pitying), and the relationship between its narrative and choreographic structures. The really ironic twist in the essay is that Croce argues that communitarian thinking has been running the governmental agencies funding the arts in the last two decades! "The arts bureaucracy in this country, which includes government and private funding agencies, has in recent years demonstrated a blatant bias for utilitarian art—art that justifies the bureaucracy's existence by being socially useful. . . . By the late eighties, the ethos of community outreach had reached out and swallowed everything else; it was the only way the N.E.A. could survive" (56). Tell it to Karen Finley.

The outrageous thing about Croce's attack is not the content—that can be debated—but the way she deliberately traduces democratic processes through her refusal to see the work itself, combined with the full privilege of her position at the *New Yorker,* and a simultaneous refusal to take responsibility for her own judgments (by placing herself, and the NEA for that matter, as captive to "self-declared cases of pathology in art [that] have effectively disarmed criticism," 58). Thus even within the practice of a radical democracy that combines certain aspects of liberalism with communitarianism, there are grounds to return Croce's salvo.

The unpleasant truth contained in this essay's last section is that in democracy antagonisms have to be met head on, negotiated, and fought through. Artists have sometimes, often, wanted to stay above the fray or at least out of its way. But we can't. To say that the national debates about the NEA or about Croce's attack on Bill T. Jones's choreography are perhaps doing the work of democracy is not to say that they are not shocking or hurtful, regrettable in themselves, or threatening in a country swinging to the right. It is to say, however, that these challenges are part of the process of cultural production in a democratic society. Why participate in such a democracy? Why accept the appellation *citizen* and engage in this struggle? Michael Walzer offers this rationale, with which I concur:

> The associational life of civil society is the actual ground where all versions of the good are worked out and tested . . . and proven to be partial, incomplete, ultimately unsatisfying. It cannot be the case that living on this ground is good-in-itself; there isn't any other place to live. What is true is that the quality of our political and economic activity and of our national culture is intimately connected to the strength and vitality of our associations.[33]

NOTES

1. Ernesto Laclau and Chantal Mouffe began working out a new theory of radical democracy in *Hegemony and Socialist Strategy: Towards a Radical Democratic Politics* (London: Verso, 1985). See also Chantal Mouffe's *The Return of the Political* (London: Verso, 1993). All others are contributors to *Dimensions of Radical Democracy,* ed. Chantal Mouffe (London: Verso, 1992).

2. Mouffe, *Dimensions of Radical Democracy*, 1–2.

3. These debates focus on the year 2000 census and the adequacy of existing racial categories in a time of unprecedented diversification and also on the question of the desirability of government classification according to skin color and ancestry. See Lawrence Wright, "One Drop of Blood," *New Yorker*, 25 July 1994, 46\ts\ff.

4. Postcolonial critics have written most perceptively about these contradictory and simultaneous inscriptions. For example, Homi Bhabha quotes Frantz Fanon ("National consciousness, which is not nationalism, is the only thing that will give us an international dimension") in the introduction to a collection of essays designed to discuss the disunity of "nation" and the "articulation of cultural difference in the construction of an *inter*national perspective." Homi Bhabha, *Nation and Narration* (London: Routledge, 1990), 4–5.

5. Sue-Ellen Case, "Performing Lesbian in the Space of Technology, Part I," *Theatre Journal* 47, no. 1 (1995): 2.

6. Particularly annoying in this regard is an otherwise very clear and incisive review of the communitarian/liberal debate by Amitai Etzioni in *New Communitarian Thinking: Persons, Virtues, Institutions, and Communities* (Charlottesville: University of Virginia Press, 1995), 16–34.

7. "The argument is something to the effect that by seeking a more secure place for the needs of the community in determining the course of social and political policies, individual and minority rights will be automatically or necessarily disregarded." Etzioni, *New Communitarian Thinking*, 2.

8. Bhabha, *Nation and Narration*, 2.

9. Chantal Mouffe, *The Return of the Political* (London: Verso, 1993), 65–66.

10. Rosemary Hennessy, *Materialist Feminism and the Politics of Discourse* (London: Routledge, 1993), 92–93.

11. Etzioni, *New Communitarian Thinking*, 27.

12. Tim Miller and David Román, "Preaching to the Converted," *Theatre Journal* 47, no. 2 (1995): 177.

13. Miller and Román, "Preaching to the Converted," 187.

14. Janelle Reinelt, "Tracking Twilight: The Politics of Location," *Theatre Forum* 6 (1995): 52–58.

15. Reviews of both *Fires in the Mirror* and *Twilight—Los Angeles, 1992* often mark the local geography involved. See for example Melanie Kirkpatrick's closing paragraph joining the performance to her location: "As I left the theatre and ventured out in the city. . . ." "A Summer Day When Emotions Boiled Over," *Wall Street Journal*, 27 May 1992. See also Clive Barnes, who personalizes his own experience of 19 August 1991 (he was in Europe at the time of the riots where the Gorbachev coup was the front-page story): "When I returned, their significance [events in Crown Heights] caught at my lungs like a whiff of gun powder." "*Fires in the Mirror* Burns Brightly," *New York Post*, 13 May 1992.

16. Anna Deavere Smith, *Fires in the Mirror* (New York: Anchor Books, 1993), xxviii–xxix.

17. On the question of whether or not her performance technique would work if she were white, I would argue no—because then the power of the dominant position would appear to appropriate weaker positions in the process of representation.

18. Charles Lyons and James Lyons, "Anna Deavere Smith: Perspectives on Her

Performance within the Context of Critical Theory," *Journal of Dramatic Theory and Criticism* 9, no. 1 (1994): 45.

19. David Savran, "Ambivalence, Utopia, and a Queer Sort of Materialism: How *Angels in America* Reconstructs the Nation," *Theatre Journal* 47, no. 2 (1995): 221.

20. I would argue the San Francisco production, but not the New York production, carried these possibilities. See Reinelt, "Notes on *Angels* as American Epic Theatre," in *Approaching the Millennium: Essays on Tony Kushner's "Angels in America,"* ed. Deborah R. Geis and Steven F. Kruger (Ann Arbor: University of Michigan Press, 1997).

21. Savran, "Ambivalence," 216.

22. Savran lays out the multiple ways Kushner weaves Walter Benjamin's "Theses on the Philosophy of History" into an intertext in *Angels* ("Ambivalence," 210–15).

23. See Fredric Jameson, *Postmodernism; or, The Cultural Logic of Late Capitalism* (Durham: Duke University Press, 1991); and Donna Haraway, "A Manifesto for Cyborgs: Science, Technology, and Socialist Feminism in the 1980s," *Socialist Review* 80 (1985): 65–68.

24. Tobin Siebers, ed., *Heterotopia: Postmodern Utopia and the Body Politic* (Ann Arbor: University of Michigan Press, 1994), 19–20.

25. Paul Ricoeur, *Lectures on Ideology and Utopia,* ed. George H. Taylor (New York: Columbia University Press, 1986), 265–66.

26. Ricoeur, *Lectures,* 16.

27. Savran, "Ambivalence," 223.

28. Jeffrey Abramson and Elizabeth Bussiere, "Free Speech and Free Press; a Communitarian Perspective," in Etzioni, *New Communitarian Thinking,* 218–19.

29. Abramson and Bussiere, "Free Speech," 226.

30. Some eloquent and complex argumentation about the Endowment crises did see print. See, for example, Peggy Phelan's two articles on the subject: "Serrano, Mapplethorpe, the NEA, and You: 'Money Talks,'" *The Drama Review* 34, no. 1 (1990): 4–15 and "Money Talks, Again: The National Endowment for the Arts and 'Obscene' Art," *The Drama Review* 35, no. 3 (1991): 131–41.

31. Abramson and Bussiere, "Free Speech," 229.

32. See Arlene Croce, "Discussing the Indiscussable," *New Yorker,* 26 Dec. 1994–2 Jan. 1995, 54–61. Page numbers hereafter cited in the text. For various responses, see "In the Mail," *New Yorker,* 30 Jan. 1995, 10–13; Richard Goldstein, "The Croce Criterion," *Village Voice,* 3 Jan. 1995, 8; Frank Rich, "Dance of Death," *New York Times,* 8 Jan. 1995, A19.

33. Michael Walzer, "The Civil Society Argument," in Mouffe, *Dimensions of Radical Democracy,* 98. For more of Walzer's ideas, see "The Communitarian Critique of Liberalism," *New Communitarian Thinking,* 16–34.

Contributors

John Bell teaches theater at New York University and Rhode Island School of Design, is a member of Great Small Works, and has worked extensively with Bread and Puppet Theatre. In addition to several articles, he is currently editing a special issue of the *Drama Review* on "Puppets, Masks, and Performing Objects in the Twentieth Century."

Marcia Blumberg is a Postdoctoral Research Fellow at the Open University, England. In addition to her current project, "Making AIDS Visible: Theatre as/and Activism," she is coediting *South African Theatre as/and Intervention* with Dennis Walder and completing her own book *Engendering Intervention in Contemporary South African Theatre.*

Elaine Brousseau is a Ph.D. candidate in English at the University of Massachusetts, Amherst, where she also teaches writing in the individualized major program. Her dissertation investigates the gender, racial, and political implications of nineteenth-century American productions of Shakespeare.

Tom Burvill is Associate Professor of English, Linguistics, and Media at Macquarie University, Sydney, Australia. He has long been associated with Sidetrack Theatre and has published in *Australasian Drama Studies, Paregon,* and *Literary Criterion.*

Una Chaudhuri is Professor of English and Chair of the Department of Drama at New York University. She is the author of *No Man's Stage: A Semiotic Study of Jean Genet's Major Plays* (UMI) and *Staging Place: The Geography of Modern Drama* (University of Michigan Press).

Jeanne Colleran is Associate Professor and Chair of the Department of English at John Carroll University, Cleveland, Ohio. She has published widely in the area of contemporary theater and fiction and is completing a book, *Critical Stages: The Place of Politics in Contemporary Theatre*.

Tracy C. Davis is Associate Professor of Theatre, English, and Performance Studies at Northwestern University. She is author of *George Bernard Shaw and the Socialist Theatre* (Praeger) and *Actresses as Working Women: Their Social Identity in Victorian Culture* (Routledge). In addition to numerous articles on performance and culture, she is presently writing a book for Cambridge University Press on the economics of nineteenth-century British theater.

Harry J. Elam, Jr. is Associate Professor of Drama and Director of the Committee on Black Performing Arts at Stanford. He is author of *Taking It to the Streets: The Social Protest Theater of Luis Valdez and Amiri Baraka* (University of Michigan Press) and coeditor of *Colored Contradictions: An Anthology of Contemporary African American Drama* (Penguin). His articles have appeared in *Theatre Journal, Text and Performance Quarterly, American Drama,* and elsewhere. He is working with Alice Rayner on a critical study of the work of Suzan-Lori Parks.

Lisa Jo Epstein is Assistant Professor of theater history, criticism, and directing in the Department of Theatre and Dance at Tulane University. She has served as an intern for CTO, Paris and currently facilitates Theatre of the Oppressed workshops in the CJ Peete Housing Project through the Tulane–Xavier Campus Affiliate Program. Support for the essay included here was provided by an American Association of University Women Fellowship.

Linda Kintz is Associate Professor of English at the University of Oregon. She is the author of *The Subject's Tragedy: Political Poetics, Feminist Theory, and Drama* (University of Michigan Press) and *Between Jesus and the Market: The Emotions that Matter in Right-Wing America* (Duke University Press), and coeditor of *Media, Culture, and the Religious Right* (University of Minnesota Press).

Josephine Lee is Associate Professor of English at the University of Minnesota. In addition to articles on modern and contemporary theater, she is the author of *Performing Asian America: Race and Ethnicity on the Contemporary Stage* (Temple University Press). She is currently book review editor for *Theatre Journal*.

Lionel Pilkington is a Lecturer in English at University College, Galway, Ireland. He is coeditor of *Gender and Colonialism* (Galway University Press), and his essays in theater history and cultural politics have appeared in *Irish University Review, Modern Drama, TDR, Etudes Theatrales/Essays in Theatre,* and *Eire-Ireland.* He is currently preparing for Routledge a book-length study of theater and politics in twentieth-century Ireland.

Alice Rayner is Associate Professor of Drama and Director of Humanities Special Programs at Stanford University. In addition to articles in *Theatre Journal, Journal of Dramatic Theory and Criticism,* and *New Theatre Quarterly,* she is the author of *Comic Persuasion* (University of California Press) and *To Act, to Do, to Perform* (University of Michigan Press).

Janelle Reinelt is Chair of the Department of Theatre and Dance at the University of California, Davis, and author of *After Brecht: British Epic Theatre* (University of Michigan Press), editor of *Crucibles of Crisis: Performance and Social Change* (University of Michigan Press), and coeditor of *Critical Theory and Performance* (University of Michigan Press) and *The Performance of Power* (University of Iowa Press). She is the former editor of *Theatre Journal.*

Jenny S. Spencer is Associate Professor of English at the University of Massachusetts, Amherst. She is the author of *Dramatic Strategies in the Plays of Edward Bond* (Cambridge University Press) and has published in *Modern Drama* and elsewhere. She is currently editor of *Theatre Topics.*

Esther Beth Sullivan is Associate Professor of Theatre at Ohio State University. Her articles have appeared in *Theatre Journal, Theatre Studies, Literature in Performance, Theatre Topics,* and elsewhere. An active dramaturg and director, she has also served as President of Women and Theatre.

Eugene van Erven is Lecturer in American Studies at Utrecht University in the Netherlands. His books include *Radical People's Theatre* (1988) and *The Playful Revolution: Theatre and Liberation in Asia* (1992). A frequent contributor to *Drama Review* and *New Theatre Quarterly,* he is currently working on a book and educational video for Routledge entitled *Swapping Stories: A Guide to Community Theatre.*

Index